AMERICAN APOCALYPSES

Cain & Abel (Erik Sandgren, 1982)

AMERICAN APOCALYPSES

THE IMAGE OF THE END OF THE
WORLD IN AMERICAN LITERATURE

DOUGLAS ROBINSON

THE JOHNS HOPKINS UNIVERSITY PRESS

BALTIMORE AND LONDON

This book has been brought to publication with the generous assistance of the Andrew W. Mellon Foundation.

© 1985 The Johns Hopkins University Press
Printed in the United States of America

The Johns Hopkins University Press, 701 West 40th Street,
Baltimore, Maryland 21211
The Johns Hopkins Press Ltd, London

The paper in this book is acid-free and meets the guidelines for permanence
and durability of the Committee on Production Guidelines for Book
Longevity of the Council on Library Resources.

Library of Congress Cataloging in Publication Data

Robinson, Douglas.
  American apocalypses.

  Bibliography: p.
  Includes index.
  1. American literature—History and criticism. 2. End of the world in
literature. 3. Apocalyptic literature—History and criticism. I. Title.
PS169.E53R6 1985   810'.9'38   84-28865
ISBN 0-8018-2528-8 (alk. paper)

Front cover stamping: Emerging Figures *(original linocut by Erik Sandgren, 1982). Illustrations reproduced by permission of the artist.*

The following publishers have generously given permission to use ex-tended quotations from copyrighted works: From Nightwood, *by Djuna Barnes. Copyright 1937 by Djuna Barnes. Reprinted by permission of New Directions Publishing Corporation and Faber and Faber Publishers. From* Giles Goat-Boy, *by John Barth. Copyright 1966 by John Barth. Reprinted by permission of Doubleday & Company, Inc. From* Invisible Man, *by Ralph Ellison. Copyright 1947, 1948, 1952 by Ralph Ellison. Reprinted by permission of Random House, Inc. From* Absalom, Absalom!, *by William Faulkner. Copyright 1964 by Estelle Faulkner and Jill Faulkner Summers. Reprinted by permission of Random House, Inc. From* Moby-Dick, *by Herman Melville, The Norton Critical Edition, edited by Harrison Hayford and Hershel Parker. Copyright 1967 by W. W. Norton & Company, Inc. Reprinted by permission of W. W. Norton & Company, Inc. From* Cats Cradle, *by Kurt Vonnegut Jr. Copyright 1963 by Kurt Vonnegut Jr. Reprinted by permission of Delacorte Press/Seymour Law-rence. From* Imaginations, *by William Carlos Williams. Copyright 1970 by Florence Williams. Reprinted by permission of New Directions Publish-ing Corporation.*

FOR HELJÄ, LAURA, AND SARA

*In the department of science, and the specialty of journalism,
there appear, in these States, promises, perhaps fulfillments,
of highest earnestness, reality, and life. These are, of course,
modern. But in the region of imaginative, spinal and essential
attributes, something equivalent to creation is, for our age
and lands, imperatively demanded. For not only is it not enough
that the new blood, new frame of democracy shall be vivified
and held together merely by political means, superficial suffrage,
legislation, etc., but it is clear to me that, unless it goes deeper,
gets at least as firm and as warm a hold in men's hearts, emotions and beliefs, as, in their days, feudalism or ecclesiasticism,
and inaugurates its own perennial sources, welling from the
center forever, its strength will be defective, its growth doubtful,
and its main charm wanting. I suggest, therefore, the possibility, should some two or three really original American poets,
(perhaps artists or lecturers,) arise, mounting the horizon like
planets, stars of the first magnitude, that, from their eminence,
fusing contributions, races, far localities, etc., together, they
would give more compaction and more moral identity, (the quality today most needed,) to these States, than all its Constitutions, legislative and judicial ties, and all its hitherto political,
warlike, or materialistic experiences.*
—*Walt Whitman*, Democratic Vistas

CONTENTS

Images of the end of the world abound in American literature, and with good reason: the very idea of America in history *is* apocalyptic, arising as it did out of the historicizing of apocalyptic hopes in the Protestant Reformation. Discovered by Europeans in the sixteenth century, America was conceived as mankind's last great hope, the Western site of the millennium. Settled by millenarian religious groups, most notably the Puritans in the Massachusetts Bay Colony, its future destiny was firmly and prophetically linked with God's plan for the world, and the national dream of an American Age, a great paradisal future to be ushered in by America, remains strong even into our own time.

Yet there remains, among many students of American literature, a strange unwillingness to allow the centrality of the apocalypse. To the extent that critics have discerned apocalyptic elements in American literature at all, they have tended either to deplore them as somehow unworthy of the American imagination, thereby edging apocalyptic works subtly out of the American canon; or they have sought to tame them, to render them ideologically "safe" by treating them as simple congeries of discrete plots and images. The image of the end of the world in American literature is regarded either as somehow frightening and therefore to be relegated to the periphery, or as so patently mundane, so unproblematically commonplace, as to be dismissible with a few passes of the interpretive hand.

My contention in this study is that American apocalypses are commonplace, at least in the sense that they are so fundamental to American writing as to be virtually ubiquitous—but, at the same time, that they are by no means unproblematically so. American apocalypses—American works that adopt *some* interpretive stance toward the end of the world—at once undermine basic American values and definitively express those values; they essay both a rejection and a signal exploration

env. apocalypse

xi

of American ideologies of the self, of nature, of God and the supernatural, and of the community. Because they present a thoroughgoing challenge both to dominant American ideologies and to our customary ways of thinking about such ideologies, American apocalypses place demands upon our understanding, in response to which thematic interpretation has often proved inadequate. In a critical tradition long given to thematic interpretation, this renders apocalypses problematic indeed.

My approach to the challenge posed by these works is broadly hermeneutical in that my own interpretive stances are located *within* the complex debate set up by the works themselves—confronting not merely American authors' hermeneutical relations to previous American texts and to the apocalyptic texts of the Bible but also the ways in which criticism implicates the critic in those relations. To ask of an American apocalypse how it conceives of the self in relation to time and place is inevitably to ask the same question of oneself. *American Apocalypses* is not explicitly self-reflexive criticism, but it proceeds with an acute awareness of the extent to which the works it examines are mirrors—its investigations therefore self-reflections.

This notion of textual mirroring figures significantly in my interpretation of what American apocalyptic writers are trying to accomplish. The image of the end of the world in American literature is an image of desire that seeks not to point beyond itself to some indefinite paradise but to embody the very mediatory locus that makes speculation about temporal and spatial transitions possible. If speculation is etymologically a mirroring, one finds American writers speculating about the self in relation to the various others of society, nature, God, the future, and the unconscious, by staring profoundly into mirror-images of transition. In theological studies of the apocalypse, a distinction is normally made between the broad category of *eschatology,* or doctrines about the last things, and the narrower category of the *apocalyptic,* a branch of eschatology that stands alongside the ethical eschatology of Old Testament (OT) prophecy, definitively seeking to explore the unveiling of the future in the present, the encroachment of a radically new order into a historical situation that has disintegrated into chaos. The root meaning of the *eschaton,* however, is not in fact the last things but the "furthermost boundary," the "ultimate edge" in time *or* space. I propose to read American apocalypses *as* investigations into the edge, the boundary, the interface between radically different realms. If the apocalypse is an unveiling (*apo* [from or away], *kalupsis* [covering] from *kalupto* [to cover], and *kalumma* [veil]), then clearly the veil is the *eschaton,* that which stands between the familiar and whatever lies beyond. In this sense the apocalypse becomes largely a matter of *seeing;* and what one sees by imagining an apocalypse depends chiefly upon how one conceives the veil. Is it a mirror that reflects the self? If opaque and therefore obstructive, does it reflect or merely deaden vision? Is it to be removed, cast off and destroyed, or transformed—rendered transparent, for example? The veil/mirror/mask/wall/ door image cluster that the topos of the end of the world becomes in American literature allows American writers to explore the possibility of an *iconic mediation,* a standing-between-extremes that (these writers hope) will permit vision without loss of self.

The two most obsessive concerns for American apocalypses involve mediations across the oppositions implicit in *time* and *judgment.* Both entail differentiations, discriminations; but the problem of time leads to questions about linearity and irreversibility (how does one undo or correct or repeat the past?) and about expectation and deferral (how does one achieve a desired future?), while the "spatial" differentiations of moral judgment prompt questions about the nature of community (how does one justify discriminations in an egalitarian society?) and about the constitution of the self (on what ethical grounds does one define the self in action?). In one sense the structure of this book reflects these preoccupations. After an introductory consideration of apocalyptic hermeneutics in chapter 1, the text moves through discussions of judgment (chapter 2) and of time (chapter 3) to two central explorations of the range of mediation (chapters 4 and 5), returning in chapter 6 to the problem of time and in chapter 7 to the problem of judgment.

In addition, however, the book is divided into two parts, which complicates these tidy summations. Indeed, as the title of my first "judgment" chapter suggests—"Signs of the Times"—time and judgment are finally inseparable questions in American apocalypses. Part I takes up the central issues in American apocalypses heuristically, moving from works that only raise those issues without attempting to solve them, to works that are profoundly aware of the problems and offer definitive American solutions to them. Part II, then, develops a historical argument in which major American writers explore the successes and failures of previous solutions and seek to arrive at new solutions. In the process, this section retraces the ground covered in Part I but now self-consciously, with full cognizance of the magnitude of the problems faced. Part I, one might say, works toward the *achievement* of a definitive American apocalypse; Part II works toward the *restriction* of that apocalypse, specifically toward a self-restriction of the American apocalypse in which the apocalyptic visionary locus is progressively dispersed or deeschatologized. As American apocalypses in Part II become increasingly more concerned with issues of time and judgment in a communal context, they also become less recognizably "apocalyptic"; these American apocalypses continue to confront the image of the end of the world, but with the express intention of defusing the vision of apocalypse, of rendering the *eschaton* not necessarily powerless but less privative, less directed toward a high Romantic isolation whose issue is clear sight at the expense of meaningful action in the world.

Chapter 1 discusses the difficulties involved in interpreting images of the end of the world, both through a review of contemporary literary-critical interpretations of the apocalypse (from Northrop Frye and R. W. B. Lewis to M. H. Abrams and Martha Banta) and through a historical overview of the hermeneutics underlying those interpretations (Daniel, St. John of Patmos, Augustine, William Blake, Henry Adams). My aim here is to elicit the fundamental logic of apocalyptic hermeneutics and to develop a provisional schematization of that logic for later reference.

Part I moves, in chapter 2, from this general perspective into specific American apocalypses by Carol Balizet and Michael Wigglesworth (with a brief stop at Jonathan Edwards), works that are revealing largely in a negative sense, in that they fail to deal adequately with the profound problems they implicitly raise. Like all the texts considered in Part I, those by Balizet and Wigglesworth are determined to eschatologize history, to establish within their obsession with dates and times an eternal perspective that will guarantee the conformance of historical developments with present desire. The implication for criticism is that hermeneutical affinities might most fruitfully be defined by logical or philosophical rather than historical horizons. The pincer movement suggested by this chapter, with Wigglesworth (1662) and Balizet (1979) poised at opposite ends of the American historical spectrum, is continued and narrowed in chapter 3, where (perhaps asymmetrically) the counterpart to chapter 2's excursus on Jonathan Edwards (1765) becomes a reading of Mark Twain's *A Connecticut Yankee in King Arthur's Court* (1889), a valiant effort to solve the American problem of time that finally fails, but fails heroically, by succumbing to gigantic dilemmas. Twain's juxtaposition of two eras, the industrial present and a barbaric past, again directs our attention away from the *flux* of time to the *eschata* of time, to beginnings and endings, to boundaries at which clear vision may be accessible but for Twain's hero, in the end, proves unattainable. In chapter 4, the pincers close on the two writers that I suggest are our seminal apocalyptists: Ralph Waldo Emerson and Edgar Allan Poe, in two works of the 1830s, *Nature* (1836) and *The Narrative of Arthur Gordon Pym* (1838). This chapter, positioned at the center of the book, argues that Emerson and Poe stand at the exact center of the American apocalypse; the two works discussed in this chapter at once present the definitive American forms of the American apocalypse inherited from the Puritans through Edwards and define for later American writers the range of issues that must be dealt with, somehow, if the American experience is to make sense.

Part II, then, traces the attempts of the writers who follow Emerson and Poe to *make* sense of the American experience on the grounds these two authors established. In each of these chapters a single text is central and two or three other texts that confront similar problems in similar ways help to illuminate it: Herman Melville's *Moby-Dick* is supported in chapter 5 by Poe's "A Descent into the Maelström," Ralph Ellison's *Invisible Man,* and Kurt Vonnegut's *Cat's Cradle;* William Faulkner's *Absalom, Absalom!* is supported in chapter 6 by Poe's "The Fall of the House of Usher," Nathaniel Hawthorne's *The House of the Seven Gables,* and Henry James's "The Jolly Corner"; and John Barth's *Giles Goat-Boy* is supported in chapter 7 by Poe's "The Masque of the Red Death" and "William Wilson," and by Nathanael West's *Miss Lonelyhearts* and *The Day of the Locust.* As the historical argument in this section progresses from Emerson and Poe to Melville to Faulkner to Barth, the apocalyptic mediation becomes not less efficacious, but less desirable, less attractive an alternative; indeed, it becomes *too* efficacious, too likely to initiate a transformation that will *endanger* the collective vision of the community. Thus, where Ishmael comes to see clearly but finds himself unable to translate personal vision into communal action, Faulkner's Miss Rosa finally achieves a victory *over* the community and *in* the community by accepting the necessary failure of apocalyptic vision, and Barth's George Giles moves through a self-restrictive apocalyptic vision to reintegration into the community. Throughout the discussions in this section, representatives of transformative apocalyptic vision, such as Ahab, Thomas Sutpen, and the mythic heroes that George admires—are understood and assimilated only in order that they might in the end be distanced, put aside or put in perspective. In this sense Part II is most fundamentally concerned with antiapocalypses, with self-restrictive American apocalypses that seek to reinterpret the image of the end of the world so as to facilitate not world transformation, not an isolate mediatory insight, but meaningful action in a communal context. Particularly in chapter 7 this concern is manifest; there we move from the apocalypse of apocalypse, the end of the end, the revelation of the impossibility of a revelation in Poe, through largely unsuccessful explorations of a meaningful work or activity in West, to the successful discovery of that activity in Barth—a move that could as well have been traced from the desperate search for an alternative to apocalyptic annihilation in Thomas Pynchon's *Gravity's Rainbow,* through the inverted parody of apocalyptic funk in Robert Coover's *The Public Burning,* to *Giles Goat-Boy.* My decision to excise lengthy discussions of Pynchon and Coover from the final version of this book should not, that is to say, be taken as evidence that Barth (along with Vonnegut, in chapter 5) is the only major contemporary writer concerned to defuse the apocalypse by communalizing apocalyptic eschatology; antiapocalypse—not apocalypse, as many critics have claimed—is the dominant topos of American postmodernism.

In the Conclusion, finally, I restate the problems of community raised by American apocalypses through a reading of two more Poe tales, "Ligeia" and "The Man of the Crowd." That Poe has by this point become the principal figure in the book should be clear; his tales are used in every chapter of Part II to introduce readings of later works on which his writing—along with Emerson's—has proved influential. My relative neglect of Emerson has less to do with the dynamics of historical influence than with the present state of Poe and Emerson criticism. F. O. Matthiessen's rehabilitation of Emerson in *American Renaissance* (1941) has inspired an impressive body of scholarship that has solidly established Emerson's centrality to American literature. The rehabilitation of Poe is just now, in the past decade and a half, getting under way, and this book is an attempt to contribute to that rehabilitation by placing Poe in the context in which his centrality is most obvious and most significant: American apocalypses.

More specifically, my treatment of Poe derives from a sense that his importance to later American writers differs markedly from Emerson's. Emerson was assimilated rapidly into the dominant culture, which involved a dogmatization of his thought that it has been criticism's task to undermine; critics have been concerned to juxtapose against Emerson's ostensible "tenets" a range of "heresies," of idiosyncrasies or inconsistencies, those ironic self-doubts and qualifications that make Emerson so interesting and complex a thinker. Emerson continues to fascinate us precisely as a rebel—a rebel against his own authority, against the orthodoxy into which the dominant culture always eagerly transforms his thought. But Poe doesn't need to be made into a rebel; he *is* one, a fact that, perhaps rather surprisingly, has tended to work against his critical recognition. Poe's influence is always actively and profoundly subversive, traditionally working first and foremost (at least in America) on the imaginations of small children, to whom teachers read his apparently harmless detective stories and tales of horror along with other "children's" classics by such successors of his as Conan Doyle and Robert Louis Stevenson. Because Poe is assimilated early, his influence over American writers is frequently denied even (or especially) where it is strongest; where it *is* recognized and admitted, as in the case of Henry James, or T. S. Eliot, it is often admitted condescendingly, like something long since outgrown. The crucial task in Poe criticism, therefore, has proven to be the demonstration not of how Poe diverges from the dominant culture, but of how he converges upon it: how he reveals its salient features by writing about seemingly unrelated things like decaying castles, angels, and polar encounters. The recognition of the centrality of American apocalypses, I contend, must ground itself on a recognition of the twin centrality of Emerson *and* Poe, and to establish that is the burden not only of chapter 4 but the whole of Part II, in which I trace their respective influences.

My own rediscovery of Poe as an adult, and my concomitant and growing sense of the importance of American apocalypses, were shaped and guided particularly by two recent studies of American literature that gave coherence to many of my vague surmisings: John T. Irwin's *American Hieroglyphics* (1980), most especially in the long middle section on Poe, and Martha Banta's *Failure and Success in America* (1978), especially in Parts V and VI, her discussion of the apocalypse. Although I find myself more attracted to Irwin's book methodologically than ideologically, and to Banta's book more ideologically than methodologically, the two taken together represent for me the excitement of American literature as it is currently being reappraised. Indeed, to the extent that *American Apocalypses* is intended as a contribution to that reappraisal, it might in one sense be imagined as an attempt to bridge the gap between the scholarly traditions represented by Irwin and Banta—to mediate between them, in the strong American tradition of mediation, in which a middle ground between extremes is always at once a loss and a willful transformation of loss into gain.

■

I want to take this opportunity to express my gratitude to Leroy Searle, who read several drafts of this manuscript and contributed more than a little to the final shape the argument takes; Leroy brought to my project an enthusiasm for the theoretical complexity of American literature and a passion for truth and value that influenced my thinking on the subject immensely. Mark Patterson, Míċéal Vaughan, and John Griffith read the entire manuscript in draft form and made useful comments, and Martha Banta, Charles Altieri, Donald Kartiganer, and Evan Watkins offered valuable criticism on portions or early drafts of the book. I would also like to thank the theologically trained members of my family—my brother David Robinson and my brothers-in-law Martti,

Markku, and Ilkka Antola—whose insights into my subject at an early stage guided my lay path into the thickets of Bible scholarship. My greatest debt is to my wife Heljä, whose suggestions and comments have been as helpful as her continuing support.

AMERICAN APOCALYPSES

ONE

APOCALYPTIC HERMENEUTICS

Our age is bewailed as the age of Introversion. Must that needs be evil? We, it seems, are critical. We are embarrassed with second thoughts. We cannot enjoy any thing for hankering to know whereof the pleasure consists. We are lined with eyes. We see with our feet. The time is infected with Hamlet's unhappiness,—

"Sicklied o'er with the pale cast of thought."

Is it so bad then? Sight is the last thing to be pitied. Would we be blind? Do we fear lest we should outsee nature and God, and drink truth dry? I look upon the discontent of the literary class as a mere announcement of the fact that they find themselves not in the state of mind of their fathers, and regret the coming state as untried; as a boy dreads the water before he has learned that he can swim. If there is any period one would desire to be born in,—is it not the age of Revolution; when the old and the new stand side by side, and admit of being compared; when the energies of all men are searched by fear and by hope; when the historic glories of the old, can be compensated by the rich possibilities of the new era? This time, like all times, is a very good one, if we but know what to do with it.
—Ralph Waldo Emerson, "The American Scholar"

"Between the novel and America," Leslie Fiedler remarks in *Love and Death in the American Novel*, "there are peculiar and intimate connections. A new literary genre and a new society, their beginnings coincide with the beginnings of the modern era and, indeed, help to define it. We are living not only in the Age of America but also in the Age of the Novel, at a moment when the literature of a country without a first-rate verse epic or a memorable verse tragedy has become the model of half the world."[1]

Is all of this true? What is striking about Fiedler's criticism is what is striking about all central American criticism, back to Emerson: it strikes us with the force of truth, directing us past timid concerns with empirical verification to an obsessive and transformative attention to the truth of myth. Like Emerson's, Fiedler's critical rhetoric is an ideologically charged examination of American ideology, a self-consciously mythic discourse that both exposes and embodies the mythic self-conceptions of the New World. And as the term *New World* suggests, as Fiedler's rhetoric itself reveals, the ideology that American writers at their most mythic invariably engage is *apocalyptic:* it is an ideology very much concerned with the end of old eras and the beginning of new eras, with the transition in space and time from an Old to a New World, from the Age of Europe (decadence, decay, death) to the Age of America (rebirth, return to primal innocence), in which America becomes the messianic model for the world.

And so one may paraphrase Fiedler's statement, by way of bracketing a range of general concerns for *this* study: "Between the *apocalypse* and America there are peculiar and intimate connections." If the modern era whose beginning coincides with the discovery of a palpable New World is in one respect the bourgeois era, the era of social and empirical common sense that has made it the Age of the Novel, in another and equally important respect it is the Protestant era, the era of radical revision of medieval conceptions of God and history that has made it—even more than the Middle Ages, which of course in many ways prepared the way for it—the Age of Apocalypse. The idea of a *material* New World, of an apocalyptic paradise in literal historical fulfillment, was foreign to the orthodox medieval imagination of Augustine or Aquinas; and it required the rehistoricizing of the apocalypse—begun by revisionist medieval clerics like Joachim de Fiore and numerous popular movements, and established in the Reformation by Luther and Calvin—for the very conception of America to become possible. The American Dream as European Dream was fundamentally a Protestant dream of historical apocalypse—a dream of a transformation *of* history *in* history that would consummate and so give meaning *to* history.

The central thesis of this book is that the whole question of the apocalyptic ideology, of the historical transformation of space and time from old to new, from corruption to new innocence, from death to rebirth, is fundamental to American literature. The great majority of our writers have insistently attempted to come to grips with the problems raised by the apocalyptic thrust of the American Dream, as most listings of mainstream American authors suggest. Emerson, Poe, Hawthorne, Melville, Twain, Henry James, Faulkner, West, Ellison, Barth: The dominant writers in my discussion are not unexceptionably canonical, but I would emphasize that all are unquestionably *mainstream* in their close attention to the shifting issues of the American apocalypse.

Indeed, one of the most revealing cultural facts to be noted about the American preoccupation with the apocalypse is that it has always been forcefully contested. The difference between the American mainstream I will be arguing for and even the *existing* canon (fifty years ago the difference was greater still) underscores what amounts to a profound ideological rift within American letters: a certain brand of commentator has long denied canonicity to American apocalypses and continues to deny it to them today, preferring to treat those works not as basic to the literature but as inhabiting some fanatical fringe worthy only of the critical attention needed to dismiss it. "We must get it out of our heads that this is a doomed time, that we are waiting for the end, and the rest of it," Saul Bellow has his Moses Herzog declaim. "We love apocalypses too much."[2] Or, put mythically, we love *sin* too much: Bellow displaces Israel's transgressions against the Deity into American transgressions against mankind, but he retains the theological tinge of his accusation. According to such commentators, to conceive an American apocalypse is not merely undesirable but an infraction, an offense against the quasi-deified body of mankind. Apocalypses—puerile fantasies of escape from the pressures of history, betrayals of mankind's holiest self-conceptions, expressions of a diseased lust for racial suicide—can therefore not be *typical* of the American literary imagination. To intimate as much is to undo the stays of the humanistic world view and precipitate a descent into despair. Apocalypses are, they must be, freaks or sports, the eccentric imaginative spawn of dangerous cranks from whom readers cannot be overly protected.

Not surprisingly, Bellow's strictures against the apocalyptic imagination are much quoted by conservative critics of contemporary American literature as part of a concerted effort to direct readers' tastes and writers' inclinations away from the likes of Barth, Coover, Pynchon, and Vonnegut and toward Bellow and his ideological kinsmen such as Bernard Malamud and (across religious boundaries) John Updike. This sort of rift is understandable in discussions of contemporary literature, where evaluative criteria remain in flux; what is

surprising is that the rift extends back to the roots of our classic literature as well. Neither the inclination toward images of apocalypse nor
the conservative reaction is a recent innovation; the break lies at the
heart of the debate over the meaning of the American experience. A
case in point is Henry James's unbending stricture on the Poeian imagination: it is *wrong,* James says, to report "strange encounters," supernatural prodigies, which can

> keep all their character [only] by looming through some other
> history—the indispensable history of somebody's *normal* re-
> lation to something. It's in such connexions as these that they
> most interest, for what we are then mainly concerned with
> is their imputed and borrowed dignity. Intrinsic values they
> have none—as we feel for instance in such a matter as the
> would-be portentous climax of Edgar Poe's "Arthur Gordon
> Pym" where the indispensable history is absent, where the
> phenomena evoked, the moving accidents, coming straight, as
> I say, are immediate and flat, and the attempt is all at the
> horrific in itself. The result is that, to my sense, the climax
> fails—fails because it stops short, and stops short for want of
> connexions. There *are* no connexions: not only, I mean, in the
> sense of further statement, but of our own further relation
> to elements, which hang in the void; whereby we see the effect
> lost, the imaginative effort wasted.[3]

Is Poe canonical or not? It is at best an open question: Poe is
read by most American schoolchildren but not by most American
graduate students. It seems reasonable to conjecture that the English
professors who will not teach Poe to graduate students are the same
professors who will not teach Barth, Pynchon, and Coover, for reasons
tied not to a wait-and-see attitude but precisely to a reaction against
American apocalypses. What this counterreaction tends to prefer in
American literature is "the indispensable history of somebody's *normal*
relation to something" that James speaks of, and it has generated a tradition of attacks on American apocalypses in recent decades, from
R. W. B. Lewis's influential "Days of Wrath and Laughter" (the seminal
work in the tradition, to which I return later in this chapter); to Robert
Alter's *Commentary* polemic against "Christian" postmodernism, "The
Apocalyptic Temper;" to the Christian polemics against the *wrong*
sort of Christian postmodernism in Bernard Bergonzi's *The Situation
of the Novel* and Nathan A. Scott, Jr.'s, " 'New Heav'ns, New Earth'—
The Landscape of Contemporary Apocalypse."[4] Just how much is at
stake in these ideological discriminations is suggested by the impassioned

rhetoric to which the thought of an apocalyptic American fiction drives these critics. Here, for example, is Alter:

> What I would like to suggest is that . . . much recent American literature has told considerably less than the truth precisely because of the apocalyptic postures it has assumed. The excitement of apocalypses is seductive and may easily give the impression of profundity and imaginative daring where neither is present. No one can be altogether impervious to the jeweled flashes and lurid flames that illuminate those doomed landscapes of the Book of Revelations, but there is no other document in either the Old or New Testament so inhuman, so spiritually irresponsible, and the same negative attributes adhere to the modes of imagination that ultimately derive from Revelations. . . . There is no room for real people in apocalypses, for when a writer chooses to see men as huddled masses waiting to be thrown into sulphurous pits, he hardly needs to look at individual faces; and so it is not surprising that recent comic-apocalyptic novelists should fill their worlds with the rattling skeletons of satiric hypotheses in place of fully fleshed characters. [5]

Alter here is explicitly attacking only the contemporary works of Ellison, Barth, Heller, and Pynchon; but implicitly, it seems clear, he is extending his argument to encompass the entire tradition of American apocalypse. Poe, too, "sees men as huddled masses waiting to be thrown into sulphurous pits," if these writers do; so too does Melville, so does Hawthorne, so do Twain and West. The conservative reaction against American apocalypses, overtly directed at contemporary fiction not yet canonized, is actually a covert attack on a much broader spectrum of classic American literature, an attempt to buttress the canon by demarcating it, to shore up its periphery by throwing out the borderline works.

The profundity of this ideological rift in American letters is perhaps best illustrated by juxtaposing Alter's polemic with another account of the same literary phenomenon—unrealistic plots and characters—that he describes pejoratively: Richard Chase's influential discussion of American "romance" in *The American Novel and its Tradition.*

> The romance can flourish without providing much intricacy of relation. The characters, probably rather two-dimensional types, will not be complexly related to each other or to society or to the past. Human beings will on the whole be shown in

ideal relation—that is, they will share emotions only after these have become abstract or symbolic. To be sure, characters may become profoundly involved in some way, as in Hawthorne and Melville, but it will be a deep and narrow, an obsessive, involvement. In American romance it will not matter much what class people come from, and where the novelist would arouse our interest in a character by exploring his origin, the romancer will probably do so by enveloping it in mystery. Character itself becomes, then, somewhat abstract and ideal, so much so in some romances that it seems to be merely a function of plot. The plot we may expect to be highly colored. Astonishing events may occur, and these are likely to have a symbolic or ideological, rather than a realistic, plausibility. Being less committed to the immediate rendition of reality than the novel, the romance will more freely veer toward mythic, allegorical, and symbolistic forms.[6]

What for Alter and the conservative reaction was peripheral, for Chase is mainstream; Henry James's polemical insistence that literature be based on "the indispensable history of somebody's *normal* relation to something" is dismissed easily with the observation that "the romance can flourish without providing much intricacy of relation." Chase is manifestly closer to Fiedler's position; but what Fiedler manages to convey, and what Lewis, Alter, Scott, and others rightly insist upon, is a sense of the *risks* involved in American apocalypses, a sense strikingly missing in Chase. This is a crucial point. For Chase, American romance is finally rather aseptic; it is rendered uninterestingly safe, sheltered, by being classified in a neat generic niche—Northrop Frye's concept of romance from his third essay in *Anatomy of Criticism.*[7] Chase gives no indication that American writers work toward shifting self-definitions by reaching toward forbidden fruit, toward paradises that will irrevocably transform all our generic notions of time and tradition, toward annihilations that will suck reality and its *normal* relations down into them like black holes. The conservative reaction to American apocalypses correctly perceives that the American apocalyptic imagination is radically iconoclastic, bound to a Romantic aesthetic according to which a thing becomes true only by being destroyed; and the conservative attacks, finally, are more indicative of the explosive power of these works than all the calm method of Chase.[8] In American romance, Chase correctly asserts, "Astonishing events may occur, and these are likely to have a symbolic or ideological, rather than a realistic, plausibility." But it seems to me that one has a better chance of recovering some of that astonishment, some of the ideoclastic and iconoclastic power of American apocalypses, if one exposes oneself to the same interpretive risks as do the writers themselves—if one wanders out onto the periphery, that is, where American writers are seeking at once to destroy and to recreate the canonical tradition, and engages the issues in all their complexity.

If one follows American writers onto that periphery, I suggest, their works may begin to assume an altogether unaccustomed cast: they become at once as ideologically seditious as the conservative reaction has made them out to be and as paradoxically central, precisely because of their peripheral stances, as Chase insists they are. The nebulous freedom American apocalypses doggedly seek by lighting out for some circumferential territory is a freedom to explore the prevailing ideologies by placing themselves in opposition to them. In this sense, the importance of the image of the end of the world in American literature is not at all formal, as many critics have argued, but ideological; not structural but *relational,* which is to say that the apocalypse is never a merely formal pattern in an American work but the author's interpretive stance on the future of the world and on the past of the text, its relation both to history as con-text and to previous apocalypses as pre-text. This suggests that to trace the operation of an author's image of the end of the world invariably leads one to consider the author's image of the end of the *text.* An author in the process of creating and ending his or her text becomes an analogue of God creating and ending the world, which suggests that literature and religion might fruitfully be made to illuminate each other—or, as Kenneth Burke would have it, that God exists, if only in language, as the principle of transcendental mediation that (in a metaphor I develop in chapter 4) ferries *refracted* (bent and distorted) meanings from author to reader, from critic to author, from text to world.[9] In this sense American apocalypses constitute a radical literature of continuity past the apocalyptic end of the text and call for a criticism of continuity as well, a criticism of negation that is not deconstructive but transcendental, in which negation does not restrict but restores meaning.

This view places American apocalypses in significant contrast to the Romantic aesthetic of iconoclasm mentioned earlier. Ideologically, American apocalypses are closely related at many points to the apocalyptic visions of the English and German Romantics, most particularly those of Blake, Coleridge, and Shelley; but important distinctions can be made between English and Continental Romantic apocalypses and American apocalypses. An impressive body of criticism surrounds the apocalyptic traditions of European Romanticism, beginning in Northrop Frye's study of Blake and taken up again by such commentators as Harold Bloom, Geoffrey Hartman, and M. H. Abrams; but one needs to be wary of facile applications of these writers' conclusions to the American apocalypse.[10] Consider, for example, this characteristic account of the Romantic apocalypse from Hartman's *Wordsworth's Poetry:*

> One term, not technical, requires special comment. By "apocalyptic," as in "apocalyptic imagination," I intend the Apocalypse of St. John (the Book of Revelation), and more generally, the kind of imagination that is concerned with the supernatural and especially the Last Things. The term may also describe a mind which actively desires the inauguration of a totally new epoch, whether preceding or following the end of days. And since what stands between us and the end of the (old) world is the world, I sometimes use "apocalyptic" to characterize any strong desire to cast out nature and to achieve an unmediated contact with the principle of things. (x)

Apparently unsystematic, this definition in fact sets up a range of apocalyptic interpretations, from the Gothic to the eschatological to the revolutionary to the visionary. I return to a similar syncretic approach later in this chapter, but for now, I wish to focus on that part of Hartman's definition that seems most problematic in terms of American literature—namely, his last sentence. Do American writers ever want to cast out nature? I contend they do not. I suggest that what Hartman calls "unmediated contact with the principle of things" is what one does *not* find in American literature, mainly because for American writers things have no "principle" apart from the images through which contact is achieved. American iconoclasm is iconically mediatory; images of nature are negated apocalyptically not in order that they might be thrown out, but that the writer might incorporate and transform them into the mediate ground for visionary contact. This mediatory thrust places American apocalypses in contradistinction to the dialectical negation of Hegel, for example, in which opposites are subsumed into a synthesis that becomes a new thesis on a higher level, moving from binary opposition to binary opposition until the final telos of Absolute Spirit is reached. In American apocalypses the image of the end of the world is made to mediate between this world and the next by standing between and embracing both, thus creating what might be called a ternary logic of intercession, in place of Hegel's binary logic of supersession. The mediated opposition is preserved iconically so as to allow writer and reader to perceive the opposites (earth and new earth, present and future) *in* their opposition without subsuming or supplanting them.

What this means is that, even at their most mythic, American apocalypses are neither the puerile escapism that critics like Robert Alter would construe them to be, destroying this world in order to escape into another, nor the cheery optimism of teleological idealism, in which the ultimate millennial synthesis is always just around the corner. Instead, American apocalypses seem to be acutely aware of both their own impossibility and their imaginative necessity; they build into their imagistic structures their own negation, but by so building preserve what is negated. *This* world in all its forms—nature, history, society, and so forth—becomes the dreaded Covering Cherub at the gateway to Eden, blocking our access to the apocalyptic tree of life. But unlike Blake's Cherub, the obstruction is not destroyed by fire but is itself converted into the mediatory icon of Christ, the self-unveiling veil that reveals by standing between.

Something like this mediatory negation, this imagistic incorporation by apocalyptic destruction, seems to be what Harold Bloom is getting at in the concluding essay, "The American Difference in Poetry and Criticism," of his recent book *Agon: Toward a Theory of Revisionism:*

> From Emerson himself through to Kenneth Burke, the American tradition of criticism is highly dialectical, differing in this from the British empirical tradition that has prevailed from Dr. Johnson to Empson. But this American criticism precisely resembles Whitman's poetry, rather than the Continental dialectics that have surged from Hegel through Heidegger on to the contemporary Deconstruction of Jacques Derrida and Paul de Man. Hegelian negation, even in its latest critical varieties, is intellectually optimistic because it is always based upon a destructive concept of the given. Given facts (and given texts) may appear to common sense as a positive index of truth, but are taken as being in reality the negation of truth, which must destroy apparent facts, and must deconstruct texts. British or Humean literary critics maintain the ultimate authority of the fact or text. Emerson, and Kenneth Burke after him, espouse the Negative, but not at all in a Hegelian mode. Emerson, both more cheerful and less optimistic than Hegel, insisted that a fact was an epiphany of God, but this insistence identified God with Emerson in his most expansive and transcending moments. Burke remarks that everything we might say about God has its precise analogue in things that we can say about language, a remark which defines American poetry as the new possibility of a Negative that perpetually might restore a Transcendental Self.

The American critic here and now, in my judgment, needs to keep faith with American poetry and the American Negative, which means one must not yield either to the school of Deconstruction or to the perpetual British school of Common Sense.[11]

This seems to me an important manifesto, in spite of—or perhaps because of—its own evident anxiety of influence, an anxiety that is typically American: the anxious awareness of one's own indebtedness to European thought despite claims of self-engenderment, of one's country's youthful belatedness in the Western critical tradition. It might well be argued, after all, that Bloom is here really only rejecting the Hegelian version of Romantic negation in order to adopt another European version—for the "American Negative" that Bloom derives from Emerson and Burke bears a striking resemblance to Keats's notion of negative capability, in which negation means not obliteration but suspension.

Indebtedness and belatedness, however, are inescapable, and determining an idea's genealogy does not therefore diminish its importance: associating the American Negative with Keats does not make it any less central to American apocalypses. The one emphasis in Bloom's manifesto that I think important to revise is not his American hubris but his restrictive drive toward a single American apocalypse, a single hermeneutic that has its roots in Emerson but will not easily account for the *range* of American literature: the drive to define "American poetry as the new possibility of a Negative that perpetually might restore a Transcendental Self." If this hermeneutic runs through Emerson, Whitman, Hart Crane, perhaps even Wallace Stevens and John Ashbery, to what extent will it define the poetry of Emily Dickinson, William Carlos Williams, or Charles Olson? How characteristic is the attempt perpetually to restore a transcendental self in Hawthorne, in Melville, in Twain, in Faulkner? Bloom's insistence on the American preoccupation with a mediatory negative is salutary, as we shall see; but it needs to be fit into a more extensive hermeneutical framework before it can adequately account for the complexity of American apocalypses. To construct such a framework, then, will be my task in the remainder of this chapter.

■

Without opposition, the apocalypse is nothing; spatial (earth-heaven) and temporal (present-future) oppositions are decided eschatologically by the moral opposition between good and evil, between God and Satan—the cosmic battle (*polemos*) that both precipitates and enacts the end. It is not surprising, therefore, that apocalyptic hermeneutics too, through the ages, should be insistently polemical, conceived always as interpretive stances not merely toward a text but also against other texts, especially other hermeneutics. *I* read the apocalyptic texts right, it is assumed. *I* possess the key to their true eternal divine sense, *I* alone can correct the errors of the ages. Whereas my hermeneutical rivals interpret the texts, and by interpreting them distort them, "reduce" their divine meaning to partial human versions of the truth, *I* have unmediated contact with God's intention, and *my* understanding "represents" God's truth on earth.

It is not difficult to imagine the motivations behind such polemics; the apocalypse is a cultural topos whose stakes are always unbearably high—whose lure is always to philosophies of all or nothing. If the world is ending much—everything, in fact—depends on the accuracy of one's interpretations, which seals the fate of one's eternal soul and the souls of one's religious group, heaven or hell, eternal delight or eternal destruction. And if the apocalypse always raises the hermeneutical stakes, it is perhaps not surprising that literary-critical interpretations of the apocalypse, despite their ostensible secularity, have been equally insistent on their exclusive rightness. The world is not ending for most contemporary critics; indeed, their idea is frequently to deny the imminence of the end and to chastise those who make such predictions. And yet, revealingly enough, their rhetoric is charged with the same urgency, the same interpretive assertiveness that has characterized apocalyptic writing since the Book of Daniel. Nor is this in any way unfortunate or lamentable. The persistence of apocalyptic rhetoric in antiapocalyptic polemics testifies to the cultural power of the apocalypse, its ability to focus attention on ultimate things.

What is unfortunate, perhaps, is the confusion in terminology that results. Robert Alter's assumption that if Barth, Heller, Pynchon, and others are "apocalyptic" writers, they must "see men as huddled masses waiting to be thrown into sulphurous pits" is only the most blatant case I have found of the potential for misunderstanding the apocalyptic thrust. The truth is that when one reads a casual reference to a novel or poem or political mood as "apocalyptic," one normally has little notion of what the writer means. Take Poe's *Narrative of Arthur Gordon Pym,* for instance, which is, surely, one of America's most apocalyptic novels. Is it apocalyptic because it conveys a sense of ontological crisis that generates existential dread, as Sidney P. Moss argues? Or is it apocalyptic because, as Todd M. Lieber maintains, it achieves an imaginative isolation from an intolerable reality, spinning out a psychological fantasy world that is more real than reality itself? Or is it apocalyptic because, as David Ketterer suggests, it points to an arabesque realm beyond our world?[12] Because each of these critics adopts a polemical interpretive stance that pointedly excludes all others, the reader is left in a quandary. The apocalypse can be any or all of these things; perhaps it is none of them.

One is tempted to tame the terminological proliferations brought on by such polemics through a cool historicism or thematism, a distancing of observer from observed in order to generate the reassuring illusion that the apocalypse is something to be studied, a theme, a cultural phenomenon, a series of historical frames: an object, that is, an other, a slide for the microscope. But even apart from the severe philosophical difficulties this illusion of objectivity presents, one should be warned off such methodological reassurance by its very coolness, by the attendant loss of power. One might, for example, group all apocalyptic hermeneutics under the pejorative "reductive" rubric, denying the biblical texts and all of their later interpretations any access to loci of truth. According to such a rubric, the Book of Revelation speaks to its own time, not to ours; it was written for a first-century audience who expected the world to end around A.D. 95, and it lost all relevance when the world did not end as predicted. We read it today, therefore, as a kind of curious quirk of New Testament times that holds a certain interest for historical-critical Bible scholars as a reductive reading of the Book of Daniel (which, in turn, is a mildly interesting reductive reading of the Book of Jeremiah), but that is of no particular significance to the modern reader.

But it should be obvious that the biblical texts have not lost their explanatory power. Whether or not we want to allow them access to a locus of truth, we must recognize the enormous grip they continue to have on our imaginations—their tremendous cultural, artistic, ideological productivity—and somehow attempt to come to terms with it. Historicist and thematic treatments of apocalyptic texts as mere reductions of reductions mark a repressive attempt to protect the imagination from the power of the apocalypse, a psychic defense against the lure of the apocalyptic all or nothing—a defense that, because it is repressive, significantly fails either to confront the apocalypse or to engage its power. To engage that power, it seems essential that apocalyptic hermeneutics not be reduced but that they be explored in and through their claims to representativeness, their insistence that their interpretations of the apocalyptic texts represent the intentions of those texts.

This insistence is surely misguided; these interpretations are surely distortive, reductive. But how can we prove it? Only by claiming to possess the true intended meaning of the texts, against which to measure the reductiveness of any given interpretation—a claim that implicates us too in the hermeneutical fray. (If I invoke here the work of exegetical Bible scholars to make a representative claim stick, that claim, too, should be read in the shifting context of hermeneutical polemics.) The power of apocalyptic hermeneutics, I suggest, surges from their polemical insistence that their interpretive distortions are *not* distortions—from their heroic attempts to generate meaning out of the loss of meaning, divine intention out of human desire. These attempts are buttressed by the invocation of unimpeachable sources: God spoke to me, an angel (or Hermes, god of interpretation) brought me the truth in a dream, or, in literary criticism, Bible scholars support my claims. Unimpeachable sources, unmediated access to intended meaning—these are critical fictions that both undermine and facilitate interpretation, that both relativize truth and make it possible to talk about truth.

My approach to apocalyptic hermeneutics is specifically relativistic, relational. My interpretive norm is what might be called "mutual representation," the assumption that any two hermeneutics, even if they ultimately fail to reach some absolute locus of truth, will in some significant way represent *each other*. That is, I seek here (and throughout the book) to place myself hermeneutically between texts, to read texts in assertive intertextual relation and thus to understand the "field" of apocalyptic hermeneutics less as a spatialized battlefield than as a temporal succession of battles, a complex chain of one-on-one conflicts between interpretations whose ground is therefore constantly shifting. If this approach conjures an illusion of interpretive three-dimensionality (and it is intended to), it should not be taken as erecting a stable interpretive structure. The schema I work toward in this chapter is a thematic fiction that may shed light for a moment but must soon be superseded and qualified by confrontations with (and among) different texts in later chapters.

Let us enter the hermeneutical fray, then, through R. W. B. Lewis's seminal essay on the "comic-apocalypses" of contemporary American literature, "Days of Wrath and Laughter." Lewis begins by setting up a pair of apocalyptic hermeneutics, which he calls the "Lutheran" and the "Augustinian" strains, and placing himself in subtle opposition to the (considerable) exegetical authority of R. H. Charles:

> "It was," Charles argues, "from the apocalyptic side of Judaism
> that Christianity was born." The statement is probably true,
> but it is misleading. The Christian vision of history is undoubt-
> edly apocalyptic: if we grant that latter term a high degree of
> dialectical flexibility. But Charles tended to identify apocalypse
> with catastrophe, and hence with an uncompromisingly glum
> view of the moral and spiritual potentialities of mankind. Given

that identification, I should prefer to say that a certain great phase of Christianity was born out of Judean apocalyptics—and I am tempted to call it "the Lutheran phase," as against the Thomistic phase, for example, or even the Augustinian; using quotation marks to indicate a strain as old as Christianity and one which seems to be in the ascendancy today, and on not unreasonable grounds. (195-96)

A few pages later, Lewis takes his own interpretive stance by identifying the "Lutheran" strain as a reductive or distortive interpretation of the Book of Revelation and the "Augustinian" as the representative or intended interpretation:

There has been as much controversial wrestling with the meanings of Revelations over the centuries as there have been shifts and rearrangements of the elements by other and later apocalyptic writers. On the one hand, for example, it seems now generally believed that phrases like "a new heaven and a new earth" and "coming down" are primarily spatial metaphors; that "a new heaven" is not God's heaven, but the visible heavens—taken metaphorically, however, as part of a radically transformed spiritual condition; while God's heaven, the divine kingdom, continues as traditionally to be the eventual domain of the blessed—but again, as the name of a spiritual estate, wherever the blessed might be simplemindedly thought to reside in physical fact. . . . The author of the Book of Revelation, for example, saw the earthly millennium in the far future, and was not, one gathers, very much interested in it. (197)

This is, *mutatis mutandis,* Augustine's allegorical interpretation of John's Apocalypse from Book 20 of *De civitate Dei.* The cosmic battle depicted in the Book of Revelation is no historical prediction, as in the "Lutheran" strain, but a spiritual allegory, a narrative metaphor for man's inner ethical growth toward God. The "Lutheran" reading of the book as an account of actual future events is easily dismissed as naively literal: "wherever," Lewis writes, "the blessed might be simplemindedly thought to reside in physical fact." Augustine believed that the earthly millennium was *now,* in the worldly reign of the Church, and he consigned the New Jerusalem to the far and therefore uninteresting future. When Lewis claims (in the traditional "representative" invocation of authorial intention) that "the author of the Book of Revelation . . . saw the earthly millennium in the far future, and was not, one gathers, very much interested in it," he is modifying (or mistaking) Augustine only very slightly.

Lewis's aim is to discredit his so-called Lutheran strain of apocalyptic by denying it scriptural sanction—a typical enough move in the history of apocalyptic polemics but one that in this case seems strangely undermotivated. Augustine, of course, had a doctrinal system to defend, a system whose internal coherence is directly threatened by the kind of historical disconfirmation to which apocalyptic prediction is susceptible. But it is difficult to imagine R. W. B. Lewis exercised by questions of doctrinal coherence. True, predictive apocalyptic is a booming and vulgar industry these days; grocery store bookracks overflow with slick paperbacks promising swift retribution to the quiescent and eternal redemption to those who buy the books. But this is irritating, not threatening. Why is Lewis so concerned to take a stance against the predictive "Lutheran" strain?

His polemic becomes even more puzzling when one realizes that it is offered in opposition to a rather well-established exegetical tradition of twentieth-century Bible scholarship, beginning with R. H. Charles in the early decades of this century and continuing, using increasingly sophisticated historical and philological methods in English through the work of H. H. Rowley, D. S. Russell, Paul D. Hanson, and others, into the present.[13] When Lewis says that "it seems now generally believed" that the Book of Revelation was intended allegorically, he means believed by dogmaticians, systematic theologians, ideologues concerned with making Christianity make sense. Exegetes, the historicists and formalists of Bible studies, disagree. Exegetes now generally believe that the writers of the biblical apocalypse did believe that the end was near; they did expect a momentous historical upheaval within a very few years of their writing and at least within their lifetimes, an upheaval that would rid them of the oppressive present and usher in a glorious new age of righteousness, presided over by Christ himself. Indeed, the exegetical evidence is compelling; and while it is too involved to probe in depth here, some sense of the pervasiveness of these predictive hopes can be gained by a quick look at the texts themselves. The New Testament writers, for example, are unanimous. Paul says that "the appointed time has grown very short" (1 Cor 7:29), Peter that "the end of all things is at hand" (1 Pet 4:7), John that "it is the last hour" (1 John 2:18), and John of Patmos opens and closes the Book of Revelation with promises of imminent relief: "The Revelation of Jesus Christ, which God gave him to show to his servants what must soon take place; ... for the time is near" (Rev 1:1, 3), and "he who testifies to these things says, 'Surely I am coming soon'" (Rev 22:20). Jesus himself, the apocalyptic Messiah, tells his disciples that "there are some standing here who will not taste death before they see that the kingdom of God has come with power" (Mark 9:1).

This suggests that Lewis's "Augustinian strain" of apocalypse is a strong misreading of the Apocalypse, as Harold Bloom would put it, in Hebraic terms a midrashic revision or, in the terms I am employing here, a hermeneutic, an interested interpretation of the Book of Revelation whose motivation can be traced.[14] The writers of the biblical apocalypses believed in an imminent end, not in an infinitely deferred one. But this means that the "Lutheran strain" too is a strong misreading of the Apocalypse. When John of Patmos described "what must soon take place," he meant by "soon" sometime around A.D. 95. Luther took him to mean not the first but the sixteenth century, and Protestant apocalyptists since Luther have invariably insisted upon the same revision, reinterpreting the predictions so as to project an end in *their* day, up to Hal Lindsey in ours, who predicts the end of the world in 1988.[15] The exegetical hermeneutic of R. H. Charles and other Bible scholars differs substantially from this predictive hermeneutic, of course. Exegetes insist that the apocalypses be read in their historical context, while the "Lutheran" and "Augustinian" strains, as named by Lewis, are both essentially interpretive means for establishing the relevance of a first-century text to the present.

In another sense, however, Luther and Hal Lindsey (along with the many others who have adopted the same hermeneutic) remain firmly within the apocalyptic tradition of the Bible; for as Lindsey revises Luther's revision of St. John, so too did St. John revise "Daniel's" revision of Jeremiah.[16] Indeed it is a defining characteristic of the biblical apocalypses to revise, and to keep revising, previous interpretations of the end in order to keep the end always in the near future; the only difference between St. John and Luther in this respect is that the former is canonical and the latter is not. For exegetes, this is of course an all-important difference: St. John is worth their attention in ways that Lindsey is not. But in terms of cultural history, the difference between canonical and noncanonical revisions of past predictions is always secondary to the revisionary motive of imminent expectation that propels both.

What the disconfirmation of apocalyptic predictions has meant for this sort of expectant interpreter is simply the necessity of refiguring the dates. The Augustinian tradition takes another tack: disconfirmation signals the necessity of shifting interpretation to a different level. Augustine correctly perceived that even if the Book of Revelation was intended as a prediction of impending doom, and even if that prediction has remained unfulfilled, it can still be made to serve another and possibly more important function. After all, this line of reasoning runs, although John never mentions individuals in the book, never mentions their central problems of distinguishing truth from falsehood, good from evil, and thereby right action from wrong, his implicit intention is to paint a picture of good and evil revealed in their true form so as to facilitate ethical choice. Most importantly for *individuals,* therefore, the Book of Revelation is not a historical prediction but an ethical allegory: God and Satan figure the two opposing poles of mankind's internal struggle, and by reading the book one is guided to make the correct choice.

The Augustinian interpretation, one might say, as opposed to the Lutheran or predictive interpretation, is more "useful," more "constructive," more "responsible," more solidly grounded in the psychological realities of human life in ongoing history. As such, it is also better suited to political conservatives—those defenders of the status quo, ideologues of the "good citizen," and protectors of law and order— than to the always implicitly revolutionary predictive interpretation. Here we have the beginnings of an explanation for Lewis's hermeneutical stance. Predictive apocalypse is an overt threat not only to dogmatic systems but also to the existing world order, in its insistence that God is to arrive momentarily to destroy it. So as long as the Christians were a persecuted minority, there was great comfort in this interpretation. But as Bernard McGinn reminds us, when Rome converted to Christianity in A.D. 313, "the destinies of *imperium* and *Christianitas* seemed to have been providentially unified, [and] many Christians felt that any expectation of the downfall of the empire was as disloyal to God as it was to Rome."[17] And so there arose a powerful need to defuse the revolutionary spirit of primitive Christianity, a need Augustine filled in *The City of God,* presenting there a deeply conservative revision of the Book of Revelation that was to remain the only orthodox position on the book for over a thousand years—until the revolutionary undercurrent in the Church grew strong enough to achieve a Reformation, and returned (most powerfully through Luther's 1545 "Preface" to the Book of Revelation) to a literal reading of the Apocalypse.[18]

This, surely, is the political context in which one must interpret Lewis's resistance to what he appropriately refers to as the "Lutheran" strain of apocalypse. Lewis has no dogmatic axe to grind; imminent prediction is no threat to any doctrinal system of his, even assuming he has one. But the revolutionary fervor of the mid-sixties *is* a potent threat to his conservative political position. The author of *The American Adam* in 1955 has turned around ten years later to find that his students have taken him seriously—that *they* are trying to become new Adams and new Eves through a revolution that Charles Reich would later term the "greening of America."[19] Lewis's veiled hostility toward contemporary American fiction, therefore, should probably be read as a measure of his apprehension that what is finally at stake in that fiction is the survival of established values. "Contemporary American fiction," he says in "Days of Wrath and Laughter," "or the vein of it which I have been mining, seems determined to draw us on toward that cliff edge, or to watch with a sort of bitter contemptuous laugh as we draw ourselves on—only to leave us there, swaying ambiguously, just before the sound of midnight" (234). What Augustine offers Lewis is not doctrinal credibility but a secure conservatism that stresses *learning* over revolution, through the infinite deferral of apocalyptic crisis.

Lewis does not expand on his sense of the Augustinian alternative to Lutheran prediction; his essay is a relatively single-minded, if complexly veiled, attack on the "wrong" kind of apocalyptic thought. But at least one of his followers has undertaken the task of unfolding the Augustinian perspective. John R. May, appropriately enough a Roman Catholic priest, in his *Toward a New Earth: Apocalypse in the American Novel* (1972), follows Lewis implicitly in his choice of texts and adds to Lewis's theoretical arsenal an impressive familiarity with systematic theology; but unlike Lewis, May takes the central American novels not as "reductive" but as "representative" of the biblical apocalypse. For both critics, the intended meaning of the Book of Revelation is ethical rather than predictive; but for Lewis American apocalypses are predictive ("time present in the contemporary American novel," he says in "Days of Wrath and Laughter," "is precisely the moment of the last loosening of Satan" [199]) and are therefore misled, escapist, puerile; while for May these apocalypses too are ethical and therefore "serious." In place of Lewis's rather dubious readings of American "comic apocalypses," which always seem to be pointing toward cataclysm no matter how uncataclysmic they are on the surface, May develops a displaced ethical symbolism in which every external conflict and renewal has an internal significance, so that, for example, "The death of the individual as typical of a phase of society or of the fate awaiting a certain unacceptable response to living" may well render a novel, in May's terms, "apocalyptic."[20] Interestingly enough, by assimilating the imagery of historical ends and paradisal beginnings to inner growth, May assimilates the biblical apocalypse of St. John to an unmistakably antiapocalyptic perspective: "Where a millenarian viewpoint is secularized," May claims, "history may be imagined . . . as a process of transformation without end" (36).

If, then, we read Lewis as aligning contemporary American novels with a "literal" (predictive in an external, historical realm of collective action) interpretation of the apocalypse and May as aligning

American fiction with an "allegorical" (ethical in an internal, psychological realm of individual moral decisions), we have so far two interpretations of the apocalypse (literal/predictive, allegorical/ethical) and two evaluations of American literature in those interpretive contexts. The alignments become rather more complex, however, when we note the similarities of May's ethical apocalypse with the internal, allegorical perspectives on the apocalypse developed out of William Blake by Northrop Frye, for example, in which Augustine's ethical emphasis on right and wrong is crucially supplanted with a Romantic emphasis on imagination and its absence, on visionary versus mundane perception. For Frye and Blake, as for Augustine, the Book of Revelation is to be read as allegory—but as Blake would put it, it is allegory addressed not to the "Corporeal Understanding" but to the "Intellectual powers," an allegory not of ethical choice but of *vision*.[21] A representative passage is Plate 14 from Blake's *Marriage of Heaven and Hell:*

> The ancient tradition that the world will be consumed in fire at the end of six thousand years is true, as I have heard from Hell.
>
> For the cherub with his flaming sword is hereby commanded to leave his guard at the tree of life, and when he does, the whole creation will be consumed, and appear infinite. and holy whereas it now appears finite & corrupt.
>
> This will come to pass by an improvement of sensual enjoyment.
>
> But first the notion that man has a body distinct from his soul, is to be expunged; this I shall do, by printing in the infernal method, by corrosives, which in Hell are salutary and medicinal, melting apparent surfaces away, and displaying the infinite which was hid.
>
> If the doors of perception were cleansed every thing would appear to man as it is: infinite.
>
> For man has closed himself up, till he sees all things thro' narrow chinks of his cavern. (39)

Blake's Romantic apocalypse, as this passage suggests, entails a revelation or unveiling initiated not by God but by man—or by the godman that every man is if he but knew it. The fiery "consumption" of the world is a consumption of our false *perception* of the world, which the poet reveals as illusion and removes, leaving only true reality, which is infinite, an apocalyptic paradise. The old husk of the world, the false reality that *we* take for real, Blake images as the Covering Cherub from Gen 3:24 and Ezek 28:14-16, the living creature that God stationed at the gate of Eden to block mankind from the tree of life, whose fruit would make human beings into gods. By destroying that Cherub—or, here, by simply ordering it to depart—the poet opens the gate to paradise and to man's natural divinity. But it is important to stress that in this revision of the biblical apocalypse, the renewed reality is always there, there right now, and transformation is only a matter of learning to *see* it.

Blake's apocalypse is also closely linked with his crucial notion of centers and circumferences, which in fact becomes the focal image of all of Frye's work. "When we pass into anagogy," Frye writes in the *Anatomy of Criticism,*

> nature becomes, not the container, but the thing contained, and the archetypal universal symbols, the city, the garden, the quest, the marriage, are no longer the desirable forms that man constructs inside nature, but are themselves the forms of nature. Nature is now inside the mind of an infinite man who builds his cities out of the Milky Way. This is not reality, but it is the conceivable or imaginative limit of desire, which is infinite, eternal, and hence apocalyptic.[22]

In Frye's Blakean apocalypse man expands from his shrunken, worm-like existence at the center of a dead and alien world into a giant visionary form—an "infinite man"—that inhabits the circumference and thus encompasses all. Otherness is subsumed into innerness; things that once were isolate are subsumed into identity, in the double sense of being identical (absolute Oneness) and of retaining, and at the same time finally attaining, their true individual identity (the Many in the One).[23]

Frye's apocalyptic hermeneutic has of course been tremendously influential, particularly in studies of English Romanticism that have appeared since his *Fearful Symmetry* in 1947. Readings of the apocalyptic visions of Blake, Wordsworth, Shelley, and others over the past three decades have almost without exception been conceived (implicitly or explicitly) as extensions of or oppositions to Frye. Interestingly enough, however, Frye has proved considerably less influential in studies of the American apocalypse, where the influence of R. W. B. Lewis remains dominant. One significant attempt to link the two interpretive traditions with specific reference to American literature did appear in the mid-seventies, however: David Ketterer's *New Worlds for Old* (1974), which takes the apocalypse to involve a "moment of juxtaposition and consequent transformation or transfiguration when an old world of mind discovers a believable new world of mind, which . . . nullifies the old system" (13). Perhaps due to Ketterer's concern with science fiction, however, fiction whose major premises are derived from the empiricist tradition that Blake indicts, he invariably insists on otherness. The apocalypse, in his reading, is brought about not through the revelation of the true world but through the *creation of other worlds,* which do not become the apocalyptic reality but only serve as catalysts for learning. That is, other worlds remain other, but by juxtaposition with an empirically defined "real" world bring about a change in sensibility. Ketterer defines three different strains of his apocalyptic fiction, all of which are characterized precisely by otherness: (1) the "visionary" strain, which offers "other worlds out of space and time"; (2) the "dystopian" strain, which offers "other worlds in space and time"; and (3) the "philosophical" strain, which portrays "the present world in other terms." The visionary strain would appear at first blush to be the most overtly Blakean of the three, but it is presented as including space flight of all things, that rationalistic reduction of the apocalypse from entrance into a spiritual heaven (the biblical vision Blake condemned as external to man) to entrance into the *natural* heavens, which are not only external but material as well. Ketterer's "visionary" strain thus becomes almost a parodic inversion of Blake's apocalypse, moving toward a greater rather than a lesser externality. The "dystopian" or "satiric" strain focuses upon antiutopian visions, endtime visions whose issue is not transfiguration but a new perspective on the "real" world; and the "philosophical" strain in Ketterer's argument finally becomes an umbrella for all three, his composite apocalypse, essentially synonymous with Robert Scholes's notion of fabulation: "Fabulation, then," Scholes says, "is fiction that offers a world clearly and radically discontinuous from the world we know, yet returns to confront that known world in some cognitive way."[24]

A key to Ketterer's revision of Frye, as I say, may lie in the scientific materialism underlying science fiction itself, a positivistic ideology in which subject remains forever subject and object object. And for the *locus classicus* of the materialistic apocalypse in our century we may look to Henry Adams, who in *The Education* set scientific materialism in opposition to the Romantic apocalypse of his own country, the vision of Emerson:

> He never reached Concord, and to Concord Church he, like the rest of mankind who accepted a material universe, remained always an insect, or something much lower—a man. It was surely no fault of his that the universe seemed real to him; perhaps— as Mr. Emerson justly said—it was so; in spite of the long-continued effort of a lifetime, he perpetually fell back into the

heresy that if anything universal was unreal, it was himself and not the appearances; it was the poet and not the banker; it was his own thought, not the thing that moved it.[25]

Surely matter is more real than mind, Adams declares. Under the circumstances, it is wisest for mind not to elevate itself too greatly, but to remain duly humble before the vast material cosmos. "If this view was correct," Adams concludes grimly in his chapter, "The Grammar of Science," "the mind could gain nothing by flight or fight; it must merge in its supersensual multiverse, or succumb to it" (461). The result in either case, of course, is the same: dissolution.

If this is true, however, one wonders why Adams felt called—or how he felt able—to write an "education." With this radical pessimism in the power of the human mind, one would have thought that he would have nothing to say—or no words to say it in. While Adams never confronts this dilemma directly, he does illustrate his awareness of the problem in a passage from the "Teufelsdröckh" chapter—a passage that is also one of his clearest statements of his apocalyptic sensibility:

> Adams proclaimed that in the last synthesis, order and anarchy were one, but that the unity was chaos. As anarchist, conservative and Christian, he had no motive or duty but to attain the end; and, to hasten it, he was bound to accelerate progress; to concentrate energy; to intensify forces; to reduce friction; increase velocity and magnify momentum, partly because this was the mechanical law of the universe as science explained it; but partly also in order to get done with the present which artists and some others complained of; and finally—and chiefly—because a rigorous philosophy required it, in order to penetrate the beyond, and satisfy man's destiny by reaching the largest synthesis in its ultimate contradiction. (406-7)

The inexorable apocalyptic movement of increased entropy, for Adams, is "the mechanical law of the universe as science explained it"—it is, in other words, material, really there, and not the product of a disordered Romantic fancy (though Adams significantly hedges with his "as science explained it"). The apocalypse is inevitable because material nature decrees it, which is in itself enough to encourage man to participate in it, by accelerating entropy. More than this, however, Adams is moved to join in the movement toward the "end" by motives that may seem both irresponsible and dangerous: let us "get done with the present which artists and some others complained of."

This is apocalypse as external material annihilation: the destruction of all life not by a God who can ensure continuity beyond the end in a spiritual state but by an indifferent material universe in which life is a not very welcome anomaly. *Otherness* is so inescapably dominant, in this view, that humans are imprisoned in subjectivity, in a mental cage that constricts as entropic dissolution accelerates, until otherness swallows up innerness.

It comes as something of a surprise, then, when Adams concludes his apocalyptic credo with a reassertion of the power of the mind: the power to know, perhaps even to survive the apocalypse or to be transformed by it, possibly to be translated to an Archimedean point from which we can see both life and death, the here and the beyond. But in a way Adams's style has already prepared us for this radical shift. For if the content of the credo tends to corroborate Adams's claim that "order and anarchy were one, but that the unity was chaos," his rhetoric announces precisely the opposite: that order and anarchy are one, but the unity is order. His opening verb "proclaim," after all, suggests ecclesiastical statements of divine truth; and the syntactic structure of the passage speaks powerfully of the human capacity for rendering disorder orderly. Beginning with a tidy summary of his paradoxical ideology ("anarchist, conservative and Christian"), Adams proceeds to define a clear goal ("to attain the end; and, to hasten it"), a series of steps by which the goal may be reached, and three reasons for undertaking the project. Even the initial statement of paradox speaks of human beings' ability to frame the contradictory in language.

And indeed later Adams offers quite a different credo, containing now at least a glimmer of hope, idealistic rather than materialistic, for the future:

> He had never been able to acquire knowledge, still less to impart it; and if he had, at times, felt serious differences with the American of the nineteenth century, he felt none with the American of the twentieth. For this new creation, born since 1900, a historian asked no longer to be teacher or even friend; he asked only to be a pupil, and promised to be docile, for once, even though trodden under foot; for he could see that the new American—the child of incalculable coal-power, chemical power, electric power, and radiating energy, as well as of new forces as yet undetermined—must be a sort of God compared with any former creation of nature. At the rate of progress since 1800, every American who lived to the year 2000 would know how to control unlimited power. He would think in complexities

unimaginable to an earlier mind. He would deal with problems altogether beyond the range of earlier society. To him the nineteenth century would stand on the same plane with the fourth—equally childlike—and he would only wonder how both of them, knowing so little, and so weak in force, should have done so much. (496-97)

The hope here, clearly, is that the power of mind to resolve complexity will increase proportionately with complexity itself; that as entropy increases in its downward march to the apocalypse, so also will men and women's ability to *control* their environment and perhaps to slow the entropic disintegration. If this truly did happen, one would not need to precipitate an apocalypse in order to gain insight into the contradictions, to achieve that largest synthesis that Adams insists is mankind's destiny; instead, one might even develop the power to *prevent* apocalyptic dissolution. These two impulses, toward and away from the apocalypse, centrally inform Adams's autobiography: the surrender to a constrictive annihilation in external matter and the assertion of the mind's power over matter as a token of continuity. In both apocalyptic hermeneutics—the one annihilative, the other continuative and even antiapocalyptic—crucial emphasis is placed precisely on otherness, on the alienation of mind from matter, of subject from object. And yet Adams's insistently dialectical imagination refuses to settle for mere difference; mind and matter are variously and complexly linked by the movement toward apocalypse, as the apocalyptic decline seems to enhance mind until, at the point of dissolution itself, man becomes capable of achieving the "largest synthesis in its ultimate contradiction." Mind and matter, one might argue, thus become interrelated parabolically, each coming to stand as a metonymic parable for the other: the surrender of mind to matter as matter's metonymy for dissolution, matter's descent into complexity as the mind's metonymy for synthetic mastery.

∎

Interestingly enough, where Lewis, May, and Frye all insisted that their readings of the Book of Revelation represented the intended meaning of the book, Ketterer more modestly settles for a definition that he admits is his own and is reductive. The problem is, he says, that the intended meaning of the Book of Revelation is no longer operative and that what we must do, therefore, is reduce that meaning to a new sense which *is* operative, a sense that Ketterer defines:

Within recent history our notion of the end of the world as something man himself may instigate, detracts considerably from the visionary coloration of a possible apocalypse. In a very real sense, the atomic bomb completed the process of secularization that apocalyptic thinking has undergone since medieval times. Consequently I submit that either the word apocalyptic has lost its meaning entirely and should become obsolete, or, if not, that it can be used coherently only in the sense defined by this book.[26]

Although Ketterer's apocalyptic definition is exegetically more modest than Lewis's, May's, or Frye's, clearly, it is no less exclusive. If we accept his claim that the atomic bomb has secularized the apocalypse beyond all representative ties to the Book of Revelation, then "apocalyptic . . . can be used coherently only in the sense defined by this book." But this only leaves us worse off than before. I don't believe, first of all, that nuclear weaponry has had any such effect on our understanding of the Book of Revelation; consider how cheerfully fundamentalists like Hal Lindsey incorporate it into their doomsday scenarios.[27] More important, the confusion surrounding the term *apocalypse* in contemporary usage stems directly from this terminological assertiveness, this polemical insistence upon reducing the term's meaning to exclusive interpretations. The claim to have the intended or representative reading of the Apocalypse at least grounds such assertiveness exegetically, regardless of the number of such assertions that might historically be made. Ketterer's claim that there *are* no representative interpretations simply opens wide the floodgates: now anyone can impose his or her own set of definitions on the material and claim absolute priority for them. This sort of maverick self-assertion inevitably leads to a state of affairs where careful commentators are forced to navigate around existing definitions like so many sandbars—Ketterer's to port, Frye's to starboard, Lewis's dead ahead—and in order to avoid going aground they must usually come up with their own polemical definition, which then becomes an obstacle for later commentators to avoid.

One alternative to this confusion, as I mentioned previously, is to chart the obstacles: to map out the terminological snags and sandbars as they have appeared and developed over the years and to plot a course for the earnest reader to follow. Such is the approach taken by M. H. Abrams in *Natural Supernaturalism* (1971), for example, and, rather more complexly, by Martha Banta in *Failure and Success in America: A Literary Debate* (1978).[28] Since both Abrams and Banta offer their taxonomies of apocalyptic visions less as preexistent realities than as heuristic critical fictions, this approach is in fact very fruitful; one comes away from both books with a rich sense of the range of apocalyptic hermeneutics that Lewis, May, Frye, and Ketterer never pretend to offer. What troubles me about both Abrams's and Banta's books, however, is that for both writers the "course" seems ultimately more important than the engagement with each obstacle. Abrams, especially, offers a rigidly historicist taxonomy that would fix the reader's progress through his texts like underwater rails, and Banta's more fluid explorations finally dissolve into the impressionist fantasy of a debate. Although both works are monumental attempts to bring order to the reigning confusion, and although the order they bring has significantly shaped my conception of the subject, I propose to take a different approach.

Something like that approach, in fact, is figured in Frank Kermode's important book, *The Sense of an Ending* (1967), in which two apocalyptic hermeneutics—"naive" or predictive apocalypse and "clerkly skepticism" or ethical antiapocalypse—become topoi that can be brought to bear on a range of cultural and ideological phenomena, most centrally our need for and resistance to "endings" in fiction.[29] An expanded version of Kermode's bipartite schema, in fact, based on the range of apocalyptic hermeneutics considered here, might present five interpretive stances or topoi by which the apocalypse might be understood: (1) the *biblical* prediction of an imminent end to history, controlled by God so as to provide for a paradisal continuation; (2) the *annihilative* prediction of an imminent end to history controlled by no God at all and followed by the void; (3) the *continuative* prediction of no end at all, but of simple secular historical continuity; (4) the *ethical* internalization of apocalyptic conflict as a figure for personal growth in ongoing history; and (5) the *Romantic* or visionary internalization of the fallen world by an act of imaginative incorporation, so that the world is revealed as the paradise it already is.

What we have here, of course, is a thematic fiction, a taxonomy by which we might organize not only the interpretive stances discussed in this chapter but the American apocalypses discussed subsequently in the course of this book. The five hermeneutics might be systematized by arraying them around a Fryean five-point circle, beginning at the apex with the biblical hermeneutic and moving counterclockwise around the circle through the annihilative, continuative, ethical, and Romantic hermeneutics back to the biblical. If we imagine each two adjacent hermeneutics in terms of what I earlier referred to as mutual representation, then each "opposition" must be thought of as mediated by a principle of convertibility, a common ground, as follows: (1) biblical and annihilative, mediated by the prediction of an imminent historical end; (2) annihilative and continuative, mediated by a "naturalistic" or secular perspective on history, with no deity to provide continuation if the world ends; (3) continuative and ethical, mediated by human survival in clock-time and yardstick-space, without radical transformation; (4) ethical and Romantic, mediated by a turning away from external history for an "idealistic" emphasis on mind, will, spirit, or imagination; and (5) Romantic and biblical, mediated by an act of imaginative transformation that brings about a real paradise. Each hermeneutic, for that matter, might also be thought of as itself a mediatory ground that contains adjacent principles of convertibility: (1) the biblical hermeneutic links cataclysmic prediction and visionary transformation; (2) the annihilative hermeneutic links end-prediction and the secular emphasis on the absence of God; (3) the continuative hermeneutic links the secular vision and the idea of survival; (4) the ethical hermeneutic links survival in ongoing history with the idealistic emphasis on mind or imagination; and (5) the Romantic hermeneutic links the internal perspective of idealism (the poet's imagination) and the vision of paradisal transformation.

Beyond these adjacent relations, it might also be useful to chart relations between wider arcs on the circle: specifically, between two hermeneutics on one side of the circle and two on the other, mediated by the fifth that stands between and in a sense contains the opposition. Thus, the biblical hermeneutic can be said to mediate between "literal" or "historical" interpretations (annihilative/continuative) and "spiritual" or "imaginative" interpretations (Romantic/ethical). The Book of Revelation "contains" all four other hermeneutics by at once predicting a literal transition from worldly history to a renewed state and encouraging its readers symbolically to undergo that transition in their own minds. This mediatory containment is to be expected, since the biblical apocalypse is the standard authority, the source used by later interpreters to derive their own versions of the future. But much the same mediatory containment might be said to operate at other points of opposition around the circle as well. The annihilative hermeneutic, for example, mediates between conflicting conceptions of life beyond the apocalyptic end. Whereas the biblical and Romantic interpretations posit a transformed paradise, the continuative and ethical interpretations treat the end as symbolic and life beyond it, therefore, as simply more of the same; the annihilative vision then stands between the this-life/afterlife opposition by positing a radical transformation, but only to the void that the continuative and ethical visions agree is the only alternative to continuation. The continuative hermeneutic might be said, similarly, to mediate between end-predictive (annihilative/biblical) and nonpredictive (ethical/Romantic) visions, itself predicting no end. And the ethical hermeneutic mediates between "secular" (continuative/ annihilative) and "religious" (Romantic/biblical) visions, retaining the ethical code of religion without the visionary eschatology espoused even by the superficially secular Romantic interpretation.

The most important mediation in a discussion of *American* apocalypses, however, is the mediation that is operative in the Romantic hermeneutic. American literature is a Romantic literature; its deviations from Romanticism are themselves definitively Romantic; and the American Dream as most mythically dreamed by our greatest Romantic apocalyptist, Ralph Waldo Emerson, is clearly the umbrella covering the entire range of American apocalypses. In terms of my diagram, it is surely appropriate that the Romantic hermeneutic specifically mediates between and encompasses the extremes of "apocalyptic" visions of an imminent, final, and total end (the biblical and annihilative interpretations) and of "antiapocalyptic" visions of historical continuation (the ethical and continuative interpretations).[30] To the extent that the Romantic hermeneutic posits a total transformation of reality through its reperception by the visionary poet, it is apocalyptic in the strictest theological sense of the word; but insofar as that transformation is entirely internal, a transformation not really of the world but of human perception, history does continue as always, now merely perceived truly. This theoretical framework suggests that by modulating the Romantic hermeneutic of Emerson, one should be able to construct working models of most American apocalypses (which is to say, *interpretations* of the apocalypse, along the mediated opposition between "apocalyptic" and "antiapocalyptic")—a suggestion that I believe will be borne out by close analysis, which then will speak for the usefulness of the diagram.

On the other hand, we should not become too attached to the diagram. Useful as such a schematization is, the reduction of texts to stripped-down illustrations of the five categories would be a mechanical and distasteful chore. Indeed the circle of apocalyptic hermeneutics will only take us so far without modification and qualification; therefore, I will offer more precise (though no less provisional) formulations of the schema in the context of specific American apocalypses throughout the book, most notably in chapters 3 and 5.

More important, the need for diagrams of this sort—however modified and qualified—raises disturbing questions that prompt some of the more involved theoretical discussions in later chapters. To what extent, for example, does the schematization of a subject imply its subsumption into an apocalyptic perspective—an extrinsic or Archimedean standpoint outside the verbal flux in an eternal beyond? To "thematize" a literary work is, as the word's etymology suggests, to reduce it to a "thesis," a *position,* a *place* in a comfortably spatialized universe where meanings do not change. Indeed, to the extent that the circle diagram resembles the cross-section of a stem, it seems to require what Ferdinand de Saussure, on the *analogy* of a stem, calls a synchronic discussion of texts, which tidily ignores the problems of change in time imposed by a diachronic perspective. Even the synchrony/diachrony distinction, for that matter, is a thematization based on the metaphorical positioning of critical inquiry by analogy with stems. It is clear that all criticism is thematization at some level, insofar as it seeks to organize a text into a new order imposed by the critic; but at what point does one decide that one's critical order is sufficient both to the understanding of the reader and to the complexity of the text? To refuse to thematize is to shirk the critic's responsibility; but to thematize too soon is to make that responsibility a sham.

The argument of this chapter (indeed like the argument of the book as a whole) should therefore be taken not as conclusive, but as heuristic: the syncretic diagram is offered not as a theme, not as a hermeneutic circle that will guide our path through individual texts, but as a single step, to be broken and deflected, in a potentially endless working through. Like the American writers with whom I am concerned, I have no ultimate "apocalyptic" conclusion to the problem of American apocalypses. What I offer instead is a series of shifting perspectives from which insights into the complexity of these works may be gained, arranged into a coherent but not syllogistic argument. Like the always predicted, always deferred apocalypse itself, ultimate understanding of American apocalypses in my analysis will be persistently approached—but never attained. *Caveat lector.*

P A R T

ONE

Trembling Sea (Erik Sandgren, 1982)

SIGNS OF THE TIMES

*Thus, weary of life, in view of the great consummation
which awaits us—tomorrow, we rush among our friends
congratulating ourselves upon the joy soon to be.
Thoughtless of evil we crush out the marrow of those
about us with our heavy cars as we go happily from
place to place. It seems that there is not time enough
in which to speak the full of our exaltation. Only a
day is left, one miserable day, before the world comes
into its own. Let us hurry! Why bother for this man
or that? In the offices of the great newspapers a mad
joy reigns as they prepare the final extras. Rushing
about, men bump each other into the whirring presses.
How funny it seems. All thought of misery has left
us. Why should we care? Children laughingly fling
themselves under the wheels of the street cars, airplanes
crash gaily to the earth. Someone has written a poem.*
                —*William Carlos Williams,* Spring and All

Is the great consummation near?

Or, more critically, by what signs can we determine its near-
ness? Jesus gives us a list of such signs in the famous "Little Apocalypse
of the Gospels" in Mark 13 (with redactions in Matt 24 and Luke 21):
wars, earthquakes, famines, persecutions . . . But these signs have appeared again and again since Jesus' hopeful prediction, and still the end
delays. Do the signs themselves have signs? How far back in a chain of
signification need one go before one attains a position of certainty?

For Jesus, the problem posed by the "signs of the times" was not a problem, and in the passage from which the phrase derives he chides the Jewish scholars for failing to read the signs aright:

> The Pharisees and Sadducees came, and to test him they asked him to show them a sign from heaven. He answered them, "When it is evening, you say, 'It will be fair weather, for the sky is red.' And in the morning, 'It will be stormy today, for the sky is red and threatening.' You know how to interpret the appearance of the sky, but you cannot interpret the signs of the times. An evil and adulterous generation seeks for a sign, but no sign shall be given it except the sign of Jonah." (Matt 16:1-4)

But the Jews of Jesus' time are understandably wary: by the arrival of Jesus they had been awaiting the Messiah for some five hundred years and had had their hopes dashed sufficiently often to demand proof. The only proof adequate to their expectation is a sign *from heaven*—which is to say, a sign not of the times at all, not from the historical realm, but directly from God. What the Jews want as evidence is a self-evidential sign, a sign that interprets itself so thoroughly that it is not subject to interpretation, a sign that stands so securely outside historical space and time that it cannot be spatially or temporally disconfirmed. Cannily, Jesus refuses—either because (as in orthodox explanations) the Jews must be given the leeway to reject his teaching in order that the Gentiles might be saved or because (in secular revision) he had no self-evidential sign to offer. The one sign he promises them is the sign of Jonah, the return from symbolic death in the whale's belly that typologically anticipates his Resurrection. This was potentially a self-evidential sign to the disciples (though among them Thomas required evidence), but still not to the Jews, to whom Jesus never appeared after he rose from the dead. What's more, the sign of Jonah was far from the messianic sign the Jews were asking for. As we shall see in chapter 5, the sign of Jonah was if anything antiapocalyptic, insofar as it presented an image of doom that brought on not doom itself but doom-averting repentance. The sign of Jonah offers the Jews no evidence whatever of future restoration; instead it anticipates (typologically in the salvation of Nineveh) the salvation of the Gentiles, the very enemies whose messianic destruction was imminently awaited.

All that Jesus leaves the Jews with, therefore, are the signs of the times: history itself, conceived as a sequence from the past through a transformative present to a redeemed future, which, if correctly interpreted, propels the interpreter *into* the future. The difficulty with the signs of the times, however, is that they are part of the very temporal sequence they supposedly undermine. The times are made to signify the end of time, but the temporal nature of that signification itself defers the end. Time is at once the vehicle of eschatological fulfillment, always bringing the awaited end closer, and the obstacle to that fulfillment, ever standing between the present and the infinitely deferred future. In other words, without a self-evidential sign from heaven, the predictive apocalyptic imagination is boxed into an anxiety-producing dialectic between the certainty of past deferrals and the uncertainty of future expectation, which continually forces predictive interpreters to reinterpret the signs of the times so as to maintain the dialectical tension. The tension must be maintained, whatever anxieties it generates. To allow expectation to slide unopposed into the historical past is to become resigned, quiescent, unexpectant; and that is to relinquish the biblical vision of apocalypse.

This talk of "signs" and "signification," however—of the *semeion ek tou ouranou* and the *semeia ton kairon*—suggests that what is really at stake in the predictive apocalyptic imagination is a conjunction or disjunction between words and deeds, between language and event, between signs and the thing itself. The Book of Revelation is a completed semiotic pattern of apocalyptic fulfillment, moving from tribulation to paradisal restoration; but its very closing words, "Come, Lord Jesus!" (Rev 22:20), insistently point up the incompletion of the pattern in the world. Or, put differently, the Book of Revelation is a semiotic of completion that contains within itself the telling trace of incompletion. The very fact of its existence, of the need for its existence, is evidence of its incompletion, and the references to the imminence of completion integrate that evidence into the text itself. This is, as Jacques Derrida argues in "Differance," the dilemma of all Western metaphysics:

> Let us begin with the problem of signs and writing—since we are already in the midst of it. We ordinarily say that a sign is put in place of the thing itself, the present thing—"thing" holding here for the sense as well as the referent. Signs represent the present in its absence; they take the place of the present. When we cannot take hold of or show the thing, let us say the present, the being-present, when the present does not present itself, then we signify, we go through the detour of signs. We take up or give signs; we make signs. The sign would thus be a deferred presence. Whether it is a question of verbal or written signs, monetary signs, electoral delegates, or political representatives, the movement of signs defers the moment of encountering the thing

itself, the moment at which we could lay hold of it, consume or expend it, touch it, see it, have a present intuition of it.[1]

The burden of the history of Western metaphysics, which Derrida traces back through Edmund Husserl, Martin Heidegger, Freud, Nietzsche, Hegel, and ultimately to Plato, is the awareness of loss (absence) and the desire for restoration (presence): the loss of Eden, in the biblical metaphysics, and the desire for its apocalyptic restoration. But Derrida directs particular attention to the double bind created by the necessary imposition of *language* between present absence and absent presence. To bridge the gap between desire and its fulfillment, "we make signs"—but "the movement of signs defers the moment of encountering the thing itself." Language, signification, is for Derrida at once mankind's only hope of bridging the gap and the gap itself. "Discursive thought, philosophy, Western man," as Eric LaGuardia has summarized this position, "thus find themselves in a predicament in which the collective desire of being to be present to itself as itself must make use of the instruments of representation to realize the desire, at the same time suppressing the knowledge that it is precisely representation which constitutes the gap between absence and presence."[2] Hope is made possible only by what Heidegger calls forgetfulness: forget the linguistic ground for hope, because to remember that would be to remember the necessity of deferral implicit in signs.[3]

Derrida's master concept for this complex of deferred signification is "differance," which he derives, by way of a French pun (*différer* as both "to differ" and "to defer"), from the Latin verb *differo* (to carry [*fero*] away [*dis*]), which also has both meanings. To differ is to discern or distinguish, to chart an interval or distance in space; to defer is to postpone, to delay or hold in reserve, to chart an interval in time. If in biblical terms spatial difference marks the interval between earth and heaven, and temporal deferral the interval between present and future, then apocalyptic differance might be said, in Derrida's terms, to be "space's becoming-temporal and time's becoming-spatial, [the] 'primordial constitution' of space and time, as metaphysics or transcendental phenomenology would call it in the language that is here criticized and displaced" (136).

Even though Derrida in "Differance" never mentions apocalyptic metaphysics, it is clear that the metaphysical tradition he traces back to Plato is crucial to the biblical apocalypses as well; indeed, the writers of the New Testament (NT) are probably the most influential propagators of the metaphysics of presence in the history of Western thought. If Derrida therefore helps one to think about the dynamics of apocalyptic expectation, surely the imagistic richness of the biblical apocalypses will also help one to think about Derrida. More important, American apocalypses offer a useful series of perspectives on the antimetaphysical perspective Derrida seeks not to inhabit, the ideological grounds from which he attacks the metaphysics of presence but on which he cannot allow himself to seem to stand. American writers, as recent interpretations are beginning to reveal, have consistently been concerned with self-deconstruction; but they deconstruct themselves, I maintain, in order to reconstruct an iconic ground in which deconstruction can *be* reconstruction, in which negated assertion can still assert.

But that is to anticipate a later stage in my argument. Here I propose to focus not on the most rigorously innovative American apocalypses but on two orthodox biblical apocalypses that demonstrate the pitfalls of predictive apocalyptic. By examining these works, that is, I propose to define the stance that classic American writers will insistently seek to move beyond. The first work to be analyzed is a recent middle-brow bestseller, titled *The Seven Last Years* (1979), by Carol Balizet, a Florida nurse. It is a novel based explicitly on the apocalyptic predictions of Hal Lindsey. The second work is another American bestseller—in fact, America's first: Michael Wigglesworth's Puritan apocalypse *The Day of Doom* (1662), an incongruously bouncy ballad about the Last Judgment. Both works are strictly orthodox: Wigglesworth was a Puritan divine, and Balizet, though professionally no theologian, is an avid reader of Lindsey's popular theology; and both works adhere closely to their doctrinal sources.

What I find most significant about the two books taken together is that while both claim to be simply elaborating on the biblical predictions of apocalypse, they emphasize wholly different segments of the biblical account, and so reflect rather different attitudes toward the coming end. Balizet's focus is entirely on the tribulation, Wigglesworth's on the Last Judgment, which means that Balizet ends her novel at almost exactly the point where Wigglesworth begins his poem: the coming of Christ. Balizet thus moots the question of the judgment, just as Wigglesworth relegates the tribulation to only a few stanzas at the opening of his poem. Progressing from Balizet to Wigglesworth, therefore, will provide a useful schema of the apocalypse in its orthodox biblical rendition, and allow an exploration of some of the problems raised by the hermeneutics of literal prediction. To do this, of course, one must scrutinize works that per se do not merit such scrutiny. But, as Northrop Frye remarks in the *Anatomy of Criticism,* "archetypes are most easily studied in highly conventionalized literature: that is, for the most part, naive, primitive, and popular literature."[4] Though my focus is less archetypal than Frye's, his dictum may stand as a motto for the readings in this chapter.

∎

The Balizet passage I propose to examine here marks a turning point in the novel, just after an earthquake signals the beginning of the seven-year tributary period that figures in the book's title and frames the temporal scope of the novel (1988-1995). It begins with the gingerly establishment of intellectual contact between Stubby Kraft, a fifteen-year-old Jewish boy, and Craig McKenzie, a nineteen-year-old nominal Christian. Metatextually, Stubby doubles here as the author, Craig as the backsliding reader who believes only in word and who, through the medium of the novel, must be brought to believe in thought and deed as well:

> "Craig, are you a Christian?"
> It was an odd question. Embarrassing, in fact.
> "Sure. I mean, I was baptized when I was ten, and I went to Sunday School and all that. Why?"
> "Something happened to me last night, Craig. During the earthquake. I'd like to tell you about it, but I don't want you to laugh at me."
> "Okay, I won't laugh."
> Stubby took a deep breath, almost a sigh. "It was the sort of thing where you know it's real, but you want to pretend it's a dream. I knew my parents were dead, after the roof fell in, and I was expecting to die, too. Then all of a sudden there was this man there. Don't ask me where he came from. But he was right there and he talked to me. He said I had been chosen and that he had some things to tell me."
> He stopped and looked hesitantly at Craig. "Do you believe in angels?"
> "I don't know, Stubby. I guess I never thought about it."[5]

Anticipated nightmare becomes undesirable reality and generates the desire to dismiss reality as dream. But what is nightmarish reality for Stubby is Balizet's dream of desire, and the formula deconstructs into a rather more anxious (perhaps embarrassing or laughable) hope: anticipated dream is figured as reality and begets the fear that it will always remain dream. What is figured here, of course, is the apocalyptic future, long the true but absent presence, now entering into the present as presence, in the bodily form of an angel, a presential body who by speaking presents himself as a self-evidential sign. Expecting to die, Stubby is confronted by a divine figure from beyond death, who verbally and imagistically prefigures the coming victory over death in the apocalypse.

The expected victory, now a certainty, is a *coming:* an active moving-in-time that restores presence and banishes absence. The future as presence encroaches upon the present as absence, eliminating the spacing and temporalizing of differance and reunifying human beings with themselves. Derrida notes in "Differance" that "the characteristics of origin, beginning, *telos, eschaton,* etc., have always denoted presence—*ousia, parousia*" (138)—by which he implicitly means the *movement* of presence. *Parousia* is the Greek cognate of the Latin *praesentia* (being [*entia*] before [*prae*] = being [*ousia*] alongside [*para*]), and Paul writes to the Philippians, for example, that they must be obedient not only in his presence (*parousia*) but also in his absence (*apousia,* "being-from") (Phil 2:12; compare also 2 Cor 10:10). The central meaning of *parousia* in the NT, however, is not mere physical presence but the apocalyptic Second Coming of Christ, which is to say, not a *being-there* but a *coming.* In this sense the term is adapted from the contemporary political designation of the official visit of a king or emperor to his provinces: Christ, the king of heaven, visited his earthly province once in the guise of the Suffering Servant; he will come again in glory at the end of the age to reannex that province, long since lost to the enemy. This *parousia* is, then, a moving-in-time/space: Christ *brings* his royal presence to earth in order to bring mankind into the presence of God.

Stubby's angel, however, does not possess the power granted to Christ to "transfer" (carry across) God's presence, to close the gap of "differance." The angel is still only a *sign* of Christ; but it is now the *semeion ek tou ouranou,* the self-evidential sign from heaven which the Jews asked of Jesus but did not receive. And it is significant that Stubby *is* a Jew; for without this self-evidential sign he would not have been converted either, and could not have served as the vehicle of salvation for his nominal Christian friend Craig. The God who sends Stubby the angel doubles metatextually as the writer herself, Balizet, who knows from the history of disconfirmed predictions the impossibility of making credible predictions solely from the signs of the times. Importantly, however, since her sign from heaven comes from a heaven displaced into language—the language of her novel—it is still a sign of the times, and as such marks not the attainment of presence but once again its deferral.

The angel now goes on to rehearse Hal Lindsey's account of *Heilsgeschichte* and the Rapture: "Daniel's" unfulfilled prophecy, according to which the world was to end 490 years after the rebuilding of the temple in the sixth century B.C., is explained by the contrivance of a magical deferral of the last 7 years until 1988–95, and the visible saints are relieved of their anxiety about the tribulations by the promise that they will be taken up before it begins.

"Well, anyhow, he said we had been wrong all along. We Jews, I mean. That Jesus had been the Messiah, and we should have known it. Then he told me how we were in a very difficult period—the last seven years before Jesus comes again. It seems that a long time ago—before Christ—God gave the Jews four hundred and ninety years to show the world what God is like, and we have seven of those years left. I don't understand that, do you?"

Craig shook his head.

"Well, it's all supposed to be in the Bible, the Book of Daniel. And he said something else, too, that's really heavy. He said all the truly committed Christians went to heaven during the earthquake."

Craig found himself nodding with mixed emotions. "It's what they call the Rapture. A kid at school told me about it."

"That explains something," Stubby went on. "When they came this afternoon to take Papa and Mama away, they never found this nurse who was right there with us. They dug through about a ton of stuff but she just wasn't there. I saw her face, Craig, just when the whole place was crashing down." Stubby looked at the older boy to see how he was taking all this. "It was like—like a light was on her."

Craig swallowed hard. "I saw exactly the same thing," he said. "I just didn't know how to tell anyone. It was a little girl. She began shining like—just shining. And the next minute, Stubby, she was gone. Vanished."

They sat in silence, grappling with impossible thoughts. (94–95)

Exegetically, the division of "Daniel's" seventy heptads into two phases with a two-thousand-year gap in between and the pretribu-lation Rapture are the weakest links in Lindsey's argument: the former is his invention, the latter an apocryphal Puritan idea.[6] What is inter-esting about Balizet's use of this material is that in order to give her readers the tribulatory sequence she must have them identify not with those who are taken up, as Lindsey does, but with those who remain after the Rapture to suffer the tribulation. This means that the Rapture must become evident only fleetingly, as an apocalyptic sign that is as ephemeral as a spoken word: present for a moment, then vanishing, as Craig says of the raptured girl, and, to those who remain, most signifi-cant *in* its absence. The absence of the sign is manifested in the novel by the absence of the "truly committed Christians," an absence that is only vaguely troubling to those who have not seen the actual transition, the disappearance. For those who (like Stubby and Craig) do view the disappearance, the transition from bodily presence to absence paradoxically becomes a sign of presence; indeed, in the economy of symbolism, Stubby's angel *is* the raptured nurse, for her disappearance is the occasion of his appearance—her *apousia* (absence's moving-in-time/space) the occasion of his *parousia* (presence's moving-in-time/space). The Rapture thus becomes not Lindsey's anxiety-ridden consolation but something like Melville's "revolving Drummond light," standing midway between our present and the tribulatory period and illuminating both.[7] For Stubby and Craig *in* the intermediate period of tribulation, the Rapture stands as a sign of the promised end that gives meaning to their suffering; for Balizet's readers in ongoing history, it stands as a sign that the deferred end approaches. But that is only to say that Balizet sets Stubby and Craig beyond the sign in order to introject the certainty it gives them back into our period before the sign. The intermediate tribulatory period is a fruitful choice of setting; it is temporally and spatially continuous with the present history of absence, but through contact with augurs of absent presence can also be shown to be contiguous with the presential future realm.

The emphasis on light, on shining, in the Rapture is also significant, for God's presence is figured imagistically in the Bible precisely by shining faces. The glory of Moses' face when he returned from the presence of God on Mt. Sinai (Exod 34:33-35) is the definitive OT version of this image; it reappears throughout the OT prophets, in visionary glimpses of divine beings, and it figures centrally in the NT account of the Transfiguration, where Christ's face and garments shine not with reflected glory (as did Moses' face) but with the glory of his hidden divinity. Indeed, as God's words in Exod 33:19-23 suggest even in translation, the Hebrew conception of the divine presence *was* God's shining face; in Hebrew, the words normally used for "presence" are *'ayin* (eyes) and *pânîm* (face). The glory (in Hebrew, *kábòd,* signifying weightiness, worthiness, parallel to *spoudaios,* Aristotle's term for the nobility of the tragic hero) of God's face was too great, however, for the human eye to view; and so God veiled his face in speaking to Moses, and the tabernacle also was fitted with a veil to protect human eyes from God's glory. In NT terms, then, the apocalypse will be literally an unveiling, as human beings will be so transformed as to be able to look upon glory without mortal danger.

The NT Greek word for glory is *doxa,* whence *doxology,* words about glory; and it is relevant that *doxa* in Plato's Attic Greek meant nothing divine at all, but, indeed, that which was to be least esteemed—*opinion,* the mere words of men that Plato placed on the bottom rung of the ladder to the Absolute. "The stone which the builders rejected has become the head of the corner" (Ps 118:22)—from an NT perspective, of course, the Koine sense of *doxa* as presential glory, as the light of God's face, is the true eternal sense that Attic Greek heathens misunderstood to mean mere opinion. But if we think of the NT *doxa* as a projection of human opinion into the heavens, from mere words to the iconic vision of divine light, it becomes possible to lay the conceptual groundwork for discussions in later chapters of American attempts—particularly of Poe's attempts—to revise the NT *doxa* into a mediatory icon that is neither "mere" verbal opinion nor entirely other iconic presence but a human-divine word-vision that points both beyond and back into linguistic figuration. This is a subject we will return to in chapter 4; but the American revision of *doxa* that is central there is implicit here as well: in Balizet's "forgetfulness," her suppression of the knowledge that the shining light Stubby and Craig see *is* just "opinion," just empty words offered in a novel by one interpreter as a sign of the end—words that, *as* words, remain as much a deferral of the end as a bridge to it.

> "There's more, Craig." Stubby drew a deep breath. "This
> angel said that the Jews were God's chosen people until Christ
> was born. Then the Christians were. Now that the Christians
> have gone to heaven, the Jews are again. Does that make sense?"
> "I don't know. My parents are Christians, sort of. They're
> still here. Why did some go and not others? Who decides?" (95)

Who indeed? God does—or Balizet does, and projects her decision onto God. It is important to know, when reading of the Florida nurse whose Rapture Stubby witnessed, that Balizet, too, is a Florida nurse. Eschatologically speaking, the decision is God's, and Christians are enjoined not to judge lest they too be judged. Ethically speaking, however, every Christian must judge insofar as she makes moral decisions. Choosing between right and wrong on one level is an internalization of judgment, an allegorization of individuals into positive and negative exemplars. The Christian becomes, a fortiori, a judge when she writes a novel about the end of the world, for then she *is* the Divine Judge of her novelistic universe, the final arbiter for questions of damnation and salvation. Who is Balizet to say that Craig and his family should not be raptured? The answer is, of course: Balizet is their creator. And to the extent that the novel is offered as a linguistic prolepsis, a novel-as-sign that points toward the apocalyptic encroachment of presence into absence, this moral decision is implicitly a projection of present desire into future fulfillment: the nurse goes up before the oppression; the nominal Christians stay and suffer.

This is in fact standard fare in predictive apocalypses. What is striking about Balizet's treatment of judgment, however, particularly in juxtaposition with Wigglesworth's poem, is that in the Balizet book, judgment is implicit. Certain rewards are meted out in the novel: the Rapture, for example, to nameless, faceless characters who appear in the novel only for the brief moment it takes for them to disappear; a restricted power to perform miracles, to those who become Christians after the Rapture; and most importantly, passage through the tribulation to the millennium, to those who persevere in their belief. But, remarkably, there are no punishments. Not even the novel's Antichrist, a green-eyed man who becomes Pope, is ever portrayed as being in any way discomfited by the approach of the end, and the novel concludes at the arrival of Christ. The destruction of evil, of all those worldly forces that torment Christians now, must be inferred; it occurs in the gray realm to be projected past the end of the novel.

Judgment is most forcefully presented in the novel in the guise of choice: not ethical choice this time but eschatological choice, that is, not an inner weighing of personal oppositions (flesh and spirit) but an outer joining with one side or the other, God's or Satan's. For Luther, man was *simul justus et peccator,* at once righteous and a sinner; in the apocalypse no such overlaps are permitted. Good is good and evil is evil, and each individual is either a saint or one of the damned. Thus, when it comes time in Balizet's novel to accept the "mark of the Beast," a simple numerical stamp required for employment and a ration card, the new Christians in the household refuse to accept it. This is the eschatological choice one *must* make: the taking of sides. For the unexpectant members of the household, it is quite simply an inevitability; one must work and eat to live, and so the mark must be accepted. As one of these says, "there's no reason for your resistance to this. It isn't like some club you either join or don't join. There isn't any choice about this" (266). But he's wrong: there *is* a choice, and the club the Christians choose to join is an exclusive one indeed. Jason, a converted drug addict, provides the historical context for the Christians:

> This decision has been coming on a long time. Thirty years ago society's morals and Christians morals were much the same— don't lie, don't steal, don't live unclean lives, love your country and your fellow man. Then society went downhill morally. Being a Christian more and more meant being different. As the world got meaner and more evil, Christians had to separate themselves. It's like the Bible says, the good got better and the evil got more evil. Now the two groups are so far apart it's almost impossible for them to live together. (268)

What is most revealing about this passage, however, is what is missing: namely, what the conjunction of society's morals and Christian morals in fact *was* thirty years before the scene in this book. It was in the early 1960s, the time of the Civil Rights movement, when American society was polarized over the color of skin. *Forty* years before this book's passage, in the early 1950s, Christians led by Senator Joseph McCarthy were concerned to separate godless Communists (the party of the Antichrist) from God's people. Fifty years before, the Christian world was splintered into a world war between forces with opposing apocalyptic designs: the Nazis, with their millennial dream of ushering in an Aryan paradise, and the Allies, led by a messianic America. In the furtherance of those designs, the Germans were incarcerating and exterminating Jews (who killed Jesus), while Americans were incarcerating those of their citizens who had Japanese roots.

Just how has society gone downhill morally? The implication of this retrospective history, it seems to me, is that the whole question of morality is a subterfuge; the real issue is not morality at all, but power. The "moral" decline in Balizet's novel involves, significantly enough, an increase in "lawlessness": terrorists and vigilantes square off in confrontations whose intended outcome is not the triumph of right but the acquisition of power; political, ecclesiastical, and parental authorities show an alarming tolerance toward the perennial infractions of the young and other oppressed (drugs, sexual license, cultism). And Balizet's sympathies are revealingly mixed. On the one hand, there is a strong nostalgia in the novel for old-time religious and political authority, in an indefinite past that may have been thirty, forty, or fifty years before the main action but that, in any case, one surmises, was coterminous with the author's childhood. Tolerance for lawlessness is an abomination and is not to be countenanced.

On the other hand, however, the authoritarian impulse that this nostalgia feeds is complexly checked, or displaced, by a principle of eschatological choice that evaluates "morality" by its power source. The rise to power of the Antichrist brings with it a consolidation of law and order that most of the novel's conservatives find congenial—a *moral* consolidation of law and order, in fact, explicitly developed out of the Sermon on the Mount and very much in the same tolerant spirit as Paul's remark to the Galatians that "There is neither Jew nor Greek, there is neither slave nor free, there is neither male nor female; for you are all one in Christ Jesus" (Gal 3:28). But the novel's Christians reject it out of hand: biblical as it apparently is, the new moral order comes from the Antichrist, not God. The *content* of morality, therefore, is secondary to the *source* of morality. But discrimination then requires one to know beforehand from which source a given moral law derives, and

Balizet does not make clear just how that happens. Certainly if one extrapolates from content to source, as human beings' limited perception within history would seem to require, Christ and Antichrist become remarkably similar: "I ask you to unshackle yourselves from the prejudices and bigotries of your past. Let us truly love all men, regardless of race, creed or color. No man should be hated or deprived because of his background. No one should be punished because of his father, his forefathers or his ancestors. Let us love all men as equals" (131). This is Balizet's Antichrist speaking—but it could just as well be Christ. Somehow the Christians *sense* it is the man of evil, and they oppose him—which raises a number of problematic questions. If the validity of a morality is determined by its eschatological source, what happens when Satan usurps God's morality? Does an otherwise acceptable morality become absolutely unacceptable once taken over by Antichrist? If the Antichrist calls for love and brotherhood, are the Christians to assume that the key to a good Christian society is the negation of love and brotherhood—stern discrimination? As the *principle* of negation, the Antichrist usurps that tenet too: "In achieving our goals for mankind, we should consider ourselves at war with those destructive people and groups who want to continue their selfish pursuits. Do not be dismayed if we are forced to use warlike measures to achieve our great goals. As a surgeon removes the cancer fearlessly, so we must fearlessly, exultantly even, remove from our society those cancerous elements which are destroying our chances for a new age of man" (132).

The Antichrist's allusions to warlike measures tips the Christians off to his real identity. Clearly, however, this familiar rhetoric of tyranny is satanically close to God's own recipe for the millennium: one splits off "those cancerous elements which are destroying our chances for a new age of man" and conforms those who remain to one's own will. There is, of course, an important functional difference between Christ and Antichrist in this case, but in one sense it is a frightening one: Christ differs from his satanic counterpart essentially in his power to conform men and women's wills and remove cancers *absolutely* and *eternally,* which obviates the charge of tyranny by eliminating the moral gap between the will of the ruler and the will of the ruled.

Eschatologically speaking, this troubling resemblance between the reigns of Christ and Antichrist is negated in eternity by God's victory over Satan—and Balizet relies on that negation at the end of her novel to skirt the knotty problems her study of power raises. But the problems will not disappear so easily. In the cosmos, perhaps, Christ and Antichrist are absolutely distinct. In Balizet's novel, however, they are simply two functionally similar characters: both set up paradisal societies that promise love and brotherhood for all, once the cancerous elements have been excised. Hence, it seems, the truncation of the novel's conclusion: Balizet cannot afford to represent the judgmental *means* of Christ's messianic restoration—the splitting off of the wicked and the conformation of the saints to his will—except by inference, lest the functional parallels with the Antichrist become manifest.

Balizet dramatizes the conformation of the human will to God's in a sublimated fantasy of the reversal of generations: like all the worldly power holders in the novel, the head of the focal household and his wife are middle-aged and doomed; there is a grandfather figure, Judge Redmond, who is saved, and a motley assortment of young people, all of whom are likewise saved except, significantly enough, the only one among them who is already well established in a profession. It is the powerless, clearly, who ultimately prevail over those in power: powerless sons over powerful fathers, who in turn succumb to their own now-powerless fathers. Thus, despite her longings for a return to old-time law and order, Balizet here aligns the reader's sympathies with the oppressed, fantasizing a rise to power that is different in kind from the power-grabbing of the doomed "world." The son gains power, in this fantasy, not by becoming an oppressive father but by imagining himself as the father's father, his own grandfather; the grandfather regains power from the usurping son by becoming the son's son, his own grandson. [8] The grandfather possesses the temporal priority over the father that the son needs to legitimize his belated claim to power; the grandson has the future, the ability to survive the father, that the grandfather needs to reestablish his primordial claim to power. And in the broadest sense, the grandfather-judge is obviously the Divine Judge, the God who in a secular age seems deposed or retired (like Judge Redmond), but who through the redemptive death of his symbolic grandson (the "Son of Man") imparts to the Christians the power of his own priority. The Christian as son is oppressed by Satan as the father of sin. But Satan is a false son of God, a fallen angel, divided off from the order of grace, and by communing with God's primordial spirit the Christian can leap over Satan, bypassing his distortive power. In this way the Christian overcomes his belatedness and not only survives the father but supplants him in eternity. The son-grandfather alignment is formalized and the evil father forever banished; the son becomes his own grandfather, becomes one with God, and the father is sent to burn in hell.

This, of course, is a fantasy reversal, a fantasy whose failure, as will be seen in chapter 6, lies in deferral: so long as the ultimate victory over time is delayed, the generational structure of time requires the numbing repetition of father-son power conflicts. The unification of man and God is deferred, man and God remain different—the failure of the desire for presence is a function of Derrida's nonconcept of differance. The explanatory power of Derrida's pun does not extend, however, to the attendant desire for the splitting off of others, for the alienation or differentiation of evil in judgment. For here the dilemma is no unfulfilled unity but too great a unity, a mixing or blurring of entities that, so thinks the expectant imagination, should be separate. Here the appropriate Greek word is not *diaphero*, a passive differing, but *diakrino* (*dia* [throughout], *krino* [to judge], from *kri* [separation]), an active dividing that produces the divine *diakrisis* (Rev 16:7) or trial in which Christ separates the saints from the damned. (*Krino* also gives us *krima*, the "sentence" that by a causal metonymy yields the English word *crime*, and in Latin *discrimino*, whence our *discriminate*.)

As the foregoing discussion of moral discriminations suggests, the apocalyptic imagination posits two distinct but interrelated diacrises, two loci of diacritical knowing: one human, the other divine. Human diacrisis is proleptic, discriminating between good and evil on earth as those differences are revealed by God from across the gap of differance—or, expressed another way, human diacrisis is projective, reifying desire and repugnance as future absolutes that can then be revealed in the present. This chapter returns to the problems of divine diacrisis in the discussion of Wigglesworth, but Wigglesworth will not solve these problems either; the attempt to work through the separations of diacrisis to an American solution, a solution that will not simply dismiss the diacritical thrust of the apocalypse in either an indiscriminate Oneness or an indiscriminate nihilism, is the central focus of chapter 7.

> Craig shook his head in bewilderment, then turned back to Stubby. "What did the angel ask you to do? Go preach?"
>
> "I'm not sure. Study, I guess. Who's going to listen to a fifteen-year-old Jewish kid? He did say things are going to get pretty hairy before it's over." Stubby's liquid brown eyes were somber.
>
> Craig stared into the dusty twilight, his mind in a turmoil.
>
> "He put a mark on my forehead," Stubby asked. "Can you see it?"
>
> Craig looked at him, then shook his head. "I can't see anything."
>
> "Maybe it comes and goes. Craig, can you help me learn about Jesus?"

"You've got to be kidding. You're the one who talks to angels. I'm just a fallen-away Baptist."

"Maybe we can learn together?" suggested Stubby. "I never read one word of the New Testament."

Craig looked at him again. Was it his imagination, or in the dying daylight had he seen on his friend's forehead, just below the dark widow's peak, a tiny glowing cross? (95)

As history's day fades into night, then, Craig too sees a sign: no angel as Stubby saw, no self-evidential sign, but a glowing symbol written on a human body, a bodily sign that anticipates the glorification of *their* bodies as well. *Was* it his imagination? It cannot be, here; there is no room in Balizet's novel for an admission of the *linguistic* nature of apocalyptic signs. If the cross on Stubby's forehead is a creation of Craig's imagination, then the impending doom is likewise a creation of Balizet's imagination. But this deconstruction of apocalyptic signs is precisely what the central American apocalypses most insistently perform: signs of doom are only linguistic, only imaginative, in order that they might be *fully* imaginative. The American apocalypse is, I will claim, archetypally a self-conscious act of the imagination, a heightening of the imagination in order to encompass present and future in a single visionary act.

Here, however, the only imagination whose operation can be admitted is God's. The cross on Stubby's forehead not only separates him from the damned (it is a mark of judgment, a diacritical mark, a sign that separates humans into different groups just as orthographical diacritics mark letters for different pronunciations), but it is also a prefiguration of the final apocalyptic transformation:

Seven times the New Testament predicted He would come with clouds, a great cloud of witnesses who had been perfected to rule and reign with Him for one thousand years. And the heavens opened and the armies of saints descended, and the multitude on the mount knelt in homage to the splendid One on the white horse.

And for the third time since the dawn of creation, the words rang out: Consummatum est! As God had said following the creation of the universe, as Christ had said on Calvary as He gave up the Ghost, so now a Voice rang out for all the earth to hear: "It is finished! I am the Beginning and the End. To him who thirsts, I will give of the fountain of the water of life freely. He who overcomes shall possess these things, and I will be his God, and he shall be My son."

The One who testifies of these things says, "Surely I come quickly." Amen. Even so, come, Lord Jesus. (345)

As Jesus shines with the divine glory ("the splendid One on the white horse"), so too do all the believers, all the future inhabitants of the millennium whose future is now becoming present, whose absence is being transformed into presence. Standing at this apocalyptic interface, in the very abyss of differance here reified iconically as an actual transformation, the believers hear Jesus pronounce the definitive apocalyptic utterance, the divine syntax whose structure charts the apocalyptic movement: "He shall be My son." Grammatically this is a copulative syntax, in which mortal man and glorified man, the material earth and the re-created earth are identified through time ("shall be") by a transformative linking verb or copula. Grammarians diagram this sentence as "S is PN" (subject is predicate nominative), but it may be more useful to imagine it as "S_1 shall be S_2," in order to emphasize the *transformed identity* of subject and predicate complement. Man remains himself, but becomes the son of God; the earth becomes not a spiritual realm but a new earth. The subject changes—but stays the same. It is significant that within the copulative utterance the two subjects do "copulate," like the intertwined bodies of lovers that the mystical strain of Judeo-Christianity (Gen 2:24, Matt 19:5) presents as the apocalyptic marriage, the figure of unification (two into one flesh) between God and man that is the presential goal of all apocalyptic thought. Christ's sacrificial mediation made possible the marriage of human beings and God in the Resurrection; in the apocalypse Christ's body becomes the "copula" that iconically enacts the consummation of that marriage. *Consummatum est*—the apocalyptic work of renovation is consummated in the completion of the copulative apocalyptic utterance. (It should be noted that in addition to delaying Christ's Coming, Balizet also defers the sexual consummation of her young hero and heroine's love, leaving the reader to surmise that it, too, will be achieved in the millennium. Perhaps at one level the "coming" of Christ as bridegroom is the climax of the sentimental romance, hyperbolized to sublimity.)

The predictive apocalyptic imagination attempts to rush across the gap of differance, one might say, by setting up the grammatical subject of the copulative syntax as "signifier," the copula as the semantic ground for signification, and the transformed subject or predicate complement as "signified"—and then simply *uttering* the sentence. Certainly this is Balizet's stratagem, and she borrows it from the Book of Revelation. However, such an account fails to consider the linguistic nature of the entire sentence—or, more accurately, it does not fail to take its linguistic base into account but refuses to do so, since it cannot afford to. What the predictive apocalyptist desires is the copulative transformation of *his language* into *God's act;* he wants his linguistic utterance to run so closely parallel to God's historical utterance that his significatory copulation will not defer but precipitate God's performative copulation. That is, the apocalyptic syntax of human language is intended to stand in the same relation to the apocalyptic syntax of God's divine creative word as subject stands to predicate nominative in that syntax.

As Derrida reminds us with his notion of differance, of course, this attempted displacement of language into history is counterproductive: the very attempt to reify linguistic act as restorative historical act defers historical restoration. Acutely aware of this significatory deferral, American writers from Emerson and Poe on are willing to go this far with Derrida. It is no use, they agree, simply to assume God speaks our language. Where American apocalyptists seek to go *beyond* the impasse to which Derrida brings language, however, is in the very conception of the abysm of differance. If one resists the temptation to displace language into history and instead *embraces* language, embraces the apocalyptic imagination as linguistic with a full cognizance of the problems involved in projecting this imagination onto the world, then it may become possible, these writers surmise, to create images of the end of the world that yield perspectives on history from within the abysm of differance. If one could inhabit the interface, the mediatory place between now and then, the apocalypse could be transformed from an expectant to a visionary sign, a sign that is not hollowed out by its relation to the future, but seeks to encompass the future in imaginative prospect. The American apocalyptic journey "into" the interface, one might say, is the poetic equivalent to Satan's task in Book I of *Paradise Lost:* to plunge into the abyss of Derridean differance self-consciously and there to build a dwelling place, to shape out of lack an iconic home—to domesticate the uncanny (*das Unheimliche*). The journey, if it succeeds, moves through deconstruction to reconstruction—or rather, it reifies deconstruction *as* reconstruction, entering the uncanny gap of differance knowingly and attempting against all odds to contain it. Derrida is probably right: it won't work. But American apocalypses, I suggest, work toward self-definition precisely by undertaking that impossible task—which implies that to deal with those works adequately we need a criticism that is willing to follow American writers beyond their self-deconstructions to their futile but heroic efforts at self-reconstruction: their attempts to turn loss into restoration, not by banishing loss in an absolute recovery of presence, but through a restorative irony that generates value *out* of loss.

■

Such an attempt is vestigially present in Balizet's novel as well, despite her absolutist mind-set that requires one to choose sides, to pick an extremist allegiance—to America or to Christ, to this world or the next—and to exclude all that is not chosen, middles as well as opposite extremes. (For this mind-set, of course, there *are* no middles: "He who is not with me is against me," Matthew reports Jesus as saying [12:30]; contra Mark 9:40 and Luke 9:50.) In writing a *novel* about the end of the world, however, Balizet finds herself forced to focus neither on the world nor on the end, but on the *transition* from world to end, the end *in* the world, that seven-year period in which the signs of apocalyptic transformation are immanent in the world and so imagistically accessible, visible to those who believe. Dedicated to writing about the exclusion of middles, Balizet finds herself—apparently by default, but in fact by the necessity of language itself—inhabiting the middle she would exclude.

This is a characteristically American discovery. Whether in unintended contradiction of their own professed ideologies, as in Balizet's case, or in self-conscious struggles with the problems of transition and representation, American writers return repeatedly to the excluded middle, the abysm of differance, and seek to make it a home. William Carlos Williams writes in "The American Background" of the predicament of the European settlers, who discovered birds that were neither thrushes nor robins, but something in-between—"*A bird that beats with his wings and slows himself with his tail in landing*":[9]

> *The example is slight but enough properly to incline the understanding. Strange and difficult, the new continent induced a torsion in the first settlers, tearing them between the old and the new. And at once a split occurred in that impetus which should have carried them forward as one into the dangerous realities of the future.*
>
> *They found that they had not only left England but that they had arrived somewhere else: at a place whose pressing reality demanded not only a tremendous bodily devotion but as well, and more importunately, great powers of adaptability, a complete reconstruction of their most intimate cultural make-up, to accord with the new conditions. The most hesitated and turned back in their hearts at the first glance.*
>
> *Meanwhile, nostalgically, erroneously, a robin.* (134)

The in-between, the torsion between the new and the old, is a definitively American dilemma. Sacvan Bercovitch cites Simón Bolívar's

famous Jamaica Letter of 1815 as indicative of a similar dilemma in
Latin America—"But we scarcely retain a vestige of what once was; we
are, moreover, neither Indian nor European, but an intermediate species
[*una especie media*] between the legitimate owners of this country and
the Spanish usurpers"[10]—and extrapolates from it the range of transitional selves Americans have conceived for themselves:

> *An intermediate species:* by implication, Bolivár's definition
> points up the distinctiveness of the colonial New England legacy.
> The Civil War left the Southern apologist stranded in a historical
> no-man's-land, midway between a defeated dream and a dream
> he refused to accept. Independence from Spain left the Latin
> American similarly stranded in time, trapped between the loss of
> historical bearings and the need for historical renewal, at once
> a victim of and a rebel against the past. He had nothing because
> he had everything—culture from Spain, politics from France,
> religion from Rome, antiquities from missionary histories of the
> Aztecs. In this context, intermediacy involved a *historical* ges-
> ture at cultural *discontinuity:* a deliberately transitional form of
> nationalism, and a concept of the American as "the son of
> Nothingness."
>   . . . In the postrevolutionary Northern United States the sense
> of intermediate identity was just as pervasive, but its meaning
> was reversed. Here it entailed a *mythical* mode of cultural *con-
> tinuity:* Hawthorne's Endicott, the iron-breasted harbinger of
> the Revolution; the hero of Franklin's *Autobiography,* whose
> success story at once recapitulates the nation's past and predicates
> its future; Natty Bumppo on the prairie, transcending all contra-
> dictions of race and culture because, as *our* representative Ameri-
> can, he synthesizes the value of nature and civilization. These
> cases are very different from one another, but all three confirm
> American selfhood as an identity in progress, advancing from
> prophecies performed towards paradise to be regained. (143)

The American self *is* a transitional self, a self caught up in the midst of
a temporal transformation that is carrying him, he believes, from the
old to the new, from Europe to the American Age—from subject to
predicate complement. All he knows, however, is the "middle," in the
realm of that bird that is neither a robin nor a thrush, and his task becomes that of standing in the middle and learning to look both ways, to
define the old and the deferred new from his intermediate position.
    Even knottier than the problem of temporal transition for
America, however, is the possibility of a moral mediation, a bridging of

the diacritical gap between salvation and damnation and between the saints and the wicked, that will surrender neither to absolutism nor to a mindless monism. Balizet and Wigglesworth, who here usefully frame the history of American literature, are satisfied with absolutism: an absolute split between good and evil, between the redeemed and the damned, operative at a spiritual level here on earth and finalized for eternity in the Last Judgment. But in the three centuries spanned by these authors' rigid diacrises, American literature seeks restlessly for a moral mediation, with some success in the works of writers such as Faulkner and Barth and with less success but with a powerful and revealing (and thus anticipatory) insight in a writer like Jonathan Edwards—that crucial transitional figure between the Puritans and Poe and Emerson who set the stage for a distinctive American idiom.

The key Edwards text in this regard would be the important posthumous discourse on *The Nature of True Virtue* (1765), which seeks insistently to mediate between rigid Calvinistic doctrines of innate depravity and the preutilitarian moral philosophies of Lord Shaftesbury, Richard Cumberland, and Francis Hutcheson. It is quite properly a Herculean task: on the one hand, human beings are absolutely corrupt and incapable of real disinterest; on the other hand, "true virtue" is to be defined as a disinterested benevolence toward all Being. Still, Edwards sensed that some mediation between the two ideologies was necessary—a sense that arose out of his perception of a thorough incompatibility between the Calvinistic doctrine of innate depravity, to which he adhered, and the Bay Colony self-conception as a millennial city on a hill, lighting the world, in which he placed his hope for an American future. If, as Sacvan Bercovitch suggests, "Early New England rhetoric provided a ready framework for inverting later secular values—human perfectability, technological progress, democracy, Christian socialism, or simply (and comprehensively) the American Way—into the mold of sacred teleology" (136), Jonathan Edwards was one of the first American thinkers to feel the need for such an inversion; and in *The Nature of True Virtue* he sought a mediatory pattern for it.

Edwards's problem and task are both diacritical—paradoxically so, for Edwards wants both to retain the Calvinist doctrine that only the few can be elected out of depravity to grace and, at the same time, to allow for the potential conversion of all mankind, beginning in the Connecticut Valley. It is fundamentally a question of inclusion and exclusion, which politically charts the conflict between democracy and theocracy. The crux of the problem is the nature and extent of judgment. If by predetermined divine diacrisis only the few could be elected, then there was something terribly wrong about the vast numbers of "surprising conversions" Edwards had facilitated. If, on the other hand, the conversions were true and redemptive, then by shining its light upon the world, the city on the hill could and *must* expand into and engulf the world. One must have judgment, if virtue is to retain any meaning at all; but for an American millennium one requires also inclusivity, or the slackening of judgment. Edwards's tacit ideal would be the incorporation of the many into the few, or the revelation of the many *as* the few; but the many must at the same time remain the many in order for that incorporative revelation to be still an election. In other words, that which is defined by exclusion must be supplemented by that which is excluded, and yet must remain exclusive. Edwards further complicates this paradoxical desire in his diacritical mode of argumentation, which works to precisely the opposite effect: true virtue, the quality by and to which the few are elected, is defined in Edwards's essay by a process of elimination, which is to say not by including but by excluding. After Edwards has devoted nearly his entire essay to an explication of everything that Hutcheson, Cumberland, and others had thought virtuous but that stands revealed as so many expressions of self-love (the love between the sexes, that of parents for children, man's sense of justice and pity for those in distress), he is left with a largely negative definition of true virtue: it is the indefinite remnant of self-love, that which is left over once self-love has been defined. Edwards's valiant attempt to overcome the terrible exclusivity implicit in Calvinist doctrine thus leads him finally back to the inevitability of exclusion:

> The *first* object of a virtuous benevolence is *Being,* simply considered: and if Being, *simply* considered, be its object, then Being *in general* is its object; and the thing it has an ultimate propensity to, is the *highest good* of Being in general. And it will seek the good of every *individual* Being unless it be conceived as not consistent with the highest good of Being in general. In which case the good of a particular Being, or some Beings, may be given up for the sake of the highest good of Being in general. And particularly if there be any Being that is looked upon as statedly and irreclaimably opposite and an enemy to Being in general, then consent and adherence to Being in general will induce the truly virtuous heart to forsake that Being, and to oppose it.[11]

Seeking to open the millennial gates to the many, Edwards thus ends at the utilitarian principle that justified the holocaust: if inclusivity requires exclusion, the millennium will require the extermination of all those who are "looked upon as statedly and irreclaimably opposite and an enemy to Being in general."

■

Edwards offers a revealing perspective on Wigglesworth's high Puritan doomsday poem, largely because Edwards is aware of the implicit contradictions of his belief in ways that Wigglesworth was not. In contrast to Edwards's frustrated attempts to democratize judgment, the Last Judgment remains for Wigglesworth something like the closing of a cosmic steel trap—nothing can stop it, all are caught forever either within or without, and as the teeth lock grimly in place there is a certain mixed shudder of horrified satisfaction at the finality of it all.

Wigglesworth draws his account not from the rather terse description of the Judgment in the Book of Revelation (20:11-15), but from the more famous passage in Matt 25, with its proleptic transcript of the actual verbal interchange between Jesus and the judged. Comparing these two potential sources for Wigglesworth's doomsday scenario, we note that there is something in the former that commends it to the modern imagination; there is a certain aesthetic satisfaction in the almost pantomimic separation of good from evil in the Book of Revelation that is lost in the Matthew passage when the damned speak and thus assume personalities. For as the judgment of the damned shifts into a quasi-realistic context, what happens is that one perversely begins to identify with them, not in repentance, as the writer desires, but in indignation. Alongside the ludicrous versification, it is this feature that the modern reader will find most disturbing about *The Day of Doom*. A thoughtful reading of the work is a positively frightening experience— one that frightens the reader not into moral obedience but into a moral revulsion from the judgment. It is one thing to agree with Paul Elmer More that "If you are going to depict an eternal hell, there's no use being finicky about the benevolence of your deity,"[12] and quite another to render Christ's vindictiveness in a humanly plausible context, suggesting that divine diacrisis is human, and finally inhuman. This is the strongest example:

> 166
> Then to the Bar, all they drew near
>   who dy'd in Infancy,
> And never had or good or bad
>   effected pers'nally,
> But from the womb unto the tomb
>   were straightway carried,
> (Or at the last e're they transgrest)
>   who thus began to plead:

167

If for our own transgression,
    or disobedience,
We here did stand at thy left-hand
    just were the Recompence:
but *Adam's* guilt our souls hath split,
    his fault is charg'd on us;
And that alone hath overthrown
    and utterly undone us. . . .

170

Behold we see *Adam* set free,
    and sav'd from his trespass,
Whose sinfull Fall hath split us all,
    and brought us to this pass.
Canst thou deny us once to try,
    or Grace to us to tender,
When he finds grace before thy face,
    that was the chief offender?   (50–51)

The infants have a strong case, and Wigglesworth bravely presents it as strong. Christ's initial reply is partially acceptable:

171

Then answered the Judge most dread,
    God doth such doom forbid,
That men should dye eternally
    for what they never did.
But what you call old *Adam's* Fall,
    and only his trespass,
You call amiss to call it his,
    both his and yours it was.   (52)

But Wigglesworth's Christ cannot leave it at that, and so goes on to tip his hand in a most disturbing manner:

177

I may deny you once to try,
    or Grace to you to tender,
Though he finds Grace before my face,
    who was the chief offender:
Else should my Grace cease to be Grace;
    for it should not be free,

If to release whom I should please,
   I have no libertee.

178

If upon one what's due to none
   I frankly shall bestow,
And on the rest shall not think best,
   compassions skirts to throw,
Whom injure I? will you envy,
   and grudge at others weal?
Or me accuse, who do refuse
   Your selves to help and heal?   (53)

Wigglesworth takes Jesus' self-defense, in substance, from the parable of the vineyard in Matt 20. What is interesting about the defense, however, is what is left unsaid: the fact that, as a Calvinist Judge, Wigglesworth's Christ has no more "libertee" in his judging than either the infants or Adam have in being judged. That is, all three have (or had) the liberty of choice, but that choice is itself predetermined by God's diacritical act at the beginning of time, the primordial Election to Grace. All Jesus really has the power to do in the Calvinist scheme is to read from the Book of Life. But if that is true, why must he make his decision to pardon Adam and not the unbaptized infants seem to be a matter of personal whim? "Whom injure I?" No one—for Jesus is finally only the instrument of a depersonalized divine diacrisis, defined for eternity at the *arche* and here enacted at the telos.

What is at stake here, ultimately, is the problem of theodicy, of the justification of what to human beings seem God's unjustifiable ways. It is the problem of the Book of Job, which pits a human will that seeks to control God against a divine will that does control mankind; it is also the problem that John Milton was struggling with at precisely the same time as Wigglesworth (*Paradise Lost* appeared in 1667, five years after *The Day of Doom*), with greater skill and complexity of poetic insight but finally without much more success. Among God-fearing Puritans both the depersonalized Election to Grace at time's origin and the personal whim of the Judge at time's end would have generated anxieties that would in turn have motivated the representation of each as a finally inadequate cover for the other. Which is less arbitrary—a personal Arbiter or an impersonal arbitration? The inescapable conclusion would seem to be that, as the words themselves suggest, arbitrariness is a necessary function of arbitrating. The paradox of the theodicy in the Book of Job is central: the ultimate justification of the ways of God to man is that God needs and can have no justification, because God (fate, history, time) is not subject to man's will. And in secular revisions of God to the inscrutable forces of fate or time, this problem is a crucial one in American literature, as chapter 3 will show. How is man to gain a measure of control over forces that by definition *are* beyond his control? To what extent can the human imagination shape its own destiny in *opposition* to the powers of the universe? Barring the possibility of such shaping, how is man to adapt himself to external forces without sacrificing his integrity?

In theological terms, of course, the primal act that made it possible (and necessary) for man to seek to shape his own destiny was precisely the act that set him in opposition to the powers of the universe and thus made successful shaping ultimately impossible. The act was the Fall of Man, which as Wigglesworth implies was a fall from a "stance" or stasis that provided stability but that also meant an infernal, almost inconceivable fixity:

> 173
> If he [Adam] had stood, then all his brood
>   had been established
> In Gods true love, never to move,
>   nor once awry to tread; . . .   (52)

"Never to move"—a chilling thought. To wipe away the Fall would be to wipe away all human action, for good and evil both. It would also be to wipe away redemption, for, as Kenneth Burke argues in *The Rhetoric of Religion,* in a logological perspective "the 'fall' and the 'redemption' are but parts of the same cycle, with each implying the other"[13]: redemption *requires* a fall and therefore logically precedes it. By analogy, the end of the cycle in the apocalypse is logically prior to all human history conceived *as* a cycle of fall and redemption: the diacritical separations of the apocalypse at once stop the cycle, perfect it, and give it its eternal or divine meaning. As Burke writes:

> Though the eventual Kingdom of God is free of disobedience,
> the principle of disobedience is not eliminated. Rather, it
> is isolated and perpetuated (even in a technical sense "purified")
> in the notion of an everlasting hell. So, in this way, the idea
> of an ultimate, all-triumphant governance of good does not re-
> move the sacrificial principle, but rather absolutizes it (as one
> might expect, inasmuch as this kingdom is entered in terms of a
> perfect sacrifice).
>   . . . And those heretics who felt that God, in his infinite
> mercy, would eventually save all men after they had been

sufficiently punished for their few years of transgression here
on earth, were in effect proposing too thoroughly to abandon
the idea of the cyclicality of order. Thus the Summa tells us,
as does the Protestant Bunyan, of the edification that the blessed
derive from contrasting their blessedness with the sight of the
hellish sufferings perpetually visited upon the damned. As seen
in the perspective of eternity, a willingness on God's part to
abandon eternal punishment would be like abandoning the *principles* of bless and curse so integral to the idea of a Covenant.
It is as disturbing to the dramatics of theology (the theory of
action carried to its ultimate conclusion) as were a playwright
to *begin* where Prospero ends, by freeing not only Ariel but
Caliban. Furthermore, even a slight disobedience might seem
absolute insofar as it is viewed in terms of disobedience to an
absolute authority. (233–34)

Burke's logological perspective on judgment, with its insistence
on the logical simultaneity or mutual implication of "bless" and "curse,"
can now shed new light on the division of apocalyptic diacrisis into two
phases or loci, the human and the divine. The notion of an everlasting
hell does not by any means *halt* the cycle of terms Burke sets up;
rather, it is logically implicated in it, so that human diacrisis before the
apocalyptic end, whether conceived as proleptic or projective, is the
same *event* as the Last Judgment (which in turn is the same event as
the primordial Election to Grace), restated in historical and psychological terms. That is, theologically speaking, the apocalypse is a historical transition from human diacrisis to divine diacrisis. But logologically
every act of diacrisis is the same, so that human diacrisis may be imagined as divine diacrisis introjected into history (power divisions between
authority and submission) and into psychology (ethical divisions between right and wrong). Divine diacrisis, in turn, may be imagined as
human diacrisis projected into heaven (the ultimate separation of self
from evil other). This would suggest that Balizet's novel, with its cautious mooting of the entire problem of diacritical judgment, may well
be read as the sublimation of political revenge into the doomsday scenario implicated in the reader's mind, while Wigglesworth's emphasis on
rigid divine diacrisis can neatly be introjected into the reader's imagination as *present* ethical discrimination. By logological implication, that
which is not made explicit in either work can thus become the central
focus in the reader's understanding.

The other aspect of this apocalyptic insistence on fixity or permanence, on a perfected stasis in which ethical choice is hypostatized
in eschatological eternity, is the image of crossing: the transference or

translation across the gaps of spatial difference (earth-heaven) and temporal deferral (now-then) that would heal the negative dialectic of differance. The hope is that *differo* will become *transfero*—or in Greek, that *anaballo* (to defer) will become *sumballo* (to throw together, to symbolize) and that *diaphero* (to differ) will become *metaphero* (to carry across, to metaphorize)—that human beings, tormented by the incompletions of differance, will be translated across the abysm into the fulfillment of desire:

> 19
> The same translates, from Mortal states
>   to Immortality,
> All that survive, and be alive,
>   i' th' twinkling of an eye:
> That so they may abide for ay
>   to endless weal or woe;
> Both the Renate and Reprobate
>   are made to dy no more.   (14)

Wigglesworth gives us his usual God's-eye view of the action here, dramatizing a serene, unanxious, impersonal (because transpersonal) divine diacrisis in which a faceless mankind is neatly divided into two groups for translation, "to endless weal or woe." But it should be clear that the apocalyptic crossing or translation is here projected *for* both the renate and the reprobate, *by* the renate alone. The translative duality of Wigglesworth's apocalyptic vision is a function of a single imagination that conceives salvation and damnation less as moves on a cosmic chessboard than as the transformation of self: specifically, the salvation of self through the splitting off of an evil other, the revelation of the hidden or masked self through the removal of the other as veil or dross. The informing image is that of the remnant, which is implicitly linked to translation in its negative or "endless woe" aspect in a passage from the Vulgate Hebrews:

> Nunc autem repromittit, dicens: *Adhuc semel: et ego movebo* non solum *terram* sed *et caelum.* Quod autem, *Adhuc semel,* dicit: declarat mobilium translationem tamquam factorum, ut maneant ea, quae sunt immobilia.

> But now he has promised, "yet once more I will shake not only the earth but also the heaven." This phrase, "yet once more," indicates the removal of what is shaken, as of what has been made in order that what cannot be shaken may remain. (Heb 12:26-27)

The distinction made here between the *mobilia,* which are shaken and removed ("woe-translation") and the *immobilia,* which are unshaken and remain ("weal-translation"), is essentially that between the dross and the remnant: between those who are to be burned in the fire forever and those who will enter the kingdom of heaven. From the remnant's perspective—the perspective from which the orthodox biblical apocalypse is conceived—this is no mere division or separation but precisely an *emergence,* a *parousia* or coming into presence of that "true" or eternal part of makind whose being had for so long been concealed and distorted by the "world," that fallen state of being that is now exposed and disposed of as mere dross. "For the creation eagerly awaits the revealing [*apokalupsin*] of the sons of God," Paul writes to the Romans (8:19), implying that the Christians are *veiled* by the world, that the image of Christ that they represent and that lies germinant in their own fleshly bodies is covered by the image of Adam, and that this image awaits its uncovering, awaits the removal of the dross that makes mankind seem to be what it is not. The key to the remnant ideology is precisely the transformed identity considered earlier in this chapter. When Balizet's Jesus says, "He shall be My son," he means both, "He *is* my son, though not yet recognized as one," and "He shall be *made* My son." Wigglesworth encapsulates this idea in a deceptively simple line from stanza 200: "Where they shall see as seen they be" (64). They are seen *now,* on earth, in their true identites by God, and shall learn to see themselves through God's eyes in the transformed future; they *shall see,* and *shall be,* what they already are.

As the reference to recognition suggests, this notion of a remnant too, like the reversal of generations, is closely tied to the movement of comedy: the hope of apocalyptic salvation is the foundling's projective desire for the *anagnorisis,* or recognition, in which his royal blood is discovered, and for the concomitant exposure and removal of false identities (sinner, pauper) and false claimants (Israel, bastards)—which symbolically are revealed as the same thing, that is, the dross. The real danger in this comic remnant ideology, of course, as Auschwitz and Buchenwald attest, is that individuals with the power to do so will impose their designs of desire onto reality. But the imagination of the remnant has special applications to the problem of American self-definition. If America is the New Israel, who are American Jews, those representatives of the Old Israel who dwell in the New? Are Americans Europeans, or are they a new breed of men? Are the descendants of Protestant Europeans the only true Americans? Who are African-Americans, Asian-Americans, Catholic Americans? What is to be done with a white Anglo-Saxon Protestant who declares himself a Communist? And, most troublesome of all, who are the "Indians," projected in name by white settlers to another continent—those "native Americans" whose discomfiting appellations as the *first* Americans relegates the American remnant itself to secondariness? Space does not permit detailed discussion of all these entanglements; simply raising the problems in this context, however, shows, I think, how deeply ingrained is the ideology of apocalypse in American thought. This implies that the centrality of American apocalypses to any understanding of American literature lies precisely in the attention those works direct to the most distinctive aspects of the American experience.

■

In his third-to-last stanza, Wigglesworth moves us decisively into a realm that he can hardly begin to image, a realm to which later American writers would return continually, seeking to expand it for the human imagination into a home. The movement is a figurative movement past figuration, past the imagination, past dream:

> 222
> O blessed state of the Renate!
>   O wondrous Happiness,
> To which they're brought, beyond what thought
>   can reach, or words express!
> Griefs water-course, and sorrows sourse,
>   are turn'd to joyful streams.
> Their old distress and heaviness
>   are vanished like dreams. (64)

For Wigglesworth, dreams are ephemeral (or nocturnal) things, not to be compared with the eternal and glorious reality of the blessed state. But this is the comparison that mainstream American writers are *most* inclined to make. Wigglesworth's apocalypse for the archetypal American imagination *is* finally a dream—a dream too closely anchored to the letter of Scripture, perhaps, and too little buoyed up by the imagination of locale, of the country itself—but a dream nonetheless. One of the most obsessive concerns for American apocalypses in the centuries since Wigglesworth has been the task of infusing the biblical revelation with the visionary force of locality, the *American* power of dream. American apocalypses, to the extent that they are American, *are* American dreams—and dream becomes the characteristic American revision of the apocalypse.

THREE

REVISING THE AMERICAN DREAM

Imagine the monster project of the moment: Tomor-
row we the people of the United States are going to
Europe armed to kill every man, woman and child in
the area west of the Carpathian Mountains (also east)
sparing none. Imagine the sensation it will cause. First
we shall kill them and then they, us. But we are care-
ful to spare the Spanish bulls, the birds, rabbits, small
deer and of course—the Russians. For the Russians
we shall build a bridge from edge to edge of the Atlan-
tic—having first been at pains to slaughter all Canadians
and Mexicans on this side. Then, oh then, the great
future will take place.

Never mind, the great event may not exist, so
there is no need to speak further of it. Kill! kill! the
English, the Irish, the French, the Germans, the Italians
and the rest: friends or enemies, it makes no differ-
ence, kill them all. The bridge is to be blown up when all
Russia is upon it. And why?

Because we love them—all. That is the secret: a
new sort of murder. We make leberwurst *of them.*
Bratwurst. But why, since we are ourselves doomed to
suffer the same annihilation?
—William Carlos Williams, Spring and All

"Although all apocalyptic writers might be said to inhabit an America of the mind," David Ketterer somewhat extravagantly claims in *New Worlds for Old,* "the central tradition clings to American soil."[1] Surely there is something to this, even if we back away from the full sweep of Ketterer's claim. Following H. Richard Niebuhr's seminal 1937 study of *The Kingdom of God in America,* an impressive body of historical research has established that American thought, from its inception in European thought, is characteristically millennial; that the American continent from the start was no mere colony, no mere territory for expansion and exploitation, but mankind's last great hope, the *sine qua non* of the world's future.[2] As the European dream of America gradually congealed into the American Dream, the millennialism of that dream increasingly took on national, or perhaps *nationalistic,* shape. America was no longer simply the place of the millennium but God's millennial agent, the Redeemer Nation chosen to lead the human race into eternal felicity—and, of course, as the Williams epigraph ironically suggests, to convert or destroy the stragglers. As writers like Ernest Lee Tuveson and Cushing Strout make clear, a large part of both the strength and the astonishing naiveté of America's foreign policy in the twentieth century is attributable to precisely this millennial strain in American thought: America still insists upon seeing itself as the world's policeman, as somehow ordained by God to bear an awesome responsibility in the millennial purification of the nations.

One should not, however, get carried away: discovering apocalypses in American life is perhaps rather too easy than otherwise. There are important differences between apocalyptic thought in the orthodox biblical sense and American millennialism, as indeed there is significant distance between American millennialism and political sloganeering such as Woodrow Wilson's promise to make the world safe for democracy or Lyndon B. Johnson's call for a Great Society. As H. Richard Niebuhr reminds us,

> Seventeenth-century Protestants could not be utopians or idealists in the popular sense of the words, for they did not share the fundamental presuppositions of utopianism—the beliefs that human ills are due to bad institutions, that a fresh start with good intentions will result in a perfect commonwealth, and that human reason is sufficiently wise, or human will sufficiently selfless, to make the creation of a perfect society possible. They were for the most part thoroughly convinced that mankind had somehow been corrupted; they knew that the order of glory had not yet been established; they were pilgrims all who did not expect to be satisfied in the time of their pilgrimage. (49)

As the discussion of Jonathan Edwards in chapter 2 suggested, there is at once a significant continuity and an ever-widening discontinuity between the Puritan apocalypse and the ideological optimism that has come to be considered characteristic of the American Dream—the "cheerful countenance" that, Tuveson notes in *Redeemer Nation,* became "a sign of one's recognition as a citizen of the chosen country" (31). In the nineteenth century, philosophical idealism, along with its social offspring liberalism, generated an apocalyptic scenario that shared little with the vision of the Book of Revelation; Niebuhr wittily caricatures it as a process by which "a God without wrath brought men without sin into a kingdom without judgment through the ministrations of a Christ without a cross" (193). And by the twentieth century, Niebuhr suggests, the American Dream is still less recognizably apocalyptic:

> The coming kingdom of late liberalism, like the heaven of senile orthodoxy, came to be a place not of liberty and glory but of material delights, the modern counterparts of those pleasures which it had laughed to scorn when it spoke of ancient superstitions. For the golden harps of the saints it substituted radios, for angelic wings concrete highways and high-powered cars, and heavenly rest was now called leisure. But it was all the same old pattern; only the symbols had changed. (196)

If American social history reveals a willful myopia, however, an uneasy desire to forget the apocalyptic ground of the American Dream, American literary history presents a series of strong correctives. To the extent that American writers are social forces, they are typically voices of opposition to the prevailing versions of the American Dream. They are stubborn revisionists, always perversely concerned to unearth old skeletons and submit them to close scrutiny, always testing beliefs that the society as a whole would usually prefer not to have tested. A good recent example is Norman Mailer, who titled his 1965 novel *AN American Dream,* using the indefinite article eloquently to take a stance in opposition to what Niebuhr calls "the coming kingdom of late liberalism." In Mailer's novel, Stephen Rojack is given all the accessory achievements of the current American Dream—he is a war hero, a congressman at age twenty-six, married to a wealthy wife, a renowned professor and author, a television personality, a Casanova—but he *kills* that dream by killing his wife, and sets off romantically (though Mailer would say existentially) in search of another American Dream, the dream of personal freedom in an earthly paradise. Like watchers for the apocalypse in all ages, Rojack finds his secularized millennial goal always deferred, always visible over the horizon, shining like a jeweled city but always turning into a mere material image of the city, the neon lights of Las Vegas, upon approach. Undaunted by deferral, Rojack pushes on heroically, not waiting for apocalyptic fulfillment like the American dreamers of Balizet and Wigglesworth but questing for it, in the American Romantic tradition that looks back to the medieval dream-quests of a Dante or a Piers Plowman. Mailer raises his voice in prophetic denunciation, one might say, by casting his sights not forward but backward in time—to the Middle Ages or, in an American context, at least as far back as Huck Finn. But even that is opposition, and, as this book's discussion suggests, it may even be that to go back *is* to go forward. The American myth of progress is grounded, as Niebuhr suggests, on a dissociation of materialistic amelioration from the mythic superstition of apocalyptic expectation, or on the suppression or "forgetting" of the association of the two. And so it has fallen to American writers to probe the American Dream by reasserting the association, by serving as memory to the willfully forgetful: opposing and exposing the current mask of the American Dream, that is, by revealing its foundation in apocalyptic hope.

The current interest in the apocalypse in American literary criticism has certain affinities with, and in important ways grew out of, the "myth-symbol" studies of American history of the 1950s, such as Henry Nash Smith's *Virgin Land* (1950) and R. W. B. Lewis's *The American Adam* (1955). The American myth as envisioned by Lewis, for example, was a myth of Eden and the Fall, a myth of an Adam who can be viewed as either falling, producing a tragic view of existence, or regressing back into primal innocence. In his useful corrective to this argument, Frederick I. Carpenter demonstrates that the American myth involved no regression at all, but projected a future return to paradise. This *progression* toward paradise, which Carpenter studiously avoids calling apocalyptic, requires a "wise innocence," a growing past fallen nature to a new innocence that, because it surrenders none of man's fallen knowledge, marks an improvement over Eden.[3] Lewis's 1965 essay, "Days of Wrath and Laughter," then, takes Carpenter's argument one step further, explicitly considering the working of apocalyptic thought in American literature—the movement now not back to a paradisal beginning but forward to a cataclysmic end.

And yet there is certainly a sense in which Lewis was right the first time, in *The American Adam*. In terms of biblical orthodoxy, of course, Carpenter is right: the apocalypse lies ahead in time, and man enters it no innocent Adam but a saint, a glorified body in the image of Christ. But the heterodox literary imagination, in America and elsewhere, has ranged a good deal more widely than this. Whether in the science fiction of the past two centuries, or in the older romances in which time-travel was symbolically spatialized (in journeys up the Nile in search of the source, for example), there have been numerous literary attempts to discover paradise by going back in time. Logologically, using Kenneth Burke's method, one might even say that the passage backward and forward in time is essentially the same apocalyptic journey, the same triumph over time in order to locate an atemporal or extratemporal ground for temporal existence. This is a preliminary or heuristic formulation that will require considerable qualification before it can adequately account for the American apocalyptic concept of time, however. As a means of refining the formulation, I propose to take a close look at the first American apocalypse to explore the problem with any kind of comprehensive rigor, Mark Twain's *A Connecticut Yankee in King Arthur's Court* (1889). Twain sends his hero, Hank Morgan, back in time thirteen centuries, in order to discover whether turning back the clock might loosen the stranglehold history has on the apocalypse. Hank's failure, heroic as it is, is immensely revealing; it demonstrates the absolute impossibility, and at the same time the absolute necessity, of the national dream.

■

Twain's "inspiration" for *A Connecticut Yankee* is recorded in an oft-quoted journal entry from the mid-1880s, an ambiguous "dream" that may have been Twain's own ("I dreamed last night that . . . "—a random nocturnal image) but that also, Twain's elliptical syntax allows us to conjecture, may have been invented entirely for future use ("Have a character dream that . . . "—a mythic expression of the national hope). The journal entry, in fact, with its complex mixtures of times and attitudes, in important ways presents in embryo the novel Twain later wrote:

> Dream of being a knight errant in armor in the middle ages.
> Have the notions & habits of thought of the present day mixed
> with the necessities of that. No pockets in the armor. No way
> to manage certain requirements of nature. Can't scratch. Cold in
> the head—can't blow—can't get at handkerchief, can't use
> iron sleeve. Iron gets red hot in the sun—leaks in the rain, gets
> white with frost & freezes me solid in winter. Suffer from
> lice & fleas. Make disagreeable clatter when I enter church. Can't
> dress or undress myself. Always getting struck by lightning.
> Fall down, can't get up.[4]

This is farce in the root sense of the word, as a man of the nineteenth century is most indecorously "stuffed" (from the Latin *farcire*) into a confining suit of armor. The dream encapsulates the novel precisely as an index of Twain's driving concern with the problems of stuffing the nineteenth century into the sixth century, the present into the past, an after (*post*) into a before (*pre*)—which indeed, etymologically speaking, makes it a "preposterous" farce. Hank is stuffed into the past-as-prison, and he engineers his escape by first modifying (through his "civilization") and finally destroying (in the Battle of the Sand-Belt) the confining suit or era—only to find that the prison or shell thus destroyed was not merely a covering or vestiture but the very body that gave him life, and without it he is not just naked but dead.

I borrow this expanded sense of "preposterous farce" from Harold Bloom's discussion in *A Map of Misreading* of the trope/image/defense cluster that he cites as the central Romantic mode of victory over time: metaleptic introjection.[5] In traditional rhetoric, metalepsis (or transumption) signifies the continuing of a trope in one word through a succession of meanings; but Bloom takes some rather interesting liberties with the trope, combining it with the imagistic cluster of early and late and with the Freudian defenses of projection and introjection to generate a complex theoretical tool. Bloom's metalepsis is double—doubly dialectical. In one dialectic, it portrays the "throwing forward" (projection) of past into future, a proleptic form of representation in which the "dreamer" (my word, not Bloom's) casts his or her own past self prophetically into the dim future. In the second dialectic, the dreamer farcically "stuffs" the before with the after (preposterous), the past with the future, self with other, in a "throwing inward" (introjection). Bloom notes in *A Map of Misreading* that the latter may become a vehicle for apocalypse (101)—and while the former is the more obvious candidate (metaleptic projection clearly being the standard trope of apocalyptic expectation), in the context of *A Connecticut Yankee* it is easy to see the aptness of Bloom's notion of apocalyptic farce as well. Hank, trapped inside that suit of armor, obsessed with technological improvements and the elimination of anything that hinders him, points unmistakably from farce to apocalypse. Metaleptic introjection becomes apocalyptic farce precisely because the past cannot contain the future; nestled uneasily in the womb of the past, the future must burst out, even (or especially) at the expense of the womb itself, and even at the expense of the future's own existence. The spectacle of the future trapped in the past is incongruous, hence ludicrous; it is funny to watch its discomfort there, as well as its misadventures getting out. But it is also an explosive incongruity, a dangerous form of humor, as the ending of Twain's novel convincingly demonstrates.

What metaleptic apocalypse offers in terms of Lewis's and Carpenter's contention over the *direction* of the American myth is a dialectic in which regression and progression stand as alternative routes to the same goal: victory over time. Metaleptically, both Lewis and Carpenter are right; and one of the tensions at the heart of Twain's novel is that between a regressive and a progressive path to bliss. Might technological progress be mankind's conveyance to a utopia? Or has it meant mankind's irrevocable fall from the paradise of Twain's pre-Civil War youth, the agrarian garden of young America? The ambivalences surrounding this movement from garden to city in Twain's attitudes toward his own life charge *A Connecticut Yankee* with a vital tension, one between regression and progression. On the one hand, as Henry Nash Smith reminds us, "Mark Twain, in common with virtually all his contemporaries, held to a theory of history that placed these two civilizations [King Arthur's Britain and nineteenth-century America] along a dimension stretching from a backward abyss of barbarism toward a Utopian future of happiness and justice for all mankind."[6] On the other hand, somewhere back before that "abyss of barbarism" lay the Garden of Eden, the primal garden from which we all fell; and Twain's progressive faith was inextricably mixed with a strong strain of nostalgia, a vestigial longing for a return to Eden, to childhood, to the womb. Justin Kaplan reports that

> in other early notes for the book, the Yankee, like Mark Twain
> yearning for Hannibal as he remembered it to have been in
> his boyhood, yearns for an Arcadian past which "exists" only in
> his dream, a pre-Boss Camelot (purified, for the moment, of
> poverty and slavery) which is as drowsing and idyllic—"sleeping
> in a valley by a winding river"—as that other fictive town, the
> "St Petersburg" of *Tom Sawyer* and *Huckleberry Finn*. And
> the Yankee, even as first conceived, has already lost the power
> and desire to escape from this dream. "He mourns his lost
> land—has come to England and revisited it, but it is all so
> changed and become old, so old—and it was so fresh and new,
> so virgin before."[7]

The apocalyptic path to happiness, one might say, lies either backward, to a lost childhood world of "freshness" and "newness," or forward to a future utopia, a technologically advanced society that is as unlike the barbarism of the distant past as day is unlike night. Two paths—and one Dream. The problem for Twain, then, became the working out of the American Dream in a novel, with its demands of temporal consistency. Hank Morgan can go back in time and return to his starting point in the present; what he cannot do is go *both* forward and backward at once, back past Camelot all the way to Eden, perhaps, and forward past the nineteenth century (not too far, Twain hopes—perfection *must* be near) to the American millennium.

As I mentioned earlier, progression to an end and regression to an origin in a logological perspective constitute essentially the same transcendental movement, from a medial position in the flux of time to a paradisal stasis in eternity. For novelists (or, for that matter, theologians), who must concern themselves with narrative sequence, the problem is in fact rather more complicated, since the irreversibility of the temporal sequence of history involves the time-traveler in numerous paradoxes that underscore the radical differences between traveling back and traveling forward in time: paradoxes that science fiction, beginning with Twain's *Connecticut Yankee,* has explored at length and that will be taken up again later in this chapter. First, however, it is useful to point out the significant parallels between progression and regression. Kenneth Burke notes in *The Rhetoric of Religion* that he is concerned with "principles," *principia* or beginnings, "first things." [8] In a literal sense a concern with the apocalypse is, contrariwise, a concern with "terms," *termini* or endings. [9] But the Latin *terminus,* like the Greek *eschaton,* is not simply an end—not simply the "last things." Just as the *eschaton* is a boundary at *any* edge of either time or space, a *terminus* may be either a *terminus a quo* (boundary from which, or beginning) or a *terminus ad quem* (boundary to which, or end). The apocalyptic "term" may thus well lie at either the beginning or the end of time; it divides time from the paradisal eternity beyond it, whether we conceive of that eternity as a primordial Eden or as a final New Jerusalem.

In English, of course, there is a curious semantic inversion by which term as boundary comes to mean precisely that which is bounded: we speak of a term of office or of pregnancy, or of a school term. But this "terminological" inversion is in fact significantly paralleled in the imagination of an apocalyptic transformation, in which the "term" of history stands to the "term" as boundary as type stands to antitype, anticipation to fulfillment. But this comparison introduces an important qualification. Type and antitype in the typological schemes of the New Testament are fixed in temporal sequence, type always pointing *forward* to an antitype in which Erich Auerbach calls "phenomenal prophecy";[10] but the term-antiterm relationship I am suggesting here would seem to subvert that sequence, positing an antiterminal fulfillment or culmination of the historical term at either the beginning or the end of time. Typologically, Adam is the "first man" (*protos anthropos*), Christ the "last Adam" (*eschatos Adam,* 1 Cor 15:45); terminologically, Christ as the messianic mediator is both *protos* and *eschatos,* first and last (Rev 22:13), which would imply a reciprocal relationship between the two temporal boundaries. In this sense, Adam or mortal man is the bounded and Christ is the boundary, Adam is the center and Christ is the circumference. Christ encloses or bounds the historical term by standing between time and eternity and embodying the transition.

But the image is more complicated still, for in the same place at the end of the Book of Revelation Jesus refers to himself also as the *arche* and the *telos:* that is, he is not merely the first and last *in* time, but also the atemporal origin or source of time (*before* the first) and its atemporal end (*after* the last). Jesus is both the mediatory boundary and the unbounded realm mediated by the boundary—the former in his redemptive role as *man* (first and last), the latter in his creative role as *God* (origin and end). This suggests that the apocalypse should be thought of precisely as a terminal inversion, in which the bounded term of history from Creation to Apocalypse is turned inside out, the boundaries placed within the bounded and what before was bounded transformed into the unbounded state of eternity. Christ as mediatory circumference becomes transformed from "inside," or bounded absence, to "outside," or unbounded presence. Time as a terminal enclosure or prison becomes, as the conclusion of Dante's *Paradiso* suggests, an infinite wheel with Christ at the hub.

This implies that, metaleptically, both the "late" mode of expectant (progressive) apocalyptic projection and the "early" mode of farcical (regressive) introjection are imagistically feasible; the apocalypse may be conceived as either the projective transformation of the self into other-as-future-self or the introjective transformation of self into other-as-original-self. The former is the orthodox route; the latter is perhaps reminiscent of neo-Platonism, as we imagine the generations rolling up one by one into Eve's womb, Eve into Adam's side, and Adam himself back into not dust, of course, but the Creative Spirit of God.

But consider Twain's problem. To attain the presential society, he must either send a character ahead in time to the telos of temporal amelioration, as Edward Bellamy had done in *Looking Backward* (1888), or he must somehow accelerate progress in order to attain the presential state *now,* by sending a character back in time to redirect the stream of history at its source. The difficulty with either approach, however, is that both make it impossible to live in the nineteenth century. Bellamy's Julian West dreams he is back in 1887 and finds the dream a nightmare; he escapes back into "reality" by reawakening in the year 2000, but for the author and reader it is a dream-reality, a deferred future whose hoped-for presence reduces the nineteenth-century present to absence. Twain's Hank, propelled by an imagination wracked with the paradoxes of what it is attempting to portray, awakes from the nightmare of the past into the waking reality of the nineteenth century, but finds that reality more nightmarish than the dream. Having dismissed reality as dream-illusion, he flees back into the illusion of the dream-past, and dies. The irreversibility of time renders the revelations of time-travel horrific: if Hank succeeds in his reverse-millennial task, he necessarily obliterates the nineteenth century, for the nineteenth century is now *in* the sixth century, and what was once the nineteenth century is now an inconceivable other. Therefore, he must fail; but to fail is to lose his presential vision, to return to the nineteenth century divested of the very American ideology of progress that makes the nineteenth century what it is. Either way, Twain's own time is revealed as illusion, as alien. The American quest for presence across time ultimately uncovers only absence.

What Twain's artistic foray into the paradoxes of time-travel teaches him, in the end, is the impossibility of the American Dream—a lesson that Edward Bellamy confronts but (in Julian's waking from dream) quickly suppresses and that Balizet and Wigglesworth never even confront. On the one hand, the peculiar reality of time gives it an immalleability, a resistance to change, which renders the fruits of progress inaccessible. Since time will not permit the acceleration or compression of the sequence that progresses from bad to good to better to best into the duration of an individual's lifetime, to remain *in* the temporal flux is to surrender to the moment, to one moment among an endless series of moments, which shifts the "perception" of progress from the realm of empirical verification into that of the projection of desire. On the other hand, the escape from time or victory over time imaged in time-travel does not put one in control of time, but undermines its reality, reduces it to an illusory absence. To travel back to the "abyss of barbarism" in the sixth century, as Hank Morgan does, or ahead to the millennium in the year 2000, as Bellamy's Julian West does, is to see the ameliorative development but, by the same token, to be denied participation in it, indeed to be excluded from its reality. To dream of amelioration from within time is to discover perceptual absence; to perceive amelioration from outside of time is to reveal its presence as dream.

But this succinct statement of the paradoxes at the heart of Twain's novel needs unpacking, through a closer look at the movement of the narrative itself. Twain realized that one of the principal obstacles to the fulfillment of human desire was human beings' puny statures: their mortality and brief life span, their frail bodies, too weak to carry out the will of an unrestrained imagination, their ultimate passivity before fate. If, as in the biblical apocalypses of Balizet and Wigglesworth, God is the apocalyptic agent, human beings are forced to play a waiting game—a game in which potentially infinite deferral guarantees no winners. Suppose instead, Twain postulates, that *man* is the apocalyptic agent—no passive Briton but an American, a hero, a world-historical figure who shapes his times rather than being shaped by them. Suppose, that is to say, the American is a god—or a devil—it doesn't matter which, so long as his power is sufficient to control his temporal and spatial environment. The American hero must therefore be either elevated to divine status so as to be able to create, like God, *ex nihilo,* or lowered to satanic status so as to be empowered to combat the tyrannies of worldly ignorance and superstition through iconoclastic revolt. Harold Bloom associates this elevation and lowering with *hyperbole,* the great Romantic trope of high and low, of the sublime and the grotesque;[11] and it is clear that Twain is at some pains to hyperbolize Hank—in both directions—throughout the novel. Hank is never seen as a mere man in Camelot; he is always apparently either superhuman or subhuman, a god or a demonic sorcerer, and nothing loath to abet the Britons in their misconceptions. "I was no shadow of a king," he gloats in chapter 8; "I was the substance; the king himself was the shadow. My power was colossal; and it was not a mere name, as such things have generally been, it was the genuine article."[12] "I was admired, also feared; but it was as an animal is admired and feared" (64). "Here I was, a giant among pygmies, a man among children, a master intelligence among intellectual moles; by all rational measurement the one and only actually great man in the whole British world . . . " (66).

In fact, there is no little warrant for this hyperbolic elevation. Hank *is* superior to the Britons, at least in every way important to an American of the nineteenth century. And as Henry Nash Smith notes, his imagination is if not divine at least titanic. "Despite the Yankee's antics and the sidesplitting predicaments he falls into," Smith writes, "his command of technology makes him at least potentially a hero of epic dimensions, a man with a world-historical mission. His plan of industrializing Arthur's Britain resembles Prometheus' defiance of the tyrannical gods for the sake of bringing to man the priceless gift of intellectual light and technological power."[13] What is interesting in this self-conception, however, is the change Hank undergoes from his initial wonderment at his hyperbolic elevation to gradual acceptance of it as not hyperbolic at all, but *natural.* So as long as his memory of Hartford stands as Hank's norm of identity, he finds his elevation to near-divine stature by the Britons slightly amusing, to be exploited for business purposes but certainly not to be taken seriously. Increasingly, however, Hank comes to hyperbolize himself, losing that sense of difference between hyperbole and norm that binds him to humanity.

By the time of his duel with Sir Sagramour, Hank has romanticized himself (and, significantly enough, the fraudulent Merlin as well) into the very god-demon his audience has long considered him:

> all the nation knew that this was not to be a duel between mere
> men, so to speak, but a duel between two mighty magicians;
> a duel not of muscle but of mind, not of human skill but of
> superhuman art and craft; a final struggle for supremacy between
> the two master enchanters of the age. It was realized that the
> most prodigious achievements of the most renowned knights
> could not be worthy of comparison with a spectacle like this;
> they could be but child's play, contrasted with this mysterious
> and awful battle of the gods. (385)

What irony remains here, what sense of the difference between hyperbole and reality, is largely habitual; when Hank starts shooting the knights the reader is increasingly convinced that he does indeed think of himself as a god.

What is interesting in this ostensible apotheosis, however, is that Hank includes Merlin in it as well. In the temporal schema with which he started, Hank's gigantic stature was directly tied to his nineteenth-century origin: the hyperbolization had in effect been brought about by temporal amelioration, so that nineteenth-century beings stood alongside sixth-century beings as would *homo sapiens* alongside an ape (or a worm, Hank would say). But here Hank places a sixth-century man on his own level—a subtle indication that there is something wrong with the ameliorative schema. Either Merlin is anachronistically gigantic, achieving through magic the stature Hank was given at birth by technological progress—which would undermine the notion that nineteenth-century science is uniquely progressive—or human stature has nothing to do with progress in time. In terms I will develop more fully in chapter 6 (Part II's counterpart to this discussion of Twain), time-travel, whether in the mind or in the world, involves the traveler in scale distortions by which people of an earlier age come to be seen either as giants from which present-day pygmies degenerated, or as pygmies from which present-day giants evolved; and to the extent that other humans serve the time-traveler as mirrors, reflections of the time-traveler's own humanity, that distortion skews self-perception as well. The attempt to define himself as a god in contrast to the puny Britons takes Hank through the discovery of Merlin as an equal, to the reverse hyperbolization of himself in the disintegration of his personality at the end.

While Hank's faith in his own hyperbolical elevation lasts,

however, he stands tall as Twain's version of the Romantic American hero: the agent, not the agency, of the apocalypse. In this sense the "syntax" of Twain's American apocalypse might be characterized not as copulative, as it was in the biblical apocalypses of Balizet and Wigglesworth, but, rather, as factitive. Since the apocalyptic "factor" is now not God but a human being, the utterance would read not "The world shall be a paradise" but "I will make the world a paradise." (Note that while the copulative syntax is embedded in this structure, the emphasis is now not so much on the transformation as on the transformer.) God is now human—or human beings are divine, setting themselves up as transformative gods who propose to enact an apocalypse upon a group of peers whom they mentally degrade to the status of creatures. If the Britons are worms, then Hank can—indeed *must*—play God to them. Since Hank lacks God's power to transform by a simple performative utterance, however, it is perhaps better to examine his factitive apocalypse not syntactically at all, but dramatically, as the outcome of a dramatic action that is coordinated by a composite playwright-director-actor: Hank himself.

Here Burke's dramatistic pentad is apposite, developed at length in *A Grammar of Motives* as the reduction of all motives to five motivational terms: act, agent, agency, scene, and purpose.[14] The factitive apocalypse, clearly, would involve a ratio of two of these, scene and act; the apocalyptic drama might be stated simply as a scene-act-scene progression, specifically from scene$_1$ through the transformative act to scene$_2$. As I mentioned previously, however, this movement is complicated by Hank's reverse millennialism; where the "postmillennial" proponents of ameliorative evolution in Twain's day sought to restore on earth a paradise that was lost at the beginning of time, Hank seeks to restore in Camelot a paradise that was lost, figuratively speaking, at the end of time, in the nineteenth century. God created the world perfect, and at its fall looked forward to a future restoration; Hank falls from a Hartford that he chooses to recall nostalgically as perfect, to a corrupted, barbaric, virtually bestial state that he strives to convert into a restoration-as-anticipation of the future Eden. In the apocalyptic terms that he imposes on his experience, he alone recalls the loss of Eden and anticipates its recovery; he is an Adam who needs no Gabriel to tell him of apocalypse: he is, in fact, Christ himself, come to deliver the Britons from their bondage to tyranny and ignorance.

(Note that in the retrospective flights of Scott, Twain's nemesis, the retreat into the medieval past was conceived not as a fall at all, but as a regressive approximation of Eden. And Hank could well have imagined his trip back in time in similar terms, working to enculturate himself as fully as possible into the already existing British society, for example. But he doesn't, for the important reason that his presential locus is not the Origin but the nineteenth-century End. The movement of time takes Scott's characters ever further from their lost paradise, and so must be *resisted* through traditionalism, whereas for Hank, the movement of time brings the lost paradise ever closer, so that it must be accelerated through revolution. Traditionalist nostalgia is not only to no avail against the structure of time, it is counterproductive: the *nostos* or return of Hank's nostalgia is directed toward a future source, not a past. On the other hand, Hank's reaction to the achievement of that *nostos* at the end—his withdrawal into delirious dreams of Camelot—suggests that there is more to his hyperbolization than simply a desire for restoration to Hartford. Hank elevates himself to divine/ satanic status in large part in order to achieve a Romantic isolation from society; a flight into the mind that, as we will see in Part II, subsequent American writers resist and undercut.)

Hank's factitive act, his revolutionary transformation, is of course his civilization, his *imitation* of Hartford that he implants in the midst of sixth-century Britain. Here is the famous description from chapter 10:

> Four years rolled by—and then! Well, you would never imagine it in the world. . . . My works showed what a despot could do with the resources of a kingdom at his command. Unsuspected by this dark land, I had the civilization of the nineteenth century booming under its very nose! It was fenced away from the public view, but there it was, a gigantic and unassailable fact— and to be heard from, yet, if I lived and had luck. There it was, as sure a fact and as substantial a fact as any serene volcano, standing innocent with its smokeless summit in the blue sky and giving no sign of the rising hell in its bowels. . . . I stood with my hand on the cock, so to speak, ready to turn it on and flood the midnight world with light at any moment. But I was not going to do the thing in that sudden way. It was not my policy. The people could not have stood it; and, moreover, I should have had the Established Roman Catholic Church on my back in a minute.
>
> No, I had been going cautiously all the while. I had had confidential agents trickling through the country some time, whose office was to undermine knighthood by imperceptible degrees, and to gnaw a little at this and that and the other superstition, and so prepare things gradually for a better order of things. I was turning on my light one candlepower at a time, and meant to continue to do so. (78-79)

Hank describes his civilization as a rich fullness of potentiality, hidden away inside fences or inside a seemingly harmless mountain—troping it (in Bloom's terms) both as a metonymy of emptiness/fullness and as a metaphor of internality/externality. The problem Hank faces is exactly analogous to the problem raised by Balizet and Wigglesworth of realizing imaginative designs in history, only now Hank's design is no syntax, nothing so impalpable as language, but a *material* fiction, a "gigantic and unassailable fact." With the positivist's blithe faith in the reality of things and mistrust of deceiving words, Hank *builds* his paradise. Whereas Balizet and Wigglesworth relied by faith on the inherent resemblance of God's syntax to their own, hoping therefore that God would pronounce the performative utterance for them, Hank constructs his paradisal society materially and plots to transform the old society by supplanting it. Significantly, however, Hank's civilization is as much a figure as any shaped by Balizet and Wigglesworth: it is a metonymy of Hartford, and specifically, in Bloom's sense, a metaphorical metonymy, an apocalyptic metonymy conceived internally in Hank's factitive imagination. Hank's civilization is a rich potentiality, a source of much anticipation and an outlet for much creative effort, only in the fullness of internality; but internality as fullness depends upon *external fulfillment,* the successful bringing out of the civilization. Paradoxically, the civilization exists as an outside fullness only inside Hank's mind, in his memory of Hartford; outside his imagination, the civilization can exist in material form only hidden away inside an enclosure that *tropes* Hank's mind. The civilization as fullness seems restricted to internality; and as long as it remains inside, Camelot remains for Hank an external emptiness.

This restriction generates a tension in Hank's apocalyptic design that finally proves fatal. Left to itself, King Arthur's civilization would in time—over thirteen centuries—bring forth Hank's civilization in the fullness of externality. But then nothing would be changed, there would be no apocalyptic transformation, no primordial revelation of the nineteenth century. Hank itches for an apocalypse in the root sense of the word: he wants to "flood the midnight world with light." But he is also shrewd enough to predict the inevitable failure of a too-rapid unveiling: "The people could not have stood it; and, moreover, I should have had the Established Roman Catholic Church on my back in a minute." Hank's dilemma combines the problem of the historical realization of imaginative designs, the problem of human stature, and the problem of change over time—three of the most central concerns in the American experience. If human beings accept their limitations (as Balizet and Wigglesworth do to an orthodox extreme), they are reduced to a waiting game in which their only hope is that there is a significant parallel between their imagination and God's, who will therefore bring on the apocalypse that they desire. If, on the other hand, men and women hyperbolize themselves into gods and seek to effect real change by altering the structure of time (and its twin constitutive forces, the structures of material reality and of people's minds), they must confront the built-in resistances of that structure. However elevated by technological knowledge to a god's power over material nature, Hank lacks a god's power over human nature and so finds himself powerless in the end to effect a revolution; however elevated by the accident of his time-travel to a god's foreknowledge of the future, he lacks a god's eternality (temporal unboundedness) and so finds himself powerless to oversee an evolution with patience. "If I lived and had luck," he says, revealing the anxiety of his impotence before both time (mortality) and fate (luck). Unless he moves quickly, he will never see the fruits of his labor; but if he does move quickly, the fruits of his labor will be destroyed.

And so, although in chapter 40 Hank paints a rosy picture of the "unveiling" of his civilization, the external fullness of his apocalyptic metonymy of Hartford, in the next chapter, "The Interdict," the Church steps in and *empties* that fullness:

> I approached England the next morning, with the wide highway
> of saltwater all to myself. There were ships in the harbor, at
> Dover, but they were naked as to sails, and there was no sign
> of life about them. It was Sunday; yet at Canterbury the
> streets were empty; strangest of all, there was not even a priest
> in sight, and no stroke of a bell fell upon my ears. . . . It was
> the INTERDICT! . . .
> Of course, I meant to take the train for Camelot. Train! Why,
> the station was as vacant as a cavern. I moved on. The journey
> to Camelot was a repetition of what I had already seen. . . . I ar-
> rived far in the night. From being the best electric-lit town in
> the kingdom and the most like a recumbent sun of anything you
> ever saw, it was darker and solider than the rest of the dark-
> ness, and so you could see it a little better; it made me feel as
> if maybe it was symbolical—a sort of sign that the Church was
> going to *keep* the upper hand now, and snuff out all my beau-
> tiful civilization just like that. I found no life stirring in the som-
> ber streets (410–12)

When externality is thus revealed as emptiness, Hank finally realizes that it's all over; he is left with no recourse but to empty out what internality remains. He gives the order to vacate the Man-factories just as the Church had vacated the streets, and when the time is ripe, detonates his secret mines and blows them up: "In that explosion all our noble civilization-factories went up in the air and disappeared from the earth" (433-34). Hank's dream of a brave new civilization in the heart of barbarism is thus reduced to the illusory fragments of dream dissipating in a bitter waking: "My dream of a republic to *be* a dream," he laments, "and so remain" (417). Two dreams: the former a fullness of the imagination projected onto reality; the latter an emptiness of reality that engulfs the imagination. Imaginative dream destroyed reduces to illusory dream; Hank is already left, at this stage prior to the final battle, with nothing.

In another sense, however, nothing is what Hank had been going on all along. The eventual emptying out of his dream into illusion is prefigured even earlier in the novel by his penchant for the gaudy illusion of showmanship, a short tolerance for the unexciting that is inextricably tied to his American dreaming. "I never care to do a thing in a quiet way," he declares; "it's got to be theatrical or I don't take any interest in it" (310-11). This is the side of Hank that Martha Banta aptly calls *Sawyerism,* "the curse placed upon those fascinated by the gaudy effects of crises."[15] Hank Morgan is a grown-up Tom Sawyer, with all the irrepressible immorality that made Tom's antics delightful, but with a new ethical attachment to his pranks, born of his "world-historical mission," that adds a degree of frightening seriousness to his tricks. Banta analyzes Twain's novel almost entirely under the rubric of this disease, suggesting finally that the book demonstrates the dangers of the apocalyptic imagination: "Mark Twain considers," she claims, "whether death offers the most effective dream-escape" (386). "The only solution to stasis, Mark Twain implies, is for the imagination to get to work with catastrophe" (398). This vision, which in the terms I suggested in chapter 1 would be annihilative apocalypse, Banta contrasts with tragedy, a more positive acceptance, despite pain, of time's built-in resistances: "Mark Twain recognized that farce (even more than melodrama) has a bang-up, fast-paced ending, while the tragedy is a world without the benefit of apocalypse—an existence in which suffering and the exactions of patience are endless. He came in time to prefer the profits of the farce, while Adams and the Jameses chose the tragic mode with its costs" (423).

Certainly in terms of the main narrative of the novel, this is true. Hank's final explosive attack on knighthood is annihilative apocalypse as puerile escape; and the groundwork for that escape is laid throughout the novel, wherever Twain provides the imagery of apocalypse. All of the apocalyptic threats in the tale, as they are usefully discussed by David Ketterer in *New Worlds for Old* (213-32) figure dream as gaudy illusion, a kind of sleight-of-mind that takes its effect partly through the ignorance of the spectators, partly through the human love of lurid spectacle. The eclipse, the destruction of Merlin's tower with fires from heaven, the firework display at the Valley of Holiness, the Battle of the Sand-Belt—all are undertaken largely for effect. Hank has more at stake in some of his apocalyptic effects than in others, but the *form* of each is explicitly designed to wow the rubes— and of course to gratify Hank's craving for glory. It is all theater; if someone is killed, so what? In a theater murders are perpetrated, and after the curtain falls the dead men stand up and wash off their make-up—while the audience cries, "Author, author!" over thunderous aplause. For Hank, Camelot is such a theater, a stage on which to act out his apocalyptic drama, with the same real men and women for both actors and audience.

The crucial difference between real theater and Hank's, of course, is that theatergoers know they are watching a drama and enjoy the illusion of reality. In Hank's theatricality, on the other hand, the illusion *is* reality, or is palmed off on the Britons as such. Hank deceives by presenting dream effects as real magic, absence as demonic presence, much as Huck Finn convinces Jim that getting lost in the fog was a dream, and has him interpret it. Jim and the Britons are the sort of literal-minded people that are easily taken in by the dream peddler; but neither Huck nor Hank can leave it at that. Both have to demonstrate their superiority by revealing the illusion *after* it has been accepted as reality, revealing presence as absence: Huck by pointing to the trash on the raft, Hank by revealing that "serene volcano, standing innocent with its smokeless summit in the blue sky and giving no sign of the rising hell in its bowels."

To crystallize this aspect of Hank's personality in Bloom's terms, one could say that Hank's penchant for gaudy effects manifestly involves him in an *ironic* dialectic of presence and absence, in which he seeks to combat Merlin's presence by revealing it as absence, through a series of illusions that he himself exposes as absence—but in so doing he inescapably leads the Britons to treat his messianic civilization (the only real presence he has) as absence also. One sees Hank's dilemma: in order to supplant Merlin's "British Dream" of chivalry with his American Dream of industrial democracy, Hank must convince the Britons that his dream is more real than Merlin's. But as soon as one introduces the concepts of "dream" and "reality," of absence and presence, it becomes almost impossible to prevent the collapse of all reality into dream, all presence into absence. The reality of dreams is too much a matter of faith for it to stand much scrutiny; to destroy one dream is to destroy them all. It little avails Hank, therefore, to insist that Merlin's dream is absence masquerading as presence, while his is a *future* presence that is available right now. What future? the Britons rightly demand. Future presence *is* an absence.

Both Hank and Merlin are essentially dream peddlers, of course, and their conflict throughout the novel is ultimately a contest for control of the Britons' minds. Twain wants to establish a radical difference between science and superstition, between technology and magic (truth and falsehood, presence and absence), by placing the two visions side by side in Hank and Merlin and testing their relative efficacy; but his imagination keeps resisting his ideological desires, revealing science and magic to be not different at all but ultimately very similar dream tools, both illusionistic devices for the manipulation of the masses. (As Henry Nash Smith points out, Hank's magic in the destruction of Merlin's tower by "fire from heaven" is as unscientific as any of Merlin's, and Merlin's magic works on Hank in the end.)[16] Like his creator, Hank would like to think of his contest with Merlin as revolving around the question of *truth*. He finally comes to realize (perhaps) that truth or falsehood is secondary, that the contest actually revolves around the question of *power*. Neither Hank's nor Merlin's vision of man and society—neither Hank's American Dream of capitalism nor Merlin's British Dream of chivalry—is *truer* than the other; both are illusions or fictions that, if successful, will grant their shapers access to ultimate channels of control.

For this sort of fiction to succeed, however—for its fictional absence to be shazammed into ontological presence—the magician/scientist requires absolute credibility, which is why we find Hank crowing throughout the novel that "Merlin's stock was flat again." But with Hank's overriding love for the kind of fiction that establishes a fradulent credibility, for effects that seek to convince the ignorant that absence is presence, he cannot himself sustain credibility long. Thus it is that when the Church imposes the Interdict, although everyone in the kingdom still believes (or *fears*) that Hank is a powerful magician, they can no longer afford to believe in his vision of mankind; and the dialectics of fullness and emptiness, of inside and outside, and of presence and absence begin to converge:

> "The Church is master now [Clarence says]. The Interdict in-
> cluded you with Mordred; it is not to be removed while you re-
> main alive. The clans are gathering. The Church has gathered
> all the knights that are left alive, and as soon as you are discov-
> ered we shall have business on our hands."
> "Stuff! With our deadly scientific war material; with our
> hosts of trained—"

> "Save your breath—we haven't sixty faithful left!"
>
> "What are you saying? Our schools, our colleges, our vast workshops, our—"
>
> "When those knights come, those establishments will empty themselves and go over to the enemy. Did you think you had educated the superstition out of those people?"
>
> "I certainly did think it."
>
> "Well, then, you may unthink it. They stood every strain easily—until the Interdict. Since then, they merely put on a bold outside—at heart they are quaking. Make up your mind to it— when the armies come, the mask will fall." (419-20)

Superstition (Merlin's tool) is an absence that is *in,* and Hank fails to educate it *out;* the Church's threat of eternal damnation, the substance of the Interdict, remains for the Britons a most powerful presence, God's judgmental presence, which banishes Hank's dream to the "bold outside," to a "mask" that must eventually "fall." Just as Hank "stuffed" the suit of armor with his own body, so he stuffs his "establishments" with hand-picked workers and their minds with hand-picked ideas; but the *divine* threat wielded by the Church remains sovereign, and all the "establishments will empty themselves" of Hank's dream.

The Battle of the Sand-Belt is then really no more than the physical enactment of Hank's failure, the emptying out of his dream into illusory absence. His boast at the close of the duel with Sir Sagramour—"name the day, and I would take fifty assistants and stand up *against the massed chivalry of the whole world and destroy it*" (397, emphasis Twain's)—decodes into a frightening dehumanization of Hank's one-time "agencies": chivalry to Hank is an "it," an abstraction, which he can destroy only by killing "them," every body that harbors Merlin's chivalric dream. "English knights can be killed," he later tells his "boys," "but they cannot be conquered. . . . We will kill them all" (435). Hank's intention is an implicit admission of defeat. Unable to rid the Britons of the parasite of superstition, unable to supplant the chivalric dream with his American dream of industrial democracy, he is forced to destroy the host body. Having done so, Hank finds himself trapped, paradoxically, inside Merlin's cave, all alone, symbolically incorporated into Merlin's mind at last. Merlin then sneaks in to cast his most successful spell, drugging Hank to sleep thirteen centuries and to wake, finally, back in his own time.

■

But here the novel takes a puzzling turn. Why must Hank return? Why must he survive his own apocalypse to confront the nineteenth century once more? The apparent reason is to provide "M.T." with the palimpsest manuscript, of course; but M. T. could just as easily have discovered the manuscript in the cave himself. Why does Hank revive—and, more puzzling still, why does he die almost immediately upon M. T.'s completion of the story?

We must seek answers to these questions in yet another version of *dream* developed in the novel, a version that provides the rationale for Hank's science-fiction excursion back in time. The novel itself is in a sense a "dream palimpsest," in which Mark Twain dreams Hank dreaming himself back in Camelot; for when M. T. first meets Hank in Warwick Castle, he already finds *himself* being transported back into Hank's dreamworld: "As he talked along, softly, pleasantly, flowingly, he seemed to drift imperceptibly out of this world and time, and into some remote era and old forgotten country; and so he gradually wove such a spell about me that I seemed to move among the specters and shadows and dust and mold of a gray antiquity, holding speech with a relic of it!" (1). Hank moves both himself and his listener "out of this world and time" into an "old forgotten country" that, mythologically, might be the land of the dead, where "specters and shadows" dwell—or, psychologically, a dreamland, a land of mythic fantasy. Like Nathaniel Hawthorne in "Young Goodman Brown," Twain is careful not to tell us whether Hank actually did go back to King Arthur's time and return, or whether it was all a dream; Hank dreamed it, and it really happened.

This joint time-travel/dream-travel, undertaken simultaneously by teller and told, is further complicated when Hank begins his narration later that evening, in M. T.'s room. Hank describes the blow on the head that somehow mysteriously sent him back in time—"Then the world went out in darkness, and I didn't feel anything more and didn't know anything at all—at least for a while" (6)—and shortly after, almost as if telling about the blow had the same effect as the blow itself, Hank begins to fall asleep. As Hank's mental world in the main narrative goes "out in darkness," so also, simultaneously, does that world in the narrative frame. The manuscript Hank hands M. T. just before dropping off is Hank's dream record of his stay in Camelot, written while holed up in Merlin's enchanted cave; and the act of reading it transposes the dream into M. T.'s imagination. Indeed, we might even assume that Hank is redreaming the entire episode while he sleeps, and that the act of dreaming and the act of reading are the same, Hank's manuscript in M. T.'s hands a synecdoche for his dreaming mind. For when M. T. finishes reading the manuscript, Hank comments on it *in his sleep*, adding the final touches that the manuscript lacks, and then dies, of no apparent cause. Healthy and chipper when he went to sleep in the opening frame, he dies mysteriously in the closing frame, almost as if the dreamworld of Camelot *were* his only reality, as he deliriously claims, and the dream over, he must die.

To read the novel in this fashion, of course, is to blur the distinction between world and mind; Hank's dream adventures in King Arthur's Court, the dream manuscript, and the dream ravings that end the novel come increasingly to look like mutually interchangeable tropes for Hank's *mind*—external parts that represent an internal whole. This terminology suggests a fifth and final borrowing from Bloom's "map of misreading": here the part/whole dialectic of synecdoche is conjoined with the inside/outside dialectic of metaphor to form a composite trope for ethical growth. Where the conjunction of metaphor with metonymy in Hank's conception of his civilization permitted us to trace the emptiness and fullness of hidden (inside) and revealed (outside) experience in the *world,* the synecdoche-metaphor conjunction directs us to the problematic part/whole relations between world and mind: between outward action (including the act of narration) and inward mental action, between experience in the world and inner growth.

Does Hank grow, then? What inward action does the novel trace? Reading the novel in terms of synecdochic metaphor, I suggest, points us to the root of Hank's true failure: for he doesn't grow, doesn't learn, and that is finally a greater failure than the mismanaging of a revolution. Like a host of American heroes before and after him—Hollingsworth, Ahab, Gatsby, Sutpen—Hank betrays a significant kinship with the obsessional personality of Job:[17] throughout the novel he really *sees* only his dreams, his imaginative recreation of reality, relegating alien reality to the status of illusion and elevating dream to the reality that must displace that illusion. Job demands that God conform to his moral standards, and he uses every form of coercion he knows to compel conformity. Hank demands that Arthur's Britain conform to his dream, and tries to annihilate it when it resists. Unlike Job, however, who does learn moderation in the end, Hank learns nothing; he remains obsessional to the last.

David Ketterer suggests that Merlin's cave, in which Hank is trapped at the end, is also Plato's cave (223); but if that is true, Hank is symbolically trapped in Merlin's cave throughout the novel. Despite his claims of Yankee practicality and common sense, Hank lives in a cavernous realm of shadowy illusions, of dreams, of gaudy effects and utopian schemes, and clings to those shadows even when representatives of reality—or rather of *alternative* illusions that would force him to acknowledge the relativism of his particular illusions—would thrust him out of the cave toward the light. In an important sense, in fact, "Plato's cave" is as much Hank's own as it is Merlin's, for the two illusionists are indeed congruent in the novel's symbolic scheme. Hank is trapped, finally, inside his own head (or inside Merlin's head); he is trapped inside the apocalyptic imagination, which would transform the world into the image of the individual's desire. The American hero's task, here as elsewhere, is to climb up out of Plato's cave not into the realm of transcendental form (that illusory realm is where he is trapped now), but into the real world of men and women, the *social* or communal world. The American solution to this problem, as Faulkner conceives it in *Absalom, Absalom!* and as Barth conceives it in *Giles Goat-Boy,* is my focus in chapters 6 and 7; for now let me simply note that Twain had the makings of a solution in the story-telling situation of Hank and M. T., and rejected it. M. T. is an innocent abroad, a Yankee in Warwick Castle; Hank is, one would think, no innocent, but still a Yankee, an American in Europe whose experience spans two continents and thirteen centuries. Together they incorporate the relevant polarities—innocence/experience, America/Europe, present/past—into a potential image of community, the community of speaker and listener by which those polarities might be collectively and progressively understood. Instead, Hank falls asleep and dies; M. T. is left with a mind, an imaginative enclosure troped by the palimpsest MS. itself, a Platonic cave in which he is, like Hank before him, trapped. Twain reaches the threshold of a solution, but backs away, will not pass through; he remains too attached to Hank's American Dream, perhaps, to view its destruction with equanimity. The dream dies and reduces reality to dream. The extremes of Hank's experience cancel each other out, and nothing remains—except bare alien reality, of course, which Hank refuses to recognize as such:

> And such dreams! such strange and awful dreams, Sandy!
> Dreams that were as real as reality—delirium, of course, but *so*
> real! Why, I thought the king was dead, I thought you were
> in Gaul and couldn't get home, I thought there was a revolution;
> in the fantastic frenzy of these dreams, I thought that Clarence
> and I and a handful of my cadets fought and exterminated
> the whole chivalry of England! But even that was not the strang-
> est. I seemed to be a creature out of a remote unborn age, cen-
> turies hence, and even *that* was as real as the rest! Yes, I seemed
> to have flown back out of that age into this of ours, and then
> forward to it again, and was set down, a stranger and forlorn in
> that strange England, with an abyss of thirteen centuries yawn-
> ing between me and you! between me and my home and my
> friends! between me and all that is dear to me, all that could
> make life worth the living! It was awful—awfuler than you can
> ever imagine, Sandy. Ah, watch by me, Sandy—stay by me every

moment—*don't* let me go out of my mind again; death is nothing, let it come, but not with those dreams, not with the torture of those hideous dreams—I cannot endure *that* again. . . . Sandy? . . . (449, ellipses Twain's)

His American Dream destroyed, Hank's apocalyptic imagination is now reversed: having achieved the *nostos* or return that informed his nostalgia while in Camelot, he flips the apocalyptic alignments and desires a return to a lost time that now lies not in the future but in the past, as in Scott. Before, the temporal movement had brought him ever closer to future restoration, inspiring in him a revolutionary spirit that, he knew, still could never successfully bridge the gap between the sixth century and the restoration of an American paradise in the nineteenth. Fortuitously enabled by Merlin to bridge the gap in a thirteen-hundred-year sleep, Hank now finds himself, pathetically, being taken ever further from a *past* restoration by that same temporal movement. Rather than retreating into a reactionary ideology of conservation (for what good would that do?), he retreats into delirium, dreaming that he only dreamed of the thirteen-century abyss that separates him from his paradise. Whatever time Hank inhabits, in whatever terms he thinks of his predicament, there remains that abyss between desire and its fulfillment: that definitive feature of apocalyptic imaginings that Twain understands but cannot get past. As my later discussions of American apocalypses will show, the archetypal American solution to Hank's imaginative dilemma is to plunge into the "abyss of thirteen centuries" that yawns between desire and fulfillment and to generate a productive energy from its iconic habitation. Like Tiresias, first man then woman then man again, Hank has passed through the extremes of his experience and thereby stands at the threshold of a mediatory understanding that could transform his life as the simple desire for restoration never could.

What the apocalyptic dream-farce of *A Connecticut Yankee* reveals, in the end, is no historical crisis but character, Hank's *ethos,* the failure of an individual to learn. Hank's final delirium, which transforms dream reality into an illusion more real than reality itself, brings us back through the novel's dream inversions to the original frame, the *fiction* in which all dreams and all realities—and all apocalypses, real or dreamed—are illusions that do not pretend to deceive. Dream as hyperbolic metonymy passes through near-total annihilation in the dream-as-irony that concludes the main narrative, emerging in the book's P.S. as an internalized synecdoche that yet retains much of the ironic awareness of absence. Hank dreams to create, to destroy, and finally to escape the necessity of choice. Synecdochic dream remains, in the end, Hank's most effective escape from death; but the escape is cheap, for it is based on a self-deluding denial of absence.

■

As the reader has no doubt noticed, the five modified Bloomian tropes generated by my reading of *A Connecticut Yankee* bear an uncanny resemblance to the five apocalyptic hermeneutics I offered in chapter 1—a resemblance that suggests a number of directions my argument might take. To note that metalepsis complexly transforms the biblical hermeneutic, hyperbole the Romantic, metonymy the continuative, irony the annihilative, and synecdoche the ethical is to set a fairly obvious (if not entirely hazard-free) course toward neat formal correspondences. Rather than follow that course, which requires no great ingenuity for the reader to work out on his or her own, I want to close this chapter by taking a brief look at how Twain returned in his last, unfinished novel, *The Mysterious Stranger*—particularly in the novel's last chapter, the one constant in the shifting textual debate [18]—to solve the dilemma to which *A Connecticut Yankee* had led him. Whereas *A Connecticut Yankee* had failed to make the move from irony's annihilative absence to synecdoche's ethical internalizations, *The Mysterious Stranger* at least sketches a rough chart for that move, succeeding where the other book failed by reconceiving the synecdochic perspective as grounds for hope, hope of an ultimate personal redemption. Hank dies as deluded as he had lived; August Feldner or Theodor Fischer finally learns, finally comes to understand, and what he understands is Twain's last thrust at an American solution to the apocalypse.

This is by no means the established reading of the chapter, however. Most critics tend to see in it unmitigated nihilism, a bitter attack on human life and human knowing that places it, as R. W. B. Lewis suggests in "Days of Wrath and Laughter," in the extreme fringes of annihilative apocalypse:

> Mark Twain ends his parable with a peculiarly inventive sort
> of metaphysical or even ontological catastrophe: not the re-
> ported end of the world in ice or fire, but the revelation that
> the world, the very universe, does not even exist and never has.
> "*Nothing* exists, " Satan informs the narrator Theodor at the
> moment of his disappearance; "all is a dream. God—man—the
> world—the sun, the moon, the wilderness of stars—a dream,
> all a dream; they have no existence. *Nothing exists save empty
> space and you.* "
> Beyond that uncovering of absolute nothingness, the apoca-
> lyptic imagination can hardly venture. [19]

Or, as John R. May summarizes this position: "The world is not literally destroyed by catastrophe; its reality, however, is dissolved by demonic fiat."[20]

What Lewis and May discover in the chapter, of course, is the ironic revelation of presence as absence, which is a central trope in the annihilative apocalypse. But not all irony is apocalyptic, and Lewis and May have to stretch this passage to make it an annihilation. In the first place, the "revelation that the world . . . does not even exist and never has" is not at all a metaphysical catastrophe and not therefore (since ontology is a branch of metaphysics) an ontological catastrophe either. If it is a catastrophe at all, it is an ethical one: August/Theodor unlearns a false ontology and learns the true one, an internal transition that gives David Ketterer his cue for the "philosophical apocalypse." If the universe never existed, it cannot be "dissolved;" and 44's, or Satan's, words to the narrator can therefore be no *fiat*. Read in this way, the chapter is solipsistic, perhaps even nihilistic—but certainly not apocalyptic, unless one considers ethical growth apocalyptic.

But notice further that 44/Satan nowhere uncovers "absolute nothingness"—what he uncovers is a world of *"empty space—and you,"* which is a rather different matter. Empty space may not be the fullness of God, humanity, the world, sun, moon, and stars—but it does exist, in an empty metonymical way. The narrator exists too. Where then is that nothingness? "And you are not you," 44/Satan tells August/Theodor—"you have no body, no blood, no bones, you are but a *thought*" (404). Still, better a thought than nothing at all. 44/Satan continues: "I myself have no existence, I am but a dream—your dream, creature of your imagination. In a moment you will have realized this, then you will banish me from your visions and I shall dissolve into the nothingness out of which you made me. . . . " (404, ellipsis Twain's). Creation *ex nihilo:* this existence as a mere "thought" is beginning to look increasingly godlike. And in 44/Satan's next paragraph he makes his finest statement of hope:

> I am perishing already—I am falling; I am passing away. In a little while you will be alone in shoreless space, to wander its limitless solitudes without friend or comrade forever—for you will remain a *Thought,* the only existent Thought, and by your nature inextinguishable, indestructible. But I your poor servant have revealed you to yourself and set you free. Dream other dreams, and better!" (404)

The narrator has thus been revealed *to himself* as a lonesome god, set free from old dreams, "pure and puerile insanities, the silly creations of an imagination that is not conscious of its freaks" (405), to *create anew:* to dream better dreams, better gods, better worlds, better individuals into shadowy existence. Twain images this revelation as loss, loss of the external world that seemed so substantial. But to despair of this loss is to remain squarely within the positivistic world view that Twain is attacking. The strong sense one gets of irony, of presence horrifically revealed as absence, suggests that Twain probably remained a positivist at heart even while undermining the very foundation of positivism; but the almost messianic tone of 44/Satan's last two sentences in the passage just cited reveals another Twain as well, a Twain finally not far from the Blake who insisted that all externality was a fallen projection. 44/Satan sets August/Theodor free, by revealing him to himself—and this is, clearly, a step not back into the abyss of nihilism but forward into some new form of self-understanding. It is in this sense that I find the chapter a *hopeful* shift from irony, with its insistence upon absence, to the inward perpsective of synecdoche. If irony prevails, all that remains is *external* absence, a terrifying alienation of matter from mind; and this would, perhaps, point to an apocalyptic annihilation. But if external absence is revealed as a synecdoche for the dreaming mind—or rather, for the mind-about-to-dream—then the question of presence and absence no longer matters. What matters is one's inner vision, which *constitutes* reality by reseeing it.

■

Re-creation by revelation, the synecdochic incorporation of externality in the internality of vision: these *are* Blakean notions, though it is clear that Twain had never read a word of Blake. But he didn't need to; he had two potent American sources for the apocalyptic visions toward which he strove, two seminal American apocalyptists to whom we turn in chapter 4:

> Every spirit builds itself a house; and beyond its house, a world; and beyond its world, a heaven. Know then, that the world exists for you. For you is the phenomenon perfect. . . . Build, therefore, your own world. As fast as you conform your life to the pure ideas in your mind, that will unfold its great proportions. A correspondent revolution in things will attend the influx of the spirit. [21]

> *Oinos.*—Then all motion, of whatever nature, creates?
> *Agathos.*—It must: but a true philosophy has long taught that the source of all motion is thought—and the source of all thought is—
> *Oinos.*—God.

Agathos.—I have spoken to you, Oinos, as to a child of the fair Earth which lately perished—of impulses upon the atmosphere of the Earth.

Oinos.—You did.

Agathos.—And while I thus spoke, did there not cross your mind some thought of the *physical power of words?* Is not every word an impulse on the air?

Oinos.—But why, Agathos, do you weep—and why—oh why do your wings droop as we hover above this fair star—which is the greenest and yet most terrible of all we have encountered in our flight? Its brilliant flowers look like a fairy dream—but its fierce volcanoes like the passions of a turbulent heart.

Agathos.—They *are!*—they *are!* This wild star—it is now three centuries since with clapsed hands, and with streaming eyes, at the feet of my beloved—I spoke it—with a few passionate sentences—into birth. Its brilliant flowers *are* the dearest of all unfulfilled dreams, and its raging volcanoes *are* the passions of the most turbulent and unhallowed of hearts. [22]

The first passage is Emerson, from the conclusion to *Nature;* the second is Poe, from "The Power of Words." Both confront the physical power of the imagination to create worlds, worlds of the imagination that are real and are not real—worlds that at once apocalyptically supplant and iconically express the world we know. What difference does it make that Emerson's American dreamer is a poet, recreating by reseeing the world in time and space, while Poe's is an angel, creating worlds of beauty and turbulence beyond the space and time of "the fair Earth which lately perished"? It is a question Poe himself would take up in his poem "Israfel," and it is closely allied to Twain's significant shift from an angelic alter ego in "The Chronicle of Young Satan" to a dream-self in "No. 44, The Mysterious Stranger." The notion of the Other as double, of the alien as mirror image, raises focal questions both of spatial relation (here and there, earth and heaven: material self and spiritual or imaginative self) and of temporal relation (now and then, present and future: self and to-be-imagined self), questions that, I suggest, iconically define the central concerns of American apocalypses as being concerns of mediation. The works we are examining throughout this study *are* most obsessively preoccupied with that transformative interface; that boundary between now and then and between here and there, the point at which the status of the self can be scrutinized in relation to the inscrutable beyond.

FOUR

DREAM'S BODY

Man is adjoind to Man by his Emanative portion:
Who is Jerusalem in every individual Man: and her
Shadow is Vala, builded by the Reasoning power in Man
O search & see: turn your eyes inward: open O thou
World
Of Love & Harmony in Man: expand thy ever lovely
Gates.
> *—William Blake,* Jerusalem *39:38-42*

Since the mind has set no limit for itself, and since no
idea completes the task of consciousness, it must perish
in some incomprehensible disaster, one curious sen-
sation of which I was speaking. These give a glimpse of
unstable worlds, incompatible with the fullness of
life; inhuman, infirm worlds, comparable with those
suggested by the geometrician when he plays with
axioms, and by the physician when he postulates other
than the admitted constants. *Dreams, anxieties, and*
ecstasies; all those half-possible states that might be de-
scribed as introducing into the equation of knowledge
approximate values, or transcendental solutions, exist
between the clarity of life and the simplicity of death,
forming strange degrees, varieties, and ineffable phases—
for there are no names for things among which one is
quite alone.
> *—Paul Valéry,*
> *"Introduction to the Method of Leonardo"*

Emerson and Poe: in many respects, the juxtaposition is an unexpected one. Emerson was early assimilated into the main current of American thought as a prophet of the liberalized national dream and has long been invoked reverently in self-help manuals, Fourth of July speeches, sentimental posters, greeting cards, and other mythical expressions of the culture. Poe, on the other hand, has never been officially assimilated. Traditionally regarded (in America, at least) as a lowbrow writer fit primarily for scaring small children, he has always exerted a more covert, more subversive influence than Emerson—an influence channeled precisely through those somehow unshakable childhood memories of a strangely visionary death, weirdly illuminated and charged with an imaginative power that abortively and yet unmistakably seeks to point *beyond*. Revealingly, in his seminal attempt in 1941 to rescue Emerson from the gentility ghetto, F. O. Matthiessen decided that Poe was of too marginal an interest to the American Renaissance and American literature as a whole for inclusion with Melville, Hawthorne, Whitman, Thoreau, and Emerson: "his value," he wrote in a brief footnote, "even more than Emerson's, is now seen to consist in his influence rather than in the body of his work. No group of his poems seems as enduring as *Drum-Taps;* and his stories, less harrowing upon the nerves than they were, seem relatively factitious when contrasted with the moral depth of Hawthorne or Melville."[1] Moral depth: if that is the criterion, of course, Poe drops out of the canon.

In the decades following Matthiessen's pronouncement, Poe criticism has shown a curious tendency to get him right in censure and wrong in praise; T. S. Eliot's and Allen Tate's famous disparagements of Poe in the forties and fifties are by and large the most accurate "early" appraisals of his work,[2] while the various attempts to rescue Poe from censure have generally tended to re-create him in the critic's own image. We have had a striking succession of such resuscitated Poes: a Freudian Poe, a Jungian Poe, an existentialist Poe, a Marxist Poe, and most recently a Poe who, through the French line of Baudelaire, Mallarmé, Valéry, Lacan, and Derrida, has become the great Proto-Deconstructor.[3] It is really only in the last decade or so that serious attempts have begun to be made to unearth a historical Poe as Matthiessen had unearthed a historical Emerson. John Lynen's, Paul John Eakin's, and others' efforts to conceive a Poe who could have written not only the tales and poems but the letters, the essays, and most particularly *Eureka* have been instrumental, as have the inquiries into Poe's textual and ideological sources by, predominantly, Burton R. Pollin and Barton Levi St. Armand.[4]

Still—Emerson is respectable, while Poe remains largely beyond the pale. Why, then, set them side by side? Two points unite them: the pervasiveness of their influence upon American literature; and the visionary force of their apocalyptic dreams. I contend in this chapter, as on a broader scale in the book as a whole, that Emerson and Poe are the two great presiding figures over American apocalypses, that between them they define the apocalyptic mainstream of American literature that has succeeded them. Or more accurately, perhaps, *mainstreams*—for the work of Emerson and Poe in the 1830s and 1840s marks a crucial watershed in American literature, from which two great currents flow into the present, currents whose intermixings in Melville, Ellison, and Vonnegut (see chapter 5), Hawthorne, James, and Faulkner (see chapter 6), and West and Barth (see chapter 7) will be the focus of our discussion in Part II of this book.

Consider, for example, the intensity of messianic expectation in both writers. In a letter to James Russell Lowell on July 2, 1844, Poe writes: "1 have been too deeply conscious of the mutability and evanescence of temporal things, to give any continuous effort to anything—to be consistent in anything. My life has been *whim*—impulse—passion—a longing for solitude—a scorn of all things present, in an earnest desire for the future."[5] In the same year, Emerson published "The Poet," which looks to the future with much the same all-absorbing hope:

> And now my chains are to be broken; I shall mount above these
> clouds and opaque airs in which I live—opaque, though they
> seem transparent—and from the heavens of truth I shall see and
> comprehend my relations. That will reconcile me to life and
> renovate nature, to see trifles animated by a tendency, and to
> know what I am doing. Life will no more be a noise; now I
> shall see men and women, and know the signs by which they
> may be discerned from fools and satans. This day shall be better
> than my birthday: then I became an animal; now I am invited
> into the science of the real. Such is the hope, but the fruition is
> postponed.[6]

Both writers, like Balizet and Wigglesworth, locate a significant hope in the future; but rather than suppressing or sublimating the problem of deferral, as did those prophets of orthodox doom, they address it directly, insistently turning their critical and self-critical attention to that abysm of differance that stands between them and the fulfillment of their desires. This means that the apocalypse for Emerson and Poe, in very different ways, is always most ironic when it is most mythically apocalyptic. Both writers, as we shall see, seek to incorporate into their apocalypses a radically ironic perspective on the necessary failure of apocalypse, and by so incorporating it, paradoxically to *transform* irony into a desperate basis for hope.

■

"When an emotion communicates to the intellect the power to sap and upheave nature," Emerson writes in "The Poet," "how great the perspective! . . . [D]ream delivers us to dream, and while the drunkenness lasts we will sell our bed, our philosophy, our religion, in our opulence" (R 3:33). "Dream delivers us to dream"—the famous phrase makes dream itself the poet's tool in the work of renovation, the medium that links world and spirit, delivering us in biblical terms from Egypt into Canaan, from the world of appearances into the world of truth. Dream is both the conveyance and the destination, both the apocalyptic angel whose light fills the poet's nocturnal eye and the paradise that the poet's dream creates. Dream drunkenness is renovation. Unlike Nietzsche's dream in his revision of this passage in *The Birth of Tragedy* (*passim*, especially Section 1), Emerson's dream *is* the Dionysiac, or it is the "treaty" that Nietzsche posits between Apollonian shaping and Dionysiac enthusiasm that produces art.

Like Twain half a century after him, however, Emerson also knew acutely the failures of dream. "Dream delivers us to dream," he reiterates in "Experience," the essay that followed "The Poet," but adds, "and there is no end to illusion" (R 3:50). "My dream of a republic to *be* a dream," Twain's Hank Morgan was to paraphrase this reversal, "and so remain."[7] If Emerson is the prophet of the American Dream, he is as much a skeptical as a visionary dreamer:

> The waking from an impressive dream is a curious example of the jealousy of the gods. There is an air as if the sender of the illusion had been heedless for a moment that the Reason had returned to its seat, & was startled into attention. Instantly, there is a rush from some quarter to break up the drama into a chaos of parts, then of particles, then of ether, like smoke dissolving in a wind: it cannot be distinguished fast enough or fine enough. If you could give the waked watchman the smallest fragment, he could reconstruct the whole; for the moment, he is sure he can & will; but his attention is so divided on the disappearing parts, that he cannot grasp the least atomy, & the last fragment or film disappears before he could say, I have it. (JMN 16:177–78)

There is an implicit history of American literature in this journal entry from 1870: it is all, in one sense, a desperate attempt to "reconstruct the whole" dream from the slippery fragments that are disappearing everywhere the divided attention turns. Emerson's complex prefiguration of the problem, his incorporation of both sides (the dream and its fragmentation) into his apocalyptic vision, has made his work notoriously hard to classify: he won't hold still long enough to be fit into a critical category. This is his strength—his American strength, which continually presents the complexities that evade classification. To deal with this problem, I propose to examine the apocalyptic vision of *Nature* in a series of shifting perspectives that will define or *display* Emerson multiply by contextual contrast, and will thereby, I hope, progressively illuminate his importance for later American apocalypses. The contexts are three, each marking a significant relationship not of direct influence but of ideological kinship: F. W. J. Schelling and German idealism, Blake and English Romanticism, and Charles Sanders Peirce and American Pragmatism. Taken in sequence, these perspectives suggest a movement from a disembodied spiritual apocalypse, through the imagistic importance of "dream's body" to apocalyptic transformation, to the problematic question of how one interprets the body of dream so as to bind ontological truth and pragmatic consequences. This chapter is titled after the middle perspective, echoing Norman O. Brown's famous title *Love's Body*, which he derives from Blake;[8] but by placing the pragmatic context of Peirce last, I want to emphasize Emerson's profound awareness of the interpretive dilemmas surrounding the Romantic notion of bodily vision, his ironic (and characteristically American) sense that if the dream of bodily transformation is true, it is not because that is the way the universe is made but because we *need* it to be made that way if our lives are to be usefully spent.

Emerson's exposure to the idealistic philosophy of Schelling in the early 1830s was largely through Coleridge, of course, whose extensive "plagiarism" from the German philosopher began to be noticed in the late 1830s and whom Emerson had first read in 1829, in James Marsh's influential American edition of *Aids to Reflection,* a book that was the prime mover behind the 1836 formation of the Transcendental Club.[9] The traces of Schelling in *Nature* are oblique, therefore, and not evidence of direct influence. (Emerson was to read John Elliot Cabot's unpublished translation of Schelling's book on freedom in the early 1840s and about the same time—1843—published the first American translation of Schelling in *The Dial.*)[10] Indeed, Peter Carafiol underscores the dangers in drawing any positive conclusions about Emerson's influences:

> Emerson's understanding of *Aids* is more difficult to assess for, unlike Alcott, Emerson acknowledged no "master" or school

and denied all influence but inspiration. He took from other writers only those phrases that spoke to something in himself, giving credit not to the writer but to the universal truth that lay in his own soul awaiting revelation. Emerson read widely and eclectically, selecting from each writer only those ideas that he could use and virtually ignoring the rest. As René Wellek has noted, in the profusion of Emerson's reading he had access to assorted original and translated texts of German philosophy and therefore did not necessarily require the mediation of Coleridge.[11]

By "Schelling," then, let us signify the profound undercurrent of German idealism that infused American Transcendentalism, via Coleridge in England, Victor Cousin in France, and F. H. Hedge in America: that core matter of Emerson's idealistic philosophy that he so variously forged into idiosyncratic shape. "The Germans," Emerson writes in his journal, "believe in the necessary Trinity of God—The Infinite; the finite, & the passage from Inf. to Fin.; or, the Creation. It is typified in the act of thinking. Whilst we contemplate we are infinite; the thought we express is partial & finite; the expression is the third part & is equivalent to the act of Creation. Unity says Schelling is barren" (JMN 5:30). This journal entry is from 1834, before Emerson had read Schelling; and revealingly, Schelling's name functions in the passage, as evidently in Emerson's entire conception of his subject, as little more than a counter: he first wrote "Unity says Boehmen," then deleted "Boehmen" and wrote "Schelling."

However distorted by Emerson's restlessly assimilative imagination, Schellingian idealism has striking analogues in the "Idealism" and "Spirit" chapters of *Nature*. Here, for example, from "Idealism," is Emerson's apocalyptic version of Schelling's teleology:

> To the senses and the unrenewed understanding, belongs a sort of instinctive belief in the absolute existence of nature. In their view, man and nature are indissolubly joined. Things are ultimates, and they never look beyond their sphere. The presence of Reason mars this faith. The first effort of thought tends to relax this despotism of the senses, which binds us to nature as if we were a part of it, and shows us nature aloof, and, as it were, afloat. Until this higher agency intervened, the animal eye sees, with wonderful accuracy, sharp outlines and colored surfaces. When the eye of Reason opens, to outline and surface are at once added, grace and expression. These proceed from imagination and affection, and abate somewhat of the angular

distinctness of objects. If the Reason be stimulated to more
earnest vision, outlines and surfaces become transparent, and
are no longer seen; causes and spirits are seen through them.
The best, the happiest moments of life, are these delicious awak-
enings of the higher powers, and the reverential withdrawing
of nature before its God. (B 1:30)

The God before whom nature reverentially withdraws at this
highest point in the teleological ascent is the world-creating Spirit, and
it is the human race, which is now apocalyptically revealed as of the
same essence as the Spirit. At that telos, for Emerson as for Schelling,
human beings become artists, performing in the work of art a constitutive creative act that repeats and enacts the original creation of the
world by Spirit. Moreover, the artist's act is by definition apocalyptic,
at once creating the world *as* created and revealing it to itself. Primitive sensation, in Schelling's terms, is succeeded by productive intuition
as the material world is generated out of the unconscious activity of
Spirit; productive intuition is succeeded by reflection, in which the
ego becomes conscious both of its separation from the act of productive intuition and of a universe of space, time, and causality; and reflection is succeeded by absolute abstraction, in which the ego returns
on itself and becomes self-conscious, recognizing itself as intelligence
through an active and free act of will. As Schelling summarizes this development in the *System of Transcendental Idealism (1800):*

> These are the phases, unalterable and fixed for all knowledge, in
> the history of self-consciousness; they are characterized in ex-
> perience by a continuous step-wise sequence; and they can be
> exhibited and extended from simple stuff [where "Things are
> ultimates," as Emerson says] to organization [the addition of
> "grace and expression"] (whereby unconsciously productive
> nature reverts into itself), and from thence by reason and choice
> up to the supreme union of freedom and necessity in art
> ["these delicious awakenings of the higher powers"] (whereby
> consciously productive nature encloses and completes itself).[12]

This discussion of Emerson's ideological congruences with
Schelling reveals, I think, that something like Schelling's idealistic
teleology is the foundation for Emerson's apocalyptic vision—but also,
and more importantly, that it is *only* the foundation, not the edifice
itself. For if *Nature* is rhetorically as well as ideologically "an idealistic
exercise in transcendence up," as Kenneth Burke says[13] ("It is essential
to a true theory of nature and of man," Emerson writes, "that it contain

somewhat progressive" [B 1:36]), it reaches its Schellingian telos in the "Idealism" chapter and then begins to work past it, toward an American idealism that would point directly into the pragmatism of Charles Sanders Peirce. The crucial transition comes in "Spirit," after the Schellingian apothegms that nature "always speaks of Spirit" (B 1:37) and that "the noblest ministry of nature is to stand as the apparition of God" (B 1:37). Here is the transitional paragraph:

> Three problems are put by nature to the mind; What is matter?
> Whence is it? and Whereto? The first of these questions only,
> the ideal theory answers. Idealism saith: matter is a phenomenon,
> not a substance. Idealism acquaints us with the total disparity
> between the evidence of our own being, and the evidence of the
> world's being. The one is perfect; the other, incapable of any
> assurance; the mind is a part of the nature of things; the world
> is a divine dream, from which we may presently awake to the
> glories and certainties of day [this "awaking" already begins to
> move us away from Schelling]. Idealism is a hypothesis to ac-
> count for nature by other principles than those of carpentry and
> chemistry. Yet, if it only deny the existence of matter, it does
> not satisfy the demands of the spirit. It leaves God out of me. It
> leaves me in the splendid labyrinth of my perceptions, to wan-
> der without end. Then the heart resists it, because it baulks the
> affections in denying substantive being to men and women.
> Nature is so pervaded with human life, that there is something
> of humanity in all, and in every particular. But this theory
> [that is, idealism] makes nature foreign to me, and does not ac-
> count for that consanguinity which we acknowledge to it.
> (B 1:37-38)

The key here is Emerson's resistance to the idealistic denial of "substantive being to men and women." Rather surprisingly, this chapter titled "Spirit" is a veiled celebration of the *body*, of the "body of man" as the "incarnation of God" (B 1:38). And when we reach "Prospects" and find Emerson's Orphic poet singing of the original human form, the gigantic body "permeated and dissolved by spirit" (B 1:42), from which we have degenerated and into which we must apocalyptically be regenerated, we begin to suspect that the source Emerson is using to modify Schellingian idealism into a congenial American form is none other than St. Paul—specifically, Paul's notion of the spiritual body. This radical shift in the book's two concluding chapters is in fact alluded to in earlier sections; in "Nature," for example, Emerson tells us: "But if a man would be alone, let him look

at the stars. The rays that come from those heavenly worlds, will separate between him and vulgar things. One might think the atmosphere
was made transparent with this design, to give man, in the heavenly
bodies, the perpetual presence of the sublime" (B 1:8). And later, in
"Language," he refers directly to Paul in the course of a eulogy to
seeds: "The seed of a plant,—to what affecting analogies in the nature
of man, is that little fruit made use of, in all discourse, up to the voice
of Paul, who calls the human corpse a seed,—'It is sown a natural body;
it is raised a spiritual body'" (B 1:19). Both allusions are to the same
passage in 1 Cor 15, where Paul analogically establishes the nature of
the resurrection:

> But someone will ask, "How are the dead raised? With what
> kind of body do they come?" You foolish man! What you sow
> is not the body which is to be, but a bare kernel, perhaps of
> wheat or some other grain. But God gives it a body as he has
> chosen, and to each kind of seed its own body. For not all flesh
> is alike, but there is one kind for men, another for animals,
> another for birds, and another for fish. There are celestial bod-
> ies; but the glory of the celestial is one, and the glory of the
> terrestrial is another. There is one glory of the sun, and another
> glory of the moon, and another glory of the stars; for star dif-
> fers from star in glory.
> So it is with the resurrection of the dead. What is sown is
> perishable, what is raised is imperishable. It is sown in dishonor,
> it is raised in glory. It is sown in weakness, it is raised in power.
> It is sown a physical body [*soma psuchikos*], it is raised a spir-
> itual body [*soma pneumatikos*]. If there is a physical body, there
> is also a spiritual body. Thus it is written, "The first man Adam
> became a living being;" the last Adam became a life-giving spirit.
> But it is not the spiritual which is first, but the physical, and
> then the spiritual. The first man was from the earth, a man of
> dust; the second man is from heaven. As was the man of dust,
> so are those who are of the dust; and as is the man of heaven, so
> are those who are of heaven. Just as we have borne the image
> of the man of dust [*eikona tou choikou*], we shall also bear
> the image of the man of heaven [*eikona tou epouranou*]. I tell
> you this, brethren: flesh and blood [*sarx*] cannot inherit
> the kingdom of God, nor does the perishable inherit the imper-
> ishable. (1 Cor 15:35-50)

Central to this passage is the notion of *image as body:* we have
borne the *image* of Adam in our present flesh-and-blood (*sarx, soma*

psuchikos), and by the typological relation between Adam and Christ in history, metaphorically linked to the relation between seed and grain in nature (*phusis*), we will bear the image of Christ in the spiritual body (*soma pneumatikos*). Paul's Christology, one might say, is an iconology: the definitive Christian icon (*eikon,* image) is the *soma Christou,* the mystical body of Christ that is the Church (as the Catholics would stress) and the Logos (as the Protestants would stress), and in both the Church and the Logos the symbolic conjunction of God and man, the celestial and terrestrial, glory and dishonor, power and weakness, spirit and nature.

Something akin to this mediatory and apocalyptically redemptive spiritual body, embodying both spirit (*pneuma* or breath) and physicality (*phusis* or nature), is what Emerson's vision is striving to encompass in the conclusion to *Nature.* It is a vision strikingly similar to Blake's myth (which Emerson, of course, did not know) of a fallen Albion, a gigantic body whose all-containing primordial internality in the Fall is externalized into the visible creation, earth, ocean, and the Starry Floor, as Blake calls the heavens. "A man is a god in ruins," Emerson's Orphic bard sings, unwittingly echoing the cosmogony of Blake, which was to remain almost unknown for nearly a century. Central to both Emerson and Blake is an emphasis not on the human unconscious becoming self-conscious, as in Schelling's "objective" idealism, but on the body as "the human form, of which all other organizations appear to be degradations" (B 1:28), and as the divine-human power or energy that fuels all life:

> As a plant upon the earth, so a man rests upon the bosom of God; he is nourished by unfailing fountains, and draws, at his need, inexhaustible power. Who can set bounds to the possibilities of man? Once inhale the upper air, being admitted to behold the absolute natures of justice and truth, and we learn that man has access to the entire mind of the Creator, is himself the creator in the finite. (B 1:38)

"This view," Emerson continues, "which admonishes me where the sources of wisdom and power lie, . . . carries upon its face the highest certificate of truth, because it animates me to create my own world through the purification of my soul" (B 1:38).

Blake of course went much farther than Emerson in both the elaboration of his visionary cosmogony and in the emphasis on the *body* as the source of the divine energy. Emerson had serious reservations about the extremes to which a visionary account of men and women's spiritual bodies might be taken, and he reacted strongly to

Whitman's extension of his own ideas in *Leaves of Grass*. But the centrality of the body to the apocalyptic renovation is clearly there, however veiled. "But, having made for himself this huge shell [of nature], his waters retired; he no longer fills the veins and veinlets; he is shrunk to a drop. He sees that the structure still fits him, but fits him colossally" (B 1:42). This is the import also of the "transparent eye-ball" passage: "Standing on the bare ground,—my head bathed by the blithe air, and uplifted into infinite space,—all mean egotism vanishes. I become a transparent eye-ball. I am nothing. I see all. The currents of the Universal Being circulate through me; I am part or particle of God" (B 1:10). Emerson is a visionary eyeball, the ocular organ of nature herself, perceived as the gigantic human body (later to be not the body but the clothing) through which the "currents" or breath (spirit, *pneuma*) of God circulate. It is a body "permeated and dissolved by spirit" (B 1:42)—which is to say a spiritual body.

Why, however, must the eyeball be transparent? Transparency allows eyes to *see through;* but why does Emerson insist here that the eye itself be seen through even as it is seeing? The question relates directly to the complexities of Emerson's notion of the spiritual body as apocalyptically mediatory—a notion that, again, he shared with Blake and that both derived from Paul. The same complexity figures in another problematic passage in rather a different but significantly kindred way, namely the famous "apocalypse of the mind" paragraph in "Idealism":

> In my utter impotence to test the authenticity of the report of
> my senses, to know whether the impressions they make on
> me correspond with outlying objects, what difference does it
> make, whether Orion is up there in heaven, or some god paints
> the image in the firmament of the soul? The relations of parts
> and the end of the whole remaining the same, what is the dif-
> ference, whether land and sea interact, and worlds revolve and
> intermingle without number or end,—deep yawning under deep,
> and galaxy balancing galaxy, throughout absolute space, or,
> whether, without relations of time and space, the same appear-
> ances are inscribed in the constant faith of man? Whether
> nature enjoy a substantial existence without, or is only in the
> apocalypse of the mind, it is alike useful and venerable to
> me. (B 1:29)

What is the "apocalypse of the mind"? "The phrase is beautifully suggestive," Barbara L. Packer remarks in her recent reading of *Nature:*

it combines both the etymological and conventional meanings of the word 'apocalypse' in that vibrant tension Emerson thought characteristic of the best poetry. The mind *is* an uncovering, a revelation of significance; it also may be the consuming fire in whose flames the dross of nature will be burnt up. Perhaps its most significant contribution to the argument of *Nature* is its implicit assertion that the mind is not a place but a process; not an isolated inner space passively receiving sense impressions, but an active power incessantly striving to reveal the meaning of creation.[14]

The phrase does indeed operate, I think, through a tension between the etymological and conventional sense of apocalypse; but Packer's description of that tension will work only with two interrelated qualifications. First, nature is never consumed in Emerson, as it is in Blake; and second, for that very reason, Emerson's reference to the apocalypse of the mind is deprecatory: "Whether nature enjoy a substantial existence without, or is *only* in the apocalypse of the mind, it is alike useful and venerable to me." Apocalypse in this context sounds less like an unveiling than a shadowy mirage: "Dream delivers us to dream, and there is no end to illusion." It seems, in fact, almost a direct reversal of the Blakean alignments of Jerusalem and Vala in this chapter's epigraph: Vala as substantial nature is *real,* and inward Jerusalem, man's redemptive emanative portion, becomes the shadow that is "only" in the apocalypse of the mind.

But this eloquent "only" establishes only half of Emerson's polemical argument. The opening paragraph of "Idealism," with its disparagement of a nature that is "only in the apocalypse of the mind," must be set against the chapter's penultimate paragraph, which sets up an important dialectic between nature as substantial and nature as apparent and then, by way of balancing the earlier inclination toward substantiality, leans distinctly toward apparency:

> It appears that motion, poetry, physical and intellectual science, and religion, all tend to affect our conviction of the reality of the external world. But I own there is something ungrateful in expanding too curiously the particulars of the general proposition, that all culture tends to imbue us with idealism. I have no hostility to nature, but a child's love to it. I expand and live in the warm day like corn and melons. Let us speak her fair. I do not wish to fling stones at my beautiful mother, nor soil my gentle nest. I only wish to indicate the true position of nature in regard to man, wherein to establish man, all right education

tends; as the ground which to attain is the object of human
life, that is, of man's connexion with nature. Culture inverts the
vulgar views of nature, and brings the mind to call that apparent, which it uses to call real, and that real, which it uses to call
visionary. Children, it is true, believe in the external world. The
belief that it appears only, is an afterthought, but with culture,
this faith will as surely arise on the mind as did the first.
(B 1:35-36)

Nature appears only: her substantiality is only apparent. Or, to
retain the full range of Emerson's dialectic, nature both does and does
not appear only, which is to say, surely, that she "transpears": for to
be transparent is to be at once visible and invisible, present to perception but unobstructive of what lies beyond. The substantial body of
nature, that is, is both physically *there,* present to the senses for what
Emerson calls commodity and beauty, and spiritually *not there,* apocalyptically absent so as to reveal the transcendental truths that it hides.
Nature, then, is both a veil (Vala) and an unveiling (the apocalypse of
the mind).

Blake has a curious passage in *The Four Zoas* that strikingly
resembles Emerson's attempt to have it both ways here; it is the beginning of Vala's restoration of Tharmas and Enion in Night of the Ninth.
Vala, Blake's external nature, is looking for Tharmas and Enion. Gazing
at her reflection in the water, she sees Tharmas, and calling to Enion she
hears her own echo, but in that moment she is transfused with light:

> She stood in the river & viewd herself within the watry glass
> And her bright hair was wet with the waters She rose up from
>   the river
> And as she rose her Eyes were opend to the world of waters
> She saw Tharmas sitting upon the rocks beside the wavy sea
> He strokd the water from his beard & mournd faint thro the
>   summer vales . . .
>
> Then Vala lifted up her hands to heaven to call on Enion
> She calld but none could answer & the Eccho of her voice
>   returnd . . .
>
> She ceas'd & light beamd round her like the glory of the morning
> And she arose out of the river & girded on her golden girdle[15]

Blake's revision of the Narcissus myth is perhaps imagistically
displaced here, but the conjunction of mirror, echo, and restoration

strongly suggests that he was shifting the myth in the direction of apocalyptic revelation. A mirror-image and an echo, clearly, are the visual and vocal forms of *reflection,* in which vision or voice is projected onto an opaque surface and returned to the projector. But opacity for Blake, as for Emerson, was a function of fallen perception; objects in their eternal form are transparent, suffused with the divine-human light, and so Blake modulates his reflective images toward the perception of *depth.* In one sense, of course, Vala looks *up* from the water and sees Tharmas "sitting upon the rocks *beside* the wavy sea;" but in another and perhaps more important sense, Tharmas *is* water, the chaotic ocean that must be given human form, and when Vala's eyes are "opend to the world of waters" she sees him *in* the water, *in* her own reflection. But what this means is that her vision is both reflective (returned from the surface of the water as *opaque*) and refractive (penetrating through the surface of the water as *transparent*). In terms of the Narcissus myth, the image Vala sees in the "watry glass" is both a surface reflection of her own face and a depth refraction of Tharmas stroking the water from his beard. Similarly, although Vala's echo returns when she calls to Enion, apparently negating signification by means of mechanical repetition, at the same time she discovers that "light beamd round her like the glory of the morning."

The two mediatory imageries, Blake's and Emerson's, are essentially congruent in their suggestion that apocalyptic revelation comes by the conversion of an opaque surface into a transparent one: not at all the *removal* of the opaque surface that obstructs vision, that is, but its transformation into a visionary medium that reveals by standing between the viewer and truth, a veil that unveils itself, a mirror that acts as a window. The source for both imageries, once again, may be St. Paul, as revealed in a particularly pregnant passage at the conclusion of 2 Cor 3, where Paul describes the apocalypse as an unveiled reflective/refractive mirroring that glorifies the viewer, filling him or her with the divine light: "And we all," he writes, "with unveiled face, beholding as in a mirror the glory of the Lord, are being changed into his likeness from one degree of glory to another, for this comes from the Lord who is the spirit" (2 Cor 3:18).[16] Here Christ *is* the veil, as Heb 10:19-20 suggests, who by his death to sin unveils the believer's face; and he is also the mediatory mirror, an opaque surface like a veil or Blake's Covering Cherub that blocks vision beyond it, but which by his redemptive power is converted into a transparent surface that reveals to the mirror-gazer his own *future* glorified body, his Christlike spiritual body, *in his own reflection.* This paradoxical mirror-imagery is most concisely presented in Paul's famous mirror passage in 1 Cor 13: we see *di esoptrou en ainigmati, through* a glass darkly, perceiving *in* a mirror the transcendental realm *beyond* the mirror.

This notion of the substantial but transparent body of nature as a mediatory icon is central to Emerson's apocalyptic vision. In his revision of Paul, nature becomes the redemptive incarnation of God that mediates between man and his creator, standing "like the figure of Jesus" (B 1:37) between us and truth and revealing truth by embodying our relation to it. "Every rational creature," Emerson writes, "has all nature for his dowry and estate. It is his, if he will. He may divest himself of it; he may creep into a corner, and abdicate his kingdom, as most men do, but he is entitled to it by his constitution. In proportion to the energy of his thought and will, he takes up the world into himself" (B 1:15). Once assimilated as an apocalyptic mediation, "the beauty of nature reforms itself in the mind, and not for barren contemplation, but for new creation" (B 1:16). New creation is a trope for art; but it is also literally what the words *new creation* denote, a reenactment of God's creation of the earth in an apocalyptic restoration. "But when a faithful thinker," Emerson says, "resolute to detach every object from personal relations, and see it in the light of thought, shall, at the same time, kindle science with the fire of the holiest affections, then will God go forth anew into the creation" (B 1:44)—God as the apocalyptic poet, that is, and the poet as God. The ME incorporates the NOT ME into himself, transforming it from alien matter to a transparent mediatory icon that both reveals and reflects the Spirit that is God and the human being; humans see God both through and in the iconic medium of nature and realize that by looking *beyond* to God they are actually looking *back* at the image of God in themselves. Nature is iconically transformed from opaque mirror to transparent mirror; iconic mediation becomes enhanced reflection.

To "transpear" is therefore not, as Eric Cheyfitz argues, to "disappear," for the transformation of nature does not consume it; that transformation constitutes not the end but the *perfection* of mediation. "The end of tradition, for Emerson," Cheyfitz writes, "appears to be a metaphor for the messianic moment when the suggestive text of nature will become transparent to the satisfaction, or finality, of the Over-soul. At that moment the traditional, or opaque, book will disappear—all mediation will end—and men 'can read God directly'; and what they will 'read' will be the Book of their own Identity, the Book of the absolute Unity, their absolute Wholeness."[17] In Emerson's apocalypse the mediatory apparition of nature does not disappear, is not cast out, but ceases to obstruct vision while remaining substantially present to perception, so that the apocalyptic dream remains firmly embodied in the physical world.

This summary of Emerson's apocalyptic vision does not, however, account for its marked divergence from Blake and indeed from the entire tradition of Romantic idealism as Emerson inherited it from English and Continental poets and philosophers. I mean its radical grounding in a highly pragmatic skepticism. Kenneth Burke noted this movement in *Nature,* in his 1966 study:

> In the case of Emerson's essay, the underlying structure is as simple as this: The everyday world, all about us here and now, is to be interpreted as a *diversity* of *means* for carrying out a *unitary purpose* (or, if you will, the *principle* of purpose) that is situated in an ultimate realm *beyond* the here and now. The world's variety of things is thus to be interpreted *in terms of* a transcendent unifier (that infuses them all with its single spirit). And by this mode of interpretation all the world becomes viewed as a set of *instrumentalities.* (Emerson more resonantly calls them, "commodities.") For we should bear it in mind that Emerson's brand of transcendentalism was but a short step ahead of out-and-out pragmatism, which would retain an unmistakable theological tinge in William James, and furtive traces even in Dewey. I have in mind the ambiguity whereby, when Dewey pleads that people use their "capacities" to the fullest, he secretly means their *"good* capacities." He thus schemes to make a quasi-technical term serve a moralistic purpose. (191)

But as Frederic I. Carpenter persuasively aruges in *American Literature and the Dream,* the missing link between Emerson and the philosophy of James and John Dewey is Charles Sanders Peirce, whose pragmatism, unlike that of James and Dewey, placed ideas before actions and insisted that actions therefore *guide* thought rather than supplant or succeed it. Peirce was, as Carpenter says, a "platonic realist," who "opposed all forms of nominalism, valuing the general above the particular"; "He believed in the power of the human will to direct man's destiny; but he thought that progress would best be achieved, not by fighting against evil but by developing human intelligence."[18] Peirce's pragmatism was in spirit far closer to the Schellingian idealism that lay at the core of Emerson's vision than to the humanistic realism of James and Dewey; and indeed, Peirce wrote to James,

> My views were probably influenced by Schelling—by all stages of Schelling, but especially by the *Philosophie der Natur.* I

consider Schelling as enormous; and one thing I admire about
him is his freedom from the trammels of system, and his holding
himself uncommitted to any previous utterance. In that, he
is like a scientific man. If you were to call my philosophy Schel-
lingism transformed in the light of modern physics, I should
not take it too hard.[19]

If this transcendental undercurrent is instrumental to our understanding of Peirce's thought, the pragmatic undercurrent in Emerson's
thought is equally instrumental to our understanding of *Nature*. Note,
for example, how Emerson couches his attack on empiricism: "What
difference does it make, whether Orion is up there in heaven, or some
god paints the image in the firmament of the soul?" *What difference
does it make*—for Blake, the question would be frivolous. To Blake, as
to Schelling, it makes all the difference in the world; it is the most
crucial ontological question of all, which must be settled one way or
the other if human beings are to move toward truth. For Emerson the
ontological question is always subordinated to pragmatic concerns:
"to what *end* is nature?" (B 1:7). "Whether nature enjoy a substantial
existence without, or is only in the apocalypse of the mind, it is alike
useful and venerable to me"—never mind ontology, this says, what
matters is nature's use and my veneration for it. And of course nature's
use for Emerson is spiritual; if idealism "only deny the existence of matter, it does not satisfy the demands of the spirit. It leaves God out of
me. It leaves me in the splendid labyrinths of my perceptions, to wander without end" (B 1:37). In Emerson, the true test of a doctrine
is in its consequences for human activity. The attacks on empiricism
and idealism are therefore substantially the same: each interpretation, taken to an ontological extreme, "leaves God out of me"—empiricism because it insists too strongly on dead matter and idealism because
it dissipates the body of nature. Ontologically, that is, it makes no
difference "whether nature enjoy a substantial existence without, or
is only in the apocalypse of the mind;" what matters is the pragmatic
consequences of adopting either position, and Emerson resolutely seeks
to chart a middle path between them, ironically undermining ontological claims by submitting them to tests of psychological and ethical
effect.

But this shift of alliances essentially serves to displace the philosophical quest for truth into a self-conscious examination of the
grounds of interpretation by which truth can be known. If truth is
pragmatic, then it is relative, always determined by its consequences in
the minds and deeds of men and women, of individuals thinking and

acting in a communal context. Thinking *and* acting: "Pragmatism is correct doctrine," Peirce wrote to James, "only in so far as it is recognized that material action is the mere husk of ideas. The brute element exists, and must not be explained away, as Hegel seeks to do. But the end of thought is action, only in so far as the end of action is another thought."[20] In other words, to crystallize Peirce's pragmatic dialectic, the supreme act is an *act of interpretation,* and the supreme thought is a *self-reflexive* thought about the grounds of interpretive action.

If Emerson's apocalyptic vision is a "reflective" one in the sense discussed here, therefore, showing individuals in the *reflection of nature* their own gigantic lineaments and transforming them into these lineaments, it is a vision whose primary focus finally becomes the *nature of reflection.* If the body of nature prompts us to idealistic speculations about an apocalyptic transformation, Emerson insists that we ask how we are implicated in that prompting. To what extent is nature's call to gaze into her transformative mirror a projection of our own desire to be transformed? What *good* does it do to imagine ourselves apocalyptically, as capable of being revealed as visionary giants? The ontological either/or of Emerson's essay, which points ahead unmistakably to what has been called the "multiple choice" method of Hawthorne and to an entire range of American metafictions, effectively dismisses ontology and advances in its stead a pragmatic concern for the grounds of human action.

∎

Much the same pragmatic irony informs the apocalyptic vision of Poe, too, who in *Eureka* claims that the ontological ground for his discussion must be the Godhead, but then insists that "of this Godhead, *in itself,* he alone is not imbecile . . . who propounds—nothing,"[21] thus echoing Emerson in *Nature:* "Of that ineffable essence which we call Spirit, he that thinks most, will say least" (B 1:37). *Eureka* is a "prose poem," therefore, that is both true and a fiction; as Poe writes in his preface to the volume, "I offer this Book of Truths, not in its character of Truth-Teller, but for the Beauty that abounds in its Truth; constituting it as true. To these I present the composition as an Art-Product alone:—let us say as a Romance; or, if I be not urging too lofty a claim, as a Poem" (16:183). Poe, like Emerson, wants to have it both ways: his cosmological treatise is true, but "an Art-Product alone"; a poem conceived as beauty, which constitutes it as true. "*What I propound here is true;*—therefore it cannot die:—or if by any means it be now trodden down so that it die, it will 'rise again to the life Everlasting'" (16:183), Poe continues, invoking his apocalyptic theme.

"Nevertheless it is as a Poem only that I wish this work to be judged after I am dead" (16:183).

The multiply shifting lenses of irony through which Poe views the apocalyptic transformation that he awaits have led many, both in his day and in our own, to reduce his vision in *Eureka* and elsewhere to an *attack* on vision, to an ironic negation of visionary truth. This inclination led critics in Poe's time to revile him as an atheist and has caused critics in our time to praise him as a deconstructionist; but Poe himself, defending *Eureka* against a theology student's hostile review, presents a rather different case. Responding to the reviewer's attack on the "atheistic" tenor of his claim in *Eureka* that nothing can be propounded of God, he points out in a letter of 20 September 1848 to Charles F. Hoffman that his exact words were: "Of this Godhead, *in itself*, he alone is not imbecile, etc."—which Poe says indicates a desire to concern himself with the Godhead *in its effects*—that is, not ontologically but pragmatically (L 381). The letter refutes the reviewer's attacks in some detail, finally impressing us with the sense that what Poe is most concerned to defend himself against is precisely the charge of *impiety*. As Barton Levi St. Armand concludes in his important study of the book, "To Poe . . . *Eureka* was an act of faith, not a clever apostasy."[22]

St. Armand here persuasively argues for a reading of *Eureka,* in fact, as a "late, original, and radical contribution" (9) to the movement of Christian natural theology or deism, which sought to understand not the *essence* of God, but the *acts* of God, through his handwriting in the world. In this sense, clearly, Poe is not at all "an American Blake," as David Ketterer argues in *New Worlds for Old,*[23] but a proponent of that "deluded" philosophy that Blake linked with Francis Bacon, Sir Isaac Newton, and John Locke. Emerson might more justifiably stand as the American Blake; but the skeptical and ironic pragmatism that imbues the apocalyptic visions of Poe and Emerson make both writers more Americans than Blakes. Both insistently ignore ontological questions in order to focus attention on practical problems of action, most particularly on the activity of interpretation. *Eureka* is a poem insofar as it seeks to convey a vision of God's creation in words and in that it knows acutely the inadequacy of words to achieve that; and it is the truth insofar as what is true *is* precisely the act of interpretation, the striving toward a knowledge of Being that must always fall short. For Poe, the apocalyptic act was less the actual transfiguration than the figural embodiment of the possibility of transfiguration in an artistic image. Poe is much more concerned with what lies beyond our world than is Emerson; Poe's is an external God, with whom the individual is united not by apocalyptic reflection here on earth, as for Emerson, but only after death—but that concern is invariably conceived in terms of the act of coming-to-know, not in terms of the knowing itself.

Part of Poe's deistic revision of Christian eschatology is also an insistence that what we think of as *spirit,* as radically alien to the material reality we know, is in fact only matter in a rarefied state. This turns Schelling, too, inside out, for where matter for him was particled mind, mind for Poe (including the mind of God) was unparticled matter. Poe's most concise statement of this notion is his July 2, 1844, letter to James Russell Lowell, from which I quoted at the beginning of this chapter:

> I have no belief in spirituality. I think the word a *mere* word. No one has really a conception of spirit. We cannot imagine what is not. We deceive ourselves by the idea of infinitely rarefied matter. Matter escapes the senses by degrees—a stone—a metal— a liquid—the atmosphere—a gas—the luminiferous ether. Beyond this there are other modifications more rare. But to all we attach the notion of a constitution of particles—atomic composition. For this reason only, we think spirit different; for spirit, we say is unparticled, and *therefore* not matter. But it is clear that if we proceed sufficiently far in our ideas of rarefactions, we shall arrive at a point where the particles coalesce; for, although the particles be infinite, the infinity of littleness in the spaces between them, is an absurdity. —The unparticled matter, permeating & impelling, all things, is God. Its activity is the thought of God—which creates. Man, and other thinking beings, are individualizations of the unparticled matter. Man exists as a "person," by being clothed with matter (the particled matter) which individualizes him. Thus habited, his life is rudimental. What we call "death" is the painful metamorphosis. But for the necessity of the rudimental life, there would have been no worlds. At death, the worm is the butterfly—still material, but in a matter unrecognized by our organs—recognized, occasionally, perhaps, by the sleep-walker, directly—without organs—through the mesmeric medium. Thus a sleep-walker may see ghosts. Divested of the rudimental covering, the being inhabits *space*—what we suppose to be the immaterial universe—passing everywhere, and acting all things, by mere volition—cognizant of all secrets but that of the nature of God's volition—the motion, or activity, of the unparticled matter. (L 257)

"No one has really a conception of spirit. We cannot imagine what is not." By interpreting what we call spirit as infinitely rarefied matter, ending ultimately in the unparticled matter of the mind of God, Poe claims to be able to know more of the universal order than empirical science, because matter extends further than empiricists had thought; since the "rudimental covering" restricts human beings to rudimental knowing, they can glimpse the rarer matter of the beyond only through inorganic intuition. But what they see is not the mental Being of God, which is inaccessible even to angelic knowing, but the progressive transition from our rudimental existence and God's Being. And that suggests that the task of art is to strive intuitively toward a perception and representation of that transition; to record intuitions of the transition to God through spatial and temporal images of the coming-to-know.

Such is Poe's intention in most of his best work: not to move beyond the spatial or temporal boundary but to stand *at* it and thus achieve a dual vision—of earth in terms of God's transcendental universe and the universe in terms of our present life on earth. Poe is most interested in the *process* of apocalyptic transformation—in the transitional medium that makes possible the movement from one level of material existence to another, from the human to the angelic. Transition: this is the focus of most of Poe's poems, of the tales of metempsychosis and doubling, the mesmeric revelations, the angelic colloquies, and the sea voyages—among these, "A Descent into the Maelström," "Ms. Found in a Bottle," and most important, *The Narrative of Arthur Gordon Pym*. We will be returning to "A Descent into the Maelström" in chapter 5, "The Fall of the House of Usher" in chapter 6, "The Masque of the Red Death" and "William Wilson" in chapter 7, and "Ligeia" and "The Man of the Crowd" in the Conclusion; in the remainder of this chapter I want to focus on Poe's novel, *Pym*.

Pym is a baffling narrative, in many respects, not the least of which is its radical attempt to bring the reader right to the transfigurational boundary—the terminus I called the line of deferral in chapter 2, and apparently to *pass* it—only to bring its narrator back to an unchanged America, where he sets about writing and publishing his memoirs. In answer to the most crucial question of all, at least to conventional expectations—that of what *happens* beyond the polar veil—Poe offers no explanation, leaving the reader with a tale but apparently no coherence, an absence precisely where one thinks there should be a presence: beyond the veil. The seeming gap in Pym's narrative has acted in *Pym* criticism as a kind of interpretive license, not only inviting but demanding that critics fill in the break with their own conjectures as to what befell Pym in the polar cataract;[24] but I will suggest that there is a way of reading the novel in which there is no gap at all, or in which the gap is there precisely to guide readers past false ontological interpretations to a pragmatic concern with the mediatory act of interpretation.

Like most of Poe's shorter pieces, the novel develops by what might be called a dynamic of intensification. That is, though the novel moves through space, from New England to the South Pole, an equally or more vital development in the narrative entails a progressive increase in *intensity*. Like Poe's poetry, his tales at their best present the reader with a single narrative situation, which is developed not through character and event but through the accumulation of details and the horrific though strangely lyrical intensification of both environmental threats and the narrator's sensations. We feel that we are being presented not with a causal development in linear time but with a tableau atemporally intensified to the point of overload, which is the telos of all Poe's finest tales: the point at which reality dissolves and, with luck, is transfigured. So also in *Pym*. In it, Poe chooses the sea voyage, as he does the land voyage in *Julius Rodman,* as the ideal picaresque vehicle to link together a series of conceivably unrelated tableaux: the *Ariel* escapade, the sequences in the hold and on the deck of the *Grampus,* the series of disasters on the island of Tsalal, and the mysterious approach to the Pole. Each of these tableaux is developed through the dynamic of intensification, moving toward the teleological point of overload; and the series as a whole is made to undergo the same process of intensification, leading to that final overload where Pym's narrative breaks off, the telos of the novel as a whole.

That telos, without much doubt, is apocalyptic. The imagery of the novel throughout is apocalyptic in origin and, by intensification, becomes more and more explicitly apocalyptic as the novel progresses, until a mighty explosion finally impresses Pym "with a vague conception . . . that the whole foundations of the solid globe were suddenly rent asunder, and that the day of universal dissolution was at hand" (3:203). The recurring imagistic patterns in the novel, which roughly anticipate the apocalyptic motifs I will be exploring in chapters 5, 6, and 7 of this book, all point in this direction: the descent-and-return, which significantly parallels the apocalyptic movement through death to rebirth (chapter 5); the shipwreck motif, involving the destruction of a worldly structure (chapter 6); and the revolt motif, conceived either as moral conflict between good and evil or as a class conflict between authority and subjects (chapter 7). The intensification of these images through the first three episodes (omitting, for the time being, the problematic "Tekeli-li" episode at the Pole) is striking:

	Descent-and-Return	Shipwreck	Revolt
Ariel	Two near-drownings	Sailboat crash	Boyish disobedience
Grampus	Immolation in hold; four near-drownings; extended extremity	Gradual reduction of brig to hulk	Murderous mutiny; thirty-eight men dead
Tsalal	Immolation in apocalyptic caverns	Spectacular explosion of *Jane Guy*	Treacherous destruction of entire crew by natives

Without the Tsalal episode, perhaps, this imagistic progression would be apocalyptic only in origin, not in import. On Tsalal the apocalypse becomes a real threat, as the "concussion" generated by the natives' engineered landslide, which buries the *Jane Guy*'s crew, suggests to Pym that "the day of universal dissolution was at hand," and the actual destruction of the *Jane Guy* provides us with a startling image of that dissolution:

> We now anticipated a catastrophe, and were not disappointed. First of all there came a smart shock (which we felt distinctly where we were as if we had been galvanized), but unattended with any visible signs of an explosion. The savages were evidently startled, and paused for an instant from their labours and yellings. They were on the point of recommencing, when suddenly a mass of smoke puffed up from the decks, resembling a black and heavy thunder-cloud—then, as if from its bowels, arose a tall stream of vivid fire to the height, apparently, of a quarter of a mile—then there came a sudden circular expansion of the flame—then the whole atmosphere was magically crowded in a single instant, with a wild chaos of wood, and metal, and human limbs—and lastly, came the concussion in its fullest fury, which hurled us impetuously from our feet, while the hills echoed and re-echoed the tumult, and a dense shower of the minutest fragments of the ruins tumbled headlong in every direction around us. (3:216)

The imagery of the explosion powerfully anticipates Poe's imagination of the apocalypse in *Eureka:* the "tall stream of vivid fire," the "sudden circular expansion of the flame," and most particularly the "magically crowded" atmosphere all point directly to the force of diffusion and "the immediate and perpetual *tendency* of the disunited atoms to return into their normal Unity" (16:210). The strange spatial protraction of the apocalypse that follows the explosion of the *Jane Guy*—the passage through the caverns and the canoe trip toward the Pole—profits from juxtaposition with the following section of Poe's discussion in *Eureka* as retroactive commentary:

> For the effectual and thorough completion of the general design, we thus see the necessity for a repulsion of limited capacity—a separate *something* which, on withdrawal of the diffusive Volition, shall at the same time allow the approach, and forbid the junction, of the atoms; suffering them infinitely to approximate, while denying them positive contact; in a word, having the power—*up to a certain epoch*—of preventing their *coalition,* but no ability to interfere with their *coalescence* in any respect or *degree.* The repulsion, already considered as so peculiarly limited in other regards, must be understood, let me repeat, as having power to prevent absolute coalition, *only up to a certain epoch.* Unless we are to conceive that the appetite for Unity among the atoms is doomed to be satisfied *never;*—unless we are to conceive that what had a beginning is to have no end—a conception which cannot *really* be entertained, however much we may talk or dream of entertaining it—we are forced to conclude that the repulsive influence imagined, will, finally— under pressure of the *Uni-tendency collectively* applied, but never and in no degree *until,* on fulfillment of the Divine purposes, such collective application shall be naturally made— yield to a force which, at that ultimate epoch, shall be the superior force precisely to the extent required, and thus permit the universal subsidence into the inevitable, because original and therefore normal, *One.* (16:210-11)

Poe recognizes, here, not only the inevitability but the *necessity* of deferral: diffuse atoms cannot collapse back into the mind of God too fast. There must therefore be a "separate *something*" that at once hastens and delays the apocalypse, brings atoms into the immediate proximity of all others without allowing them to combine. "*Up to a certain epoch*"—Poe knows the power of temporal deferral, and makes it into an actual force that opposes the "*Uni-tendency*" in accordance with the "general design." He also knows, of course, that the terms of his argument require the ultimate victory of the "*Uni-tendency*" ("unless we are to conceive that what had a beginning is to have no end," he says, begging the question of the beginning), but what his description conveys most powerfully is not the victory but the *tension,* the conflict of forces that hold individual atoms in suspension between diffusion and unification, always attracted toward unity and moving toward it, but always restrained by the power of repulsion. This transitional tension for Poe is the state in which we now exist, the state from which we intuit the yielding of repulsion to attraction: the ultimate unificatory event that will "permit the universal subsidence into the inevitable, because original and therefore normal, *One.*"

This notion of a transitional tension clearly has important interpretive applications to the ending of *Pym.* The events that follow the material dissolution of the *Jane Guy*—its "diffusion" into repelled atoms—imagistically trace a transition from endtime to rebirth, from diffusion to unity. Pym and his companion Dirk Peters move through the symbolic landscape of the caverns, with their apocalyptic inscriptions and their associations with Egypt and Babylon, over a cliff down which Pym plunges half-suicidally, in the famous "longing to fall" scene, to the water, where they fight off the natives, taking one as hostage, and escape in a canoe toward the Pole. Demonic images gradually drop away and are replaced by surrealistic images of paradise—the water grows warmer, the canoe moves faster, white birds circle their canoe crying "Tekeli-li!", and as they grow progressively drowsier and dreamier, they begin to see a gray vapor extending all across the southern horizon:

> The range of vapour to the southward had arisen prodigously in
> the horizon, and began to assume more distinctness of form.
> I can liken it to nothing but a limitless cataract, rolling silently
> into the sea from some immense and far-distant rampart in
> the heaven. The gigantic curtain ranged along the whole extent
> of the southern horizon. It emitted no sound.
> *March 21.* A sullen darkness now hovered above us—but from
> out the milky depths of the ocean a luminous glare arose, and
> stole up along the bulwarks of the boat. We were nearly over-
> whelmed by the white ashy shower which settled upon us and
> upon the canoe, but melted into the water as it fell. The summit
> of the cataract was utterly lost in the dimness and the distance.
> Yet we were evidently approaching it with a hideous velocity. At
> intervals there were visible in it wide, yawning, but momentary
> rents, and from out these rents, within which was a chaos of flit-
> ting and indistinct images, there came rushing and mighty, but
> soundless winds, tearing up the enkindled ocean in their course.

March 22. The darkness had materially increased, relieved only by the glare of the water thrown back from the white curtain before us. Many gigantic and pallidly white birds flew continuously now from beyond the veil, and their scream was the eternal *Tekeli-li!* as they retreated from our vision. Hereupon Nu-Nu stirred in the bottom of the boat; but upon touching him, we found his spirit departed. And now we rushed into the embraces of the cataract, where a chasm threw itself open to receive us. But there arose in our pathway a shrouded human figure, very far larger in its proportions than any dweller among men. And the hue of the skin of the figure was of the perfect whiteness of the snow. (3:241-42)

Pym and Peters rush toward the veil like the disunited atoms in *Eureka* toward unity—but do not quite reach it, held back by the power of repulsion, apparently, which in this case is obviously Poe himself. It is an impressive finish to an often awkward and uneven novel; Poe writes as powerfully here as anywhere in his finest work. But what is happening? Is this an apocalypse? Pym's return has provoked any number of fanciful speculations by critics, such as that Pym's dreamy state means that he is hallucinating and that the white figure he thinks he sees can be explained away naturalistically, as the white sails of a ship, for example, which rescues the two and returns them to America.[25] There is no textual warrant for such speculation; but then, there is no textual evidence to disprove it, either.

The most brilliant speculative reading of the novel, John T. Irwin's astonishing two-hundred-page Lacanian interpretation in *American Hieroglyphics,* presents an explanation of the polar encounter that is also naturalistic, but with such a wealth of persuasive detail that it is a good deal harder to dismiss than the "white sail" reading. Irwin notes that this final event in Pym's adventure occurs on March 22, the vernal equinox in the Northern Hemisphere, but which at the South Pole is the beginning of winter, at which the sun would hover just above the horizon, immediately behind Pym and Peters. It is reasonable to conjecture, therefore, that the white figure is either Pym's own shadow cast by the sun onto the white curtain, or a hallucination, but, says Irwin, "whether one interprets the gigantic shape that Pym sees in the mist as a natural optical illusion (a white shadow) or a spectral illusion (a mental image that, by a reversal of intensity in a liminal state, appears to have the independent status of a visual image), the figure displays in either case a shadowy character in the sense of being unrecognizably self-projected."[26] The white curtain thus becomes like a piece of paper on which Pym—or Poe—etches the figural illusion, or, in Irwin's words, "a movie screen, providing a background against which the figure stands out, and veiling, in this case, the abyss of the infinite in which vision is lost" (224). Pym crosses no transcendental boundary, therefore; he descends into the gaping hole at the Pole (Symmes' Hole, a *natural* rather than supernatural hole) and emerges in the far North. Hence his return.

But this reading is grounded in the assumption that Poe didn't *believe* in a transcendental beyond for Pym to enter—or to glimpse—and so was concerned to reduce all apparent signs of such a beyond to illusions, self-projected specters. To allow Poe his visionary metaphysics in this context is to admit the possibility that the white figure is projected onto the misty veil *from above or behind the veil,* which itself is imaged as a "limitless cataract, rolling silently into the sea from some immense and far-distant rampart in the heaven" (3:241). This suggests that Poe may be drawing *unironically* on the NT imagery of white shadows, which Irwin (via Coleridge, Wordsworth, and such phenomena as the Brockengespenst), so painstakingly deconstructs (205-15). For in the NT imagery of transcendence, the white shadow is precisely the sort of doxic body-image that Pym sees over the misty veil. White shadows appear throughout the NT as emanations of divine beings: in the Annunciation, the angel Gabriel tells Mary that the Holy Spirit will "overshadow" (*episkiasei*) her and beget on her a holy child (Luke 1:35); similarly, in the Transfiguration Jesus and God approach the state of doxic body-mediation from opposite states, as Jesus' earthly body is glorified and God's disembodied spirit takes bodily form as a "bright cloud" that again "overshadows" the disciples (Matt 17:5; compare also Heb 9:5).

Now unlike a natural shadow, the NT *skia* (shadow) is cast not by a light-source past an opaque obstruction, but by a source of light that is itself a body, a substance characterized not by opacity (the absence of light) but by glory (the divine presence). As Paul says, metaphorically associating *skia* with *gramma,* the letter of OT law, "these things are only a shadow of what is to come; but the substance [*soma*] belongs to Christ" (Col 2:17). Or, in the more explicitly Platonic terms of the writer to the Hebrews, "the law has but a shadow of the good things to come instead of the true form [*eikon*] of those realities [*pragmaton*]" (Heb 10:1). Metaphorically speaking, that is, the Jews were people capable only of looking down at the ground around them; seeing a shadow, they took it for a divine *pragmaton* and subjected themselves to its rule—the rule of law. The Christian thus becomes one who looks up to discover that the law is only a shadow of the good things to come: still bright enough to foreshadow God, but too distant, too faded to render more than a faint image of the glory of the divine body, the *soma Christou* or messianic substance, that casts it. One might thus see in the spatial path of a shadow, from the point at which it is perceived to the body that casts it, a trope for the temporal distance between the present and the *ta mellonta,* the apocalyptic "things that are about to be."

On the other hand, Poe did know the Romantic revisions of this imagery, and it is not implausible to read the polar encounter Romantically as well, regarding the white figure as a god-shadow cast not by Christ but by Pym himself. This is not to reduce the shadow to an illusion, unless one prefers one's own prejudices to Poe's; rather, it is to assimilate the ending of *Pym* to the apocalyptic vision of *Nature,* in which the poet looks deeply into the natural world and sees himself reflected there as God, as a giant human form that he recognizes as his own true self. Suggestive as such a reading unquestionably is, however, it still seems inadequate to the sense one gets of a figural boundary at the Pole, an apocalyptic line of deferral that Pym is bound to cross, borne by the mighty current. Emerson's poet stands still in nature and *sees;* Pym *rushes* toward the veil. There is a spatiotemporal dynamic in Pym's revelation that is largely lacking in Emerson, and it directs Pym *past* the boundary, past the figural into the transfigural "chaos of flitting and indistinct images" beyond the veil.

But this suggests that Poe is modifying the same Pauline imagery that we saw Emerson revising in *Nature:* whereas for Emerson, nature-as-window becomes nature-as-mirror, revealing other (the external God standing behind the transparent glass) as self, for Poe the veil-as-obstruction unveils itself, marking a boundary in order to indicate the difference between before and beyond. In the optical terminology I invoked earlier in the context of Blake, Emerson modulates *refraction,* which reveals the self as future other, into *reflection,* which reveals future other as self. Poe, on the other hand, modulates Romantic reflection, in which the white figure is revealed as his own giant shadow, into refraction, in which the shadow, even if it is his own, is also God's. One might diagram Emerson's reflective apocalypse somewhat as follows: A sees in X (the mediatory icon) B-as-A, indicating that what is initially perceived as other is discovered to be self. Or, more accurately perhaps: A_1 sees in X B-as-A_2, since in the very act of seeing other as self, one is transformed into the other's image, self as god, or as giant human form. Poe's refractive apocalypse, on the other hand, would diagram like this: A_1 sees in X A_2-as-B, which is to say that one perceives in the mirror one's own glorified face as it will look in the future state, and recognizes it as God's.

This refractive apocalyptic vision I am suggesting Poe presents is manifestly a restatement of the biblical hermeneutic explored in chapter

2; but Poe's puzzling ending to *Pym* signals his important departure from the orthodox apocalypse, thus establishing, alongside Emerson's Romantic hermeneutic, the standard American version of the biblical apocalypse. In an orthodox *Pym*, the white figure that loomed over the polar veil would be taken as a self-evidential sign, certain proof not only to Pym but to the reader that the end is near. But as the wide range of conflicting interpretations of that sign in *Pym* criticism indicates, the white figure's signification is not at all self-evident but is profoundly ambiguous. As John Irwin notes, the idea of a self-evidential sign is itself inherently problematic:

> From this abyss of world-dissolving thought about thought,
> the only escape would seem to be some kind of self-evidential
> sign able to evoke immediate conviction. But the problem
> implicit in the logical concept of self-evidence remains that of
> of whose self is being evidenced—the in-itself or the for-itself.
> In order for a self-evidential sign really to operate, it would
> have to suspend or abrogate thought in a kind of mystical im-
> mediacy. A self-evidential sign would have to be an unmediated
> sign, a self-interpreting sign, since any mediation would in-
> volve the uncertainty of interpretation. But with the concept of
> an unmediated sign, epistemology reaches the borders of
> mysticism. (96)

But while this stricture has obvious applications to Stubby's angel in Balizet's *The Seven Last Years,* where the movement *is* pre-cisely toward an escape from what Irwin calls "world-dissolving thought about thought," I am not at all sure it applies to the ending of *Pym*. The truncated state of that ending seems to indicate that Poe is not in the slightest interested in abrogating thought about thought and its world-dissolutions. One needs a self-evidential sign only if one wants to avoid the "uncertainty of interpretation," as Irwin notes; but that is exactly what Poe does *not* want to avoid. The telos of Poe's novel, as I suggested earlier, is not the transcendental beyond at all, but the point of overload at which the transfigurational process begins, that crucial transition whose function is precisely to mediate vision. What Poe is concerned with is the domestication of the uncanny that I mentioned in chapter 2: the effort to plunge not into presential Being but into the abysm of differance that forever separates presence from absence, and there to generate an iconic dream-body that will permit a visionary habitation of the gap. The entire passage from Tsalal to the Pole, with its warming climate, its surrealistic seascape of whirling white birds and white ash, and the rapidly accelerating velocity of the current, is an imagistic exploration of that differance; but the crucial confrontation occurs at the polar veil itself, with the differance problematically mediated by the iconic resemblance between Pym and the white figure. As Pym rushes into the polar cataract, as the veil over which the white figure looms encloses him, Poe achieves the critical act of interpretive embodiment, the act of mediation that links the here and the beyond by containing them in a single image. The white figure, that is, is not a self-evidential sign but precisely a mediatory icon, which does not suspend or abrogate interpretive thought but *requires* it, insists that the reader perform the act of interpretation initiated by Poe.

Read this way, the novel's conclusion in effect swallows up the narrative that precedes it, including the problematic preface: for the thrust of the iconic mediation at the Pole is toward a *perspective* on journeying in the world that can only be attained at the interface marked by the veil. In a sense, Poe simply suspends the problem of Pym's return, just as Emerson suspends the problem of nature's substantiality; whether Pym returns or not is no longer important. As Paul John Eakin suggests, the novel's ending is double: "Pym survived—but he died. The key to the mystery is lost—but here it is" (16). Realistically speaking, it is important to know what became of the narrator; indeed, by the conventions of realistic fiction he *had* to return in order to tell his tale. But *Pym* is no realistic novel, and Poe manipulates the conventions of realism precisely in order to achieve the act of iconic mediation at the Pole. As Eakin argues:

> The equivocation . . . of the double ending of *Pym* does not cast
> the existence of meaning in doubt but rather man's capacity
> to apprehend it. . . . Whether Poe's endings take the hero to the
> brink of the abyss or plunge him into the gulf beyond, they
> all confirm that Poe and his heroes believe in a significant uni-
> verse; they believe in its buried treasure and they dream of the
> man who could find it out and cry "Eureka!" to an astonished
> world. (21)

It is important to note, however, that that very doubt of the human capacity to apprehend meaning necessarily does cast the existence of meaning in doubt—hence Poe's complex irony. What is crucial for Poe is not the meaning itself, but the interpretive act of constituting meaning through imagistic mediation. In this sense one might even say that the novel's ending is not double at all; for Pym returns only by realistic convention, not in the narrative itself. If we take the novel in the order in which Poe gives it to us, without attempting to reconstruct a hypothetical chronology, then the authoritative voice that narrates the novel is not Pym but Poe himself, in a series of narratorial personae: first, as the returned Pym who writes the preface; next, as the voyaging Pym who disappears into the polar veil; and finally as the anonymous editor who concludes the truncated tale.

This is, of course, a most tentative and uncertain interpretation; but if, as I suggest, the uncertainty of interpretation is the rhetorical focus of the novel, it is appropriate that its readers be required to enter into the interpretive dilemma as well. In their seminal study of Poe's composition of *Pym*, J. V. Ridgely and Iola S. Haverstick demonstrate that Poe wrote the novel (rather unsuccessfully, they conclude) without much prior planning, on the one hand, as if it were to remain entirely picaresque, but also, on the other hand, with a clear sense of an ending in mind—hence the many narrative discontinuities and disunities that their analysis discovers.[27] Even accepting these critics' evidence, however, one is not necessarily forced to accept their conclusion that the novel is therefore a failure. All it means is that Poe's method of composition in *Pym*, like Twain's after him, was essentially heuristic—which in turn is to say that Poe's artistic search for the Pole is essentially the same as Pym's geographical search and that Pym's voyaging allows Poe to work through the problems that block access to the mediatory stance at which interpretation is both problematical and possible.

In this sense, there *is* no gap; Poe takes Pym right up to the polar veil, where he (Poe) wants to be, and there parts company with his persona, sending him into the "chaos of flitting and indistinct images" and assuming a new (editorial) persona in order to explore the transitional passage from Tsalal to the Pole. Pym is disposed of as no longer necessary; and Poe slyly hints that he *has* indeed disposed of Pym, killed him off when his usefulness was expended, by having the editor describe the strange coincidence of his death: "It is feared that the few remaining chapters which were to have completed his narrative, and which were retained by him, while the above were in type, for the purpose of revision, have been irretrievably lost through the accident by which he perished himself" (3:243).

The coincidence, of course, is too great; Poe thus signals to his reader that he is pulling a narrative trick by which one should not be fooled. The "accident" in which Pym died, my reading suggests, is the polar encounter, and the "lost" chapters perished with him because they never existed. This reading would essentially assimilate the ending of *Pym* to the ending of "MS. Found in a Bottle," except that the bottle, which by realistic conventions contains the text, is replaced in *Pym* by the authority of Poe himself. But that is really only to say that the text's container as *place* is replaced by a container as *act*—an act of interpretation that is necessarily uncertain and that, by Poe's insistence that the reader identify in the end not with Pym but with the uncertain author(ity) that wrote it, draws the reader into that uncertainty as well. By leaving the tale deliberately "incomplete," Poe both tempts his readers to complete it for themselves and reveals the pitfalls of any completion they might conceive. What constitutes for Poe the heart of the refractive apocalyptic vision is not at all the object of vision, ever soon to be attained, but the act of vision, ever to be not just performed but repeated.

If Poe and Emerson both look to the future, then, it is to an apocalyptic future not as Being but as Doing—a mental (artistic or philosophical) Doing that, in terms of their apocalyptic hopes, may reflectively transform human beings and their world into their true primordial selves (Emerson) or refractively project them into a transfigured beyond (Poe), but a future that in terms of Poe's and Emerson's pragmatic irony is important not for what it will probably fail to achieve but for the sake of interpretive Doing itself. Reflection and refraction in Emerson and Poe are mediated, one might say, by the ironic knowledge that truth is endlessly deferred; but the interpretive acts of reflection and refraction are their attempts, against all odds, to transform deferral into an iconic home, a medium in which their very failure to achieve their apocalyptic goals can become success.

TWO

Across The Ambiguous Plain (Erik Sandgren, 1982)

FIVE

CALL ME JONAH

> *But desire itself is an activity within a certain lack, and
> the logic of our desiring fantasies leads ultimately to
> the annihilation of all otherness. In order for plenitude
> to replace absence, the world we desire must replace
> the world we perceive. Desire is intrinsically violent
> both because it spontaneously assumes this annihilation
> of everything alien to it, and because its fantasies in-
> clude a rageful recognition of the world's capacity to
> resist and survive our desires. . . . Desire depends on
> the withdrawal of a satisfaction; even though our desir-
> ing fantasies include certain pleasures, they also dra-
> matize a spontaneous fury at those invincible forces
> (both in the world and in ourselves) which have con-
> demned us to the loss of ecstasy, to experiencing plea-
> sure as part of a lack.*
> —*Leo Bersani,* A Future for Astyanax

"But desire itself is an activity with a certain lack, and the logic of our desiring fantasies leads ultimately to the annihilation of all otherness": Leo Bersani's trenchant critique of desire and character in literature intersects at all key points with the problem of imagining an apocalypse, for the central issue for the apocalyptic imagination is the relation of desire to its fulfillment and the origin of desire in lack or unfulfillment. The apocalyptic satisfaction withheld from the expectant is the ultimate one: the total adequacy of the world to desire. And as Bersani and Jacques Derrida insist, the pleasure derived from the imagination of such satisfaction is necessarily self-deconstructive, since to imagine presence is to redouble one's dissatisfaction with absence.

Twain's *A Connecticut Yankee* is probably the best American illustration of Bersani's thesis that "the logic of our desiring fantasies leads ultimately to the annihilation of all otherness," and that this annihilation inevitably leads to the deconstruction of the self. The self-conscious imposition of desire onto a recalcitrant reality leads through the annihilation of otherness back to the annihilation of dream itself, of desire, of that which constitutes the self. What Hank Morgan destroys, in the end, is not knighthood, but himself; his slaughter of 25,000 knights is far less effective against an undesired reality, which survives his attack, than against his own imagination, which doesn't.

Poe and Emerson seek to chart another path: a path through both the annihilation of other and the deconstruction of the self to the *reconstruction* of self and other in a dialectical tension between desire and the lack in which it is conceived. My studies in Twain suggest that the logic of desire leads to the ultimacy of annihilation, only when the *expression* of desire projects the dissolution of the dialectic in which desire and lack are mutually defined; to accept the inevitability of unfulfillment, as Poe and Emerson do (indeed as Twain seems to do in *The Mysterious Stranger*), is to hold back from annihilative ultimacy, and in that sense ironic pragmatism is redemptive. Hank Morgan (or Adolf Hitler, or Jim Jones) is the biblical diacritical mind carried to its furthest humanistic extension, in which human beings arrogate to themselves the power to dissect desire from lack, to break out of the limiting dialectic and thus to establish an image of desire on earth. Indeed, that arrogation is implicitly present in the orthodox imaginations of Michael Wigglesworth and Carol Balizet as well, earthly revenge there only being projected onto a God whose desire coincides with his people's, and who is omnipotent. A pragmatic awareness of the origins of desire in lack, of the projective nature of proleptic "revelation," and therefore of the probable failure of every statement of apocalyptic hope, acts in Emerson and Poe as the crucial anchor in reality that checks driftings toward the imagination of annihilation.

What it does not check, however, is self-deconstruction. The notion of a self that exists only as lack and that seeks to fill itself with the products of its own self-constituting imagination (which also has its basis in lack), necessarily calls into question the assumption that the self exists either as Being or Will. What remains of the self for Poe and Emerson is a congeries of discrete acts, which *may* add up to an apocalyptic transformation "without having in my thoughts any occurrence of special good fortune"[1] as Emerson says, or may be carried by the rushing current of God's or Poe's transitional imagination—guided, that is, by some mind that is capable of collecting the discrete acts into a purposive and transformative Self-as-Act—but that also may not.

If Poe presents his refractive apocalyptic vision in dialectical tension with irony, however, and Emerson his reflective vision in the same tension, both writers are concerned in the works considered in chapter 4 to introject pragmatic doubts into their vision of the redemptive act, so that failure can become an element (even a paradoxical guarantee) of success. The emphasis in both writers is on hope, on the chance of success, irony figuring therefore less as an obstruction to vision than as an inward limitation. If, however, one imagines refraction, reflection, and irony as three vertices of a triangle, irony as the mediating third term between Poe and Emerson, then clearly the American writers who follow those two definitive American apocalyptists and react against them take us progressively further away from reflection and refraction toward a convergence in irony—or, to move away from the diagram, toward an awareness that failure is the *starting point,* not merely a pragmatic check on the imagination. What American writers in the wake of Emerson and Poe begin to stress is the enormous *risk* involved in American apocalypses—a risk that can be exposed and resisted, these writers claim, only by being taken, which means that the exposer necessarily exposes himself or herself to the very hazards to which he or she points. The radical apocalyptic visions of Emerson and Poe finally lead us, revisionary writers insist, not toward the fulfillment of desire but right back into irony, an explosively self-destructive irony whose issue may be the annihilation of matter (historical cessation) or of mind and signification (linguistic cessation), but which in either case pushes apocalyptic desire to an undesirable and inevitable end.[2] The catch is that the desire to oppose this collapse back into irony is itself subject to the same limitation: if the apocalyptic imagination must fail, so too must the perception of that necessity. Yet, at a deeper level the imagination of failure goes hand in hand with the imagination of success, and American writers have always charged their work with intensity precisely by combatting what they recognize as the inevitability of failure. My task in Part II, then, will be to trace the path American writers have sought out of the mind-numbing dilemmas generated by the failure of the apocalyptic imagination: a path that would transform the iconic mediations of the American apocalypse from tools for the counterproductive and finally self-destructive enhancement of desire into tools for the self-restriction of desire.

■

There is no better place to begin an exploration of self-restrictive American apocalypses than Melville's persistently problematic novel *Moby-Dick,* which mirrors the magnitude of its subject in the strong visionary reflective mode of Emerson, precisely in order to call that mode into question. Listen to Ishmael, in "The Fossil Whale":

> One often hears of writers that rise and swell with their subject, though it may seem but an ordinary one. How, then, with me, writing of this Leviathan? Unconsciously my chirography expands into placard capitals. Give me a condor's quill! Give me a Vesuvius' crater for an inkstand! Friends, hold my arms! For in the mere act of penning my thoughts of this Leviathan, they weary me, and make me faint with their outreaching comprehensiveness of sweep, as if to include the whole circle of the sciences, and all the generations of whales, and men, and mastodons, past, present, and to come, with all the revolving panoramas of empire on earth, and throughout the whole universe, not excluding its suburbs. Such, and so magnifying, is the virtue of a large and liberal theme! We expand to its bulk.[3]

The image of the whale becomes in Ishmael's imagination a mirror that reflects not mere Ishmael but a visionary giant, a "Colossus" (136) as he calls it in "The Mast-Head," who bestrides not only the ocean, not merely all whales and all human beings, but all time and space, time from origin to end and space from the depths of the sea to the furthest reaches of the cosmos.

For Melville, that is, as for Emerson and Poe, the act of interpreting the book of nature was potentially a radically transformative one: the effect of a "large and liberal theme" is to *magnify,* to expand the mind of the interpreter so as to encompass not only the theme but all that contains the theme, to become in fact the visionary container of creation. But Melville, far more than Emerson in *Nature* or Poe in *Pym,* clearly perceived the dangers of this poetic; or, rather, to avoid taking sides, Melville's imagination ran far more insistently to the mediatory compromise of an ironic perspective than did Emerson's and Poe's (and so indeed he gives us the "magnifications" of the passage quoted above in a tone of bemused hyperbole). For Emerson and Poe, the chief danger was failure: that the human race might not after all be transformed by its engagement with the world. For Melville, the chief danger was success: that human beings' engagement with the world might indeed transform them, but that the transformation might be to some wholly undesirable state, of madness or of the simple nonexistence of death. Where for Emerson Narcissus gazed deeply into the mirror of nature and became what he beheld, and for Poe Narcissus gazed through the mirror of nature to his future image in the depths, for Melville—as in the original Narcissus myth—the depth is death, the image no transformative reflection but a call to suicide. "And still deeper the meaning of that story of Narcissus," Ishmael warns us early on, "who because he could not grasp the tormenting, mild image he saw in the fountain, plunged into it and was drowned. But that same image, we ourselves see in all rivers and oceans. It is the image of the ungraspable phantom of life; and this is the key to it all" (14).

The terrible paradoxes of this image—tormenting yet mild, the key to it all yet ungraspable—map out at this early stage the iconic dialogue Melville's novel will seek to explore. If it is true that in order to live men and women *must* gaze deeply into the image of Narcissus— if they must in some fashion go to sea, confront the whale, confront the phenomenon of Ahab—how do they do so and yet avoid plunging into it to their deaths? Is there a transformation that is not suicidal? Ishmael's artistic dilemma throughout will be to bring the reader to the crucial act of mirror-gazing in all its complexity, its dangers and attractions, in order to chart some sort of compromise transformation, some iconic reduction of the apocalyptic visions of Emerson and Poe that will allow the reader—and himself—to engage the phantom of life without drowning in it. In the famous water-gazing passage from "The Mast-Head," Ishmael tries again, this time more fully, to express his sense of the crucial duality of the Narcissus myth, at once vitally necessary and mortally dangerous:

"Why, thou monkey," said a harpooner to one of these lads, "we've been cruising now hard upon three years, and thou hast not raised a whale yet. Whales are scarce as hen's teeth whenever thou art up here." Perhaps they were; or perhaps there might have been shoals of them in the far horizon; but lulled into such an opium-like listlessness of vacant, unconscious reverie is this absent-minded youth by the blending cadence of waves with thoughts, that at last he loses his identity; takes the mystic ocean at his feet for the visible image of that deep, blue, bottomless soul, pervading mankind and nature; and every strange, half-seen, gliding, beautiful thing that eludes him, every dimly-discovered, uprising fin of some undiscernable form, seems to him the embodiment of those elusive thoughts that only people the soul by continually flitting through it. In this enchanted mood, thy spirit ebbs away to whence it came; becomes diffused through time and space; like Wickliff's sprinkled Pantheistic ashes, forming at last a part of every shore the round globe over.
    There is no life in thee, now, except that rocking life imparted

by a gently rolling ship; by her, borrowed from the sea; by the sea, from the inscrutable tides of God. But while this sleep, this dream is on ye, move your foot or hand an inch; slip your hold at all; and your identity comes back in horror. Over Descartian vortices you hover. And perhaps, at mid-day, in the fairest weather, with one half-throttled shriek you drop through that transparent air into the summer sea, no more to rise for ever. Heed it well, ye Pantheists! (140)

The crux here is the masthead philosopher's visionary perception of "the mystic ocean at his feet [as] the visible image of that deep, blue, bottomless soul, pervading mankind and nature"—a pantheistic enhancement of the Narcissus myth in which the reflected image reveals to sight the soul of *all* nature, human and nonhuman, and most particularly here of both viewer and viewed. The loss of identity in "the blending cadence of waves with thoughts" is the collapse of self into a self-containing other; the merging of soul with soul, of man with nature, marks the collapse of difference between self and other, so that the undifferentiated spirit "ebbs away to whence it came; becomes diffused through time and space; like Wickliff's sprinkled pantheistic ashes, forming at last a part of every shore the round globe over."

To the pantheist, of course, this loss is gain; it is an apocalyptic union, the elimination of alienative difference. And, in fact, Ishmael portrays that gain in its full attraction. At the same time, however, he is acutely aware of the gain as *loss:* "There is no life in thee, now," he says, implying that life *is* differentiation, and the collapse of difference is a kind of death—indeed, an anticipatory figure of death, since to lose one's identity/spirit/life is to lose that sense of place and task that prevents the plunge into the sea. As the enhanced analogy with Narcissus suggests, that plunge is the physical enactment of the visionary union; something like the plunge is the act toward which Poe propels Pym at the misty polar veil. But for Melville the problem of deferral is now crucial; what happens when the masthead philosopher moves and "his identity comes back in horror" is that he recovers a sense of his physical distance from the water *as* a deferral of the envisioned mystic union. The union can occur only fleetingly, in the visionary imagination; to achieve the union in transformative act one must move, and to move is to defer the union by restoring the difference between self and other. As he falls toward the desired goal, the masthead philosopher is given a moment to recognize that it is *not* the goal, that desire apparently fulfilled is desire forever deferred—deferred by death in the very medium that was to mean fulfillment.

Melville's revisionary reading of Emerson's apocalypse is further

complicated in the tale of Pip, whom Melville presents at one level as a
successful Emersonian hero, a successful water-gazer who achieves
mediatory contact with the "heartless immensity" and is apocalyptically transformed by it. But, of course, Melville's account of Pip's transformation is radically ambivalent:

> Now, in calm weather, to swim in the open ocean is as easy to
> the practised swimmer as to ride in a spring-carriage ashore. But
> the awful lonesomeness is intolerable. The intense concentra-
> tion of self in the middle of such a heartless immensity, my God!
> who can tell it? . . . By the merest chance the ship itself at last
> rescued him; but from that hour the little negro went about the
> deck an idiot; such, at least, they said he was. The sea had jeer-
> ingly kept his finite body up, but drowned the infinite of his
> soul. Not drowned entirely, though. Rather carried down alive
> to wondrous depths, where strange shapes of the unwarped
> primal world glided to and fro before his passive eyes; and the
> miser-merman, Wisdom, revealed his hoarded heaps; and among
> the joyous, heartless, ever-juvenile eternities, Pip saw the mul-
> titudinous, God-omnipresent, coral insects, that out of the fir-
> mament of waters heaved the colossal orbs. He saw God's foot
> upon the treadle of the loom, and spoke it; and therefore his ship-
> mates called him mad. So man's insanity is heaven's sense; and
> wandering from all mortal reason, man comes at last to that ce-
> lestial thought, which, to reason, is absurd and frantic; and weal
> or woe, feels then uncompromised, indifferent as his God. (347)

Outward spatial depth is here mystically reflected as inward
mental depth, and Pip becomes an idiot, a holy fool, as indifferent as
Emerson at his most mystical: "The name of the nearest friend sounds
then foreign and accidental," Emerson says in the "transparent eye-
ball" passage from *Nature.* "To be brothers, to be acquaintances,—
master or servant, is then a trifle and a disturbance" (B 1:10). Pip
becomes "indifferent" to his fellow human beings quite literally: relations between brothers, between master and servant, friendships marked
as such by the *names* of friends, all depend on the differentiation of
person from person, and that is precisely what Pip loses in his visionary
transformation into madness. But as Sharon Cameron stresses in *The
Corporeal Self,* this is still an apocalyptic transformation as loss, a concentration of self as isolation, a drowning of the soul in which the soul
is cut adrift in boundless watery space.[4] Pip's "indifference" is not,
after all, a mystical unity but an inability to draw distinctions, a paralysis of differentiation; Pip does not "lose" his life as identity but finds it

compressed or concentrated into a tight knot of undifferentiated matter, like the mind of Poe's God before the explosion into multiplicity.
Pip enacts the Emersonian vision of incorporative unity in terms that
strikingly anticipate the Emersonian revisionism of Emily Dickinson,
who gives us transformative containment as self-incarceration: "I've
known her—from an ample nation—/Choose One—/Then—close the
Valves of her attention—/Like Stone—".[5] The incorporative Romantic
apocalypse is revealed as not an expansion but a constriction, a closing
of the gates that shuts the soul in with itself in a prison of its own making, a self-immolation in the self that ultimately excludes everything.

This constrictive fate enacted by Pip is precisely what Ahab
seeks to avoid, of course: Ahab pursues the whale, he tells us, specifically
in order to escape the prison of the self by smashing the constricting
walls. But there is rather more to Ahab than that. Ahab not only sees
himself in Pip and shares Pip's fate in the end, but seeks to avoid this
fate through very much the same Emersonian locus of visionary incorporation to which Pip succumbs. The key passage here is the concluding paragraph of "The Chart," Ishmael's pivotal diagnosis of Ahab's
disease:

> Often, when forced from his hammock by exhausting and intol-
> erably vivid dreams of the night, which, resuming his own in-
> tense thoughts through the day, carried them on amid a clashing
> of phrensies, and whirled them round and round in his blazing
> brain, till the very throbbing of his life-spot became insufferable
> anguish; and when, as was sometimes the case, these spiritual
> throes in him heaved his being up from its base, and a chasm
> seemed opening in him, from which forked flames and light-
> nings shot up, and accursed friends beckoned him to leap down
> among them; when this hell in himself yawned beneath him,
> a wild cry would be heard through the ship; and with glaring
> eyes Ahab would burst from his state room, as though escap-
> ing from a bed that was on fire. Yet these, perhaps, instead of
> being the unsuppressable symptoms of some latent weakness,
> or fright at his own resolve, were but the plainest tokens of its
> intensity. For at such times, crazy Ahab, the scheming, unap-
> peasedly steadfast hunter of the white whale; this Ahab that had
> gone to his hammock, was not the agent that so caused him
> to burst from it in horror again. The latter was the eternal, living
> principle or soul in him; and in sleep, being for the time dis-
> sociated from the characterizing mind, which at other times em-
> ployed it for its outer vehicle or agent, it spontaneously sought
> escape from the scorching contiguity of the frantic thing, of

which, for the time, it was no longer an integral. But as the mind does not exist unless leagued with the soul, therefore it must have been that, in Ahab's case, yielding up all his thoughts and fancies to his one supreme purpose; that purpose, by its own sheer inveteracy of will, forced itself against gods and devils into a kind of self-assumed, independent being of its own. Nay, could grimly live and burn, while the common vitality to which it was conjoined, fled horror-stricken from the unbidden and unfathered birth. Therefore, the tormented spirit that glared out of bodily eyes, when what seemed Ahab rushed from his room, was for the time but a vacated being, a formless somnambulistic being, a ray of living light, to be sure, but without an object to color, and therefore a blankness in itself. God help thee, old man, thy thoughts have created a creature in thee; and he whose intense thinking thus makes him a Prometheus; a vulture feeds upon that heart for ever; that vulture the very creature he creates. (174–75)

The psychology Ishmael here sets up, his tortured syntax mirroring the tortured psyche of his subject, is precisely a psychology of transformative incorporation revealed as the path to schizophrenia. The "clashing of phrensies" that results from the resumption of intense daytime thoughts in "exhausting and intolerably vivid dreams of the night" heaves Ahab's "being up from its base" and opens an infernal chasm in him, the eschatological psychic landscape revealing to Ahab (or at least to Ishmael) a violent conflict between metonymies of the self. The combatants are a separative self, the "characterizing mind" that individuates by assigning characteristics, and a unifying self, the "eternal, living principle or soul in him," the "common vitality" that all people share. In the terms suggested by the "Mast-Head" passage just discussed, the former is that aspect of the psyche that remains cognizant of difference, of the separation between itself and the outside world, and so protects the water-gazer from the "living principle's" longing to be reunited with the "deep, blue, bottomless soul, pervading mankind and nature." One is tempted to say, following Ahab himself, that the "characterizing mind" *is* Ahab, while the "living principle" is only *in* him; but Ishmael stresses that "the mind does not exist unless leagued with the soul." The psyche is the conjunction of a principle of individuality with a principle of commonality. Inside Ahab's psyche, however, the conjunction has become a deadly conflict, as the "characterizing mind" progressively generates out of its own will a "purpose" as a "kind of self-assumed, independent being of its own," thus alienating the living principle, normally employed by the characterizing mind as its outer vehicle. The monomaniacal obsession that produces the independent purpose renders that vehicle a "frantic thing," and the conjunction itself a "scorching contiguity" from which the living principle seeks escape as soon as is possible—which is to say, at night, in dreams. Thus split off from the usurper, the living principle is tormented and torments Ahab with dreams of hell; it is a "vacated being," a shell emptied out by its splitting off from the "characterizing mind," a somnambulistic being that is *formless* precisely because the characterizing mind was the agent that gave it form.

Clearly, here, Ahab contains his world, but contains it in inner division. Pip's horrific concentration of self is there, for instance, in the vacating of the "living principle," the perversion of the common vitality, joining human beings to each other and to nature into a "tormented spirit"; and the isolation to which Pip is reduced is intolerably heightened when brought into "scorching contiguity" with the self that cast it adrift. Ahab has incorporated Pip into a visionary Romantic self precisely in order to isolate him, to split him off and deny his doubling of Ahab, so that in "The Log and the Line," Ahab stares at Pip in a willed lack of recognition: "And who art thou, boy? I see not my reflection in the vacant pupils of thy eyes" (427). Of course he doesn't: what Pip reflects is the "vacated being" that glares out of Ahab's eyes only in dreams of the night, vacated by the purposeful mind that has given birth to itself by the denial of commonality.

Ahab incorporates Starbuck too, whose insistence on the "common vitality" or "living principle" in Ahab is both more conscious than Pip's and potentially more effective. Starbuck for Ahab comes to represent something like the differential bond between the two metonymies of his divided self, the communal link between the individual and the collective, between the separative and the unifying self. "Close!" Ahab cries in "The Symphony," "stand close to me, Starbuck; let me look into a human eye; it is better than to gaze into sea or sky; better than to gaze upon God. By the green land; by the bright hearth-stone! this is the magic glass, man. I see my wife and my child in thine eye" (444). In Starbuck the separative self and the unifying self have been brought into a coercive ethical alignment in which everything that threatens to sunder the bond is shunned as evil, everything that supports it clasped as good. This ethically controlled bonding makes Starbuck the one man on board the *Pequod* whose psychological makeup could conceivably thwart Ahab's mad quest; he not only knows that the will must be bound to the "common vitality" of mankind and why it must be so bound, but he construes that binding in a coercive manner that drives him to oppose the captain's will. Ahab overmasters his ethical coercion, however, by the sheer force of that monomaniacal purpose, external mastery doubling the internal mastery that had produced the "unbidden and unfathered birth" out of the clash of selves. Ahab's surrender to the image of commonality (wife and child) that he sees reflected in Starbuck's eyes—a surrender he conceives virtually as a sin, a sin against the self-created god of his purpose—is therefore only temporary. Turning from the false gods of "green land" and "bright hearthstone" by which he swears in "The Symphony," in "The Chase—Second Day," Ahab once again disavows any claim the living principle might have on his will by ordering Starbuck *not* to mirror him, to "vacate" or blank out the reflective surface of his face: "Starbuck, of late I've felt strangely moved to thee; ever since that hour we both saw—thou know'st what, in one another's eyes. But in this matter of the whale, be the front of thy face to me as the palm of this hand—a lipless, unfocused blank. Ahab is for ever Ahab, man" (459). In the context of Ishmael's psychology, this last ejaculation is a telling reduction; Ahab as whole self, as at once an individuated and universal self, as the "mind" in league with the "soul," now *is* Ahab as "characterizing mind"; Ahab is a metonymy of himself, hyperbolized by sheer will into the whole.

When Starbuck senses in the earlier passage that Ahab's new mood is already passing, he steals away, appropriately enough "blanched to a corpse's hue with despair" (445)—for the depletion of color in his face dramatizes Ishmael's earlier statement that, split off from the "characterizing mind," the "living principle" is "a ray of living light . . . but without an object to color, and therefore a blankness in itself." But this also means that any object that doubles the "characterizing mind" in its isolation from the light of the "living principle" must *remain colorless;* and it is significant that the instant color goes out of Starbuck, the colorless Parsee replaces him as Ahab's double: "Ahab crossed the deck to gaze over on the other side; but started at two reflected, fixed eyes in the water there. Fedallah was motionlessly leaning over the same rail" (445). The shadowy Parsee doubles not the "living principle," but that monomaniacal "characterizing mind" that pursues the whale and that, unlit by conjunction with the "common vitality" of the soul, remains mysteriously insubstantial: "Such an added, gliding strangeness began to invest the thin Fedallah now; such ceaseless shudderings shook him; that the men looked dubious at him; half uncertain, as it seemed, whether he were a mortal substance, or else a tremulous shadow cast upon the deck by some unseen being's body" (438). The shadow is cast by Ahab, of course, or by that unseen part of Ahab that has taken on "a kind of self-assumed, independent being of its own," as Ishmael says explicitly when Ahab and the Parsee gaze fixedly at each other "as if in the Parsee Ahab saw his forethrown shadow, in Ahab the

Parsee his abandoned substance" (439). In the Parsee, that is, Ahab's monomaniacal purpose is revealed as the colorless, insubstantial, sinister thing it is.

The Parsee ultimately points Ahab to the white whale; and Moby Dick of course is Ahab's most definitive double, the object of his purpose that *constitutes* the purpose. As Ishmael makes clear in "The Whiteness of the Whale," the pale color of the whale, that "corpse's hue," is the exact analogue of the sinister colorlessness of Fedallah: "Is it that by its indefiniteness it shadows forth the heartless voids and immensities of the universe, and thus stabs us from behind with the thought of annihilation, when beholding the white depths of the milky way? Or is it, that as in essence whiteness is not so much a color as the visible absence of color, and at the same time the concrete of all colors; is it for these reasons that there is such a dumb blankness, full of meaning, in a wide landscape of snows—a colorless, all-color of atheism from which we shrink?" (169). Indefiniteness, heartless voids and immensities, annihilation—"of all these things," Ishmael says, "the Albino whale was the symbol" (170), and as such the dream double of the uncolored mind that would destroy it.

This connection between Ahab and the white whale is especially important in Ahab's famous quarterdeck speech to Starbuck:

> Hark ye yet again,—the little lower layer. All visible objects, man, are but as pasteboard masks. But in each event—in the living act, the undoubted deed—there, some unknown but still reasoning thing puts forth the mouldings of its features from behind the unreasoning mask. If man will strike, strike through the mask! How can the prisoner reach outside except by thrusting through the wall? To me, the white whale is that wall, shoved near to me. Sometimes I think there's naught beyond. But 'tis enough. He tasks me; he heaps me; I see in him outrageous strength, with an inscrutable malice sinewing it. That inscrutable thing is chiefly what I hate; and be the white whale agent, or be the white whale principle, I will wreak that hate upon him. Talk not to me of blasphemy, man; I'd strike the sun if it insulted me. (144)

Here the paradoxes of inside and outside begin to converge in an unbearable replication or complication of images; for Moby Dick is to Ahab both an alien other that at once conceals and reveals "some unknown but still reasoning thing" *in the world,* and a mirror or double that shows him the blank image that at once conceals and reveals the vacated, split-off, "frantic thing" *in the self.* René Girard notes that etymologically "the mask displays combinations of forms and colors incompatible with a differentiated order that is not primarily that of nature but of the culture itself. The mask mixes man and beast, god and inanimate object," and thus conjoins them, embodies both differentia in a single image.[6] By this mediatory function of masks, Girard suggests, the mythic monster that the hero seeks to slay is revealed as his own "monstrous double"—which, in turn, suggests that what Ahab would destroy is the glass that shows him back himself. Sharon Cameron's incisive reading of Ahab here comes close to expressing the full complexity of Ahab's dilemma:

> In such a fluid conception of bodies, the self's exterior and its interior are incapable of distinction: who can "stop to . . . find [one's leaks]; or how hope to plug [them], even if found." But while Ahab's image voices its fear at loss of the self's parts— at their leaking into the world—fear obscures the way in which this particular image of exit allows the self a wanted "out." As I have suggested, the corollary to the idea of false embodiment— believing that otherness can be reduced to a single body—is the expulsion from Ahab's body of those feelings he wishes alien to it: grief to Pip, rage to God. For if you cannot become Bulkington, cannot absorb the landscape, then you must postulate a reductive singularity within and without yourself, achieving singularity by doing away with characteristics legitimately—but intolerably—part of the two identities in question. Unable to stand parts of himself he would repudiate as "other," Ahab first projects them outward, lets them leak into the world—in the concreteness of his image conceives of such exorcism as physically possible. These parts, once outside his person, are attributed to another body. Thus, Ahab conceives of them as having a body manifestly different from his own, and then construes that body as evil *because* it is outside of himself, *because* it is not his own. The hope would be to vanquish otherness and the evil with which Ahab now identifies it. Then the alien body could be reappropriated, but purged of its unwanted attributes: made beautiful rather than monstrous, mystical rather than sexual, elemented of a single feeling rather than of ambivalent ones. From the cleanness of such a body, one might actually wish to be born. (48-49)

What Cameron fails to mention is that before Ahab can project the repudiated self into the world, he must first *introject the world into his self*. In order to pursue the whale, he must contain his crew, bring them into his vision, incarnate his vision in them so that the entire whaling ship will be an extension or expansion of himself. This Ahab achieves. But the next step is to contain the whale, for if he could contain the whale as mediatory icon he could see through to the "unknown but still reasoning thing" whose presence he intuits behind the whale's blank mask, recognizing (in Emerson's terms) the NOT ME as the ME and thereby containing all creation in a single visionary body. Ahab brings other into the self precisely in order to align the whale with the hunter in a mutually defining relation that will generate an Ahab as visionary giant.

But Melville will not allow Ahab this Emersonian apocalypse. The drive toward unity of whatever kind is exposed in this novel as a reductive or repressive exclusion of the other; the other for Melville can never entirely be assimilated to the self, since the assimilation of one instance of otherness inevitably requires the exclusion of another instance. In order to assimilate the whale into a self-defining mono-maniacal self, Ahab must exclude or project outward the "common vitality" or "living principle or soul in him," must split off that force within himself that would deflect him from his quest; but the self that is repressed or excluded as other returns as the "unknown but still reasoning thing" dimly reflected in the mirror of the whale, so that the quest for the whale finally becomes a fantastically involuted quest of self-discovery. Because the self that Ahab seeks is a self that opposes the quest, however, and because the questing self is doubled and icon-ically constituted by the very thing the quest must destroy, the Ro-mantic apocalypse in Melville's revision becomes a vicious circle or closed circuit of imagings in which self-discovery is suicide. Reaching to strike through the mirroring mask, Ahab sees the reflection of his own hand coming back to strike through *him*.

The apocalyptic suicide of Ahab is, of course, the death also of his entire crew, with the significant exception of Ishmael. As the white whale goes down, carrying Ahab and Fedallah with him to the depths of physical death, the surface of the ocean opens up in a gigantic whirl-pool that Melville took straight out of Poe:

> For an instant, the tranced boat's crew stood still; then turned. "The ship? Great God, where is the ship?" Soon they through dim, bewildering mediums saw her sidelong fading phantom, as in the gaseous Fata Morgana; only the uppermost masts out of water; while fixed by infatuation, or fate, to their once lofty perches, the pagan harpooneers still maintained their sinking lookouts on the sea. And now, concentric circles seized the lone boat itself, and all its crew, and each floating oar, and every

lance-pole, and spinning, animate and inanimate, all round and round in one vortex, carried the smallest chip of the Pequod out of sight. . . .

Now small fowls flew screaming over the yet yawning gulf; a sullen white surf beat against its steep sides; then all collapsed, and the great shroud of the sea rolled on as it rolled five thousand years ago. (469)

The image of the vortex that yawns in the middle of the sea and swallows the great ship entire is modeled directly on the ending of *Pym,* even to the screaming birds flying over the gulf. What Melville adds to Poe's ending, however, is a rationale for his narrator's survival—an important addition. In *"Pym* and *Moby-Dick:* Essential Connections," Grace Farrell Lee suggests that "Melville learned well from Poe's narrative dilemma: he bifurcated his voyager into a narrator who could survive the action and tell the story and an actor who could not." "Ishmael survives first," she says, "because he comprehends the nature of his journey as a meditative, yet dangerous, dive at death, and second, because he distances himself from the dive at death which Ahab takes."[7]

True enough. But what is a *meditative* dive at death? Meditation in Ishmael's case is clearly related in some sense to his awareness of alternatives, his ability to stand on a middle ground between extremes and look in both directions without leaping. Ishmael's meditative dive at death is manifestly a *compromise* with death—or perhaps merely a compromise with the dive, since, as Lee implies, he dives not *to* but only *at* death. This insistence on meditation as compromise does lie behind Ishmael's survival—but in complex ways that require some sorting out.

A preliminary step in that sorting out might be to look at that other vortex tale of Poe's, "A Descent into the Maelström," in which the sailor-hero does escape the whirlpool for a clearly defined reason. Martha Banta's account of the tale, for example, is immediately suggestive:

All minds potentially possess the imagination of disaster. But to imagine disaster does not need to be the same as its creation or as submission to its force. The vortex may image the mind, but the mind can still save itself from the vortex. The brother in Poe's "A Descent into the 'Maelström'" perishes because his frightened mind merges with the destroying whirl, but the narrator escapes. Driven toward the imagination of disaster by the way events horrendously control him, the narrator uses his dread to create the imagination of success by which he is released from the destructive waters.[8]

In this reading, the apocalyptic image itself becomes the key to success; the hero who, faced with apocalyptic destruction, can keep his wits about him and convert the threat of disaster into the mere image of disaster will survive. What is most debilitating in the perception of imminent disaster is terror, the fear of death that subordinates all other feelings and thoughts to it and thus makes ratiocination impossible. In order to escape the whirlpool, therefore, Poe's sailor-hero must surrender his fear of death and bring his imagination to bear on it. "It may appear strange," he reports, "but now, when we were in the very jaws of the gulf, I felt more composed than when we were only approaching it. Having made up my mind to hope no more, I got rid of a great deal of that terror which unmanned me at first. I suppose it was despair that strung my nerves."[9] "After a little while I became possessed with the keenest curiosity about the whirl itself. I positively felt a *wish* to explore its depths, even at the sacrifice I was going to make; and my principle grief was that I should never be able to tell my old companions on shore about the mysteries I should see" (1:240).

Richard D. Finholt offers a cogent explanation of this shift in the sailor's state of mind in light of Poe's cosmology, noting that the terror engendered by the fear of death is for Poe only the first step in the eschatological movement; it is followed by a lucidity that emanates from the mind of God:

> At the moment of lucidity, the hero's thoughts are vibrating in tune with the thoughts of the Universal mind. This is possible because at the origin of the universe when God sent the spirit of diversity, the principle of Repulsion, into the nature of all particled matter, he also found it necessary, Poe says in "Mesmeric Revelation," to "incarnate portions of the divine mind" into that particled matter called man. Poe postulated that as the human organism *approaches death* it tends to move away from the organization of the sensual life and to become more in tune with the incarnate "universal mind" within itself (he calls this the "Heart Divine" in *Eureka*), and, as this hitherto latent essence comes to life, it "vibrates" in "unison" with "the unparticled matter" which is the essence of the universe. The movement of the sailor in the Maelstrom, then, can be interpreted as a movement from the periphery of God's thoughts ever and ever closer to their center, ever and ever closer to the more perfect motion of Unity and wholeness, and, as he moves, his thoughts become more and more refined, approaching the perfection of the "unparticled" essence. It is thus no wonder that his old companions recognize him "no more than they would

have known a traveler from the spirit-land"; for that is where his mind has been.[10]

As the two brothers approach the horrific vortex, it impinges upon their terror-stricken imaginations as a black deathly enclosure, a "pit" of absolute absence like the one that threatens the narrator of "The Pit and the Pendulum." Having overcome his fear of death, however, the sailor realizes that this pit-image was itself generated by his fear, and that what lies at the bottom of the vortex is no absence at all but unity with God in an apocalyptic unparticled state. Terror conquered, absence is revealed as presence. Finholt continues:

> It might be argued that it should be the hero's brother who achieves the final reunion with God since he is the one who travels the whole cycle of the Maelstrom to its center and to his own destruction. However, it must be remembered that his mind is frozen by the terror of the sensual life and can never, therefore, vibrate to the tune of the Maelstrom. The progress of the hero is as much mental as physical; he can thus travel closer to the unparticled essence of the Maelstrom, as is evidenced by the fact that he gains the ability to ascertain the mode of escape implicit in God's conception of the Maelstrom. Since the Maelstrom is a *thought* of God, we should conceptualize it as being like a sentence; the hero's mind travels down its vortex the way a reader's eye follows the words of a subject—predicate—object configuration. The meaning of the sentence is not in the period that the reader's eye arrives at—it is in the thought generated by the words seen as a whole. Similarly, the essence of the Maelstrom is not to be found at its physical termination— the unifying center is not a locality, remember, but a principle—and it is toward this principle that the hero's mind moves, as his body moves toward the center of the vortex. (363)

Finholt's syntactical analogy usefully recalls my considerations of deferred predication in chapter 2; the sailor-hero of Poe's tale returns with a *proleptic semantic* gained by his confrontation with God's apocalyptic syntax. In place of the actual predicate complement, the actual apocalyptic end, he returns with an *image* of that complement: the experience of near-disaster gives him an insight into the meaning of disaster without having himself to surrender to it. "A Descent into the Maelström" thus offers a paradigm of the returned hero: swallowed up in an enclosure that in its blackness and threat to human life figures death, he moves, by a redemptive act of imagination, *past* deathly terror to a proleptic image of unity with God (the rainbow at the center of the whirl), and thus is enabled to escape, to return, and to tell the tale. It is a paradigm of apocalyptic threat converted to apocalyptic image—essentially an antiapocalyptic paradigm, whose biblical pre-text, I suggest, is not the Book of Revelation at all but the Book of Jonah, a tale of descent and return in which the cataclysm is *averted*.

The Book of Jonah is obviously of some importance to Melville in *Moby-Dick,* as well. In fact, I will contend in this chapter that Melville uses his apocalyptic imagery hermeneutically in much the same way the writer of the Book of Jonah does: to displace apocalyptic hopes (and fears) into an image of apocalypse that is finally antiapocalyptic, redemptive in a secular sense. This position is anticipated to some extent by Daniel Hoffman in his excellent essay "Moby-Dick: Jonah's Whale or Job's?"[11] In the remainder of this chapter I want to place Melville's treatment of the Jonah motif that Hoffman hints at in an apocalyptic perspective. Melville explores the imagery of descent and return, of death-enclosures and escape, of whales and vortices, not merely to choose between Job and Jonah, as Hoffman (and, more simplistically, Nathalia Wright in a later article)[12] suggests—but in order to take an interpretive stance on the apocalypse.

∎

The Book of Jonah presents a striking alternative to the eschatological thrust of OT prophecy. In its historical context of emergent postexilic apocalypticism, of passionately ethnocentric messianic expectation, the Book of Jonah stands out as an exceptional call for cosmopolitan tolerance, a tolerance that would place personal spiritual growth ahead of racial discrimination, ethics ahead of apocalypse. Jonah is the perfect Jew of his time—his messianic expectation is strong, his ethnocentrism implacable—and so, in the world of this book, he becomes an apocalyptic prophet against his will, a rebel against God's holy command: not because he has any particular antipathy toward the doomsayer's role, but because he is afraid that his apocalyptic preaching might prevent apocalypse. He is an apocalyptic bigot, a Jew who resists preaching anything to the great Gentile city, Nineveh, lest it repent and be spared. In an OT context, of course, the Gentiles are of the company of the NT Antichrist, the forces of earthly evil whose destruction is eagerly awaited as the prerequisite of apocalyptic restoration. To encourage their repentance, therefore, was to postpone the messianic kingdom, the elevation of the Jewish nation out of bondage into paradise. And so, when the word comes down to Jonah, he flees it:

> Now the word of the LORD came to Jonah the son of Amittai, saying "Arise, go to Nineveh, that great city, and cry against

it; for their wickedness has come up before me." But Jonah rose
to flee to Tarshish from the presence of the LORD. He went
down to Joppa and found a ship going to Tarshish; so he paid the
fare, and went on board, to go with them to Tarshish, away
from the presence of the LORD. (Jon 1:1-3)

Being a rather literal-minded chauvinist, Jonah believes that
God *lives* in Israel and can be escaped by geographical flight. As soon as
the ship gets out to sea, however, God raises a tempest that threatens to
destroy it—an "apocalypse" that can be averted only through Jonah's
repentance, just as the destruction of Nineveh can be averted by *their*
repentance. Jonah does not immediately come forward; only after lots
have been cast and Jonah singled out as the cause of the ship's distress
does he reluctantly offer himself as propitiatory sacrifice: "Take me up
and throw me into the sea," he tells the crew; "then the sea will quiet
down for you" (Jon 1:12). With anticipatory irony, the sailors are portrayed as Gentiles (praying to their *gods*) who are yet decent men, more
selfless than Jonah. Whereas Jonah is willing to let the crew die lest
Nineveh be *spared,* they would rather risk death than cast out a stranger
who admits his own guilt. Jonah finally convinces them to heave him
overboard, however, and the first apocalyptic threat passes: the sea is
calmed. As a result, the sailors are awed by the power of Jonah's God,
and offer sacrifices not to their gods, but to Yahweh. God's purpose is
not to destroy the Gentiles, but to convert them.

Jonah is now swallowed by the whale, remaining in its belly for
three days and three nights, until finally he sends up a prayer of repentance and is deposited on dry land, where God again instructs him to
preach doom to the Ninevites. He does, and as he feared, they do repent,
and God does spare them. This angers Jonah considerably; ostensibly
repentant, he retains his chauvinism, and so he removes himself outside
the city to sulk—and, he hopes, to watch the Gentile city's demise.
There God comes to him in a final attempt to teach him a larger perspective: raising a plant to shade Jonah from the sun, God causes it to
wither overnight as a kind of material allegory for Jonah's edification:

But God said to Jonah, "Do you do well to be angry for the
plant?" And he said, "I do well to be angry, angry enough to
die." And the LORD said, "You pity the plant, for which you
did not labor, nor did you make it grow, which came into
being in a night, and perished in a night. And should I not pity
Nineveh, that great city, in which there are more than a hundred and twenty thousand persons who do not know their right
hand from their left, and also much cattle?" (Jon 4:9-11)

One wonders just how intentional this concluding bathos is; to describe the Ninevites as not knowing their right hand from their left is to *reduce* them to the status of cattle, and to end the book on the bathetic note of "and also much cattle" reduces the enterprise it describes to absurdity. God is a Humane Society liberal who feels sorry for a bunch of dumb animals. By implication, however, the *opposite* to this animal state, represented by Israel through Jonah, is not much dearer to God; Jonah does know his right hand from his left, knows God from idols, Jews from Gentiles, but that knowledge generates only an apocalyptic selfishness (a kind of "eschatological splitting," as I call it later) that hungers for the destruction of enemies. God's is a broader perspective that encompasses both the knowledge and the bitter ethnocentrism of the Jews, and both the ignorance and the humble repentance of the Ninevites, and that implicitly *equates* the two peoples in such a way as to hint at a human brotherhood. God threatens to destroy the Gentile city for their ignorant wickedness—but also threatens to destroy Jonah, the tale's figure for Israel, for his knowledgeable chauvinism, and finally *spares* and *teaches* both. Read in terms of image and theme, the Book of Jonah points clearly to an imagistic reversal of the apocalypse—an invocation of apocalyptic threats (structural collapse in ship and city) in order to replace the ideology of apocalypse with a "liberal," antiapocalyptic tolerance.

This reading, however, neglects the tale's most famous episode—Jonah's descent into the belly of the whale. Why must Jonah be swallowed up? How is his repentance tied to the mythic descent? A look at the tale's rhetoric clarifies much of its obscurity. As is twice emphasized in the opening paragraph of the book, Jonah flees "from the presence of the LORD," which is to say, in Hebrew terms, from God's face. He seeks a place where God cannot *see* him—where he can *absent* himself from God's command and thus also from God's wrath at his disobedience. This ironic inversion of the religious desire for presence into a desire for absence is symbolically a death wish; the only place of absence in the Hebrew cosmology is Sheol, the land of the dead. And when Jonah is swallowed up by the whale, he *figures* his absence in terms of Sheol:

> I called to the LORD, out of my distress,
>   and he answered me;
> out of the belly of Sheol I cried,
>   and thou didst hear my voice. . . .
> Then I said, "I am cast out
>   from thy presence;

how shall I again look
> upon thy holy temple?" (Jon 2:1, 4)

But with Jonah's death comes also conversion:

> When my soul fainted within me,
>> I remembered the LORD;
> and my prayer came to thee,
>> into thy holy temple. . . .
> Deliverance belongs to the LORD! (Jon 2:7, 9)

The absence of Sheol is thus converted here into presence in God's holy temple; cast out of God's presence into the land of the dead, Jonah *prays,* and the prayer (synecdoche of Jonah, whose name means "dove") flies from Sheol-absence to temple-presence, leading ultimately to deliverance. Tropologically speaking, the irony of Jonah's flight from presence into absence has been converted into the synecdoche of prayer, outward flight from God's face into inner mental speech, which flies back to God's presence. In the whale's belly, the absence Jonah seeks is revealed as *internality,* specifically the internality of a prison; to escape, Jonah must unlearn his simplistic notions of externality, and go *out* by first going *in.* That is, Jonah's path out of the whale's belly lies not through the whale's skin, an outward direction that a mythic hero (or an Ahab) would take, but through the inwardness of his own mind. When Jonah prays, he imagistically turns inside-out, the outward predicament of being trapped in a whale's belly becoming itself the illusion that is replaced with an internal dialogue, an inward communion between Jonah-as-prayer and God-as-spirit. That this inwardness delivers Jonah back into the outside world suggests that activity in that world without the inward journey Jonah undergoes is doomed to insubstantiality; one goes out by first going in, and synecdochically inverting internality into externality.

When Jonah emerges from the whale's belly, however, his learning is far from complete. When God stops the apocalypse, Jonah's bigotry reemerges as an angry death wish—he again prefers to die rather than see a Gentile city spared. As Jonah sees it, God has cheated Israel and made a liar out of him: he had, after all, predicted no contingent destruction but a predetermined apocalypse: "Yet forty days, and Nineveh shall be overthrown" (Jon 3:4). But another way of conceiving Nineveh's salvation is to imagine Jonah's prophecy not as a metaleptic projection, Jonah's bigotry *become* future other in the form of destruction, but as metonymical reduction, in which Nineveh's wickedness is destroyed not by the apocalypse *imaged* by Jonah, but by the apocalyptic image itself—by signifier rather than by signified, in the structuralist idiom. In other words, frightened by the apocalyptic image, the Ninevites destroy their *own* wickedness metonymically in repentance; cataclysm, etymologically the "washing down" of the world in the Flood, becomes the "washing away" of the Ninevites' evil. And Jonah is taught, this time, by the same metonymical process: instead of having him swallowed up by another whale, God presents Jonah with a metonymic image of destruction, a plant that grows and dies *next to* the great city. And, one assumes (the book ends on the rhetorical question that presumably precedes Jonah's final insight), just as Jonah's image of the end of the world instructed Nineveh, so also will this image instruct Jonah.

Rhetorically, then, the Book of Jonah records a three-phase movement from ignorance to wisdom. In the first, or ironic, phase, Jonah flees a presence that is at once a *fullness* and a *limitation* (a limitation of perspective to the ethnocentrism sanctified by Jewish tradition) into a deathly absence, a psychological isolation from both God and his Holy Nation, that is revealed as *inward*. The constrictions of this inwardness, however, impinge on Jonah's mind in the image of prison, motivating the second, or synecdochic, phase. Here Jonah escapes mental imprisonment by inverting inside and outside, going out by going in, thus learning to operate in the outside world with a broader perspective gained through his inward journey. But in order to carry "insight," inward vision, into the outside world, he must understand the nature of *signs*. This is the lesson learned in the third, or metonymical, phase. Responsible activity in the world requires neither a solipsistic withdrawal into an inward fantasy world nor a projective drive to transform the world into an image of one's inwardness, but a metonymical compromise between image and reality. One offers an image of the end of the world not in the belief that (through the supernatural intervention of a sympathetic God) reality will conform to it, but in the hope that the image might encourage others to undergo one's own transitional experience. Like Augustine's allegorical displacement of the Book of Revelation, the Book of Jonah traces the internalization of apocalyptic threats into a learning process in which the learner progresses by discovering first the inward path to expanded perspectives and then the necessity of *compromising* with inward vision in confrontation with the world.

■

It should be clear by now how the Book of Jonah serves as a basis for Poe's "Maelström" tale. There, too, the sea-voyager travels into a deathly enclosure, inverts absence into presence by an imaginative act that allows him to escape the enclosure, and returns to offer an *image* of the disaster, a metonymical reduction of the apocalypse, to the tale's narrator, high on the precipice above the vortex. What remains for this chapter is to explain how the Book of Jonah shapes *Moby-Dick*—and this is by no means a simple task. If the imagistic conjunction of Jonah's whale and Poe's whirlpool suggests that the relevant enclosure in the novel is the final vortex created by the whale's descent, which swallows the *Pequod,* for example, that suggestion is complicated considerably by the images of reflection and refraction discussed here previously. "How can the prisoner reach outside except by thrusting through the wall?" Ahab asks—a question that indicates both his imprisonment in the whale's belly *throughout* the novel and his insistence upon fighting his way out rather than achieving the synecdochic escape of Jonah. What is his prison? Does it contain Ishmael too? Pip is carried down to the depths and returns, in a manner of speaking, to tell the tale; is he to be considered a successful Jonah figure?

What I am attempting to do here is to construct a vessel that will contain *Moby-Dick,* but that is a delicate operation, to say the least, for *Moby-Dick* is a novel that resists containment and will break most vessels one tries to fit it in. Instead of turning directly to Melville, therefore, let us make a brief excursus into more readily workable material so as to establish the Jonah pattern in the American novel, construct the vessel, only then returning to *Moby-Dick* to enlarge and reconstruct—let us hope not break—the vessel. I want to look specifically at two novels, Ralph Ellison's *Invisible Man* and the novel from which I take my chapter heading, Kurt Vonnegut's *Cat's Cradle*—both of which experiment with the Jonah motif in both structure and character, in simpler (though not simplistic) and pedagogically more illustrative ways.

In *Invisible Man* the Jonah motif is central. Not only is the novel plotted around a series of symbolic descents and returns, deaths and rebirths, but its macrostructure itself reflects the three phases of Jonah's ethical growth: (1) ironic phase—main narrative; (2) synecdochic phase—prologue; (3) metonymical phase—epilogue. This may seem a simplistic reduction of the novel to the terms of my Jonah motif, but if one reads the novel as an *elaboration* of this bare outline, I think it makes sense.

Consider, first of all, the parallels between Ellison's main narrative and the first chapter of the Book of Jonah. Like Jonah, Ellison's narrator moves through the novel in *flight,* an external and unconscious (though increasingly conscious) flight from a series of paternalistic manipulators (Bledsoe, Lucius Brockway, Brother Jack) who use him ostensibly in his own best interests, but in fact entirely for their own gain. This flight repeatedly leads him into apocalyptic situations that, as in Poe's *Pym,* develop by a sequential dynamic of intensification, each cataclysm more explosive than its predecessors: the battle royal in chapter 1, the pandemonium at the Golden Day in chapter 3, the boiler-room explosion at the Liberty Paint factory in chapter 10, and the Harlem riot in chapter 25. As the apocalypses intensify, the reader's sense that the end of the world is in the offing grows, until in the Harlem riot it seems the end does finally impend, as interpreted by R. W. B. Lewis:

> The chaos is total and ubiquitous. It represents the considered program, as it were, of the agents of Antichrist for drawing the world onward to the great catastrophe—with the manifest intention of seizing power in the post-catastrophic wreckage. For Ellison has elevated his political theme, the familiar authoritarian strategy of making disaster serve the ends of conquest, into universal apocalyptic significance. [13]

Even within the main narrative, however, this reading is questionable. Note how Lewis hedges on agents, for example. If they are of the biblical Antichrist, there is no need to seize power *after* the apocalypse, since Antichrist holds power now. And Lewis's "as it were" indicates that he really wants to use Antichrist metaphorically, to describe the displaced apocalyptic characteristics of political power-holders like Bledsoe and the Brotherhood—which is in fact the only Antichrist for which there is textual warrant. The problem is, if "Antichrist" is no more than an aggregate of powerful human beings, then the "great catastrophe" is only partial, and can have no "universal apocalyptic significance." Chaos may be ubiquitous, but it is by no means total. If men survive the great catastrophe to seize power in the "post-catastrophic wreckage," then it *wasn't* the great catastrophe.

Lewis's apocalyptic reading of *Invisible Man* becomes even more dubious when Ellison's narrator takes us out of the main narrative, out of history, into the mental landscape, the underground haunt—the whale's belly—of the prologue and epilogue. For the invisible narrator follows Jonah out of the external world of ships/riot and geographical travel into the internal world of dark imprisonment; as Jonah is swallowed by the whale, the invisible man is swallowed by the manhole in which he hides from his white pursuers:

> "You goddam black nigger sonofabitch," someone called, "see how you like this," and I heard the cover settle over the manhole with a dull clang. . . . [Ellipsis mine] Then I thought, This

is the way it's always been, only now I know it—and rested back, calm now, placing the brief case beneath my head. I could open it in the morning, push off the lid. Now I was tired, too tired; my mind retreating, the image of the two glass eyes running together like blobs of melting lead. Here it was as though the riot was gone and I felt the tug of sleep, seemed to move out upon black water.

It's a kind of death without hanging, I thought, a death alive. In the morning I'll remove the lid . . . Mary, I should have gone to Mary's. I would go now to Mary's in the only way that I could . . . I moved off over the black water, floating, sighing . . . sleeping invisibly. [Ellipses Ellison's]

But I was never to reach Mary's, and I was over-optimistic about removing the steel cap in the morning. Great invisible waves of time flowed over me, but that morning never came.[14]

Here, at the close of the ironic phase in his Jonah-progress, the invisible man finds himself locked underground in total darkness, which he describes as at once "a kind of death" and a descent into invisible sleep. "This is the way it's always been," he now realizes, "only now I know it"—it's always been dark, he's always been invisible. The reality he thought was substantial is revealed as illusion—apparent presence is revealed as absence, and the absence of total dark is revealed as the only presence he has ever known.

Once the absence of his invisibility has been revealed as *internality,* as the inwardness of his underground prison, the invisible man begins the labor of converting inwardness into outwardness, dark into light—the synecdochic phase of his progress described in the prologue. Another way of describing this second phase might be to see in it an inversion of Plato's allegory of the cave: outside the cave, under the sun, the invisible man learns negatively, he *unlearns,* a process figured by the encroaching chaos of apocalypse; in the cave, he begins in the darkness of shadowy ignorance and gradually generates *truth* (figured both by the artificial light of 1,369 lightbulbs and the sound of the blues on the phonograph) out of his own imagination. By synecdochic substitution, the apocalyptic dynamic of intensification here becomes a dynamic of *internalization.* Reality is turned inside out; the external historical reality that physically encloses his haunt becomes itself enclosed by the internal reality of the mind, lit by electric light, filled with the vibrations of the blues, wound up in the string of words that produces the novel.

Like Jonah's three days and three nights in the belly of the whale, of course, this is a solipsistic retreat; but it is a solipsism that is both necessary and fruitful, for it marks the narrator's realization of his invisibility and therefore of the imperative of transforming it. His task in this second phase is to reverse the part-whole, inside-outside alignments imposed on him by the outside world, discovering in his invisibility the true reality and in the white blindness that fails to see him the illusion that till now has passed for reality. As he says in the opening words of the prologue:

> I am an invisible man. No, I am not a spook like those who haunted Edgar Allan Poe; nor am I one of your Hollywood-movie ectoplasms. I am a man of substance, of flesh and blood, fiber and liquids—and I might even be said to possess a mind. I am invisible, understand, simply because people refuse to see me. Like the bodiless heads you see sometimes in circus side-shows, it is as though I have been surrounded by mirrors of hard, distorting glass. When they approach me they see only my surroundings, themselves, or figments of their imagination—indeed, everything and anything except me. (7)

"You wonder," the narrator goes on, "whether you aren't simply a phantom in other people's minds. Say, a figure in a nightmare which the sleeper tries with all his strength to destroy" (7). The synecdochic reversal recorded in the prologue, one might say, is an iconological reversal, in which the shadowy nightmare image perceived as a mental phantom by whites is revealed as physical body, the *soma phusikos* or *sarx*, "flesh and blood, fiber and liquids," and the bodily reality above ground is conceived as illusory shadow. Mirrors, then, as the invisible man points out, create not images of the true substance, but *desubstantiate* by reflecting a distorted image, an illusion projected onto the night. When a white man insults the narrator on a dark street, he beats the man and nearly kills him—but suddenly "it occurred to me that the man had not *seen* me, actually; that he, as far as he knew, was in the midst of a walking nightmare! . . . Then I was amused. Something in this man's thick head had sprung out and beaten him within an inch of his life" (8). The confrontation is the product of competing iconologies: whereas the narrator conceives both self and other as substantial, as embodied minds, the white man, in a secularized inversion of medieval demonology, images the narrator as a black spirit in the illusory guise of a body—an illusion that would later, no doubt, mystify him by leaving visible bruises.

What the apocalyptic events throughout the ironic main narrative destroy, therefore, is not the world but the invisible man's vision of the world as projected through the lenses of the white man's iconology. The realization that he is invisible marks the nadir of his ironic flight and necessitates the synecdochic reimaginings of the prologue; there, trapped in his underground hole, the narrator turns his world upside down—or, like Dante climbing down Satan's chained body, finally comes to see the world right-side up. The difficulty with this synecdochic understanding, however, is that while it reconciles the invisible man to *himself,* it does not go far toward reconciling him to the *world.* The explosion of the white man's iconology in the narrator's mind does nothing to erase it in the world, in the minds of others; and without such erasure, obviously, the narrator's *social* circumstances can never change. "Hence again I have stayed in my hole," he tells us in the epilogue, "because up above there's an increasing passion to make men conform to a pattern" (499). The narrator now understands and knows what he doesn't want; but what is there left for him to want? Why should he come out of his hole? What can he *do* in the world above ground? What is needed is some route to compromise that will not destroy the invisible man's new-found inward integrity—and the last few pages of the epilogue record just this search, the search for a passage into Jonah's last phase of metonymical compromise. The narrator offers two alternatives: "Until some gang succeeds in putting the world in a strait jacket, its definition is possibility. Step outside the narrow borders of what men call reality and you step into chaos—ask Rinehart, he's a master of it—or imagination" (498).

Chaos—or imagination. Chaos is what remains when one rejects the prevailing ideological fiction and has nothing to offer in its place—an ironic formlessness that Rinehart, the great swindler, represents and exploits. Rinehart is *free*—but for Ellison, freedom in a surrealistic world of shifting images is meaningless, and the narrator rejects it. What is needed is *imagination,* the recreation of reality in a more human form. Although the narrator never quite tells us what he plans to do with his life above ground—what the form of his metonymical compromise will be—my guess is that he intends to publish his novel, the novel that he has been writing in his underground haunt: the novel that has guided *him* to insight by the very act of writing and that may guide others as well. The clue to this reading appears in the last two paragraphs of the novel, in the narrator's twofold reversal of his prologue position. Whereas earlier, before the narrator had written the novel, he denied any claim to social responsibility and insisted on his own substantiality, here, guided by artistic creation to deeper truths, he offers a new manifesto:

I'm shaking off the old skin and I'll leave it here in the hole. I'm coming out, no less invisible without it, but coming out nevertheless. And I suppose it's damn well time. Even hibernations can be overdone, come to think of it. Perhaps that's my greatest social crime, I've overstayed my hibernation, since there's a possibility that even an invisible man has a socially responsible role to play.

"Ah," I can hear you say, "so it was all a build-up to bore us with his buggy jiving. He only wanted us to listen to him rave!" But only partially true: Being invisible and without substance, a disembodied voice, as it were, what else could I do? What else but try to tell you what was happening when your eyes were looking through? And it is this which frightens me:

Who knows but that, on the lower frequences, I speak for you? (503)

Just when did he become "without substance, a disembodied voice"? He did so, I suggest, when he came to conceive himself not as a political activist nor as a solipsistic hermit, but as a *fictional speaker*. Invisibility, that is, is here reified as the imaginative power of voice, the narrator's inward vision metonymically reduced to black words on a white page that both move and illuminate as no political action can, because they allow readers to reify *their* invisibility as well. The novel is Ellison's version of Jonah's plant—a visible reduction of inward vision that transcends compromise by *teaching*, by implanting itself, as it were, in the reader's imagination. Thus, far from predicting the imminent end of the world, Ellison's novel takes us through the symbolic landscapes of Jonah's descent and return, embodying for us not apocalypse but ethical growth—growth toward *ethos*, a fully developed and integrated self.

■

In contrast to *Invisible Man,* Vonnegut's imagery in *Cat's Cradle* is extreme: here the world *ends*, with no hope of continuation. It is (along with the tales by Poe and Nathanael West that we will be considering in chapter 7) one of the most *final* endings in the top rank of American literature and so offers a useful counterpoint to the endless struggle of Ellison's world that will help us to place in perspective the near-final ending of *Moby-Dick*. Significantly, however, through the use of the Jonah motif I have been developing here, Vonnegut signals to the reader that his imagination of doom is not at all *predictive,* but cautionary. It stands in relation to *us,* its readers, as Jonah's apocalyptic warning to the Ninevites: as an ostensible prediction that will *not* come true if we take heed.

Call me Jonah. My parents did, or nearly did. They called me John.

Jonah—John—if I had been a Sam, I would have been a Jonah still—not because I have been unlucky for others, but because somebody or something has compelled me to be certain places at certain times, without fail. Conveyances and motives, both conventional and bizarre, have been provided. And, according to plan, at each appointed second, at each appointed place this Jonah was there. [15]

Vonnegut's parody of Melville's famous opening line indicates his desire to reinterpret the significance of the Jonah motif; but at this point in the novel Vonnegut doesn't seem to *have* much of a Jonah motif, nor does it ever become much more explicit than it is here. Where is his whale? Where is his plant? How does being in the right place at the right time qualify John as a Jonah? Vonnegut's opener is a good line, a funny line—but it's not a throwaway. By the end of the novel, the world is ending; the miraculous substance called *ice-nine,* invented by Dr. Felix Hoenikker to help Marines freeze swamps in order to facilitate warfare, has frozen all of the earth's waters and every-thing—including humans—that contain water. Very few of the survivors (who continue to survive until they eat some of the blue-white *ice-nine* crystals) understand what is happening to them; it is just a random apocalypse, an apocalyptic accident that wipes out mankind for no particular reason.

But random apocalypses are unavertable; to avert an apocalypse one needs *studied* aversion. And so we have John/Jonah, the narrator, the one person who understands what is happening, for the very reason that he has been at "certain places at certain times." As God enlight-ened Jonah, so John's God—Vonnegut himself—has enlightened him as to the cause behind the apocalypse: the casual misuse of technology. Within the novel's world, this enlightenment is bootless; it cannot stop the apocalypse, which ends the novel on a seriocomic note of despera-tion, as the mock remnant faces tenuous life in a hostile environment, or suicide:

> "Bokonon?"
> "Yes?"
> "May I ask what you're thinking?"
> "I am thinking, young man, about the final sentence for *The Books of Bokonon.* The time for the final sentence has come."
> "Any luck?"
> He shrugged and handed me a piece of paper.

This is what I read:

If I were a younger man, I would write a history of human stupidity; and I would climb to the top of Mount McCabe and lie down on my back with my history for a pillow; and I would take from the ground some of the blue-white poison that makes statues of men; and I would make a statue of myself, lying on my back, grinning horribly, and thumbing my nose at You Know Who. (191)

From behind Vonnegut's desperate jesting there emerges a powerful moral concern for the dangers of human stupidity; he creates metonymies of destruction (the novel, and the human "statue" of Bokonon) as what he calls *wrang-wrangs,* people or things that steer others "away from a line of speculation by reducing that line, with the example of the *wrang-wrang*'s own life, to an absurdity" (71). And if it is too late for the novel's world—like Ahab-as-Jonah, John-as-Jonah will never return from the apocalyptic whale's belly—it most decidedly is not too late for the world that contains the novel. *We* are the Nineveh Vonnegut is persuading to put aside wickedness, though the wickedness is not here a sin against God but a sin against mankind and mankind's chances of survival. Hence Vonnegut's opening parody of Melville: without the Jonah allusion, there would be no real reason to seek out a return from the whale's belly, a continuation past the novel's apocalyptic end. Identifying with Jonah, *we* return, and with good luck learn his lesson of metonymical compromise.

∎

Melville's first extended interpretation of the Book of Jonah in *Moby-Dick* is, interestingly enough, an ironic misinterpretation of the book, in the form of Father Mapple's Puritan sermon on that text. By making Father Mapple get it all wrong, Melville at once distances the unbendingly dualistic Puritan interpretation and moves hermeneutically back closer to the spirit of the original text. Father Mapple's reading of the book, in fact, most nearly approximates the eschatological mind-set of the intractable Jonah, for he presents as the message of the book precisely the religious bigotry that the writer seeks to demolish. Jonah's task, according to Father Mapple, is "to preach the Truth to the face of Falsehood!" (50). Truth and falsehood: Israel and Nineveh, that is, Jews and Gentiles, Christians and heathens, Puritans and papists—which is all to say, *my side* and *the other side.* Significantly, however, truth is precisely what Jonah does *not* preach to the Ninevites. When his prediction of doom does not bring on doom, he is proved a liar, at least within the terms of his naive dualism. It is this naive dualism that Father Mapple presents as the vision of Jonah's God:

This, shipmates, this is that other lesson; and woe to that pilot
of the living God who slights it. Woe to him whom this world
charms from Gospel duty! Woe to him who seeks to pour oil
upon the waters when God has brewed them into a gale! Woe
to him who seeks to please rather than to appal! Woe to him
whose good name is more to him than goodness! Woe to him
who would not be true, even though to be false were salvation!
Yea, woe to him who, as the great Pilot Paul has it, while preaching to others is himself a castaway! (50)

This may be good Puritanism, but it is not the Book of Jonah;
Father Mapple is wrong on every point. He cries "Woe!"—but the God
of the Book of Jonah called not for destruction but repentance; not for
punishment and exclusion but forgiveness and integration; not for
bigoted dualism but liberal tolerance. Jonah does pour oil on the waters
when God has brewed them into a gale, by repenting—and so too do the
Ninevites. Jonah refuses to preach apocalypse to Nineveh not because
he is "appalled at the hostility he should raise" (50)—what better hostility than the hostility of the Gentiles?—but because he *wants* to appal
and is afraid his preaching will *please* his enemies the Ninevites by
saving them. Truth and falsehood are a bit more complex in the Book
of Jonah than they are for Father Mapple: for to be true to Jewish law,
as Jonah is, is to be false to God, and to be false for Jonah is not salvation but imprisonment in the whale's belly. As Bainard Cowan points
out, this alignment of Father Mapple with the apocalyptic bigot Jonah
itself points forward to Ahab:

> Mapple's twisting of the message of Jonah to its opposite in
> an earnest conviction of personal rightness and an intolerance
> of opposition suggests in its largest lineaments the attitudes
> of Ahab. Mapple and Ahab share a hatred for profane dark-
> ness, a desire to "kill, burn, and destroy all sin," and an assump-
> tion that one can infallibly discern the ultimate import of
> things. Allegorical in the crude sense of substituting a value-term
> for a reality, theirs is ultimately a profoundly anti-allegorical
> attitude in rejecting the activity of interpretation as the condi-
> tion whereby man lives in the world. It is a position that finally
> rejects mediation—truth is not to be gained from the created
> world, or from the words of others, nor, finally, as with Jonah's
> intransigence, even from the interposing word of God.[16]

We will return to the significant problem of mediation later; for now,
let me emphasize the uncompromising dualism of Ahab, Father Mapple,

and Jonah alike, their apocalyptic fanaticism that tends toward the splitting off and destruction of all that opposes their will.

Ishmael, clearly, presents a highly desirable imaginative alternative to this fanaticism. Ishmael, one might even say, stands for something like the easy tolerance God would teach Jonah. Certainly Ishmael's theological sophistry in the very next chapter, by which he persuades himself to join Queequeg in idolatry, is meant to conceal (playfully, and very thinly) a total disregard for moral and cosmic dualisms:

> I was a good Christian; born and bred in the bosom of the infallible Presbyterian Church. How then could I unite with this wild idolator in worshipping his piece of wood? But what is worship? Do you suppose, now, Ishmael, that the magnanimous God of heaven and earth—pagans and all included—can possibly be jealous of an insignificant bit of black wood? Impossible! But what is worship?—to do the will of God—*that* is worship. And what is the will of God?—to do to my fellow men what I would have my fellow man do to me—*that* is the will of God. Now, Queequeg is my fellow man. And what do I wish that this Queequeg would do to me? Why, unite with me in my particular Presbyterian form of worship. Consequently, I must then unite with him in his; ergo, I must turn idolator. (54)

The "magnanimous God of heaven and earth" that Ishmael invokes, of course, is a far cry from the jealous Puritan God, as he is also from the God of most OT prophets; but he *is* the God of the Book of Jonah, and it is significant that Ishmael should tacitly reject Father Mapple's reading of Jonah here only a few pages later. Ishmael's sophistry is a mask for *flexibility,* the spirit of compromise—and flexibility is motivated by friendship, human ties ousting a priori principle as the ground for action.

It would not be unreasonable to assert, therefore, that in bifurcating his voyager into a narrator who survives and an actor who does not, as Grace Farrell Lee puts it, Melville was specifically bifurcating a Jonah figure into a compromiser capable of tolerance and a fanatic who is not; a representative of excluded middles and a representative of extremes; a prophet of something like "love," or human contiguity, and a prophet of apocalypse, of destructive discontinuity. This interpretation, of course, simplifies Ishmael and Ahab considerably—and I want to try to maintain a light touch here, not insisting too strongly on my character typology. The reason I find it useful to think of Ahab and Ishmael as two faces of a composite Jonah figure, however, is that it then becomes possible to place each at a crucial *transition point* in the Jonah motif, the progress of the Book of Jonah. Ahab, as we shall see, stands somewhere at the juncture between the ironic and the synecdochic phases, Ishmael at the juncture between the synecdochic and the metonymical phases.

Why is this useful? In his discussion of *Moby-Dick,* Daniel Hoffman provides a truncated account of the Book of Jonah, ending—like most accounts of the book, in fact—with Jonah's deliverance from the whale's belly. The result is, tellingly, an incisive reading of Ahab that fails to do justice to Ishmael. "Where Narcissus proves a solipsist," Hoffman writes, "the rebel Jonah at last acknowledges the God beyond himself. In consequence Jonah is not, like Narcissus, a suicide, but is reborn, literally resurrected from his death inside the whale. These experiences of Jonah's prove to be prototypes of several adventures suffered not only by Ishmael and Ahab but also by the harpooners Tashtego and Queequeg and by the demented cabin-boy Pip" (257).[17] Ishmael does move past the suicidal tendencies of Narcissus, as we saw earlier; but it is crucial to see how he also moves past the repentance of Jonah in the whale's belly, past the inside-outside inversion that Ahab never achieves, to a metonymical compromise with visionary insight. Ishmael survives the destruction of the *Pequod,* but it is doubtful whether he is "reborn, literally resurrected from his death inside the whale"—and in the context of the complete tale of Jonah it is equally doubtful whether Jonah's deliverance from the whale's belly is a literal rebirth either. Like Jonah, Ishmael emerges from the belly of the whale with one problem—Ahab's—solved, but with the greatest problem of all yet unsolved: how to live in the world with the complex knowledge his confrontations with Ahab and the whale have afforded him.

Hoffman notes, quite rightly, that "Melville consistently presents Ahab, his Antichrist, in the guise of an unrepentant Jonah," even of an "Anti-Jonah" (259). As Ahab presents himself, certainly, he is anything but the rather odious little vermin portrayed in Jonah: "Now, then, be the prophet and the fulfiller one," he cries. "That's more than ye, ye great gods, ever were. I laugh and hoot at ye, ye cricket-players, ye pugilists, ye deaf Burkes and Bendigoes!" (147). Here is no man who turns tail and runs; here is no shirking prophet, afraid to prophesy lest his threats not be fulfilled: Ahab hyperbolizes himself into a Romantic world-recreating hero and, swallowing his crew as the whale swallowed Jonah, sails straight into calamity.

But Ahab is a Jonah, finally, his own hyperbolic self-presentations to the contrary. He is less powerful, less in control of his own fate, less a match for the gods than he thought. His defeat by the white whale exposes his quest as finally little more than Jonah's ironic flight. He is not fleeing, as Jonah is, from God's face; he is rather fleeing from the recognition that God's face is not his own: that he *is* only mortal. But it is still flight. And if the final destruction marks his swallowing by the whale, his imprisonment in the dark interiority of death, he himself recognizes at isolated moments that he is always already imprisoned by the whale: "How can the prisoner reach outside," he says, "except by thrusting through the wall?"

Ahab's problem, of course, is that the wall behind which he is imprisoned, the whale in which he is trapped, is material existence, nature or *phusis,* the physical reality of the whale, the ship, and his own body, which conspire, he thinks, to thwart his inner vision. "And as when Spring and Summer had departed," Ishmael remarks at the end of "The Cabin-Table," "that wild Logan of the woods, burying himself in the hollow of a tree, lived out the winter there, sucking his own paws; so, in this inclement, howling old age, Ahab's soul, shut up in the caved trunk of his body, there fed upon the sullen paws of its gloom!" (134). As Ahab finds himself trapped in the prison of his vengeance, in the interiority of the pasteboard mask taken as an enclosure to be smashed, so also does he find his frail old body imprisoning a soul that would be divine. This Platonic and Christian anger at the soul's bodily incarceration leads in Ahab both to a self-destructive anger at the body, a desire to discipline and finally to demolish the body that the soul might be freed—even if only into nonexistence—and toward a Romantic desire to expand the body to match the soul's self-conception:

> Hold; while Prometheus is about it, I'll order a complete man
> after a desirable pattern. Imprimis, fifty feet high in his socks;
> then, chest modelled after the Thames Tunnel; then, legs with
> roots to 'em, to stay in one place; then, arms three feet through
> the wrist; no heart at all, brass forehead, and about a quarter
> of an acre of fine brains; and let me see—shall I order eyes to see
> outwards? No, but put a sky-light on top of his head to illu-
> mine inwards. There, take the order, and away. (390)

Here is Emerson's visionary giant reduced to a mechanical contrivance—a Frankenstein, a Talus, a gigantic cyborg made to order—whose magnitude will sustain the soul's strivings toward divinity and whose eyes are programmed to see only what the soul introjects: not life, but divine *desire*.[18] Even this, however, constitutes a radical destruction of the body; where Emerson saw his giant body in the magic glass of nature, Ahab would scrap his old frail one in order to replace it with a heartless monster. Trapped in a carnal prison that constrains his fulfillment of desire, Ahab's divine-willing soul would thrust through the wall—and in so doing, of course, self-destruct. The whale as the mask that hides the "unknown but still reasoning thing," the body as the prison that restrains Ahab's self-engendered purpose—both must be destroyed that spirit might be conjoined with spirit, the NOT ME with the ME, God with man in a transformative apocalypse whose issue is the deification of the hero. Like Jonah, Ahab flees toward freedom, toward a self-contained freedom where God's absence will empower Ahab's divinity—but with every step he takes the walls close in on him. Locked into a vision of the world in which heroic action—violent reprisal as the "living act," the glorious transformative deed—is the only conceivable response to reality's encroachments on the human condition, Ahab strikes out at the walls that enclose him, and is buried under their rubble. Close as he occasionally comes to Jonah's synecdochic inversion of outside and inside—with Starbuck in "The Symphony," for example—Ahab never quite allows himself that "easy" way out. He is symbolically trapped in the whale's belly throughout the novel, trapped in the world, trapped in life itself—so that his incarceration becomes finally a living death, a death in life itself. His death and final descent into the watery depths, lashed to his enemy's side, only seals his failure to learn.

Indeed the infrequent moments when Ahab is seriously tempted by visions of compromise seem almost the influence of his narrator, Ishmael; for it is precisely that path from inside to outside, from synecdoche to metonymy, that Ishmael finds and Ahab does not. One might almost say that Ishmael finds the American escape from the endless hostility of Harold Bloom's family romance of influence, and nearly teaches it to Ahab, paradoxically, in the narration of Ahab's story. Ahab's soliloquy at the end of "The Deck," for example, is obviously a thrust in the direction finally taken by Ishmael:

> Oh! how immaterial are all materials! What things real are there, but imponderable thought? Here now's the very dreaded symbol of grim death, by a mere hap, made the expressive sign of the help and hope of most endangered life. A life-buoy of a coffin! Does it go further? Can it be that in some spiritual sense a coffin is, after all, but an immortality-preserver? I'll think of that.
> But no. So far gone am I in the dark side of death, that its other side, the theoretic bright side, seems but uncertain twilight to me. (432–33)

What Ahab sees in the coffin life-buoy is an image that promises a complex access to truth: an image that reduces the visionary truths of life and death to a single representation and in so doing mediates between them, inclines the imagination toward a mixed or dialectical perception. But Ahab turns away from the invitation to mediated insight, not merely because he is too far gone to think of heaven, but because he is too much the transcendental idealist to tolerate iconic mediation. His thirst is for immediate vision, and he knows intuitively that whoever follows the image's path to truth must finally contend with the possibility that the path ends at the image. Images do not point, they veil; mediation is finally no path at all, but a wall to be smashed. The coffin life-buoy, with its iconic confusions of inside and outside, before and behind the ocean's reflective surface, stands between life and death—or between life as mortality and life as immortality, and between death as entrapment in the material world and death as a gateway to freedom—and so calls Ahab to question his monomania, to place under skeptical scrutiny the idealism that drives him toward apocalypse. The coffin life-buoy is a metonymy of death that points toward the preservation of life; but it is also a metonymy of life that reminds the viewer of his or her mortality and thus of the futility of striving for apocalyptic transformation.

In Ishmael's hands, of course, the coffin life-buoy ultimately becomes more crucial even than that. Carved with the encyclopedic hieroglyphics that Queequeg has transferred to it from the tattoos covering his body, it finally becomes the float, a metonymy of Ishmael's book itself, on which Ishmael/Jonah is saved:

> Many spare hours he spent, in carving the lid with all manner of
> grotesque figures and drawings; and it seemed that hereby he
> was striving, in his rude way, to copy parts of the twisted tattoo-
> ing on his body. And this tattooing, had been the work of a
> departed prophet and seer of his island, who, by those hiero-
> glyphic marks, had written out on his body a complete theory
> of the heavens and the earth, and a mystical treatise on the
> art of attaining truth; so that Queequeg in his own proper per-
> son was a riddle to unfold; a wondrous work in one volume;
> but whose mysteries not even himself could read, though his own
> live heart beat against them; and these mysteries were there-
> fore destined in the end to moulder away with the living parch-
> ment whereon they were inscribed, and so be unsolved to the
> last. And this thought it must have been which suggested to
> Ahab that wild exclamation of his, when one morning turning

away from surveying poor Queequeg—"Oh, devilish tantalization of the gods!" (399)

What is important to note here is the number of removes we are
from truth: there is a theory and an art of attaining truth, which only
exists in its written form (a treatise), which Queequeg cannot read but
transfers rudely to the coffin life-buoy. Truth is multiply mediated by a
series of written traces, each of which loses something of the message it
transcribes. In Ahab, this loss or reduction provokes only anger, impa-
tience. An imagistic compromise with truth is forever a simply negation
of truth that must itself be negated if truth is to be attained. The danger
is that the negation of negation may reveal no truth at all but the void:
"Sometimes I think there's naught beyond." Ahab, we might say, is a
deconstructor with the courage—or the madness—to pursue his negative
convictions to their ultimate end. "Oh, devilish tantalization of the
gods!" Tantalized by images of truth, he would strive toward truth by
destroying its image, and so must be forever frustrated.

But for Ishmael iconic mediation is no tantalization: it is a
richness, a reductive fullness that fills visionary privation by reducing
it to a publicly inscribed message, a book.[19] "What things real are
there," Ahab cries, "but imponderable thoughts?" Writing is ever inferior to thought, the book inferior to the truth it records—until one
accepts the writing *as* the truth, the act of writing (and of reading) as
an interpretive activity that generates the only truth that matters.
"Only in the heart of quickest perils; only when within the eddyings
of his angry flukes; only on the profound unbounded sea, can the
fully invested whale be truly and livingly found out" (378), Ishmael
says, implying that the point of the hunt that is *Moby-Dick* is not the
meaning but the *finding out*. The whale, like Queequeg and his coffin,
may be covered with hieroglyphics that, like the "mystic rocks" Ishmael recalls along the Mississippi, must "remain undecipherable"
(260); *Moby-Dick,* like Moby Dick, may never lead us to the encyclopedic truth it seems to promise. But the reduction of truth fulfilled
to an image of fulfillment is all the truth we need and all the truth we
will ever attain.

If *Moby-Dick* is potentially the most apocalyptic novel ever
written in America, then the survival of Ishmael past the apocalyptic
vortex, past the absolute and final absence of the belly of Jonah's
whale, ultimately subordinates the vision of apocalypse to a written
metonymy of apocalypse, a gourd that points us finally toward a more
secularly redemptive vision. Ishmael writes the encyclopedic narrative that figures the apocalypse, but places the apocalyptic figure in a

context that defuses and redirects its power. The end of the *Pequod* is an image of the end of the world—but it is a cautionary image, an allegorical image that displaces apocalyptic images in the *world* metonymically into the iconic mediations of the *word*. Ishmael survives the apocalypse, as his quotation from Job in the epilogue suggests, in order to write a novel about—and against—the apocalypse: "AND I ONLY AM ESCAPED ALONE TO TELL THEE" (470). To tell *about* the apocalypse, for Melville, was to take the only measure that might be effective toward circumventing it.

THE HOUSE OF FICTION

"*Strange, I had never seen the Baronin in this light before,*" *the Baron was saying, and he crossed his knees.
"If I should try to put it into words, I mean how did I
see her, it would be incomprehensible, for the simple
reason that I find that I never did have a really clear
idea of her at any time. I had an image of her, but
that is not the same thing. An image is a stop the mind
makes between uncertainties. I had gathered, of
course, a good deal from you, and later, after she went
away, from others, but this only strengthened my
confusion. The more we learn of a person, the less we
know. It does not, for instance, help me to know
anything of Chartres above the fact that it possesses a
cathedral, unless I have lived in Chartres and so keep
the relative heights of the cathedral and the lives of its
population in proportion. Otherwise it would only
confuse me to learn that Jean of that city stood his wife
upright in a well; the moment I visualize this, the deed
will measure as high as the building; just as children
who have a little knowledge of life will draw a man and
a barn on the same scale.*"

"*Your devotion to the past,*" *observed the doctor,
looking at the cab metre with apprehension, "is perhaps
like a child's drawing.*"

*The Baron nodded. He was troubled. "My family is
preserved because I have it only from the memory of
one single woman, my aunt; therefore it is single, clear
and unalterable. In this I am fortunate; through this
I have a sense of immortality. Our basic idea of eternity*

is a condition that cannot vary. *It is the motivation of
marriage. No man really wants his freedom. He gets a
habit as quickly as possible—it is a form of immortality."
"And what's more," said the doctor, "we heap re-
proaches on the person who breaks it, saying that in so
doing he has broken the image—of our safety."*
                                        —Djuna Barnes, Nightwood

In *Exiled Waters: Moby Dick and the Crisis of Allegory,* Bainard Cowan
points to an ultimately redemptive, but still disturbingly ambiguous,
rift in Ishmael's solution to the problem of the sea and the land, which
is to say, of the Romantic self-constitutive imagination and society: in
writing a book, Ishmael at once incorporates American society into
his imagination and is thereby irrevocably exiled from it, orphaned,
excluded from the community by his imaginative insistence upon transforming it. "The triumph of Ishmael," Cowan writes,

> would be the widespread recognition that community is genu-
> inely constructed not out of fathers and sons but out of exiles
> and orphans, not on the land, in Nantucket or New Bedford,
> but only on exiled waters. Yet this understanding has great dif-
> ficulty fitting itself to the fathers' structure of power without
> negating itself. Ishmael does not become a captain; instead he be-
> comes a fabulator, and his empire is not maritime but discur-
> sive. His is a city that like the proto-allegorist Plato's will exist
> only in discourse.[1]

From a Romantic perspective, of course, one might claim that
this city that exists "only in discourse" has a distinct advantage over
real cities in that, even if it does negate itself, it nevertheless goes on
existing; Ishmael's fabulation both negates and preserves the apocalyptic quest and destruction of Ahab, at the same time as it preserves
and negates its own compromising alternative to apocalypse. What is
more, Ishmael's first-person narration implies and indeed constitutes
a communal dialogue with the reader in which community *becomes*
discursive; if communion in the sociopolitical realm of fathers and
sons is oppressive, we can at least commune in the realm of fiction,
specifically in a self-conscious fiction that would mediate between
fiction and reality by reminding us that the realm we inhabit *is* a fiction, not a reality.

From another viewpoint, however, this move—restricting one-self to the realm of fiction—constitutes a profound loss. Edgar A. Dryden speaks in *Melville's Thematics of Form* of "the troublesome task of defining the writer's relationship to the pseudo reality which is society and to the conventions and formulas which structured it," and remarks: "This is, of course, the problem which Ishmael's method allows him to avoid altogether. Because he is unwilling to be an actor in the world's play, Ishmael retreats from both nature and society by becoming a teller of stories. For him it is necessary that the writer remove himself from the prison of 'hereditary forms and world-usages' (*P*[*ierre*], V, 104), which cut him off from the truth of the universe."[2] If society is a pseudoreality and the truth of the universe a transcendental one to be grasped only by withdrawing from social structures, then of course Ishmael's solution is the only adequate one: to retreat into fiction. But will this Platonic conception of society and truth suffice? Is it enough to construct self-conscious cosmologies that at once deny reality to society and undermine the transcendental reality of fictions?

In *After the New Criticism,* Frank Lentricchia offers a powerful critique of this poetic of what he calls conservative fictionalism, maintaining that, in its determination to withdraw from the social world, the poetic is ultimately a late form of aestheticism:

> Another difficulty is that in his self-conscious recognition of a gulf between fictive discourse and being, the poet forges another link to his not-so-distant aestheticist kin by holding up a sign that says "No road through to action." . . . To return to one of Kermode's illustrations: the unself-conscious or innocent mythicist and pragmatist might murder Jews, but the fiction-maker's self-consciousness will keep him from doing that because it will keep him from all *doing,* saving as well as murdering. . . . The counsel of self-consciousness in the aestheticist mode does not urge the uncovering and bringing to bear of alternative perspectives which in dialectical interplay might offer constraints to the excesses and blindnesses of single-minded ideology. The counsel of aestheticized self-consciousness is, rather, paralysis and despair. From a valid perception of the difficulty of human vision and humane action, it leaps to the metaphysical conclusion that all perspectives, no matter how subtly, how flexibly managed, are inherently vicious, and that moral security lies only in withdrawal from action and refusal of all points of view except the view that no view is any good. Self-consciousness of this sort is the modernist intellectual's rationalization of his alienation and impotence.[3]

In the tradition of Emerson and Poe, of course, Melville would say that this is not quite true: one does encourage action in the world, specifically the act of interpretation. But such action may, finally, be a subterfuge. In what social context does the interpretation take place? What effect does it have on society? What *good* is it, apart from its constituting a personal retreat from the numbing and paradoxical demands of social existence? Lentricchia continues:

> This specially endowed, fictive literary language, because it is washed clean of mythic and pragmatic reductionist tendencies in the poet's self-consciousness, permits the poet to say anything he pleases, no matter how repugnant. Since his playfulness has presumably placed him beyond the domain where his linguistic acts are regarded as *acts* with practical implication, the poet can never be charged with moral irresponsibility. Self-consciousness, then, by producing an awareness of the fictiveness of fictions, produces the knowledge which saves us from being caught up in the net of moral relations. Somewhere along the line, however, we must ask ourselves whether this late version of aestheticism is sufficient protection against the claims—moral, social, political—that can be levied on the discourse of intellectuals, or, an easier question to answer, whether a tiny community of *literari,* cherishing the insulation afforded by their brand of self-consciousness, has ever, can ever, or should ever want to make aestheticism operative in the world. (57)

These are questions that, as Dryden suggests, Melville was to explore more explicitly (though no more successfully) in *Pierre;* and as we shall see, they were central concerns particularly for Hawthorne. William Faulkner, however, is the American writer who (heavily influenced by Hawthorne) most insistently and comprehensively treats of the dialectic between the individual and his or her society, most decisively perhaps in his masterpiece, *Absalom, Absalom!,* which takes us from individualistic isolation in frail and impotent fictions to some sort of communal inclusion that may be redemptive.

Miss Rosa Coldfield, the aged spinster who among *Absalom, Absalom!*'s four central characters is the only one to have known the shadowy Thomas Sutpen personally, illustrates this shift most clearly. She begins in Ahab's self-imprisoned state, shut off from communal reality:

> *Instead of accomplishing the processional and measured milestones of the childhood's time I lurked, unapprehended as*

> *though, shod with the very damp and velvet silence of the*
> *womb, I displaced no air, gave no betraying sound, from one*
> *closed forbidden door to the next and so acquired all I knew*
> *of that light and space in which people moved and breathed*
> *as I (that same child) might have gained conception of the sun*
> *from seeing it through a piece of smoked glass—*[4]

In *"I lurked . . . from one closed forbidden door to the next,"* Miss Rosa is trapped inside herself, behind the closed door of her own flesh, not just behind *"that veil we call virginity"* (148) but behind selfhood itself, the very being-in-the-world as an *individual* being that separates man (and woman) from others. And Faulkner places his novel directly at the doorway, at that invisible yet apparently impassable boundary between self and other that is, so importantly in this novel, also a boundary between present and past/future, between the *is* and the *once-was* or the *might-have-been.* Here is Miss Rosa again:

> *living is one constant and perpetual instant when the arras-veil*
> *before what-is-to-be hangs docile and even glad to the light-*
> *est naked thrust if we had dared, were brave enough (not wise*
> *enough: no wisdom needed here) to make the rending gash.*
> *Or perhaps it is no lack of courage either: not cowardice which*
> *will not face that sickness somewhere at the prime foundation*
> *of this factual scheme from which the prisoner soul, miasmal-*
> *distillant, wroils ever upward sunward, tugs its tenuous prisoner*
> *arteries and veins and prisoning in its turn that spark, that*
> *dream which, as the globy and complete instant of its freedom*
> *mirrors and repeats (repeats? creates, reduces to a fragile*
> *evanescent iridescent sphere) all of space and time and massy*
> *earth, relicts the seething and anonymous miasmal mass which*
> *in all the years of time has taught itself no boon of death but*
> *only how to recreate, renew; and dies, is gone, vanished: noth-*
> *ing—but is that true wisdom which can comprehend that there*
> *is a might-have-been which is more true than truth, from which*
> *the dreamer, waking, says not "Did I but dream?" but rather*
> *says, indicts high heaven's very self with: "Why did I wake since*
> *waking I shall never sleep again?"* (142-43)

What lies beyond the arras-veil at which all existence stands is knowledge—knowledge of that might-have-been of which men and women only dream, and in waking from dream find vanished. For Miss Rosa, the concrete form that might-have-been takes, its objective correlative as it were, is *"Charles Bon, Charles Good, Charles*

Husband-soon-to-be" (148), whose image she says should *"adorn the barren mirror altars of every plain girl"* (147), for gazing at her own image in the mirror each girl imagines the mirror as an altar in which the image is sacramentally transformed into the desired other, the husband-soon-to-be that objectifies desire. And yet, tellingly, Miss Rosa never even sees Bon; sight even of the material image, the somatic icon, of the might-have-been is deferred.

And indeed as this chapter's epigraph from *Nightwood* suggests, there is forever a fatal gap between an image and its object, between an image of the truth and absolute knowledge of the truth. "An image is a stop the mind makes between uncertainties," the Baron says, and Miss Rosa's image of Bon-as-image is a yet more tenuous stop. "The more we learn of a person, the less we know." To create an image of a person, a town, a cathedral, an act, is to defer absolute knowledge of that act. Devotion to the past, like devotion to the future, is like a child's drawing in the sense that all attempts to recover the past in a future repetition and to correct it are necessarily distortions of scale and perspective, for what an image of the past or the future cannot bridge is the gap between early and late, between one's own lateness and the earliness of the past or the recovered earliness of the future. As the Baron says, there is a powerful safety in an image of the past, especially when (as in his case) it is single, unified, "clear and unalterable," for an unvarying image provides a sense of time frozen, time conquered in the cessation of action. But the safety inherent in such an image is fragile, necessarily, for time cannot be stopped; in the apocalyptic deferral of the end and the endless receding of an origin, time defeats images of fixity, and with them human security.

There is another side to this defeat, however, as Evan Watkins notes in his incisive reading of Faulkner's novel: the flux of time, by defeating images of security, also makes possible a mode of understanding by incompletion, a mode that Faulkner attempts persistently in his works to inhabit.

> Being alive in the present means feeling the loss of the past, the inability ever to comprehend fully history as the object of one's present awareness. Yet that feeling of loss is the guarantee of one's future, is finally at one with the future because it, too, is an absence, toward which the present resolves itself. If the past were wholly given to present experience there could be no genuine present or coming-to-be of the future because the future could never become past, could never violate the crystal integrity of a completed object. Historical understanding is

possible just because it is never complete, because one's present consciousness can merge with the dehiscence of present into future, can, that is, become aware of itself in time and hence make it possible for one to have a history, just as Faulkner can at once be speaking inside the novel and aware of himself speaking as he shapes the novel from the beginning. Thus the "dream" sense of *Absalom, Absalom!* as instantaneous and eternal is finally at once [*sic*] with its temporal articulation, arising from the awareness of a continual movement of self-transcendence toward the future that like the past is felt as a loss, an absence. The temporal movement of the novel is a present, continual appropriation of the loss of the past which contains within itself both the coming-to-be of the future and the lapse of future into past. [5]

This delicate balance, however, this at-onement of instantaneity and temporal articulation, is by definition always incomplete, and in that sense always a "failure," for only by failing to complete itself does such an appropriation of the loss of the past succeed. This necessity of failure is something that, of all four principal characters in *Absalom, Absalom!* (whose novelistic action consists entirely of speaking, listening, and reading), only Miss Rosa understands with any clarity. The other three work fitfully toward such an understanding; for Quentin, especially, more than for either his father or his Harvard roommate, a definite understanding of the interrelationship between completion and incompletion, between success and failure, and between pushing through closed doors and standing impotently outside, is crucial—but finally unattainable. Miss Rosa is central in the novel by virtue of having suffered the frustrations now confronted by Quentin and thought them through: "The greatness of section 5," as Watkins says,

> is that Faulkner talks about himself through Rosa talking about Sutpen, realizing in fact that it is the only way to talk about himself, not only because Rosa belongs to him as a character in his novel but also because he belongs to her. In committing himself to creating her as a character, he has at the same time committed himself to her creating him as a novelist before his own equilibrating self-consciousness and before his readers. He must accomplish with Rosa what she accomplishes with Sutpen. (202) [6]

But Quentin, Miss Rosa's younger male self in significant respects, is also a major figure because he *hasn't* thought his frustrations through as clearly as Miss Rosa; because his thinking about deferral and incompletion is still in process toward the recognition that it must always *remain* in process; and because, failing to understand that, Quentin ultimately finalizes failure by drowning himself.

This suggests that the novel's central issue is *time,* specifically in this context the problem of defining the self and the community (each in relation to the other) in time. Watkins rightly stresses the victory Miss Rosa achieves in chapter 5, but her victory must be balanced against Quentin's defeat, particularly since it is with Quentin's anguished and self-denying cry—"*I dont hate it! I dont hate it!*" (378)—that the novel ends. If Miss Rosa stands at the center of the novel and expounds the complexities of self and community in time that she has now come at last to understand, Quentin stands at the end, after Miss Rosa's death, and reiterates his bewilderment, his failure, finally, to understand the import of his own storytelling. Quentin's failure will ultimately take us back to Miss Rosa's qualified success, which in turn will suggest some ways of appraising the novel's success. But to get there we must follow a roundabout path, a path that will take us through Poe and Hawthorne before leading back to the possibility of *victory.*

John T. Irwin's speculative Freudian and Nietzschean reading of Faulkner in *Doubling and Incest/Repetition and Revenge* is probably the best starting point for a discussion of Quentin. In Irwin's analysis, on which my discussion of Balizet in chapter 2 partially relied, the ostensibly redemptive image of the past that Djuna Barnes likened to a child's drawing becomes a mode of revenge against the father, whose earliness with respect to the son renders him in the son's eyes always a giant who "will measure as high as the building." The "child's drawing" of the two drawn on the same scale—Quentin's version of the past as a heightened image of the father (Sutpen and Jason Compson both)—freezes the father's earliness and therefore grants the son a surrogate victory or revenge over time and the father (over Father Time) by making Quentin the primordial creator, Father Time his willed creation. "Quentin's act of narration in *Absalom,*" Irwin suggests, "is an attempt to seize his father's authority by gaining temporal priority,"[7] for to gain temporal priority would be to stop time, or at least to spatialize it into a fixed image controlled by the son. Irwin states: "If Quentin were really able to repeat the events of the summer of 1909, then it would *be* the summer of 1909 again. Time would not have irrecoverably passed, but, as the Christian image of eternity, would be totally spatialized so that the past would continue to exist at the present moment as if it were a place to which we could go" (80).

But Quentin is not able; and in his quest for revenge against time and the father he essentially only dooms himself to time's victimization, for, as Irwin says, "narration does not achieve mastery over time; rather, it traps the narrator more surely within the coils of time" (122). Out of the endless repetition of this attempted revenge there then arises a historical sequence in which repetition is always a trap, and always the *same* trap. Irwin's account of this sequence bears quoting from at length:

> In this mechanism of a repetition in which the active and passive roles are reversed, we have the very essence of revenge. But we must distinguish between two different situations: in the ideal situation, the revenge is inflicted on the same person who originally delivered the affront—the person who was originally active is now forced to assume the passive role in the same scenario; in the other situation, the revenge is inflicted on a substitute. This second situation sheds light on Sutpen's attempt to master the traumatic affront that he suffered as a boy from the man who became his surrogate father, to master it by repeating that affront in reverse, inflicting it on his own son Charles Bon. This scenario of revenge on a substitute sheds light as well on the connection between repetition and the fantasy of the reversal of generations and on the psychological mechanism of generation itself. The primal affront that the son suffers at the hands of the father and for which the son seeks revenge throughout his life is the very fact of being a son—of being the generated in relation to the generator, the passive in relation to the active, the effect in relation to the cause. He seeks revenge on his father for the generation of an existence which the son, in relation to the father, must always experience as a dependency. But if revenge involves a repetition in which the active and passive roles are reversed, then the very nature of time precludes the son's taking revenge on his father, for since time is irreversible, the son can never really effect that reversal by which he would become his father's father. The son's only alternative is to take revenge on a substitute—that is, to become a father himself and thus repeat the generative situation as a reversal in which he now inflicts on his own son, who is a substitute for the grandfather, the affront of being a son, that affront that the father had previously suffered from his own father. (116-17)

This kind of repetition as substitutive revenge, Irwin notes, constitutes a form of doubling, in which, according to Otto Rank, the double marks off "the distance between the ego-ideal and the attained reality" (cited in Irwin, 33). "The double evokes the ego's love," Irwin says, "because it is a copy of the ego, but it evokes the ego's fear and hatred as well because it is a copy with a difference" (33)—a difference that is both spatial and temporal and thus, in Derrida's pun, a "differ-ance." Spatially, the double traces a complex web of brother-sister (and, in *Absalom,* black-white) relations: Quentin imagines himself in *The Sound and the Fury* as Dalton Ames in his sister's arms and as Can-dace in Dalton's arms, when he faints like a girl (double as image of self: love), and he imagines himself killing Candace in a sexual *Liebestod* and killing Dalton Ames to avenge his sister's honor (double as image of other: hatred).[8] Temporally, the double charts father-son relationships, which in *Absalom* are further complicated by Quentin's multiple iden-tifications with the father-son and brother-sister conflicts of the Sutpen family. In each case, Irwin suggests, doubling constitutes an impassable barrier between self and other—an abysm of differance that forever sep-arates desire from its fulfillment.

Forever: the bleak vision that Irwin's reading ascribes to Faulk-ner's work is in keeping with—and indeed largely derived from—what Norman O. Brown calls the radical pessimism of Freud's agonistic or dualistic conception of the psyche.[9] Man's instincts, for Freud, are for-ever locked in conflict between life and death, a conflict that neither instinct can win until physical and mental death ends the instinctual struggle. This instinctual dualism, Brown reminds us, underlies Freud's profound disbelief in the possibility of a cure; so long as doubling, for example, is conceived as agon, as binary conflict, the sickness of inner division will be the *norm* of psychic reality and cure will be an illusion and therefore itself a symptom of the sickness. As an interpretive strat-egy for reading Faulkner, however, such a stance essentially only makes the inwardly divided Quentin a spokesman for the author, or at the least a touchstone by which the work can be understood. I suggest that in *Absalom* the crucial Quentin/Miss Rosa axis precludes such an as-sumption; and that Miss Rosa's acceptance of incurability *as* cure offers a mediated third term to the binary health/sickness opposition, thus directing us past the false promise or threat of an agon for which both Sutpen and his symbolic son Quentin hold out. In a sense Faulkner *is* looking for a cure to the sickness of the South, which is the sickness of Sutpen, Miss Rosa, and Quentin. But his novel finally insists that the only possible cure transcends the notion of cure—that diagnosis and cure, sickness and health are themselves the misleading terms of a binary doubling or agon that expresses or exposes Sutpen's innocence. Miss Rosa steps outside Sutpen's shadowy agonistic world to a cure that is not a cure, to a health that is a new understanding of health and sick-ness, when she finally comes to see that Sutpen's innocence was "*not articulated in this world"* (171)—in the *real* world that will not conform to an abstract agon.

As I mentioned previously, Miss Rosa typically images the frustration of desire by closed doors. If we juxtapose her notion of time as the endless coming to a closed door with Quentin's notion of time as an endless frustrated act of revenge against the father, the novel's central metaphor clearly becomes the father's house, that structure built by the father to outlast himself as an image of his own authoritative (or authorial) primordiality. Leroy Searle notes that throughout the novel "movement is oriented by houses, rooms, and entryways—from office to gallery to dormitory room—with a constant and acute awareness that the essential space all would enter is the *house* of Sutpen, both as a literal structure and a genealogical metaphor. The action of each chapter, then, involves the opening of a door to understanding—or coming to a door that cannot presently be passed."[10] If closed doors mark the differential impasse between doubles, between self and self-image, the definitive act of curative mediation will be the opening of and passing through a closed door. And if the House of Sutpen (understood broadly enough to encompass Sutpen's one-hundred square miles of land and his dynasty that never materializes) is Sutpen's image against time, his "child's drawing" that asserts his mastery over genealogy as history, then in some sense *Absalom* is a "house of fiction" that constitutes *Faulkner's* image against time—a creation that, expanded to encompass all Yoknapatawpha County, belongs to one "William Faulkner, sole owner and proprietor," as Faulkner proclaims on his map at the end of *Absalom.* The question then becomes: to what extent, and by what means, does Faulkner in his own house-building successfully overcome the contradictions he discerns in Sutpen's? If the House of Sutpen is an American apocalypse that succumbs to its own inner conflicts, how is Faulkner to maintain and even escalate those conflicts in his own fictional house without allowing that fiction to succumb to them?

■

The context in which answers to these questions must be sought, I suggest, is a historical one: an American *tradition* of Gothic housebuilding, a literary history of American apocalyptic architecture that raises and profoundly explores the crucial issues implicit in the idea of an apocalyptic house of fiction. "Every spirit builds itself a house," Emerson's Orphic bard proclaims in the passage from *Nature,* quoted earlier:

> and beyond its house, a world; and beyond its world, a heaven. Know then, that the world exists for you. For you is the

phenomenon perfect. What we are, that only can we see. All
that Adam had, all that Caesar had, you have and can do. Adam
called his house, heaven and earth; Caesar called his house,
Rome; you perhaps call yours, a cobler's trade; a hundred acres
of ploughed land; or a scholar's garret. Yet line for line and
point for point, your dominion is as great as theirs, though without fine names. Build, therefore, your own world.[11]

Thomas Sutpen called his house Sutpen's Hundred—not acres,
but square miles. But if in Sutpen's American Dream we trace Faulkner's sense of the poverty or the insidiousness of Emerson's prophetic
hope, in *Absalom* as a whole we trace yet another version of that same
hope, the hope that a verbal house will withstand the contradictions of
time and judgment as a material house never can. The critical relation is
that of *built* apocalypse to *written* apocalypse, of American house to
American fiction—and I suggest that our best guide to this relation is
not Emerson but Poe, whose complexly self-reflexive tale, "The Fall of
the House of Usher," is perhaps the definitive work in the tradition and
a seminal influence behind *Absalom.* Significantly, whereas Emerson
conceived his visionary house in terms of expansion, Poe conceives his
in terms of constriction; the world that human beings build to encompass alien reality in a vast human form is revealed in Poe as a prison:

> *I was fourteen then, fourteen in years if they could have been
> called years while in that unpaced corridor which I called child-
> hood, which was not living but rather some projection of the
> lightless womb itself; I gestate and complete, not aged, just over-
> due because of some caesarian lack, some cold head-nuzzling
> forceps of the savage time which should have torn me free, I
> waited not for light but for that doom which we call female
> victory which is: endure and then endure, without rhyme or rea-
> son or hope of reward—and then endure.* (144)

This is Faulkner, of course, but it seems to come straight out of Poe;
its corollary is Madeline "enwombed" in the crypt, consigned to *her*
"female victory" but less willing than Miss Rosa to endure. In fact,
Roderick Usher paints the scene Miss Rosa describes; he too, like his
sister, has lived his life in horrific experience of the *"unpaced corridor"* that is the projection of the lightless womb: "A small picture,"
Poe's narrator says in this central ekphrasis,

> presented the interior of an immensely long and rectangular
> vault or tunnel, with low walls, smooth, white, and without

> interruption or device. Certain accessory points of the design
> served well to convey the idea that this excavation lay at an ex-
> ceeding depth below the surface of the earth. No outlet was
> observed in any portion of its vast extent, and no torch, or other
> artificial source of light was discernible; yet a flood of intense
> rays rolled throughout, and bathed the whole in a ghastly and
> inappropriate splendour. [12]

The Ushers are trapped in the house as Ahab is trapped in the prison of
his monomania, as Miss Rosa is trapped behind closed doors: all are in-
carcerated, finally, in selfhood, in a fearful, anticommunal individuality
that, following Emerson, finds all presence inside but inexorably constricts into absence.

As elsewhere, Poe's lens here is cosmological as well as psychological; he is symbolically concerned in this tale with the fate not only
of the human *mind* but also of the human *race,* of the world and human history: the "time-honoured" and "very ancient family" of Usher"
(3:275) is the family of man, their house the world as God's architectural creation. Earl J. Wilcox notes that in naming his family, Poe was
probably thinking of the Archbishop Ussher (also spelled "Usher");
Ussher's *Annales Veteris et Novi Testamenti* (1650-54) established the
scriptural chronology that was accepted until after Poe's time, [13] which
would link the House of Usher with all biblical history, from the Creation to the Apocalypse, and indeed with the planet itself, the "frame
of this world" that, Paul says in 1 Cor, is "passing away" (1 Cor 7:31).
Paragei gar to schema tou kosmou toutou: the Vulgate renders this
praeterit enim figura hujus mundi, which suggests that the *schema* or
"frame" of this world, God's architecture, is a *figure,* a divine trope
which bears the mark of its "fictor" or shaper. [14]

What this submerged allusion to biblical history seems to suggest is that Poe is using the idea of a house—structure and family
dynasty—to confront the twin problems of time and figuration. Thomas
Sutpen, in his American dream of creating an architectural image of
victory over time, archetypally aspires to God's control over time:

> yet he sitting there on the one afternoon of his leave as though
> he had a thousand of them, as if there were no haste nor urgency
> anywhere under the sun and that when he departed he had no
> further to go than the twelve miles out to Sutpen's Hundred and
> a thousand days or maybe even years of monotony and rich
> peace, and he, even after he would become dead, still there, still
> watching the fine grandsons and great-grandsons springing as
> far as eye could reach. . . . (271)

To imagine a millennium is to oppose time with a figure; and to imagine the success of that figural gesture is to hyperbolize oneself into a god. Poe's family, not the builders but only the last inhabitants of the house, can have no such hyperbolical aspirations; but, like Thomas Sutpen, they perceive themselves caught up in a web of destiny whose culmination must certainly be horrific:

> To an anomalous species of terror I found him a bounden slave. "I shall perish," said he, "I *must* perish in this deplorable folly. Thus, thus, and not otherwise, shall I be lost. I dread the events of the future, not in themselves, but in their results. I shudder at the thought of any, even the most trivial, incident, which may operate upon this intolerable agitation of soul. I have, indeed, no abhorrence of danger, except in its absolute effect—in terror. In this unnerved—in this pitiable condition—I feel that the period will sooner or later arrive when I must abandon life and reason together, in some struggle with the grim phantom, FEAR." (3:280)

Like most of Poe's characters for whom death is only a cessation, Usher is a "bounden slave" to dread, a dread that casts a Gothic gloom over all life and makes him wish for death *now* in place of his unbearable fear. Usher's terror is at bottom a terror of *time,* death being in this sense only the terminus to individual time; he dreads the "events of the future" because they are temporal and so beyond his control. In this sense his assault on time is congruent with Sutpen's; whereas Sutpen destroys his architectural image against time by denying his son, Charles Bon, by refusing the doubling of a younger man who might survive and supplant him, Roderick commits imagistic suicide by immolating his twin sister, whose cataleptic attack renders her a living image of deathly stasis. Bon and Madeline, one might say, represent to their destroyers horrific images of encroaching time, of *passing* time that erodes figures of permanence and stability by moving beyond them. As in Ahab's quest for the white whale, however, the destruction of the deathly double is physically as well as imagistically suicidal; to efface the image of self is to obliterate the iconic ground for self-definition, and, like both Moby Dick and (more complexly) Charles Bon, Madeline returns to destroy her suicidal double. Since the twins are themselves doubled by the house, as they collapse upon each other the house collapses on them, immolating both in death as Roderick had his sister in life:

> From that chamber, and from that mansion, I fled aghast. The storm was still abroad in all its wrath as I found myself crossing

the old causeway. Suddenly there shot along the path a wild
light, and I turned to see whence a gleam so unusual could have
issued; for the vast house and its shadows were alone behind
me. The radiance was that of the full, setting, and blood-red
moon which now shone vividly through that once barely-
discernible fissure of which I have before spoken as extending
from the roof of the building, in a zigzag direction, to the
base. While I gazed, this fissure rapidly widened—there came a
fierce breath of the whirlwind—the entire orb of the satellite
burst at once upon my sight—my brain reeled as I saw the mighty
walls rushing asunder—there was a long tumultuous shouting
sound like the voice of a thousand waters—and the deep and
dank tarn at my feet closed sullenly and silently over the fragments of the "HOUSE OF USHER." (3:297)

What the narrator witnesses is the disfiguration of the architectural figure: the end of human history and the disintegration of the
planet, in Poe's cosmological scheme, but also, of course, the end of
figuration itself, of human language. The figure disfigures itself, specifically, in order to point beyond itself to a transcendental realm. The
widening of the fissure becomes for the narrator the opening of a door,
the rending of a veil, revealing behind it for the first time in the story
the light of the full moon, which then *bursts* upon the narrator's sight.[15]
As a figure for the transfigural, however, the moon cannot function as a
self-evidential sign, for figures (in either the linguistic or the typological
sense) are always open to interpretation; the relation of house to moon
as either sign to referent or type to antitype is necessarily mediated by
an interpretant, which in this case is another sign, another type, another
figure, the tale itself. The disfiguration of the house of fiction occurs
within another and undisfigured house of fiction that doubles its author—
Poe—and *survives*. The paradoxes of Poe's ending suggest that the tale
should be read not as the decentering of narrative by the deferral of
meaning, as Joseph Riddel argues, nor as the simple ontological vision
of transfiguration that John Lynen finds in the story.[16] Rather, figuration, disfiguration, and transfiguration conspire in uneasy alliance at the
end of the tale to show forth the transitional *act* of opening the door.
As in *Pym* and "A Descent into the Maelström," Poe brings us to the
apocalyptic interface, the line of deferral at which vision becomes possible through the veil, the ocean, or the opened door, and leaves us
there. The images that we see there—the white figure, the rainbow, the
moon—remain radically ambiguous, figures of transfiguration that en-
forcedly underscore their own impossibility, yet at the same time seek
to stake out a ground for interpretation.

■

In *William Faulkner: The Yoknapatawpha Country,* Cleanth Brooks is at some pains to link Thomas Sutpen with "the robber barons of the Gilded Age building a fake Renaissance palace on the banks of the Hudson"[17]—with *northern* capitalists, that is, whose phony culture only just masks the naked steel of industrial might. Although in important ways this linkage is simplistic—Sutpen's agrarian capitalism is insistently southern and radically opposed to the industrial capitalism of the North—in another sense the connecting of Sutpen's American dynasty with the northern American Dream establishes an important context for Faulkner's novel and reminds us of Faulkner's immense debt to Hawthorne. For Hawthorne's northern Gothic permeates this novel; the House of Sutpen in the end perhaps owes less to Poe's House of Usher than to Hawthorne's Puritan House of Pyncheon—which, as Maurice Beebe reminds us, was conceived in and developed out of Poe's earlier house.[18] Indeed, if "The Fall of the House of Usher" stands as the seminal work in the strong American tradition of Gothic house-building, *The House of the Seven Gables* gives the American house its most influential form; here, for example, from Hawthorne's preface, is the standard American claim to total ownership that Faulkner echoes in his map inscription:

> The Reader may perhaps choose to assign an actual locality to
> the imaginary events of this narrative. If permitted by the
> historical connection, (which, though slight, was essential to his
> plan,) the Author could very willingly have avoided anything
> of this nature. Not to speak of other objections, it exposes the
> Romance to an inflexible and exceedingly dangerous species
> of criticism, by bringing his fancy-pictures into positive contact
> with the realities of the moment. . . . He trusts not to be con-
> sidered as unpardonably offending, by laying out a street that
> infringes upon nobody's private rights, and appropriating a
> lot of land which had no visible owner, and building a house, of
> materials long in use for constructing castles in the air.[19]

The House of Pyncheon is a "castle in the air" whose existence is threatened apocalyptically not by evil, but by reality; the danger inherent in the "dangerous species of criticism" is that "positive contact with the realities of the moment" would destroy the "fancy-pictures" of the house. If Hawthorne wants here to insist on the imagistic *value* of his house of fiction, however, or its function as a stay against time, he elsewhere places equal stress on its ephemeral nature, its fragility in the face of reality. In chapter 11, for example, the "castle in the air" has become the "airy sphere" of a soap bubble, which Clifford, newly returned from prison, blows out into the street:

> Behold him, scattering airy spheres abroad, from the window into the street! Little, impalpable worlds, were those soap-bubbles, with the big world depicted, in hues bright as imagination, on the nothing of their surface. It was curious to see how the passers-by regarded these brilliant fantasies, as they came floating down, and made the dull atmosphere imaginative, about them. Some stopt to gaze, and perhaps carried a pleasant recollection of the bubbles, onward, as far as the street-corner; some looked angrily upward, as if Clifford wronged them, by setting an image of beauty afloat so near their dusty pathway. A great many put out their fingers, or their walking-sticks, to touch withal, and were perversely gratified, no doubt, when the bubble, with all its pictured earth and sky scene, vanished as if it had never been. (2:171)

Whereas in the preface Hawthorne had been concerned to protect his house of fiction, that "little, impalpable [world] with the big world depicted, in hues bright as imagination, on the nothing of [its] surface," from the destruction that contact with reality would bring, here the destruction of his airy spheres seems inevitable, in any number of senses. Since the surface of these spheres *is* a "nothing," they burst of their own accord soon enough; in the rare cases where a passerby sees and appreciates their brief beauty, the passerby recollects it only "as far as the street-corner"; and "a great many" people find a perverse satisfaction in bursting the bubbles. The house of fiction is to be valued so highly, Hawthorne's dual perspective suggests, precisely because it is ephemeral, and is perversely to be destroyed whenever it aspires to permanence—which is to say, whenever it aspires to replace the "big world" it reflects.[20]

This dual conception of the house of fiction as both valuable and impermanent is adumbrated in Hawthorne's fictional treatment of the House of Pyncheon throughout the novel. The house is portrayed as the iconic double of the Pyncheons themselves, by the iconic mediation of the portrait of its builder, Colonel Pyncheon, that hangs in the parlor. Or to be precise, every male heir of the colonel who resembles him becomes the house's somatic icon and the house his architectural icon, the iconic ground of resemblance being the fateful portrait. At the colonel's death the narrator speaks of the "portrait of Colonel Pyncheon, beneath which sat the original colonel himself" (2:18); but by the time of the novel's main events, the somatic icon is "original" only in a reconstructed temporal sequence. Long since dead, the "original" colonel remains as an absence to be filled by a succession of later Pyncheons—all of whom die mysteriously of Maule's curse.

The mediatory function of the colonel's portrait as the ground of doubling between house and owner is further complicated by an agent of the "enemy," the son of the original owner of the plot whom Colonel Pyncheon had had executed for witchcraft. Matthew Maule, invited to build the House of the Seven Gables for the colonel, installed in the symbolic center of the house—behind the colonel's portrait—a "recess" in which he hid the hieroglyphic deed to the Pyncheons' Indian territory. Hawthorne's early description of the deed and the territory is richly suggestive of both Sutpen's Hundred and Yoknapatawpha County:

> The family of Colonel Pyncheon, at the epoch of his death, seemed destined to as fortunate a permanence as can anywise consist with the inherent instability of human affairs. It might fairly be anticipated that the progress of time would rather increase and ripen their prosperity, than wear away and destroy it. For, not only had his son and heir come into immediate enjoyment of a rich estate, but there was a claim, through an Indian deed, confirmed by a subsequent grant of the General Court, to a vast and as yet unexplored and unmeasured tract of eastern lands. These possessions—for as such they might almost certainly be reckoned—comprised the greater part of what is now known as Waldo County, in the State of Maine, and were more extensive than many a dukedom, or even a reigning prince's territory, on European soil. When the pathless forest, that still covered this wild principality, should give place—as it inevitably must, though perhaps not till ages hence—to the golden fertility of human culture, it would be the source of incalculable wealth to the Pyncheon blood. Had the colonel survived only a few weeks longer, it is probable that his great political influence, and powerful connections, at home and abroad, would have consummated all that was necessary to render the claim available. But, in spite of good Mr. Higginson's congratulatory eloquence, this appeared to be the one thing which Colonel Pyncheon, provident and sagacious as he was, had allowed to go at loose ends. So far as the prospective territory was concerned, he unquestionably died too soon. His son lacked not merely the father's eminent position, but the talent and force of character to achieve it: he could, therefore, effect nothing by dint of political interest, and the bare justice or legality

of the claim was not so apparent, after the colonel's decease, as it had been pronounced in his lifetime. Some connecting link had slipped out of the evidence, and could not anywhere be found. (2:17-18)

Ths missing "link," of course, is the "deed"—which, as the word's root sense suggests, is the textual record of a deed or action without which the action never officially occurred. The loss of the hieroglyphic deed separates the Pyncheons from their primordial paradise as absolutely as the signs of the times separate the expectant from apocalyptic restoration. The Pyncheon family is deeded a new American Eden that Hawthorne slyly associates with "Waldo County": the Pyncheons have taken Emerson at his word and have built their own world. Here, in fact, is the national dream, conceived in slight but crucial revision of Emerson as *commodity,* as "the source of incalculable wealth." Indeed, in the Pyncheon claim we are on precisely the same ground later explored by *Thomas* Pynchon in *Gravity's Rainbow;* the family that Hawthorne wrongly thought extinct when he named his house *is* Thomas Pynchon's family, which Pynchon himself transformed into the Slothrop family in *Gravity's Rainbow,* and in a broader sense into the Calvinist Elect that form the System.[21] The Calvinist Eden for Pynchon, Faulkner, and Hawthorne is no place of personal freedom but a "source of incalculable wealth" and the key to inordinate power over one's fellow human beings. The sole difference between Hawthorne's ostensibly sunny novel and Pynchon's considerably bleaker vision in *Gravity's Rainbow* is that Hawthorne's Pyncheons *lack* the text that would give them dominion over paradise, while Pynchon's System has had it all along. Hawthorne seeks to tame his Calvinists, suppressing his sure knowledge (shared by Pynchon) that they are beyond taming.

Hawthorne in the end does give his new comic society ultimate power over the old order, of course; Judge Pyncheon dies of Maule's curse, and the current member of the Maule clan, Holgrave, gives over his feud with the Pyncheons and marries one, joining the divided families and giving the novel the happy ending Hawthorne so wanted for it. The final enactment of this comic reversal entails the iconic destruction of the house, as Holgrave reveals the secret recess in which his ancestor had hidden the deed:

The artist put his finger on the contrivance to which he had referred. In former days, the effect would probably have been to cause the picture to start forward. But, in so long a period of concealment, the machinery had been eaten through with rust; so that, at Holgrave's pressure, the portrait, frame and

all, tumbled suddenly from its position, and lay face downward
on the floor. A recess in the wall was thus brought to light, in
which an object so covered with a century's dust that it could
not immediately be recognized as a folded sheet of parchment.
Holgrave opened it, and displayed an ancient deed, signed with
the hieroglyphics of several Indian sagamores, and conveying
to Colonel Pyncheon and his heirs, for ever, a vast extent of territory at the eastward.

"This is the very parchment, the attempt to recover which
cost the beautiful Alice Pyncheon her happiness and life," said
the artist, alluding to his legend. "It is what the Pyncheons
sought in vain, while it was valuable; and now that they find the
treasure, it has long been worthless." (2:315-16)

Here the proprietor of the secular apocalypse himself, Colonel
Pyncheon (along with all those of his descendants iconically linked with
him, up to Judge Pyncheon), is revealed as the veil that concealed the
deed, covered the text that might have guaranteed the attainment of
the Calvinist paradise. Removed, the iconic veil lies facedown on the
floor; like the deed itself, it is now an old useless piece of paper, an illusion, an absence to be destroyed by simply exposing it as such.

But to reveal the text and the mediatory icon as absences is to
reveal the house itself as absence, as itself an illusory text or icon that
can be dissipated as easily as the others. Hawthorne, concerned to keep
his ending sunny, is clearly tempted nonetheless to set the House of
Pyncheon on fire, to have his characters, Maule and Pyncheon now
joined, stand around the pyre and rejoice gloatingly at its flames, like
the zealous citizens in Hawthorne's "Earth's Holocaust." But as that
sketch clearly indicates, such a fiery destruction would in fact solve
nothing:

How sad a truth, if true it were, that man's agelong endeavor
for perfection had served only to render him the mockery of the
evil principle, from the fatal circumstances of an error at the
very root of the matter! The heart, the heart,—there was the little
yet boundless sphere wherein existed the original wrong of
which the crime and misery of this outward world were merely
types. Purify that inward sphere, and the many shapes of evil
that haunt the outward, and which now seem almost our only
realities, will turn to shadowy phantoms and vanish of their
own accord; but if we go no deeper than the intellect, and strive,
with merely that feeble instrument, to discern and rectify
what is wrong, our whole accomplishment will be a dream so

unsubstantial that it matters little whether the bonfire, which I
have so faithfully described, were what we choose to call a real
event and a flame that would scorch the finger, or only a phosphoric radiance and a parable of my own brain. (10:403-4)

Earlier, Hawthorne's narrator says that he looked for his own
works "with fatherly interest, but in vain. Too probably they were
changed to vapor by the first action of the heat; at best, I can only
hope that, in their quiet way, they contributed a glimmering spark or
two to the splendor of the evening" (10:397-98). Build your own
world, Emerson advised; but that is the dream of both the writer and
the capitalist, and in demolishing the capitalist's fiction Hawthorne
knows that he is implicitly destroying his own as well. To reveal the
House of the Seven Gables as useless illusion to be discarded is to reveal
The House of the Seven Gables as the same kind of illusion. To supplant the capitalist house of fiction with another revision of the Emersonian dream is implicitly to validate *houses,* even capitalist ones.
Writing from this viewpoint, obviously Hawthorne sees that *all* new
houses must be offered as already and always ripe for destruction—
indeed that he must participate in that destruction himself. Thus in
"Earth's Holocaust" Hawthorne burns up his own books *in* one of
those books; or he imagines the fiery consumption of his and all books
in order to write another book, which again envisions destruction. The
burning of the House of Pyncheon would have been aesthetically a
more satisfying ending to *The House of the Seven Gables* than the
transportation to Judge Pyncheon's summer house, but the issue for
Hawthorne would have remained the same: the permanence or impermanence of fictional houses and the relative value we ascribe to their
survival or destruction. For Hawthorne, the American house of fiction
must continually be destroyed; but the apocalypse can be effective only
in "a phosphoric radiance and a parable" of the writer's brain, which is
to say that one house of fiction is always required to destroy another.
Hawthorne's apocalypse is, in Emerson's phrase, an "apocalypse of the
mind"; for the mind must continually destroy its own inventions if it
is to prevent them from petrifying into dangerous myths, like the myth
of a Calvinist paradise of commodity and power. The uneasy paradox,
at once promising and threatening, is that fictional houses always survive their own destructions. The house of fiction, that is, necessarily
becomes a house of metafiction. [22]

For Hawthorne's narrator, reveling in the formation of the new
comic society in the judge's summer house, this metafictional self-
destruction is ostensibly a move *beyond* fiction, back into society.
But Hawthorne is at once too conscious of the social context of fiction

and too conscious of the fictive ground of society to be satisfied with
that. The failure of Hawthorne's ending is essentially a failure to take
us past the debilitating dichotomy between reality and fiction that
prompts the writer to empty fictions self-consciously out into reality
and to reveal reality as a fiction. Is a *mediation* possible between fiction and reality? Can they be made to work dialectically, in reciprocal
constitution rather than dichotomous deconstruction? If individuals
align themselves with fiction and their society with reality, how can
they become integrated into the society without either losing their fictional identity or reducing the society to illusion? Hawthorne's tentative and severely qualified solution to the problem in *The House of the
Seven Gables* is inadequate, as Hawthorne himself manifestly knew; but
what solution would be adequate? How are American artists to transform their society without fictionalizing it? How can they live in society
without being deformed by it?

■

An entire range of answers to these questions is proposed by Henry
James, the writer from whom I take my chapter title, for James was the
supremely self-conscious—and self-consciously *social*—Hawthornean
ephebe who always insistently directed his explorations of privative
vision back into the issue of the community. The James tale that most
fruitfully charts the transition from Hawthorne back to Faulkner is
"The Jolly Corner," a near-explicit revision of both "The Fall of the
House of Usher" and *The House of the Seven Gables,* in which James
gives form to the sentient spirit of the ancestral house in the ghostly
alter ego of his protagonist, Spencer Brydon. After three nights of stalk-
ing the apparition, it finally "appears" to Brydon in a ray of the rising
sun:

> It was as sharp, the question, as a knife in his side, but the an-
> swer hung fire still and seemed to lose itself in the vague dark-
> ness to which the thin admitted dawn, glimmering archwise
> over the whole outer door, made a semicircular margin, a cold
> silvery nimbus that seemed to play a little as he looked—to
> shift and expand and contract.
> It was as if there had been something within it, protected by
> indistinctness and corresponding in extent with the opaque
> surface behind, the painted panels of the last barrier to his
> escape, of which the key was in his pocket. The indistinctness
> mocked him even while he stared, affected him as somehow
> shrouding or challenging certitude, so that after faltering an in-
> stant on his step he let himself go with the sense that here
> *was* at last something to meet, to touch, to take, to know—

something all unnatural and dreadful, but to advance upon which
was the condition for him either of liberation or of supreme
defeat. The penumbra, dense and dark, was the virtual screen of
a figure which stood in it as still as some image erect in a niche
or as some black-vizored sentinel guarding a treasure. Brydon
was to know afterwards, was to recall and make out, the particular thing he had believed during the rest of his descent. He
saw, in its great grey glimmering margin, the central vagueness
diminish, and he felt it to be taking the very form toward
which, for so many days, the passion of his curiosity had yearned.
It gloomed, it loomed, it was something, it was somebody, the
prodigy of a personal presence.[23]

The "semicircular margin" of light glinting through the arched
window over the door thus becomes at once the medium of vision and
a screen or shroud concealing visionary certitude: the door to self-
knowledge, to which Spencer has the key, but a door that he must
somehow both *pass through* and *see through*. The very attempt to see
his own ghost, to see the apparition of himself as he would have been
had he stayed in America and lived in that house for the thirty-three
years previous is precisely the solipsistic house of fictional reflections
in which he is trapped, and from which he must escape through the
front door; but the ghost he has been pursuing now confronts him
as the door, the veil whose removal would be but one more index
of apocalyptic solipsism. Mirror-gazing, one might say in the spirit
of John T. Irwin's appraisal of Faulkner, is at once solipsism's only
cure and most telling symptom. Spencer Brydon, one assumes, is
trapped.

But James gives his tale a significant twist. Spencer Brydon *is*
trapped, on his own, trapped behind the door of the self that both
promises and blocks escape. But he awakens from the ambiguous sleep
into which he falls not alone, not isolated in the house of fiction, but
in the arms of his companion, Alice Staverton, who, they now discover,
has also seen the apparition, in a dream. Revelatory vision shared is
thus transformed into a *social* medium, a channel by which self-love
flows into other-love; and Alice becomes the potentially redemptive
third, the loving woman who in the sentimentalist fiction brings Spencer out of himself, but more importantly here the vocal presence
that makes possible an interpretive dialogue. James's narrator had
earlier remarked that "they had communities of knowledge, 'their'
knowledge . . . of presences of the other age" (607), and it is toward a
community of knowledge, or at least a communal interpretation of
ambiguous signs, that James's couple works:

"In the cold dim dawn, you say? Well, in the cold dim dawn of this morning I too saw you."

"Saw *me*—?"

"Saw *him,*" said Alice Staverton. "It must have been at the same moment."

He lay an instant taking it in—as if he wished to be quite reasonable. "At the same moment?"

"Yes—in my dream again, the same one I've named to you. He came back to me. Then I knew it for a sign. He had come to you."

At this Brydon raised himself; he had to see her better. She helped him when she understood his movements, and he sat up, steadying himself beside her there on the window-bench and with his right hand grasping her left. "*He* didn't come to me."

"You came to yourself," she beautifully smiled.

"Ah I've come to myself now—thanks to you, dearest. But this brute, this awful face—this brute's a black stranger. He's none of *me,* even as I *might* have been," Brydon sturdily declared.

But she kept the clearness that was like the breath of infallibility. "Isn't the whole point that you'd have been different?"

He almost scowled for it. "As different as *that*—?"

Her look again was more beautiful to him than the things of this world. "Haven't you exactly wanted to know *how* different? So this morning," she said, "you appeared to me."

"Like *him*?"

"A black stranger!"

"Then how did you know it was I?" (639-40)

How indeed? Alice and Spencer continue their discussion for the remaining page or so to the end of the story, without reaching any momentous or final conclusions about the constitution of the self; but one senses that they have found a solution, a redemption, a love that is redemptive not because it takes Spencer *out* of his solipsism but because it composes a dialogical community in which to explore it. The interpretive discourse that closes the tale, with its minute concern for the shifting boundaries of identity ("Saw *me*—?/"Saw *him,*" "*He* didn't come to me"/"You came to yourself," "you appeared to me"/". . . how did you know it was I?"), ultimately turns away from the apocalyptic question of self-revelation to the communal question of establishing a medium of communication, a dialogical bond between self and other that supplants the privative ray of visionary light in which the ghost appeared: that replaces *vision* with the communal power of *words.*

■

This returns us to Faulkner's Gothic House of Sutpen; for if Faulkner, like Poe and Hawthorne, mires his tale in the epistemological ironies of self-consciousness—if he, too, would bridge the differential gap between self and other by the interposition of a pragmatic metafiction that asserts the truth of fiction by denying the fiction of truth[24]—he also follows James in shifting the verbal mode of storytelling from monologue to dialogue. When Miss Rosa explains in chapter 1 that she is telling the story of Sutpen to Quentin so he can turn it into a novel, he thinks, *"only she dont mean that, . . . It's because she wants it told"* (10). But it would be more accurate to say that she wants it not just *told* (she's been telling the story to herself for forty-three years), but *told to someone;* and thematically Quentin is the ideal listener (though Miss Rosa cannot be expected to know this) because he faces precisely the same problem of imprisonment in the flesh, of embattled virginity and love-hate for the father, that Miss Rosa faced in the story she tells. Miss Rosa (like Mr. Compson in the chapters following) repeatedly invokes the town's opinion of Sutpen and the events surrounding him as a kind of tragic chorus whose views represent communal norms; but to that set of norms Faulkner opposes the community of two, established in the speaker-listener locus that is less rigidly prejudicial, more open-ended, more flexible than the town, because it is self-critical, self-revisionary, and therefore always tentative, always in process.

Most significant in this image of storytelling as dialogue is the emphasis Faulkner places on the interactional *complexity* of speaking and listening. Quentin sits in Miss Rosa's office and stares with some disbelief at the "bolt upright" little figure of the old woman, "until at last listening would renege and hearing-sense self-confound and the long-dead object of her impotent yet indomitable frustration would appear, as though by outraged recapitulation evoked, quite inattentive and harmless, out of the biding and dreamy and victorious dust" (7–8). It is when listening "reneges" and hearing-sense "self-confounds" that the ghost of Sutpen appears in the room: an imaginative reconstruction of the long-dead focus of the tale achieved by Miss Rosa's indomitable frustration, which significantly anticipates the novel's supreme reconstruction in chapter 8. It is, however, paradoxically *Quentin's* reconstruction out of *Miss Rosa's* frustration; which is to say that it is the creation of both, or neither. "Her voice would not cease, it would just vanish" (8)—Quentin's wandering attention is troped by the vanishing of a voice, which, however, does not cease, and in that sense does not vanish either, but is transformed into something shared, a common ground between Quentin and Miss Rosa that conjures up Sutpen's ghost; for "the ghost mused with shadowy docility as if it were the voice which he haunted where a more fortunate one would have had a house" (8). The ghost appears when Miss Rosa's voice vanishes, but it is precisely the voice that he inhabits, which continues to stand (though "vanished") as a surrogate house, a fictional or linguistic house. "Then hearing would reconcile and he would seem to listen to two separate Quentins now" (9)—the reconciliation of hearing with speech generates now another ghost, the ghost of Quentin himself, who inhabits Quentin's "hearing-sense" as Sutpen inhabits Miss Rosa's voice, and the internal dialogue between Quentin and his ghost moves toward a paradigm of the narrative mediation established throughout the novel:

> the two separate Quentins now talking to one another in the long silence of notpeople, in notlanguage, like this: *It seems that this demon—his name was Sutpen—(Colonel Sutpen)—Colonel Sutpen. Who came out of nowhere and without warning upon the land with a band of strange niggers and built a plantation— (Tore violently a plantation, Miss Rosa Coldfield says)—tore violently. And married her sister Ellen and begot a son and a daughter which—(Without gentleness begot, Miss Rosa Coldfield says)—without gentleness. Which should have been the jewels of his pride and the shield and comfort of his old age, only— (Only they destroyed him or he destroyed them or something. And died)—and died. Without regret, Miss Rosa Coldfield says— (Save by her) Yes, save by her. (And by Quentin Compson) Yes. And by Quentin Compson.* (9)

This is Quentin in inner dialogue with his own ghost, of course; but the possibility of such dialogue is created by the intense and subverbal dialogue in which he is engaging with Miss Rosa, that intervoice or "long silence of notpeople, in notlanguage," in which the ghosts of both Quentin and Sutpen exist and which in a sense "creates" the ghostly substances of Quentin and Miss Rosa. The mediatory hearing-speech of notpeople in notlanguage becomes Faulkner's central device throughout the novel for establishing a communal mediation between speaker and listener; and as Leroy Searle notes, it is always marked typographically by italics. Paradigmatically, Searle states, this early speech in italics

> cannot be assigned to a single character, even though it represents an individual act of articulation. It arises from listening so deeply (or constantly) that speech need no longer be vocal and is almost spontaneous; yet it is not private thought, but speech

of intense participation, in which the words of others become one's own. In telling a story, it is therefore a unique point of entrance by which the past becomes present as a speaking voice— whose 'owner' is collective.

The duality of this collective hearing-speech is a complex inter-action between the functions of information and motivation, which means that to operate in that intervoice is to understand all information in terms of personal motives and motives as information. Apart from italicized passages of hearing-speech, Quentin remains baffled by Miss Rosa's narration; in italicized speeches he shows evidence of a mediated insight, a communal working-through of what he is hearing that is made possible by the intervocal union or intimacy with the speaker, Miss Rosa. The intervoice of hearing-speech here established as the com-munal mediation between speaker and listener becomes the key that opens the door to knowledge, knowledge of the eternal presence and inaccessibility of the might-have-been that is more true than truth. Faulkner's consistent representation of that intervoice typologically by italics suggests that italicized passages should receive particular atten-tion in our reading of the novel—not at the expense of passages in roman type, of course, but in *contrast* to them. For although in quoted speech represented in roman type all the characters seek understanding by im-posing on the facts more or less inadequate formulae—Miss Rosa's demonizing in chapter 1, Mr. Compson's notions of gentlemanly honor in chapters 2 through 4, Shreve's ironic reductions of love to lust and the South to a B-grade movie—in italicized hearing-speech they operate by what Searle calls "some logic of discovery, that is neither indepen-dent of facts, nor dependent solely upon facts that are manifest." Mr. Compson explicates the self-bound logic of formulization in chapter 4:

They are there, yet something is missing; they are like a chemical formula exhumed along with the letters from that forgotten chest, carefully, the paper old and faded and falling to pieces, the writing faded, almost indecipherable, yet meaningful, familiar in shape and sense, the name and presence of volatile and sentient forces; you bring them together in the propor-tions called for, but nothing happens; you re-read, tedious and intent, poring, making sure that you have forgotten nothing, made no miscalculation; you bring them together again and again nothing happens: just the words, the symbols, the shapes them-selves, shadowy inscrutable and serene, against that turgid back-ground of a horrible and bloody mischancing of human affairs.
(101)

"Just the words, the symbols, the shapes themselves, shadowy inscrutable and serene"—Mr. Compson could be Jacques Derrida, defining the hollowing out of a trace. The ultimate failure in storytelling, the ultimate reduction of stories to hollowed-out formulae, is of course Sutpen's—the outsider in the community who remains an outsider, locked out of communal interaction even with himself, because he refuses to recognize his story *as* his, and so doggedly blocks all response from his listener, whether he is talking to General Compson or himself. In this sense the failure of doubling that Irwin diagnoses in the novel is fundamentally a failure of storytelling, a failure to ground narration in a vital and self-revisionary communal mediation. It is a failure to which Sutpen succumbs monolithically; but Quentin fails too, more complexly, and in an important sense with less reason, for he has at least had the experience of intervocal mediation to work from.

Conversely, then, the centrality of Miss Rosa's italicized chapter in the novel is that it explores and expands the communal intervoice, forges it into a powerful tool for penetrating through the masks of personality to the motivations and frustrations beneath. Chapter 5 is Miss Rosa's counterpart to Quentin's dialogue with his ghost in chapter 1, that "long silence of notpeople, in notlanguage"; indeed, though it lacks attribution to speaker and setting, we may surmise that it is Miss Rosa's intervocal version of the narration to which Quentin intermittently listened in chapter 1: the hearing-speech that takes over, in this instance, when *speech* reneges and *speaking-sense* self-confounds. Searle suggests that "If in the creative metaphor of word and speech, Sutpen is the father of them all as they are enclosed in formulae, Miss Rosa is mother or midwife by which Sutpen may be reborn in the characters' understanding"; but it may in fact be more complicated than that. Miss Rosa as eternal virgin, locked behind *"that veil we call virginity,"* is as imaginatively sterile a mother as Sutpen is a father, precisely because no communion takes place, no mingling of hearing and speech in procreative act. So long as Miss Rosa remains trapped behind her selfhood of demonizing formulae, like Sutpen behind the selfhood of dynastic or millennial formulae, she cannot give birth to understanding; she can only perish and leave behind a confusing memory of her absent words. In chapter 5, brought to imaginative commingling by intervocal mediation, she does indeed become the mother or midwife of understanding, poised at the *"arras-veil before what-is-to-be"* and prepared to *"make the rending gash."* And, significantly, where in chapter 5 she records her failure, stopped by Clytie, to pass through the door to view Bon's dead body, in chapter 9 we see her bursting through the closed door, past Clytie, to find Bon's brother and murderer, Henry Sutpen, achieving the conjunction of intuition ("There's something living in that house. . . . Something living in it. Hidden in it. It has been out there for four years, living hidden in that house" [172]) and confirmation. Shreve's tribute to her in chapter 9 is significant:

> All right. You dont even know about her. Except that she re-
> fused at the last to be a ghost. That after almost fifty years she
> couldn't reconcile herself to letting him lie dead in peace. That
> even after fifty years she not only could get up and go out there
> to finish up what she found she hadn't quite completed, but
> she could find someone to go with her and bust into that locked
> house because instinct or something told her it was not fin-
> ished yet. (362)

Shreve typically reduces Miss Rosa's gesture to bathos, but she has in fact accomplished something: "she refused at the last to be a ghost." And just as Quentin's presence made it possible for her to go out to the house, it was Quentin's presence as *listener* that made it possible for her to achieve the intervocal mediatory vision of rending the arras-veil in chapter 5, and that thus precipitated her decision to stop lurking outside closed doors and march determinedly through. This is why, in fact, Miss Rosa wanted her story not only told, but told *to someone:* only in the interaction of a self-revisionary community can the individual break out of the prisonhouse of selfhood and work toward the recognition of value and truth.

Apart from chapter 5, the most revelatory transition into itali-cized intervoice occurs in chapter 8, where the door between present and past is opened and entered and the truth of Bon's drop of black blood revealed. But here Faulkner introduces a feature for which our discussion of hearing-speech between *characters* will no longer suffice. For the first time in the novel the general narrator, not one of the four characters, shifts into italics, explicitly recording the imaginative merg-ing of Shreve with Quentin and the two boys with Henry and Bon, but implicitly pointing to a larger and more problematic merging as well:

> Shreve ceased again. It was just as well, since he had no listener.
> Perhaps he was aware of it. Then suddenly he had no talker
> either, though possibly he was not aware of this. Because now
> neither of them were there. They were both in Carolina and
> the time was forty-six years ago, and it was not even four now
> but compounded still further, since now both of them were
> Henry Sutpen and both of them were Bon, compounded each
> of both yet either neither, smelling the very smoke which had
> blown and faded away forty-six years ago from the *bivouac*

*fires burning in a pine grove, the gaunt and ragged men sitting
or lying about them. . . . (351)*

In this subtle heightening of Hank Morgan's dream-travel back
in time, complexly linked with his auditor/author M. T., Shreve's loss
of listener and speaker signals the transition into the intervoice of hearing-speech; but now the general narrator is the speaker, which suggests
the establishment of an intervocal community not between character
and character but between *novel and reader.* Faulkner is attempting,
that is, to expand the scope of the mediatory intervoice in order to include his reader in the same exploratory act of narrative interpretation
as his characters, a striking experiment that attempts to solve the narrative dilemma Twain faced in *A Connecticut Yankee* by pushing the
possibility of temporal and figural mediation to its limits. Unprece-
dented as this attempt is in the general narrator's voice so far in the
novel, it is significantly anticipated in the transition from chapter 1 to
chapter 5. For there we find the general narrator either echoing Miss
Rosa's words as she attempts to describe the bodily nature of memory
in chapter 5, or else assimilating her words to those he had used to
describe the narrative situation in chapter 1:

> Her voice would not cease, it would just vanish. There would be
> the dim coffin-smelling gloom sweet and over-sweet with the
> twice-bloomed wistaria against the outer wall by the savage quiet
> September sun impacted distilled and hyperdistilled. . . . (8)

> *Once there was—do you mark how the wistaria, sun-impacted
> on this wall here, distills and penetrates this room as though
> (light-unimpeded) by secret and attritive progress from mote to
> mote of obscurity's myriad components?* (143)

The implication of this seeming approach to intervoice between
the general narrator and Miss Rosa is that the imaginative achievement
of communal hearing-speech is not merely a freak accident restricted
to a specific time and place, but it enters into, and brings speaker and
listener into, meaningful participation in a larger community. If the
general narrator can join in a dialogue of sorts with one of the characters whose narrations he is presenting, then perhaps the very act of
writing a novel is an intervocal act of communal mediation, in which
Faulkner hears-speaks with his characters meaningfully by exploring
the language and stories of the community. And if, by analogy, Quentin
as listener enters into an intervocal dialogue with the novel's reader
(the general narrator's listener), then perhaps the novel is itself the

intervocal ground of mediation, of communal interaction, between Faulkner and the reader. Put this way, of course, it appears that we have come this far in order to prove a truism; but the community's acceptance of this sense of a novel's function *as* a truism returns us to the formal experimentation in the novel by which Faulkner explores and reaffirms that sense. What is truistically asserted in that vision of novelistic function is that fiction stands neither Romantically as the path to truth that reveals society as a pseudo-reality, nor anti-Romantically as the illusion that reveals the illusoriness of all fictions, itself included—but rather as the dialogical bond that makes a society possible, by embodying and intensifying the communal interchange across temporal and moral differences, in which common values are established, challenged, and revised. *Absalom* in this light should be read as the innovatory working out of a poetic that Faulkner expressed in a famous remark in the University of Virginia interviews:

> I think no one individual looks at truth. It blinds you. You look at it and you see one phase of it. Someone else looks at it and sees a slightly awry phase of it. . . . It was . . . thirteen ways of looking at a blackbird. But the truth, I would like to think, comes out that when the reader has read all these thirteen ways of looking [he] has his own fourteenth image of that blackbird which I would like to think is the truth.[25]

Faulkner's fictional analogue to Stevens's poem, then, becomes a novel in which there are four, or thirteen, or an uncountable number of ways of looking at Thomas Sutpen, but the true one emerges from readers' engagements with those ways, from their working through to a version that is not merely idiosyncratic, not merely personal, but the product of their intervocal dialogue with the novel, and through the novel with the larger community.

This conception of *reading* as an intervocal act of communal mediation is in fact anticipated at crucial points in the novel as well: specifically in Quentin's two acts of reading a letter, one from Bon to Judith in chapter 4, and the other from his father about the death and burial of Miss Rosa in chapters 6 and 9. In both cases, the letters are printed in italics, once again signalling the operation of intervoice; and the mediatory function of those letters is made explicit both in the general narrator's remarks on the situations in which the letters are read and in the strategic placement of the letters in the movement of the novel. Bon's letter to Judith is handed to Quentin by his father at the beginning of chapter 4 and not read until the end of the chapter, so that it immediately precedes and sets the stage for Miss Rosa's italicized chapter. And Quentin reads the first half of his father's letter about Miss Rosa's death at the beginning of chapter 6, immediately after her central chapter, but cannot finish it until the very end of the novel, following his incorporation into the reconstructive intervoice of Shreve and the general narrator in chapter 8, and after his memory of the trip out to the Sutpen house and confrontation with Henry in chapter 9. Here, for example, is the account of Quentin's reading of Bon's letter to Judith and the first few lines of that letter:

> Quentin hearing without having to listen as he read the faint
> spidery script not like something impressed upon the paper by
> a once-living hand but like a shadow cast upon it which had
> resolved on the paper the instant before he looked at it and
> which might fade, vanish, at any instant while he still read:
> the dead tongue speaking after the four years and then after al-
> most fifty more, gentle sardonic whimsical and incurably pes-
> simistic, without date or salutation or signature:
>
> *You will notice how I insult neither of us by claiming this to*
> *be a voice from the defeated even, let alone from the dead. In*
> *fact, if I were a philosopher I should deduce and derive a curious*
> *and apt commentary on the times and augur of the future from*
> *this letter which you now hold in your hands— . . .* (129)

Hearing without having to listen, Quentin is already wrapped up in a hearing-speech with his father when he begins to read; and the undated letter becomes in his reading not a textual record of voice but an actual living voice, "speaking after the four years and then after almost fifty more," a voice that can vanish as his father's or Miss Rosa's voice vanishes into the intervoice of hearing-speech. It is not, Bon himself insists, a letter from the dead, even though for Judith it soon becomes that; even though for Quentin almost fifty years later it certainly is that; and even though for Faulkner's readers it is the voice of the never-lived. But in the context of Faulkner's intervocal novel, Bon is absolutely right to insist that the voice is not dead, for the "I" who augurs of the future and the "you" who holds the letter in hand are at once Bon, Mr. Compson, and Faulkner, and Judith, Quentin, and Faulkner's reader. By the sheer power of "literality" in letters, Faulkner conflates the two acts of writing (his and Bon's) with the three acts of reading (Judith's, Quentin's, and the reader's) into a single communal dialogue in which the "now" of *"this letter which you now hold in your hands"* is quite literally *now,* an eternal present that does not attempt to spatialize but communalizes time, establishes a dialogue across history that asserts the continuity of the most compelling concerns of human endeavor and the values that inform them, even as it recognizes the necessary discontinuities implicit in ongoing time.

The novel's second letter occupies an even more decisive position in the narrative's structure, framing as it does the second half of the novel and bringing the problematic ninth chapter to a guardedly optimistic close. The first half of the letter, which Quentin reads in chapter 6, focuses entirely on the isolate soul, Miss Rosa as a discrete self or subject for whom death is the ultimate alienation:

> *My dear son,*
> *Miss Rosa Coldfield was buried yesterday. She remained in the coma for almost two weeks and two days ago she died without regaining consciousness and without pain they say, and whatever they mean by that since it has always seemed to me that the only painless death must be that which takes the intelligence by violent surprise and from the rear so to speak, since if death be anything at all beyond a brief and peculiar emotional state of the bereaved it must be a brief and likewise peculiar state of the subject as well. And if aught can be more painful to any intelligence above that of a child or an idiot than a slow and gradual confronting with that which over a long period of bewilderment and dread it has been taught to regard as an irrevocable and unplumbable finality, I do not know it. And if there can be either access of comfort or cessation of pain in the ultimate escape from a stubborn and amazed outrage which over a period of forty-three years has been companionship and bread and fire and all, I do not know that either—* (173-74)

Quentin stops reading here, and for the next four chapters, deep into the cold night of his joint narration with Shreve, leaves the letter on the table before him like a partially opened door, looking at it from time to time, weighing in his mind whether he is yet ready to open it: "the rectangle of paper folded across the middle and now open, three quarters open, whose bulk had raised half itself by the leverage of the old crease in weightless and paradoxical levitation, lying at such an angle that he could not possibly have read it, deciphered it, even without this added distortion" (217). It is not until the end of chapter 9, after Shreve's and his mediatory reconstruction of the past has degenerated back into mutual misunderstanding, after Quentin and Shreve have once again become isolate, Shreve sardonic, Quentin sullen, and both locked into their respective persons, that Quentin can at last make out the words:

> Quentin did not answer, staring at the window; then he could not tell if it was the actual window or the window's pale rectan-

gle upon his eyelids, though after a moment it began to emerge. It began to take shape in its same curious, light, gravity-defying attitude—the once-folded sheet out of the wistaria Mississippi summer, the cigar smell, the random blowing of the fire-flies. "The South," Shreve said. "The South. Jesus. No wonder you all outlive yourselves by years and years and years." It was becoming quite distinct; he would be able to decipher the words soon, in a moment; even almost now, now, now.

"I am older at twenty than a lot of people who have died," Quentin said.

"And more people have died than have been twenty-one," Shreve said. Now he (Quentin) could read it, could finish it—the sloped whimsical ironic hand out of Mississippi attenuated, into the iron snow:

—or perhaps there is. Surely it can harm no one to believe that perhaps she has escaped not at all the privilege of being outraged and amazed and of not forgiving but on the contrary has herself gained that place or bourne where the objects of the outrage and of the commiseration also are no longer ghosts but are actual people to be actual recipients of the hatred and the pity. It will do no harm to hope—You see I have written hope, not think. So let it be hope.—that the one cannot escape the censure which no doubt he deserves, that the other no longer lack the commiseration which let us hope (while we are hoping) that they have longed for, if only for the reason that they are about to receive it whether they will or no. The weather was beautiful though cold and they had to use picks to break the earth for the grave yet in one of the deeper clods I saw a redworm doubtless alive when the clod was thrown up though by afternoon it was frozen again. (377)

Quentin does not actually pick up the letter, this description implies; instead, he sees it reflected in the window until the partially opened door of the letter *becomes* a window, the opaque repelling surface of the paper becoming transparent to his gaze and revealing the words to him. It has taken him an entire winter's evening to reach the "now" when he might finish the letter; the imaginative effort of working through the Sutpen story with Shreve has now finally enabled him to "decipher" the remaining portion of the letter without picking it up. And here the divergence of roman and italic type becomes most marked. For as the quoted speech of the two boys continues to reflect their alienation from each other—their retreat out of the intervocal "marriage" of chapter 8 back into their disjoined selves, a retreat that intensifies almost to the breaking point after the letter—the letter itself directs the reader past their alienation to a mediatory vision of community. The "place or bourne" at which Mr. Compson, with gentle irony, imagines Miss Rosa arriving is the afterlife, of course, that place beyond time where all the dead are no longer ghosts but living presences again; but in the expanding perspective set up by the "literality" of the letter, it is no afterlife at all, no time out of time, but the novel itself, the complex interweaving of all those voices not as ghostly records of once-living beings but as actual living voices, participating in the intervocal community evoked by the novel, into which Faulkner's reader is invited along with the rest.

These last few pages of the novel, then, proceed by a significant alternation of divisive alienation—Quentin from Shreve, Quentin from himself, Quentin from the South—and communal integration; and if the novel ends on an alienative note, Quentin's anguished denial of his hatred for the South, that alienation must be read in the overall context of a novel that as house of fiction insistently seeks to open its closed doors to the intervoices of community. Indeed, in this sense Clytie's apocalyptic destruction of the house by fire constitutes less a metafictional disfiguration of figure, as in Hawthorne and Poe, than a transformation of fiction into communal mediation by the burning down of doors. The burning of the House of Sutpen, in effect, ritually enacts Miss Rosa's victory over it by reducing its doors, behind which she lived most of her mental life, to ashes.

The image of Miss Rosa's victory over death is of course severely attenuated—the living redworm dies by the afternoon—but that very attenuation becomes the key to her victory, since for Faulkner one conquers time not by stopping it in a heavenly present, but by integrating oneself into the flux and rendering that integration and that flux meaningful by participating in a shared voice. In this sense Faulkner's solution to the alienation implicit in the idea of doubling marks an imaginative step past the ironies of Hawthorne and Poe. For his novel directs the reader to open the door not onto the absence of a dusty and obsolete text, which must be replaced by another text that will in turn become obsolete, as in *The House of the Seven Gables,* nor onto a problematic figure for transfiguration that as figure decreases itself, as in "The Fall of the House of Usher," but on *language*—a language shared by a community and therefore that both explores and partakes of the community's common values and common concerns. For Faulkner, language becomes potentially redemptive not as hieroglyphic records of actions, nor as transcendental images that point beyond themselves to truth, but as voice, caught up in the flux of time and engaged in the activity of maintaining and revising a community.

SEVEN

THE RITUAL ICON

I was angry with my friend;
I told my wrath, my wrath did end.
I was angry with my foe:
I told it not, my wrath did grow.

And I waterd it in fears,
Night & morning with my tears:
And I sunned it with smiles,
And with soft deceitful wiles.

And it grew both day and night.
Till it bore an apple bright.
And my foe beheld it shine,
And he knew that it was mine.

And into my garden stole,
When the night had veild the pole;
In the morning glad I see;
My foe outstretchd beneath the tree.
—William Blake, "A Poison Tree"

Nathaniel Hawthorne realized, as have so many American writers after
him, that the structure most in need of apocalyptic destruction was not
the earth, not human existence, but the creations of his own imagination, his *fictions,* which obscured social realities even in revealing them.
Fictions are at once the primary vehicles and the primary targets of
destruction: one fiction is needed to destroy another, and yet a third
to destroy that. Fictions harden into realities, or versions of reality

that deaden our vision to what is really out there, and so must be under-mined and dismantled. "I was beginning to lose the sense of what kind of world it was," Miles Coverdale complains in *The Blithedale Romance,* "among innumerable schemes of what it might or ought to be. It was impossible, situated as we were, not to imbibe the idea that everything in nature and human existence was fluid, or fast becoming so; that the crust of the earth in many places was broken and its whole surface portentously upheaving; that it was a day of crisis, and that we our-selves were in the critical vortex. Our great globe floated in the atmo-sphere of infinite space like an unsubstantial bubble."[1]

Coverdale finds himself, along with the other Blithedalers, "situated" by millennial schemes, by fictions of flux and transition that so distort phenomenal reality as to make it seem that the world is dissolving into apocalyptic chaos—that it *is* a day of crisis. Coverdale plainly wants to say that it is not a day of crisis, but thus situated by fictions of flux he is at a loss to say just what the world *is* like. "I was beginning to lose the sense of what kind of world it was," he says, implying with his definite article (*"the* sense") that what is progres-sively and probably irrevocably being lost in the influx of apocalyptic fictions is reality itself—but at the same time, by the very awareness of that loss, he also reveals that "reality" as a mere mental construct of primordiality or originality. It is a fiction of transcendental sta-bility that is apocalyptically destroyed by a fiction of flux, by a "criti-cal vortex" that sucks illusions of mundane reality down into it like Poe's Maelström—that reduces the "great globe" itself to a fiction, an "airy sphere" that *looks* like the world but in fact, as the soap-bubble scene from *The House of the Seven Gables* reminds us, only reflects reality on the "nothing" of its surface—a reflection that *constitutes* reality but in its nothingness also undermines the constitution.

Coverdale is portrayed as a representative of the old stable "sense," the old and unchallenged fiction of stability hardened into habit and custom in the town; and his solution to the upheaval of his "sense of what kind of world it was" *is* typically to retreat back to town. But this is a tenuous solution at best; once the illusion of reality is dissolved, there is no going back. Indeed, Coverdale's imagination of his choices is severely limiting; if the progressive loss of one's sense of reality reveals it for a traditionalist fiction, then one is forced to choose between equally undesirable alternatives: self-delusion in a willed acceptance of the traditionalist fiction as reality, or self-dissolution in a surrender to the radical fiction of flux. In either case, reality remains unknowable; the choice is between fictional *constitutions* of reality that are implicitly eschatological: is social reality to be construed as an image of an eternal and unchanging paradise or as a transitional chaos?

As Faulkner's treatment of communal mediations across time suggests, of course, this is reductive; social reality has a historical otherness that resists fictional reconstitution but that can only be vitalized by a constant dialogical interchange whose impact *is* precisely to reconstitute society. Still, Hawthorne's sense of the fictional choices available for the reconstitution of society, however circumscribed those choices are by society's resistance to radical change, is acute. To effect change, does one imagine a paradise, in so doing projecting an image of stability that resembles the traditionalist model one seeks to overthrow and that therefore implicitly negates the proposed transformation? Or does one imagine a state of transition that, because it is "grounded" in an image of flux, may in fact (as conservatives fear) precipitate the disintegration of all social order without a coherent model by which to reconstitute it? The problems of fiction and reality and of change and conservation for the constitution (and constant reconstitution) of a society are central American concerns that I want to explore at some length in this last chapter. Specifically, I want to approach these problems through an examination of an image that is at once fictional and a real communal act and is thus an important mediator across the fiction/reality opposition: the ritual icon of sacrifice, one of mankind's oldest methods for maintaining a community. As a pathway to this image, consider for a moment Hawthorne's literary pre-text for the "great globe" allusion, Prospero's famous speech from *The Tempest*:

> Our revels now are ended. These our actors
> (As I foretold you) were all spirits, and
> Are melted into air, into thin air,
> And like the baseless fabric of this vision,
> The cloud-capp'd tow'rs, the gorgeous palaces,
> The solemn temples, the great globe itself,
> Yea, all which it inherit, shall dissolve,
> And like this insubstantial pageant faded
> Leave not a rack behind. We are such stuff
> As dreams are made on; and our little life
> Is rounded with a sleep.[2]

Shakespeare's metadrama, like Hawthorne's metafiction, destroys visions with vision and makes the destroyed vision trope the inevitable end of the destroyer as well. But like Bon's "*now*" in the letter to Judith, "this vision" in Shakespeare's text possesses a literality that militates against destruction, since the text's ability to bridge the temporal gap between the vision's writing (and performing) and its reception by reader or viewer in an important sense guarantees its survival. "This vision" is Prospero's masque, the play that contains the masque, as well as the worldly existence that contains the play; but the hierarchical ordering of these containings is rendered significantly ambiguous by Shakespeare's pun in "the great globe." Which container are we to privilege: the masque or Prospero's words about the masque? The Globe Theatre or Shakespeare's written text? The planetary globe or the globy bubble of fiction? Does the end of the play trope the end of the world? Or does our ability to speak of "this vision" in a literal "now" make the world's survival trope the survival of the text?

What is at issue here is creators' attempt to define themselves by their relation not only to their creations but to *the* creation—and specifically by the relation between their desire for permanence in art and their perception of impermanence in the world. If the work of art can be made to stand as the artist's double, will its survival guarantee the artist's survival beyond death? Or will the artist's mortality ensure the impermanence of the work of art? And if the artistic creation is a dim analogue of God's creation, does the artist thereby become analogically a god, or does his or her mortality require the apocalyptic dissolution of God's creation as well? The artistic triad word-world-wordsmith, in which each complexly doubles the other two, is grounded in—and constitutes a self-critical exploration of—the analogy between artist and God, in which the power to which the artist aspires is precisely God's power over time and space. If the artist could exist as God does outside time and space, he or she could control both the temporal and the spatial movement of "differance"—could subjugate both deferral and diacrisis—and so bring on the end on his or her own terms.

Probably the most radical American attempt to come to grips with this problem is Poe's "The Masque of the Red Death," which takes on Shakespeare's *The Tempest* directly in order to confront the ultimacy of apocalyptic doubling, from which Shakespeare in the end backed away.[3] In both works a Prospero, the name linking each to a prophetic hope (*pro,* before, *spero,* to hope or look forward to), converts a retreat from world to mind-image into a stay *against* the world, expanding interiority-as-absence into a presence that would *contain* the world and so reduce it to the terms of the artist's creation. God created the world, in which death and contagion (Poe) and sinister, murderous political plots (Shakespeare) prevail; Prospero creates the castellated abbey (Poe) and the island (Shakespeare) as *new worlds* of imagination that incorporate and correct the old world of death. The "masque" in both worlds thus becomes in an important sense Prospero's double, the introjected image of self that expands to encompass and transform all otherness.

And, indeed, in Shakespeare this Romantic apocalypse (a retrospective but accurate appellation) achieves a measure of success: Prospero brings the old political society to his island in microcosm, he integrates it into the island's magic, and when at last he has that world entirely in his power and might destroy it at will, he realizes that it doesn't need destroying. He has converted it into an image of himself; the "other" from which he was originally split off has become his double, thus enabling his triumphant return.

In another sense, however, Prospero has not succeeded. If of his two worlds, Milan and the island, one is rightfully his own but now is alienated, and the other was alien but is now his own, he stands to Caliban precisely as Antonio stands to him: as usurper. Caliban is in fact the key to the play in this sense, for he is at once the rightful owner of the island and the one character in the play not transformed into an image of Prospero. By stealing the island from Caliban and converting its otherness to an image of self, Prospero essentially made it a transformative icon, a created double that would mediate between his desire and the alienated dukedom in Milan. Caliban, like Ariel, becomes an instrument of Prospero's transformative will—but not like Ariel a willing one. When properties change hands at the end of the play, then, it becomes crucial to know what will happen after Caliban regains control of the island; this in effect decides whether the "great globe" will dissolve, for in the end the island becomes the "world" that is left behind by Prospero's art. Prospero demonstrates his power over the island first, and through the island over Milan. But what is to become of the island after Prospero's departure? What is the extent of art's influence over nature? If Caliban is "a devil, a born devil, on whose nature / Nurture can never stick" (4.1.188-89), what good has Prospero's nurture been? It is uncertainty about this question that makes Prospero uneasy throughout the last two acts of the play, but Shakespeare never quite confronts the problem directly. In act 5, Prospero recognizes in Caliban a split-off image of self ("this thing of darkness I / Acknowledge mine" [5.1.275-76]), but the Prospero-Caliban doubling is not developed, and Caliban's single allusion to the possibility is entirely inadequate: "I'll be wise hereafter, / And seek for grace" (5.1.295-96). If he means this, and if Shakespeare means him to mean it, his transformation into a *true* double of Prospero (the reintegration of the "splinter," that which was split off) is not sufficiently motivated; if it is ironic, then Prospero's art in the end has failed, but we cannot be sure how or why it has failed.

This is precisely where Poe picks up the story. For in "The Masque of the Red Death," Caliban is Prospero's double from his first appearance, and the ground of resemblance is precisely the masque from which he has ostensibly been split off:

In an assembly of phantasms such as I have painted, it may well be supposed that no ordinary appearance could have excited such sensation. In truth the masquerade license of the night was nearly unlimited; but the figure in question had out-Heroded Herod, and gone beyond the bounds of even the prince's indefinite decorum. There are chords in the hearts of the most reckless which cannot be touched without emotion. Even with the utterly lost, to whom life and death are equally jests, there are matters of which no jest can be made. The whole company, indeed, seemed now deeply to feel that in the costume and bearing of the stranger neither wit nor propriety existed. The figure was tall and gaunt, and shrouded from head to foot in the habiliments of the grave. The mask which concealed the visage was made so nearly to resemble the countenance of a stiffened corpse that the closest scrutiny must have had difficulty in detecting the cheat. And yet all this might have been endured, if not approved, by the mad revellers around. But the mummer had gone so far as to assume the type of the Red Death. His vesture was dabbled in *blood*—and his broad brow, with all the features of the face, was besprinkled with the scarlet horror.[4]

Prospero here seeks to "mask" the Red Death not by covering it up but by locking it outside and by turning the mask that now remains on the *inside* into a "masque," an arabesque dance in which the specter of death is transformed by the visionary imagination into images of life: the seven-room suite that marks off the seven ages of man, the mad revel of the dance. Indeed, for Prospero there is no horror in the transformed *image* of the Red Death: his seventh room is itself decorated in the red and black that figure the Red Death, which suggests that the Red Death mummer out-Herods Herod not simply by reminding the revelers of what they are fleeing but by revealing in the mask/masque itself the *reality* of the Red Death. "His vesture was dabbled in *blood*"— not blood transformed imagistically into blood-red decor or the flickering of lamps through blood-red panes, but *actual* blood, "the scarlet horror."

The word-world-wordsmith triad, that is, here becomes masque-mask-Prospero, in which the multiple doublings all contribute to the revelation that the imagistic inversion by which Prospero banished death to the outside, and expanded the mask as inside into an arabesque masque, has failed. The masque does mask the void, as is clear when Prospero stabs it and it collapses to the floor, empty, a *mere* mask. The mask of the Red Death mummer is the split-off image of death, the frightening image of self that Prospero had sought to banish into otherness; the masque, then, is the doubled image of death, death imagistically controlled by transformation into a creation of the artistic imagination. Prospero's retreat into the castle is an act that might be called "eschatological splitting," in which the image of self that horrifies is split off in order that one might live (forever, in the orthodox apocalyptic imagination) with doubled and redoubled images of the self that pleases.

Something like this is the vision Shakespeare gives his Prospero as well; but from Poe's point of view Shakespeare is unwilling to take the ultimate step and recognize in Caliban the crucial and self-destructive mediator between Prospero and his masque. For Prospero the masque is a rather tiresome display of his powers: "I must / Bestow upon the eyes of this young couple / Some vanity of mine art. It is my promise, / And they expect it from me" (4.1.39-42), and when thoughts of Caliban recall him to his duties as lord of the island, he breaks it off. But this denigration of the masque and of Caliban both—the one to a mere vanity, the other to a mere subject—obscures the important analogy by which the entire action of the play is Prospero's masque (as the play is Shakespeare's masque) and, as such, is no mere vanity but a deadly serious attempt to transform an alien reality into an image of self. By the same anaology, Caliban is no mere subject but the splinter that *remains* a splinter, remains alienated from the artist and yet at the same time doubles the artist clearly enough to reveal the inescapable otherness of his own self-image. The identification of Prospero, masque, and death mask in Poe's tale ultimately unmasks the void that underlies the human vision of self-transformation. The expansion of mind into a presence that will encompass and transform the world stands revealed as a futile effort to cover up the deathly absence that remains inside, a futile effort to incorporate otherness into self. Alienated death reappears inside and reveals the interiority of self as alien also. The Red Death mummer doubles Prospero; but it is a dead mirror, as it were, a mirror that reflects neither Prospero's true gigantic self, as in Emerson's *Nature,* nor his future self, as in Poe's *Pym,* nor even his present self, but a blank. And since Prospero reflects that blank back to the mummer, since all in this story are masked in the same way, by costumes and by their bodies—those "rudimental coverings" that Poe speaks of in his cosmological writings—the doubling in this story sets up an endless replication of images whose end is madness.

This is a monstrous impasse—an impasse that stops the apocalypse dead, for it denies the possibility of a meaningful unveiling. What happens when one draws back the curtain, removes the mask, opens the door, and sees the image of self behind—but the image is blank, and recedes in blank reflections of reflections into infinity? A meaningful self-image is essential to the apocalypse, but this is precisely what Poe will not give Prospero. It is, of course, possible to thematize the story by analogy with Poe's other works—"The Colloquy of Monos and Una," for example, with its explication of the transition from death to the life beyond, or "Mesmeric Revelation," with its mesmeric prolepsis of material transformation. But "The Masque of the Red Death" gives us none of that, and indeed other tales still reveal the pitfalls of such thematization. For instance, "The Conversation of Eiros and Charmion," Poe's most explicitly apocalyptic angelic colloquy, moves from Aidenn to "Thus ended all" (4:8), and "The Facts in the Case of M. Valdemar" moves from the mesmeric revelation to the instantaneous decomposition of Valdemar's frame into "a nearly liquid mass of loathsome—of detestable putridity" (6:166). *That* is what remains: not heaven, but a loathsome absence.

Significantly, the key act of (self-)recognition for Prospero is the act of murder, specifically a ritual murder or sacrifice in which he seeks to protect his enclave from outside contagion (physical and mental) by eliminating an image of the undesirable. Even more significantly, it fails: fails not to reveal Prospero to himself, but to consolidate his community against the external threat, for his conception of that attempted consolidation was based on a false sense of self. Prospero thought he was a *person;* he thought his courtiers were people too; but in the ritual act of sacrifice he discovers in the mummer's blank reflection the absence of self and is killed by the very attempt to kill the blank self-image.

The ritual icon of sacrifice is an issue of some consequence to my discussion, of course, for in it culturally lie the two most persistent images of apocalypse: the vision of the remnant, in which the dross is sacrificed in order that it be split off and God's true people be revealed from behind its obscuring veil; and Augustine's internalized vision of ethical growth, in which the old self is sacrificed not to split it off but to bring it to the attention of the new self, that it might be recognized, assimilated, and subjugated. The definitive sacrifice biblically, of course, was Christ's death on the cross: Jesus died "for our sins," as the phrase goes. But what does that mean? Jesus died both *as God* and *as mankind's sin,* which is to say that mankind sacrificed both a divine other and a human self, but in so doing became one with the other and alien to the self. This crisscrossing of identifications muddies the waters of dogmatic interpretations considerably; for it can be argued equally reasonably (and with equal scriptural warrant—the arguments for both sides are contained in chapters 6–8 of Paul's epistle to the Romans) that sin was always foreign to human beings and was simply banished forever from their makeup in Christ's sacrificial death, or that sin is an inextricable part of human nature and was *conquered* but not banished in Christ's death. The former interpretation sees in Jesus's death-as-sin the destruction of the other that was deceitfully masquerading as self; the latter sees in it the defeat of the sinful self by the divine other, a defeat that stands as an iconic paradigm for ethical emulation. If in the former interpretation the iconic ritual of sacrifice becomes an act of what I have called *eschatological splitting* (salvation instantly guaranteed by the splitting off of sin in conversion), in the latter it becomes an act of *ethical doubling,* since it effects no radical permanent change, but simply provides the weapons for continuing the struggle against one's own sin.

Eschatological splitting and ethical doubling are essentially thematizations of the self-other conflict by means of the organizing image or theme of sacrifice. Much theological debate constitutes an attempt to determine which thematic reduction is "correct," scriptural, more useful, or more dignified. Jacques Ellul's book *Apocalypse: The Book of Revelation,* for example, is an extended attempt to reduce the apocalypse to ethical doubling; René Girard undertakes much the same reduction with the ritual of sacrifice in *Violence and the Sacred.*[5] Ethical doubling tends in fact to be the thematization of the conflict preferred by what Frank Kermode calls skeptical clerics;[6] it is intellectually more tenable because less simplistically repressive than eschatological splitting, since it does not require the *denial* of the self-image and so does not prompt its reification in the form of persecution. But it is equally dualistic, and the desired result of both is mastery; if eschatological splitting in its extreme form produced the Jewish holocaust, ethical doubling in an extreme form enforced the Jonestown suicides.

Blake, in fact, would call both thematizations of iconic sacrifice "negations," dualisms in which opposites (here good and evil selves) are conceived as mutually exclusive. The evil self mastered through ethical doubling *remains* evil, and in effect is split off from the good self internally. But Blake's notion of "contraries," by which he at once opposes and integrates negations, is equally (though more complexly) a thematization of the self-other problem. Rejecting the notion of sacrifice as a Druidic version of war and rape, Blake substituted for it an apocalyptic theme in which the sacrificial victim circumvents the sacrifice by *reseeing* the self-other relation, perceiving in the divine or communal authority that prescribes sacrifice no external force but a fallen projection of self that, so perceived, simply disappears.

That Blake was apparently aware of the thematic reduction implicit in his apocalyptic vision suggests a tentative solution to the endless labyrinths of self-other reflections: rather than deferring themes indefinitely, one thematizes, but thematizes transparently, revealing *through* the theme the labyrinth on which it is based. Indeed such a solution, which I have been suggesting is the characteristic American solution, is apparently what Blake is attempting in the gnomic lyric from *Songs of Experience,* "A Poison Tree," that I have taken as this chapter's epigraph. What the poem seems to be saying thematically is that God, the creator of the garden, is mankind's foe—that God, not Satan, caused Adam and Eve to eat the apple. Reduced to that theme, the poem renders Blake's adaptation of the Gnostic revisionary exegesis of the Fall—or, indeed, if the garden is of Gethsemane and the tree is the cross, of the Crucifixion as well—as follows: God killed his own son, like a Druidic priest a human sacrifice. What this reading ignores, however, is that the poem nowhere makes explicit the identification of the speaker with God. Suppose it is instead Los, Blake's visionary poet-blacksmith; then the wrath is a holy wrath, an apocalyptic wrath directed against the false projection of God that must be destroyed. The growing of a poison tree in this context might then be assimilated to Los's forging of bodies for Urizen or for the spectrous dead, or to the setting of the Limits of Contraction, suggestively called the Limit of Adam (friend?) and the Limit of Satan (foe?). Los's creation of bodies is redemptive in Blake's symbolism because it consolidates error, giving form to vague misperception; but the recipients of the bodies conceive it as a death, an imprisonment, just as Los conceives the con- strictions of Urizenic law as imprisonment.

This is all to say, of course, that the poem transparently con- tains its own dethematization; it reveals its own inherent congruence with what it seeks to attack. But in a sense this is inescapable. Litera- ture is always necessarily the thematic concretion of abstract language: Blake's poem insists by the use of images (garden, tree, apple) that the problem is not simply one of abstract dramatic function (friend, foe), but is precisely thematic. What *is* the relation of God to human beings? To write a poem or a fiction about the avoidance of thematization is inevitably to reduce that avoidance to a theme. The decisive question, then, becomes: At what point or in what form is thematization justified? It is always a necessary simplification—but how and when is it necessary?

■

An excellent American illustration of the dilemma is Poe's most famous doubling tale, "William Wilson," which entirely defers thematization for its *characters* while offering the reader tentative themes with which to think through the problem. By the end of the tale, the narrator has killed off his double and discovered to his horror not only that he has killed himself but that the two self-images, the two doubles, have be- come indistinguishable in death:

But what human language can adequately portray *that* astonishment, *that* horror which possessed me at the spectacle then presented to view? The brief moment in which I averted my eyes had been sufficient to produce, apparently, a material change in the arrangements at the upper or farther end of the room. A large mirror,—so at first it seemed to me in my confusion—now stood where none had been perceptible before; and, as I stepped up to it in extremity of terror, mine own image, but with features all pale and dabbled with blood, advanced to meet me with a feeble and tottering gait.

Thus it appeared, I say, but was not. It was my antagonist—it was Wilson, who then stood before me in the agonies of his dissolution. His mask and cloak lay, where he had thrown them, upon the floor. Not a thread in all his raiment—not a line in all the marked and singular lineaments of his face which was not, in the most absolute identity, *mine own!*

It was Wilson; but he spoke no longer in a whisper, and I could have fancied that I myself was speaking while he said:

"You have conquered, and I yield. Yet, henceforth art thou also dead—dead to the World, to Heaven and to Hope! In me didst thou exist—and, in my death, see by this image, which is thine own, how utterly thou hast murdered thyself."
(3:324-25)

Poe moves bravely past the facile themes offered by allegory: Wilson kills his conscience and so is barred entrance into heaven. Such an interpretation will not work here, however, because this ending leaves us no certainty as to who has killed whom; the dying double speaks with the voice of the surviving double, and by the potentially infinite reflections of both mirror-image and echo the two become indistinguishable: not one but not two either. "Not a thread in all his raiment—not a line in all the marked and singular lineaments of his face which was not, even in the most absolute identity, *mine own!*" If the image, by the negation of negation, is not not-other, is it identical with the self? Poe invokes the metaphorical duplicity of "identity" to call the identity of the speaker into question: the speaker is "identified" both by his difference from the dying double (he kills the double in order to establish a separate identity) and by his sameness with the double (in the iconic ritual of sacrifice, he recognizes that he *is* the other, and yet is not).

The blankness of the doubled image is not so explicit here as it was in "The Masque of the Red Death," but it is significant that the narrator never tells us that the other Wilson *is* his double—until, of course, the problematic self-sacrifice at the end, when it appears that the double is not after all a double, but himself. The narrator views his double repeatedly throughout the story, but it is not until he kills him (apparently) that he sees in the other's face his own exact likeness. The only time he comes close to revealing (or perceiving) the other's image of himself is in the nocturnal visitation that precipitates his departure from the school:

> Close curtains were around it, which, in the prosecution of my plan, I slowly and quietly withdrew, when the bright rays fell vividly upon the sleeper, and my eyes, at the same moment, upon his countenance. I looked;—and a numbness, an iciness of feeling instantly pervaded my frame. My breast heaved, my knees tottered, my whole spirit became possessed with an objectless yet intolerable horror. Gasping for breath, I lowered the lamp in still nearer proximity to the face. Were these—*these* the lineaments of William Wilson? I saw, indeed, that they were his, but I shook as if with a fit of the ague in fancying that they were not. What *was* there about them to confound me in this manner? I gazed;—while my brain reeled with a multitude of incoherent thoughts. Not thus he appeared—assuredly not *thus*— in the vivacity of his waking hours. The same name! the same contour of person! the very same day of arrival at the academy! And then his dogged and meaningless imitation of my gait, my voice, my habits, and my manner! Was it, in truth, within the bounds of human possibility, that *what I now saw* was the result, merely, of the habitual practice of this sarcastic imitation? Awestricken, and with a creeping shudder, I extinguished the lamp, passed silently from the chamber, and left, at once, the halls of that old academy, never to enter them again. (3:312-13)

What *does* he see? He tells us only by negation: "Not thus he appeared—assuredly not *thus*—in the vivacity of his waking hours." Reading back from the end of the tale, we can construe his hints about the same name, the same contour, and so forth, to mean that the narrator does see his own image in Wilson's face; but that is not what he says, and indeed it would not make much sense. If Wilson is so like him in the daylight, why should he be so horrified at what he sees in the night? Why can he not describe what he sees? His retreat into the linguistic capitulation of proforms—"thus" and "these"—signals his ability only to *point,* not to articulate. "Were these—*these* the lineaments of William Wilson?" If he sees his own image as in a mirror, there is no question; the features are of course those of William Wilson, of both

William Wilsons, self and other. No, what the narrator sees in the double's face is something alien: a blankness like what Prospero saw in the Red Death mummer, or, since Wilson seems to be some sort of shape-shifter, the features of a demon or angel, a golem, a grotesque from outside human experience. "Was it, in truth, within the bounds of human possibility, that *what I now saw* was the result, merely, of the habitual practice of this sarcastic imitation?" *No,* the question implies: it is without the bounds of human possibility. And indeed when the narrator steals from his own bed to Wilson's he must wander "through a wilderness of narrow passages" (3:311) in that old two-story house whose architecture is so opaque to the understanding:

> But the house!—how quaint an old building was this!—to me how veritably a palace of enchantment! There was really no end to its windings—to its incomprehensible subdivisions. It was difficult, at any given time, to say with certainty upon which of its two stories one happened to be. From each room to every other there were sure to be found three or four steps either in ascent or descent. Then the lateral branches were innumerable—inconceivable—and so returning in upon themselves, that our most exact ideas in regard to the whole mansion were not very far different from those with which we pondered upon infinity. During the five years of my residence here, I was never able to ascertain with precision, in what remote locality lay the little sleeping apartment assigned to myself and some eighteen or twenty other scholars. (3:303)

"There was really no end to its windings"—this is no ordinary house, clearly, but an architectural image of the cosmos, in which there is no clear boundary between earth and heaven, between life and the afterlife, but an infinite series of gradations in ascent or descent. It is here that the narrator first meets his double, who, despite their shared name, is not at first perceptibly a double and who apparently does not sleep in the same apartment as the "eighteen or twenty other scholars." If between each two rooms there are steps up or down, then in his visit to the double's sleeping closet the narrator necessarily undergoes a change in *level.* Are we to infer that the double is an angel? Poe will not say. Who is the other William Wilson? Where does he come from? What power does he have to adapt his features to the narrator's, to appear at precisely the decisive moments in the narrator's evil life, dressed in precisely the same clothes? Whether or not he presents a blank image to the narrator in the night, he remains a blank cipher to him throughout; his "imitation" of the narrator *is* meaningless, for it never reveals itself to him as other than profoundly ambiguous.

Daniel Hoffman suggests that the recognition and sacrifice of his double drives the narrator mad;[7] perhaps it does, for in the endless replication of images does lie madness. But then it becomes crucial to distinguish Poe from his narrator, for Poe most decidedly does not go mad here. This is a sane tale about madness, which suggests that artistic representation is a doubling that is more stable because more imagistically focused. William Wilson goes mad, if he does, because he is lost in the perspectivizings of infinite reflections. But Poe does not give us infinite reflections at all; rather he offers a tentative key to the labyrinth of self-other imagings. Think of interpretive dilemmas, he says, in terms of the recognition and destruction of the self-image. This *is* a thematization of a potentially bottomless abyss of meaning; but it is a thematization that seeks to establish not meaning itself, but the grounds on which meaning might be apprehended. As in the case of the Red Death mummer who out-Herods Herod, the thematic key here seems to be the figure of the sacrificed Jesus, in all its thematic variations: the problem of power or authority (Jesus as rebel and Herod as king, or Jesus as king and Herod as apostate); the problem of self-definition and self-destruction (the self defined by resemblance to the other or by the destruction of the other, which by resemblance is a destruction of the self); the problem of diacrisis (of evil split off from or incorporated into good, of good and evil identified but not unified); and so forth. What Poe offers us in "William Wilson," this suggests, is less an infinite deferral of meaning than a series of ways of thinking about the possibility of meaning.

■

Probably the clearest fictional exposition of that series in recent years is John Barth's well-known tale, "Lost in the Funhouse." Barth's funhouse, like Poe's antechamber at the end of "William Wilson," also sets up an endless replication of images without exit and comments (as Poe does not) self-consciously on the failure of language to *signify*. "What is the story's theme?" one of the narrative voices keeps asking, impatient for meaning. But there is no theme; there is only apparently aimless exploration of what happens when thematization no longer works.[8] The house of fiction from chapter 6 has here become a maze, created for fun, but fun only for those who unimaginatively follow the arrows. "Shortly after the mirror room, he'd groped along a musty corridor, his heart already misgiving him at the absence of phosphorescent arrows and other signs. He'd found a crack of light—not a door, it turned out, but a seam between the plywood panels—and squirming up to it, espied an old man" (83-84), and so forth, the implication being that where signs are lacking, the entire idea of an apocalyptic revelation becomes profoundly problematic. "If you knew all the stories behind all the people on the boardwalk, you'd see that *nothing* was what it looked like" (87)—but you can't know all the stories, and so the attempt to see *through,* to achieve an unveiling, reveals the "nothing" that *everything* looks like. The thirteen-year-old hero of the story, Ambrose, dreams of a woman who would "see him entire, like a poem or story" (88), but, knowing that no such woman exists, despairs of ever achieving self-definition: "Stepping from the treacherous passage at last into the mirror-maze, he saw once again more clearly than ever, how readily he deceived himself into supposing he was a person. He even foresaw, wincing at his dreadful self-knowledge, that he would repeat the deception, at ever-rarer intervals, all his wretched life, so fearful were the alternatives. Fame, madness, suicide; perhaps all three" (89-90).

Barth's tale is a supremely self-conscious exploration of the dead ends in the funhouse; and it works through, finally, to a tentative solution: one must become an artist, an artist not, however, as Prospero was, but a self-conscious artist, always cognizant of the self-deceptions implicit in artistic creation, of the extent to which one's artistic creation doubles the void:

> He wonders: will he become a regular person? Something has gone wrong; his vaccination didn't take; at the Boy-Scout initiation campfire he only pretended to be deeply moved, as he pretends to this hour that it is not so bad after all in the funhouse, and that he has a little limp. How long will it last?
> He envisions a truly astonishing funhouse, incredibly complex yet utterly controlled from a great central switchboard like the console of a pipe organ. Nobody had enough imagination. He could design such a place himself, wiring and all, and he's only thirteen years old. He would be its operator: panel lights would show what was up in every cranny of its cunning of its multifarious vastness: a switch-flick would ease this fellow's way, complicate that's, to balance things out; if anyone seemed lost or frightened, all the operator had to do was.
> He wishes he had never entered the funhouse. But he has. Then he wishes he were dead. But he's not. Therefore he will construct funhouses for others and be their secret operator—though he would rather be among the lovers for whom funhouses are designed. (93-94)

Wishing oneself dead, or out of the funhouse, or a lover, is where we began in chapter 2, with the wish-fulfilling dreams of apocalypse in

Balizet and Wigglesworth; we have come this far only to perceive the problem clearly. "At this rate," as Barth's persona keeps complaining, "our protagonist will remain in the funhouse forever" (75). But that is the point; there is no escaping the "funhouse," the "abysm of differ-ance," the irremediable gap between desire-as-lack and its apocalyptic fulfillment. Thirteen-year-old Ambrose Mensch here dreams up a solu-tion; but it is a very sketchy solution indeed: "if anyone seemed lost or frightened, all the operator had to do was." That is precisely the blank that Prospero and William Wilson see in their doubles' faces, and it must be filled, Barth suggests, with artistic representations, verbal funhouses that remain cognizant, even painfully cognizant, of the void on which they are based. To create a funhouse is to expand the abysm of differance into a home, without ignoring the homelessness (*das Un-heimliche*) that it displaces. It is a house of fiction that does not neces-sarily need to be destroyed, but only firmed grounded in the irony that distinguishes it from reality, for it offers solutions that reality never dreamed of and that real people must not be allowed to hope are real solutions.

"Must not": this is, clearly, not merely an aesthetic or onto-logical problem but a profoundly ethical problem as well. "Therefore he will construct funhouses for others"—what *is* the relationship be-tween the artist and society, mediated by the funhouse of art and signaled here by the telling preposition "for"? Barth knows that art is not, finally, despite all his protestations to the contrary ("Muse spare me [at the desk, I mean] from Social-Historical Responsibility, and in the last analysis from every other kind as well, except Artistic"[9]), separable from communal concerns. The artist has a function in society that is not reducible to the pieties of John Gardner's moral argument nor to the epistemological simplicities of the argument from mimesis against which Barth is reacting in the "Muse, Spare Me" essay—but which is nevertheless essential to the health not only of the society but of the artist as well.[10] I want to return to explore that societal function in the context of Barth's great novel of community and (self-)sacrifice, *Giles Goat-Boy*, later in this chapter; but to set the stage for Barth's complex solution, let us trace the less formidable treat-ment of the artist's function in society in two sacrifice novels by Nathanael West, *Miss Lonelyhearts* and *The Day of the Locust*.

■

Miss Lonelyhearts is, at one level, an attempt to mediate allusively be-tween two biblical texts, the apocalypse and the temptation of Christ in the wilderness; as such, it stands as a kind of American *Paradise Re-gained*, which also mediates between those two texts by internalizing the restoration of paradise, displacing the raising of Eden "in the waste

wilderness" into the divine mind of Jesus Christ.[11] The parallels between West's novel and Milton's brief epic are in fact striking enough
to be taken seriously: whereas Milton has Satan describe Jesus as "Proof
against all temptation as a rock/Of adamant, and as a center firm"
(4:533-34), West tells us that "Miss Lonelyhearts stood quietly in the
center of the room. Shrike dashed against him, but fell back, as a wave
that dashes against an ancient rock, smooth with experience, falls back.
There was no second wave."[12] As in *Paradise Regained,* this rocklike
immovability is Miss Lonelyhearts's only successful defense against a
satanic Shrike: "'Don't be a spoilsport,' Shrike said with a great deal
of irritation. He was a gull trying to lay an egg in the smooth flank of
a rock, a screaming, clumsy gull" (132). Milton's Satan is of course the
same kind of master-rhetorician as Shrike—opposing to Christ "Not
force, but well-couched fraud, well-woven snares" (1.97) by "the persuasive rhetoric/That sleeked his tongue" (4.4-5)—but in the end he,
too, is profoundly disconcerted by Christ's immovability.

The thematic reduction that this alignment of Miss Lonelyhearts with Christ and of Shrike with Satan immediately suggests, however, is absurd. As John R. May contends, this reading makes Shrike a
Satan-figure who tempts Miss Lonelyhearts to presumption ("The rock
is the sign of Miss Lonelyhearts' presumption; it is a traditional image
for the unchanging fidelity of God"),[13] and if Miss Lonelyhearts is punished for that presumption with death, Shrike's victory signals the "last
loosening of Satan," or impending apocalypse.

That this is a false reduction of the novel is evident in West's
insistence on aligning his antagonists the other way as well: Shrike,
after all—whose name is a near-anagram of Christ—is the one who keeps
talking about Christ; and while his is a devastating rhetoric in which the
real alternative of Christ is destroyed, that rhetoric *becomes* his image
of order, his rock, which guarantees his invulnerability throughout the
novel. If Milton's Christ throughout *Paradise Regained* remains "unmoved," then Shrike is clearly the dominant Christ figure here; for
Shrike is unmoved by the suffering that Miss Lonelyhearts perceives
precisely because he can retreat into the illusory world of rhetoric, a
paradoxical discovery of order in absence that significantly parallels
Christ's own deferral of presential order to an absent future. Shrike's
rhetoric, for Miss Lonelyhearts, represents a temptation to order
analogous to Betty's more naive belief in order, as well as to his own
hopeless wishing for an apocalypse—all temptations he knows he must
stay away from, for they will only exacerbate his sickness. Miss Lonelyhearts is driven throughout the novel by an acute perception of suffering that simply will not reduce either to Betty's simplicities or to
Shrike's rhetorical sophistication:

A man is hired to give advice to the readers of a newspaper [he explains to Betty]. The job is a circulation stunt and the whole staff considers it a joke. He welcomes the job, for it might lead to a gossip column, and anyway he's tired of being a leg man. He too considers the job a joke, but after several months at it, the joke begins to escape him. He sees that the majority of the letters are profoundly humble pleas for moral and spiritual advice, that they are inarticulate expressions of genuine suffering. He also discovers that his correspondents take him seriously. For the first time in his life, he is forced to examine the values by which he lives. This examination shows him that he is the victim of the joke and not its perpetrator. (106)

If Milton's Christ represents order and Satan a restless wandering through chaos, clearly West aligns Miss Lonelyhearts with the latter. Miss Lonelyhearts is restless throughout the novel because he sees too well that all order, indeed all *language,* is a wholly unjustified reduction of the human truth of suffering to nonexistence. As a newspaper writer, he deals in words and is taught to manipulate words by his feature editor, Shrike; but that manipulation soon goes sour on him. The letters he receives are "inarticulate expressions of genuine suffering"—which is to say that genuine suffering exposes the reductive dangers of articulation, for to articulate suffering in his responses to the letters is always to falsify the suffering.

West's problem, of course, is that he is writing a novel about the inauthenticity of articulation. His novel launches a powerful assault on the entire Western tradition of the apocalyptic unveiling of order, but by doing so *verbally,* it partakes in the very tradition that West attacks. This is, of course, the central dilemma in American writing: How does one forge an order that will not harden into a rock of repression? By what authority can one destroy all authoritarian images of order? Miss Lonelyhearts undergoes his negative revelation in the end, gives in to the temptation to become "proof against all temptation," and becomes the rock: "He approached Betty with a smile, for his mind was free and clear. The things that muddied it had precipitated out into the rock" (136). But schizophrenia (which we may define as a form of ethical splitting, perhaps) is no answer to the writer's dilemma. Having devalued the apocalyptic transformation of chaos into order, he must seek a new transformation, a new reduction, perhaps, but one that will not falsify the chaotic facts of inarticulate human existence.

Early in the novel, Miss Lonelyhearts has a sudden memory from childhood that seems to offer West a tentative way out:

One winter evening, he had been waiting with his little sister for
their father to come home from church. She was eight years old
then, and he was twelve. Made sad by the pause between playing
and eating, he had gone to the piano and had begun a piece by
Mozart. It was the first time he had ever voluntarily gone to the
piano. His sister left her picture book to dance to his music.
She had never danced before. She danced gravely and carefully,
a simple dance yet formal. . . . As Miss Lonelyhearts stood at
the bar, swaying slightly to the remembered music, he thought
of children dancing. Square replacing oblong and being replaced by circle. Every child, everywhere; in the whole world
there was not one child who was not gravely, sweetly dancing.
(84–85, ellipsis West's)

Miss Lonelyhearts quickly dismisses his memory—"What in
Christ's name was this Christ business? And children gravely dancing?
He would ask Shrike to be transferred to the sports department" (85).
But the dance remains a possibility—a possible reduction of flux to
order in which order is ephemeral, always passing away: "Square replacing oblong and being replaced by circle." The being-replaced of the
dance is Yeats's Romantic image for art, of course, repeated in Eliot's
Four Quartets as "the still point of the turning world."[14] But West, as
opposed to Yeats and Eliot, remains profoundly mistrustful of that
image; the image, too, West understands, is a falsification of the inarticulate flux of human suffering.

In *The Day of the Locust,* West supplants the image of the
dance with a painting—Tod Hackett's painting of "The Burning of Los
Angeles," which significantly enough is a painting in progress, a "picture he was soon to paint" (261). The novel becomes, finally, an exploration very similar to Poe's of the relationship between art and the
apocalypse: the power of *images,* ritual icons of sacrifice and painted
icons of a burning city, to avert, or at least give meaning to, apocalypse.
Painting allows Tod to see, for example, as writing had allowed Ambrose
Mensch to see, that *"nothing* was what it looked like;" in the act of
visualizing the "crowd" for his painting, Tod comes to perceive it
through new eyes:

New groups, whole families, kept arriving. He could see a change
come over them as soon as they had become part of the crowd.
Until they reached the line, they looked diffident, almost furtive,
but the moment they had become part of it, they turned arro-
gant and pugnacious. It was a mistake to think them harmless
curiosity seekers. They were savage and bitter, especially the

middle-aged and the old, and had been made so by boredom and disappointment.

All their lives they had slaved at some kind of dull, heavy labor, behind desks and counters, in the fields and at tedious machines of all sorts, saving their pennies and dreaming of the leisure that would be theirs when they had enough. Finally that day came. They could draw a weekly income of ten or fifteen dollars. Where else should they go but California, the land of sunshine and oranges?

Once there, they discover that sunshine isn't enough. They get tired of oranges, even of avocado pears and passion fruit. Nothing happens. They don't know what to do with their time. They haven't the mental equipment for leisure, the money nor the physical equipment for pleasure. Did they slave so long just to go on an occasional Iowa picnic? What else is there? They watch the waves come in at Venice. There wasn't any ocean where most of them came from, but after you've seen one wave, you've seen them all. The same is true of the airplanes at Glendale. If only a plane would crash once in a while so that they could watch the passengers being consumed in a "holocaust of flame," as the newspapers put it. But the planes never crash.

Their boredom becomes more and more terrible. They realize that they've been tricked and burn with resentment. Every day of their lives they read the newspapers and went to the movies. Both fed them on lynchings, murder, sex crimes, explosions, wrecks, love nests, fires, miracles, revolutions, war. This daily diet made sophisticates of them. Nothing can ever be violent enough to make taut their slack minds and bodies. They have been cheated and betrayed. They have slaved and saved for nothing. (411-12)

Here Tod portrays the crowd in terms of the "nothing" that these jaded midwesterners have slaved and saved for. California, set up in the mythology of the West as a biblical Promised Land of sun and oranges, a paradise on earth reserved for the great holy remnant of mankind, is a joke—an emptiness that derides the newcomers. Movies and newspapers offer a fictitious excitement that makes life seem real but, revealed as illusion, is worse even than unreality, for it is the promise of reality negated. Positive images of reality are inverted into negatives, good things turned not into bad things but into nothings—yet never quite dismissed as nonexistent. *Nothing* is finally revealed as the only *something* there is, an absence with all the destructive force of a presence. "Nothing can ever be violent enough to make taut their slack minds and bodies"—which is to say, *only* nothing, a fierce and malicious void, can be violent enough to make reality seem real. But even that must fail, because the midwesterners' minds and bodies *are* slack. Inside each one of them is a piece of the void, for which material existence is exile, and the only home, the only stasis, is annihilation. Absence is the only presence; outside and inside seem indistinguishable.

The crowd's anguish is strikingly similar to William Wilson's at the end of his tale, with the significant exception that, like Melville in *Moby-Dick,* West gives it to us secondhand, and so allows us to see a problematic order in it. West's crowd is no Ahab, of course, no Prospero; it *is* perhaps closest to William Wilson, in its tormented subconscious perception of separation from and attraction to mysterious images of self, images that somehow always remain inadequate to desire. Diacritical separation in these individuals' lives is suffered, not sought; it is the experience of a hiatus between the expectation of rich multiplicity and the perception of undifferentiated vacuity. What they seek is a *sufficient image* that will allow them to harness and redirect their violence born of frustrated desire. That is, they seek vicarious fulfillment: they flock to premieres in the hope that sight of a movie star will sate their hunger for glamor; they wait for an airplane to crash in the hope that the image of violent death will satisfy their need to inflict violent death. They seek, essentially, ethical doubles, ritual icons of the self, identification with which may yield them a means of control over desire and its fulfillment. And when in the riot at the end they are provoked to violent sacrifice, they sacrifice one of their own, Homer Simpson, not in order to split him off but to assimilate him ritually, to achieve by iconic doubling control over violence.

Needless to say, their attempt at control fails. The interpretive task posed by the novel is precisely to explain the failure of the image, its failure to forestall the crowd's violence and, at the end, to forestall Tod Hackett's descent into madness. What has happened to the image in this novel that renders it powerless against the disintegration of society into chaos?

Norman O. Brown offers a number of perspectives on the problem in *Life Against Death,* specifically in the chapter cited earlier regarding Freud's instinctual dualism. For Brown, a dualistic conception of the instincts to life and death dooms all human endeavor to neurotic conflict; the reduction of the ritual icon to either an eschatological splinter or an ethical double, to use the terms I have employed here, necessarily implicates the image in unresolvable conflict. Brown calls for an instinctual *dialectic,* which is therefore a redemptive dialectic that is implicitly Hegelian in force:

The neurotic animal is the discontented animal; man's discontent
implies the disruption of the balanced equilibrium between
tension and release of tension which governs the activity of animals. Instinctual repression transforms the static homeostasis
principle in animals into the dynamic pleasure-principle in man;
homeostasis can exist only under conditions of instinctual satisfaction. It is the search for instinctual satisfaction under conditions of instinctual repression that produces in man the restless
quest of the pleasure-principle for a quality of experience denied
to it under conditions of repression. The restless pleasure-
principle is the search for psychic health under conditions of
psychic disease, and therefore is itself a symptom of the disease,
just as Freud said the progress of psychic disease may also be
regarded as an attempt to cure.

By the same token, if man could put an end to repression and
obtain instinctual satisfaction, the restless pleasure-principle
would return to the Nirvana-principle, that is to say, a balanced
equilibrium between tension and tension-release. If therefore
the Nirvana-principle "belongs to the death-instincts" and the
pleasure-principle belongs to Eros, their reunification would
be the conditions of equilibrium or rest of life that is a full life,
unrepressed, and therefore satisfied with itself and affirming
itself rather than changing itself. Thus interpreted, psychoanal-
ysis reaffirms ageless religious aspirations. For Nirvana, if it
expresses the rhythm of the lowest forms of organic life, also
expresses the highest aspirations of Buddhism. And how Nirvana differs from that eternal rest not only of the spirit but also
of the body which St. Augustine promises as man's ultimate
felicity, is a distinction which I leave to the theologians.

The reunification of Life and Death . . . can be envisioned
only as the end of the historical process. Freud's pessimism, his
preference for dualism rather than dialectics, and his failure
to develop a historical eschatology are all of a piece. To see how
man separated from nature, and separated out the instincts,
is to see history as neurosis; and also to see history, as neurosis,
pressing relentlessly and unconsciously toward the abolition
of history and the attainment of a state of rest which is also a
reunification with nature.[15]

The ethical transformation of the sacrificial icon into an assimi-
lable double is, clearly, in Brown's terms, a "search for psychic health
under conditions of psychic disease, and therefore is itself a symptom

of the disease." Since the repressive mastery of death ultimately only strengthens death, the ritual icon of life triumphant over death must eventually become counterproductive; as the ritual icon grows more masterful, the gap between the image of life (associated with the masters) and the reality of death (the frustrated desire for life in the mastered) becomes exaggerated. The icon that is intended to satisfy desire in fact only feeds it, and so is revealed not only as ineffectual but as actually pernicious. The insufficiency of the ritual icon to satisfy desire is a function of its supersufficiency to generate it.

West's central figure for the counterproductive ritual icon in *The Day of the Locust* is Faye Greener, the beautiful girl who, as an image of paradise achieved, as the eternal rest of Absolute Body, is doubled in the novel both by little Adore and by California itself, the Promised Land of sun and oranges. West persistently portrays Faye, in fact, in terms of the homeostatic state of rest, of self-sufficiency, that Brown associates with paradise: she is a bird, "enjoying the release that wild flight gives" (321); her beauty is "structural like a tree's, not a quality of her mind or heart," so that "even whoring couldn't damage it" (346); she is a cork, "riding a tremendous sea. Wave after wave reared its ton on ton of solid water and crashed down only to have her spin gaily away" (406). West's narrator calls Faye ambitious; but in fact we never see her dissatisfied with her lot. Even her flipping through dreams like a deck of cards really doesn't indicate a tension, a discontented quest for pleasure. Faye's remarkably *static* dreams are sufficient for her; her endless repetition of them is not tedious, as it would be for an adult, but naively satisfying, as it is to the children of Brown's paradise of Absolute Body.

But the image of paradise Faye presents to the men in the novel has a divided effect on them, for it both feeds and fails to satisfy their desire. Faye is an image of homeostatic childhood—"just born, everything moist and fresh, volatile and perfumed" (364)—that by its iconic supersufficiency generates desire in others, but due to its instinctual stasis is insufficient to the satisfaction of desire. The frustration this clash produces in men is redirected toward the source both of desire and of frustration in the form of violence; Tod Hackett, for example, seeking the gratification of love, dreams only of the gratification of rape: "Her self-sufficiency," the narrator explains in the clearest statement of the problem, "made him squirm and the desire to break its smooth surface with a blow, or at least a sudden obscene gesture, became irresistible" (365).

He does resist his desire, of course—which is to say, he represses it and surrenders one more time to the frustrations of repetition. The same is true a fortiori of Homer Simpson, the shy midwesterner whose

sexual desire is so far repressed that he is reduced to an almost vegeta-
tive existence: "But whether he was happy or not is hard to say," the
narrator tells us. "Probably he was neither, just as a plant is neither. He
had memories to disturb him and a plant hasn't, but after the first bad
night his memories were quiet" (298). To be a plant is to be homeo-
statically impervious like Faye—structurally beautiful as a tree, invul-
nerable as a cork—or like Miss Lonelyhearts, hard as a rock, the image
of eternal rest ironically inverted into absence. But Homer, like Miss
Lonelyhearts, cannot sustain that state long; he really is disturbed, by
memories—memories of the desire Romola Martin had awakened in
him, *images* of instinctual satisfaction that disturb him by emphasizing
the gulf between desire and its fulfillment. When Homer meets Faye,
Romola Martin rediviva, he soon feels *alive* again, "more alive than he
had at any time since Romola Martin" (314)—but also, necessarily,
more miserable. The reawakening of desire enlivens him, but thereby
takes him out of the precarious homeostasis of plant life.

The problem of desire and its lack of fulfillment is worst, however—most explosive, most dangerous—in the crowd of people who
have come to California to die. For them, *all* images are vicarious; their
lives are surfeited with iconic doubles that are supposed to satisfy them
but, like Faye for Tod and Homer, only make the unfulfillment of
desire all the more painfully evident. Their hero-worship of the stars,
most particularly, has long since failed to satisfy them, because it has
become inextricably mixed up with their own self-hatred: loathing of
the repressed self is transferred to the self's external double, and their
attentions increasingly incline toward violent sacrifice, sacrifice now
as *failed* ethical doubling, an iconic ritual that is powerless to control
violence. "At the sight of their heroes and heroines," the narrator predicts, "the crowd would turn demoniac. Some little gesture, either too
pleasing or too offensive, would start it moving and then nothing but
machine guns would stop it. Individually the purpose of its members
might simply be to get a souvenir, but collectively it would grab and
rend" (409).

Collectively: what is most frightening about the riot scene that
soon ensues is that the failure of communal ethical doubling causes the
rapid proliferation of violence. By the miracle of modern communica-
tions, mob violence can be extended imagistically to engulf the entire
country; the Hollywood riot is broadcast to the rest of the country by
a young man whose "rapid, hysterical voice was like that of a revivalist
preacher whipping his congregation toward the ecstasy of fits" (409).
The media know the people's need for iconic doubles, for ritualized
images of violence that will vicariously satisfy their hunger for violence;
but they don't know—or they willfully ignore—the inevitable result of

such images. Any violence that occurs in Los Angeles will immediately be converted by the media into a ritual icon of violence for the whole country and, by the apocalyptic escalation of repressive ethical doubling, will eventually tilt the whole world into chaos: "The Angelenos would be first, but their comrades all over the country would follow. There would be civil war" (335). All each crowd needs is an "objective," some event to direct their attention and spur them to vent their frustrated violence as a concerted mob—and Homer provides it. Driven to the breaking point by Faye, he sacrifices *her* double, Adore, and the crowd "grab and rend" him. Nonritual repetition of sacrifice escalates violence, and the apocalypse becomes reality.

In *The Day of the Locust* West presents a vision of the nation's future that is almost unrelievedly bleak: the end impends, and it will most probably mean annihilation. More than in *Miss Lonelyhearts,* however, West here works toward one slim hope: the hope of art. Tod Hackett is the one character in the novel who is able to use the violence of others as a ritual icon from which to learn. If his painting opens his eyes to the crowd, it opens them no less inward to himself. "He began to wonder if he himself didn't suffer from the same ingrained, morbid apathy he liked to paint in others. Maybe he could only be galvanized into sensibility and that was why he was chasing Faye" (365). What he learns—what little he learns, in the end—he both learns from and pours into his painting of "The Burning of Los Angeles." By identifying with the crowd he paints, Tod sees the insufficiency of society's ethical images to control violence and so offers instead an eschatological image of violence that is intended as the crowd's answer to societal control. His apocalyptic painting, one might say, is a ritual icon designed to appeal to the crowd not by ethical but by eschatological doubling: he portrays no ethical mastery of life over death, but the eschatological liberation of death from life. The apocalypse in his painting is the iconic double of the apocalypse before Kahn's Persian Palace Theater, and he intends it to supplant both Faye, whose egglike self-sufficiency indirectly or symbolically sparks most of the violence in the novel, and the chaos of apocalyptic violence itself:

> When the bird grew silent, he made an effort to put Faye out of
> his mind and began to think about the series of cartoons he
> was making for the canvas of Los Angeles on fire. He was going
> to show the city burning at high noon, so that the flames would
> have to compete with the desert sun and thereby appear less
> fearful, more like bright flags flying from roofs and windows than

a terrible holocaust. He wanted the city to have quite a gala
air as it burned, to appear almost gay. And the people who set it
on fire would be a holiday crowd. (334)

Faye as ethical double is a siren, luring men to their destruction
by driving a wedge between the desire she awakens and its fulfillment;
Tod's painting of the apocalyptic gala seeks as eschatological double to
heal the division, to bring desire and its fulfillment back together again
by revealing to the viewer his desire's true locus: not, that is, in paradise, but in self-destruction. An apocalyptic gala is a *desirable* self-
destruction, a violent catastrophe that proclaims: "*This* is what we
want, not rest but flames!" And if Tod's painting successfully supplants
the pernicious image of Faye in his imagination (compare p. 365), there
may be a chance—a slim chance, which does not materialize in the
novel—that the painting may supplant actual apocalypse as well:

> Despite the agony in his leg, he was able to think clearly about
> his picture, "The Burning of Los Angeles." After his quarrel
> with Faye, he had worked on it continually to escape torment-
> ing himself, and the way to it in his mind had become almost
> automatic.
>
> As he stood on his good leg, clinging desperately to the iron
> rail, he could see all the rough charcoal strokes with which he
> had blocked it out on the big canvas. . . . He had almost forgot-
> ten both his leg and his predicament, and to make his escape
> still more complete he stood on a chair and worked at the flames
> in an upper corner of the canvas, modeling the tongues of fire
> so that they licked even more avidly at a corinthian column that
> held up the palmleaf roof of a nutburger stand.
>
> He had finished one flame and was starting on another when
> he was brought back by someone shouting in his ear. He opened
> his eyes and saw a policeman trying to reach him from behind
> the rail to which he was clinging. (419-20)

Here is art as a necessary, possibly even redemptive, but finally
unsuccessful escape from apocalyptic reality. Most importantly, Tod
escapes not only by imagining an apocalypse but by *working,* creating
a work of art: "to make his escape still more complete he stood on a
chair and worked at the flames in an upper corner of the canvas."
There *is* no chair here at the iron rail, to which he is so desperately
clinging before Kahn's Persian Palace Theater; the act of painting is an
iconic ritual, a ritual of the mind that heroically though futilely seeks

to negate the apocalypse swirling around him in order to replace it with a visionary image. The crowd's ritual icon—the slaughtered Homer—is here countered with an icon not of killing but of *making*.

Unfortunately, it doesn't work. Tod is brought back from his work by the police, who rescue him from the apocalypse but in so doing somehow expose him to its mental violence. With his rescue, the escape into the *work* of art is dissipated and Tod surrenders to the subverbal chaos of the apocalypse, to the sirenic call of death: "He was carried through the exit to the back street and lifted into a police car. The siren began to scream and at first he thought he was making the noise himself. He felt his lips with his hands. They were clamped tight. He knew then it was the siren. For some reason this made him laugh and he began to imitate the siren as loud as he could" (421).

If Tod (like Prospero) fails, however, West (like Poe) may after all have succeeded. Tod never does paint his picture; West did write his novel, and in it embodied Norman O. Brown's instinctual *dialectic*—a dialectic not as a teleological progress to paradise (which, Brown notwithstanding, should probably be seen as simply another "search for psychic health under conditions of psychic disease"), but as iconic mediation. In *The Day of the Locust* West ultimately gives us a complex ritual icon that contains both apocalypse and apocalyptic art, successful negation and unsuccessful preservation, and in the tradition of the American Negative preserves what it negates. As Donald R. Torchiana suggests, West triumphs over his annihilative theme by permitting us "to view the local chaos of Hollywood as a timeless image."[16] But the image, if timeless, is specifically an image of people *in action,* in the communal action of self-destructive sacrifice and the private action of self-preserving art, of apocalypse and antiapocalypse.

■

This brings us back to Barth, for Barth's project from *The Floating Opera* (1956) to *Sabbatical: A Romance* (1982) has been precisely to restrict *his own* American apocalyptic imagination: to subvert the national dream as it guides his own creative work, in the drive both to an encyclopedic inclusiveness (the Emersonian attempt to transform the world apocalyptically by incorporating it into the ideal body of the work of art) and to a nihilistic negation (the Poeian or Westian attempt to break out of the maddening replication of images by smashing the mirrors that constitute the self). Barth has been called both names, idealist and nihilist, and not without reason. The idealistic urge to (re)create and the nihilistic urge to destroy are the opposing poles of the apocalyptic authorial self that Barth is at pains throughout his fiction to "decreate," to disperse into less privative, communally more fruitful icons of the self.[17]

I am tempted to explore this self-decreation in *LETTERS* (1979), in one sense Barth's most self-reflexively "apocalyptic" novel. His seventh book, it assumes the task of constructing an eschatological or eternal perspective on all his fiction to date. One might almost say that in *LETTERS* Barth "judges" the characters of the earlier books diacritically: Joe Morgan and Jake Horner from *The End of the Road* (1958), the Cooke/Burlingame line from *The Sot-Weed Factor* (1960), and a Bray-figure "from" *Giles Goat-Boy* (1966) and *Chimera* (1972) are damned, as it were, assigned fates that signal what John R. May would call their "unacceptable response to living" (35), while Todd Andrews from *The Floating Opera* and Ambrose and Magda Mensch from *Lost in the Funhouse* (along with the one new character, Germaine Pitt, Lady Amherst) are assigned various forms or indices of secular salvation.

But Barth's diacritical drama, his authoritative (because authorial) apocalyptic interpretation of the moral values reflected by his fiction through the 1970s, is in another sense just one more apocalyptic stance to be exposed and rejected—of a piece with the various callous, manipulative, or self-glorifying apocalyptic fictions that run through Barth's work. If it is wrong for Todd Andrews to try to fix the meaning of his life through an apocalyptic act of suicide, it is equally wrong for Barth to fix the meaning of *The Floating Opera* through an apocalyptic act of diacritical midrash—and, of course, equally wrong for me or any other literary critic to fix the meaning of *LETTERS*. It is wrong, in other words, to pronounce on the wrongness of anything (and at the same time, as this sentence illustrates, probably unavoidable), for such pronouncement requires an apocalyptic perspective on human action to which we have no access.

That, at any rate, is the negative thrust of Barth's work: away from all absolutisms (though the denial of *all* absolutisms is another absolutism), away from the eternalizing movement of apocalyptic visions. The positive thrust is more nebulous—and rightly so, for a programmatic alternative to absolutism would hardly be an alternative at all. Barth usually thematizes his alternative to absolutism under the rubric of the "tragic view," by which he seems to mean an acceptance of relative values in a compromised environment, and an existential confrontation with and ultimately an almost mystical affirmation of human mortality and all other checks on the idealizing imagination.[18] In *LETTERS*, in fact, the "apocalyptic" judgment reduces thematically to an opposition between apocalyptic schemes (damned) and tragic acceptances (saved): between mad, idealistic visions of world transformation and rather mundane versions of loving, self-sacrificing world affirmation.

As *LETTERS* moves into *Sabbatical,* Barth increasingly shifts this thematic concern into his rhetorical mode. In the tradition of Faulkner in *Absalom, Absalom!,* Barth uses the form of the epistolary novel in *LETTERS* in order to establish and explore a communal dialogue, which becomes the narrative mode of *Sabbatical,* with its "conception" of storytelling as the mediatory fruit of social (and sexual) intercourse. But Barth's most graphic, and perhaps most hazardous, exploration of the visionary's rapprochement with the community comes at the conclusion of *Giles Goat-Boy.* I want to end this chapter and the main body of this book with a brief look at this, one of the boldest and yet at the same time one of the most surprisingly obvious of American endings.

Giles Goat-Boy is an overt, self-conscious exploration of the myth of the world-redeeming hero, as explicated anthropologically by Lord Raglan and Joseph Campbell, theologically of course by the Book of Revelation and the entire Christian Bible, the Bible as it is organized by the Book of Revelation.[19] Barth modulates the myth initially in archetypal American, specifically Emersonian directions: George Giles's apocalyptic task, he comes to realize by the end of the main narrative, is not to slay the monster but to incorporate his world, to become not a world-transforming god but a *man,* truly human because filled—swelled, to gigantic or "Grand-Tutorial" (messianic) stature—with humanity. At every stage of his long path to herohood George encounters the traditional helpers and opponents of myth, but, rather than simply conquering or learning from them, in each instance he *assimilates* them: the animality of the goat Redfearn's Tom, the proud human physicality and sexuality of G. Herrold and Croaker, the mysterious femininity of Anastasia Stoker, even the unctuous opportunism of the false messiah, Harold Bray. This Emersonian progress culminates at the rout of Bray, at the close of the main narrative, in a scapegoat ceremony with a mediatory twist: Bray is the scapegoat that is driven out, but not as split-off evil; Tommy's Tommy's Tom, grandkid of Redfearn's Tom, is the sin offering, George's double killed not for the mastery of sin but for the final ritual acknowledgment of George's goatly (bestial, bodily) nature; and Max Spielman, George's Jewish mentor, is executed for a murder he didn't commit, in a self-consciously futile but love-affirming gesture of self-sacrifice that directs George's fate twelve years later. Sacrifice in each case becomes the vehicle neither for eschatological splitting nor for ethical doubling, but for an Emersonian incorporation, the assimilation of all life: George's hero-task is to draw up his world into himself. Harold Bray transforms himself into all the central figures in George's history in turn, and finally into an image of George himself, in which guise George finally routs him, suggesting that Bray himself contains the world as otherness, as the NOT ME, within his antimessianic role, and that George assimilates that otherness in his "sacrifice" of Bray. George concludes his main narrative on a calm note of achieved triumph, a note of order within chaos that seems a mythic redemption of his society:

> I looked up. In the pall above my flaming keeper something
> large and obscure appeared to rise, rolling and spreading like the
> smoke itself. The crowd's dismay turned to panic: people leaped
> from the stands, swarmed over the barricades in both directions,
> fell upon their knees and girlfriends, clouted neighbors, clutched
> loved ones. Bravely the band played New Tammany's anthem un-
> til overrun. Guards scrambled into the moat, either to arrest
> or to protect me; at their head grinned Stoker, cursing as he
> came. His wife I discerned high up in the bleachers, one hand
> upon her belly, watching with anxious love above the crowd;
> Mother knitted placidly beside her. And upon us all, gentle
> ashes—whose if not my gentler keeper's?—commenced to fall.
> Another term, surely, they would be mine; not now, for though
> my youthful work was done, that of my manhood remained
> to do. What it was I clearly saw, and what it would come to.
> Nonetheless I smiled, leaned on my stick, and, no troubleder
> than Mom, gimped in to meet the guards halfway.[20]

This is a note of triumph, despite all; and when George goes on to record a Posttape, in which that triumph is severely qualified by a powerful sense of futility, in which the Romantic incorporation of otherness is mitigated by a perception of continuing alienation, the reader is justifiably baffled. There is a hiatus between the novel's main narrative and the Posttape, a hiatus as wide as that between George's childhood in the goatpens and his adulthood on Main Campus. The Posttape marks, in fact, the return threshold in Campbell's hero-cycle (between "my youthful work" and "that of my manhood," as George says—between success and failure, as his sure foresight here predicts), but in problematic ways that have proved a significant obstacle to the tale's readers, beginning, ironically, with "J. B.," the comic persona of Barth who "edits" George's first-person narrative. In a Postscript to the Posttape, J. B. insists that the Posttape is spurious, precisely because in it George embraces the tragic view and rejects "Gilesianism," the apocalyptic religion founded by George's followers, to which J. B. is an avid convert:

Which brings us to the real proof of its spurious character. Even if none of the above-mentioned discrepancies existed, the hopeless, even nihilistic tone of those closing pages militates against our believing them to be the Grand Tutor's own. Having brought us to the heart of Mystery, "He" suddenly shifts to what can most kindly be called a tragic view of His life and of campus history. Where are the joy, the hope, the knowledge, and the confident strength of the man who routed Harold Bray, affirmed the Candidacies of His Tutees and readied Himself to teach all studentdom the Answer? "Not teachable" indeed! And the unpardonable rejection of Greene, of Anastasia, of His own son, in favor of a sickly mulatto boy with the improbable name of *Tombo*—. . . . (710)

J. B. is wrong on virtually every count. The tone of the Posttape is not nihilistic, only resigned to defeat; George himself makes clear in the main narrative that mystery must be exploded into the tragic view; George only claimed to know and to be able to teach the Answer when he didn't know it; and Tombo is preferred over his disciples precisely because he *isn't* a disciple, but a potential successor: "If fate grant him time enough . . . and grant me to spirit him out of peril into some obscure pasturage—*he will learn,* will my Tombo! Yes, and one day hear, in his far sanctuary, a call, a summons . . . " (706, last ellipsis Barth's). J. B. deliberately misreads the Posttape because he wants to construe the main narrative as a gospel, an Answer, and the Posttape significantly undermines any such attempt. Barth deliberately misleads his reader because he knows in himself the powerful call of the American apocalypse, the lure of the Emersonian dream of incorporative transformation, and knows also that he must confront that lure on its own terms, in terms of his own inclination toward it. If some critics (most notably Raymond Olderman[21]) have bought J. B.'s version of the novel, the obvious answer would seem to be that there *is* no answer: that the novel is a hoax, a vast, ill-conceived trick, in which the "author" steps in and misreads the novel, only to be himself misread by the "Publisher," who suggests in a Footnote to the Postscript to the Posttape that the Postscript itself is spurious. These metafictional inversions of inversions have led many of the novel's critics to treat it as a self-consuming fiction, a narrative that demonstrates only the inauthenticity and impossibility of narrative itself: an ironic text, an existentialist treatise in the literature of silence in which any meaning is bad faith.[22]

But this, as I have argued elsewhere, is as much a misreading of the novel as is J. B.'s pious exegesis.[23] As should be clear by now, the metafictional self-reflections that conclude Barth's novel take a stance in a strong American tradition of such self-reflections, which, as I have suggested, are intimately linked to the problems of imagining an apocalypse. Since to destroy an image of the world is in some sense to destroy the text that images that world, apocalyptic confrontations in American literature tend almost invariably toward self-conscious explorations of the validity of literary creation. It is the American attempt to have things both ways: to tell compelling stories that compel by offering powerful metaphors for the interpretation of reality, and at the same time to remain cognizant of the necessary failure of those metaphors to *accomplish* an interpretation. The flux of time and the timeless image combine to direct pragmatic attention at once to human beings' need for themes and to their need to decreate false themes, including their own.

More than this, Barth leads his reader into the labyrinth of self-reflections at the end of the novel precisely in order to restrict his own apocalyptic imagination: to submit the privative thrust of the American apocalyptic vision to a restrictive scrutiny that will permit a transgression of the boundary between the isolate imagination and the community. Indeed, this restriction is anticipated earlier in the novel, in the passing flashes of insight that suggest to George and his mentor, Max, that he, George, is the greatest danger facing mankind: that it is precisely his misguided attempts to impose a visionary design on the world that pose the greatest threat. The surest way to save the world, George finally learns, is to stop *trying* to save it. Apocalypse in this novel is not the culmination of the Romantic hero's quest, but the disastrous consequence of the attempt to reduce life to Romantic terms. Significantly enough, Max Spielman's last words of advice to George before he begins his three catastrophic rounds of Tutoring couch a guardedly optimistic view of the future not at all in terms of visionary transformation brought about by the lone hero, but in terms of the community's gradual ethical growth. The student body (or human race), he says, is in its adolescence and thus is susceptible to accidental apocalypse. There *was* a "possibility of catastrophic accident: adolescents took chances and were by nature strenuous and impulsive; Campus Riot III might occur after all and studentdom be EATen [the novel's nuclear holocaust], as a prep-school boy might resort to delinquency or suicide, or be killed in a motorcycle race" (255). But, "By George," Max says, "I think the odds for *survival* are pretty good. Some kids don't make it through adolescence, but most do" (255).

And, indeed, the human race does make it through the novel, mainly because George grows out of adolescence and learns to leave it alone—learns not to force it into the straitjacket of his Emersonian imagination. In the Posttape Barth takes George the ultimate step: to surrender to the community the power not only to control its fate but to control the visionary's as well.

> My self-wound watch runs fast; anyhow I have small time left, and so futile is this work now approaching its end, I am sore tempted to abandon it unfinished and go gambol in the April air myself. *She* [Anastasia] thinks it done already, whose notion it was I render my tale during this my recentest and last detention. Her great nagging faith has alone sustained me, for better or worse, through the monstrous work—this "Revised New Syllabus," as she calls it, which she is convinced will supersede the Founder's Scroll [Bible]. I smile at that idea, as at the olive lad she calls our son, and in whom I see as much of Stoker, of Croaker, indeed of Bray, as of myself. Supposing even that the Scroll *were* replaced by these endless tapes, one day to feed Him who will come after me, as I fed once on that old sheepskin—what then? Cycles on cycles, ever unwinding; like my watch; like the reels of this machine she got past her spouse; like the University itself.
>
> Unwind, rewind, replay.
>
> No matter. Futility and Purpose, like Pass and Fail, themselves have meaning only for her sort, and her son's (in whose dark eyes I see already his mother's single-mindedness). For me, Sense and Nonsense lost their meaning on a night twelve years four months ago, in WESCAC's Belly—as did every such distinction, including that between Same and Different. Thus it is, and in no other wise, I have lingered on the campus these dozen years, in the humblest capacity, advising one at a time undergraduates to whom my words convey nothing. Thus it is I accept without much grumble their failings and my own: the abuse of my enemies, the lapses of my friends; the growing pains in both my legs, my goatly seizures, my errors of fact and judgment, my failures of resolve—all these and more, the ineluctable shortcomings of mortal studenthood. (699-700)

George's work is futile—but he does it anyway, because "Futility and Purpose, like Pass and Fail, themselves have meaning only for her sort," Anastasia's sort, J. B.'s sort, the sort who cling to apocalyptic (or any other exclusive) fictions. Futility and purpose are both teleological concepts that presuppose a culminating meaning, a telos, to life, and George, enlightened, has grown past the sense of a telos. George is no longer interested in crusades, in causes, even in a war against causes.

A war, after all, requires opposing forces, and tidy opposition is precisely the fiction George now attempts to unteach—futilely, but no matter. "Thus it is," he says, "and in no other wise, I have lingered on the campus [earth] these dozen years, in the humblest capacity, advising one at a time undergraduates to whom my words convey nothing." His teaching is an unteaching that in its attacks on the nothings of teleological fictions conveys nothing.

This sounds nihilistic, perhaps, but it is not; it seems a denial of the fictional ordering of reality into end-oriented narratives, but it is not. It is, in the end, simply a resignation to the inability of those fictions to *change* anything. It is a quintessentially pragmatic—and *American*—concern for consequences that drives George to the futile effort of teaching the last twelve years of his life, and, in the end, the consequences are less perhaps for the taught (who do not understand him) than for the teacher. As George's rejection of the Eastern Grand Tutor, The Living Sakhyan or Dalai Lama, indicates, he has no patience for a world view that leads to paralysis; ideas about the world are tested only by action *in* the world, and George finally denies the distinctions between Sense and Nonsense and between Same and Different, not ontologically (because they don't exist) but ethically and pragmatically (because their effects on human beings in a communal context are pernicious). "Thus it is I accept without much grumble their failings and my own: the abuse of my enemies, the lapses of my friends; the growing pains in both my legs, my goatly seizures, my errors of fact and judgment, my failures of resolve—all these and more, the ineluctable shortcomings of mortal studenthood." This acceptance is the proof of George's vision: it allows him to recognize his own humanity and that of his fellows. George's Romantic incorporation of the community into his heroic vision in the main narrative is thus not exactly negated in the Posttape but revealed as being finally the incorporation of his vision into the human community; his ultimate achievement as a world-redeeming hero is not apotheosis or deification, the elevation of a human being to the singular status of a god, but "apoanthroposis" or humanization, the recognition of a shared humanity in which George is neither the same as nor different from any other man or woman. There is no pride, therefore, in George's decision to teach "in the humblest capacity"—this is no self-humbling for the history-books—but, rather, a simple acceptance of the emptiness of all fictions that would drive wedges between members of society.

This is a lesson that, however germinant in the pragmatic thrust of American apocalypses, American heroes have typically tended in the end to reject: Ahab is perhaps the *locus classicus,* along with Hank Morgan, Thomas Sutpen, and others. Indeed, even where American heroes have moved toward a recognition of the truth of this lesson, their recognition has most often proved nearly impossible to carry out in a communal context (Ishmael) or has had to be articulated for them after their deaths (Miss Rosa). The threat of the community, even in these powerfully affirmative visions, remains strong and frightening. The community's threat, of course, is the deformation of a Romantic American selfhood: the American artist fears the loss of his or her uniqueness, of the ability to stand outside and see through illusion to truth. How can society be transformed if the imaginer of transformation is deformed by the mass? For George, deformation is inescapable; the artist's task is therefore not to flee deformation, into the isolation of the mind (the forest, the sea, the house), but to dwell in it actively even if activity is futile, transforming deformation itself precisely by affirming it through the futile attempt to transform. The ultimate deformation of the artist by society is death, perhaps; and George looks forward to his own execution in the last few pages of the novel with a calm resignation that clearly triumphs over death. Having domesticated the uncanny, having made of the abysm of differance an iconic home, as Ishmael and Miss Rosa do, American artists must finally learn to domesticate society by permitting it to domesticate them.

What George Giles reaches in the end is a profoundly ethical recognition of the *ordinariness* of life in the community: of ordinary toil without result, of ordinary humanity without hyperbolization. If George reaches this recognition through an extended and extreme confrontation with the spectre of apocalypse, that may only signal the power of the American apocalypse to consider its own processes in a pragmatically affirmative fashion, to become self-conscious without thereby blocking its mediated path to insight. Self-consciousness, in this light, becomes a pathway not out of the community into a paralyzed isolation in which meaningful action is impossible, but back *into* the community, where action becomes meaningful precisely because the fictional meanings that paralyze human beings are undone. "A knife cuts," George says, "a fish swims; a Grand Tutor, among other things, drives from the campus such as Bray. There was no glamour to the work, nor any longer to the term" (670). The American apocalyptist, among other things, maintains the community by challenging it; the American apocalypse destroys *itself*, finally, in order to direct us back to human life.

COMMUNAL TIES

τὸ δὲ σῶμα κινεῖται φορᾷ· ὥστε καὶ ἡ ψυχὴ μεταβάλλοι
ἂν κατὰ τὸ σῶμα ἢ ὅλη ἢ κατὰ μόρια μεθισταμένη.
εἰ δὲ τοῦτ' ἐνδέχεται, καὶ ἐξελθοῦσαν εἰσιέναι πάλιν
ἐνδεχοιτ' ἄν· τούτῳ δ' ἔποιτ' ἂν τὸ ἀνίστασθαι τὰ
τεθνεῶτα τῶν ζῴων. (406b1–5)

Now the motion of the body is motion in space: there-
fore the motion of the soul is also motion in space
whether the whole soul so move, or only the parts, the
whole remaining at rest. But, if this is admissible, the
soul might also conceivably quit the body and re-enter;
and this would involve the consequence that dead ani-
mals may rise again.

οὐκ ἔστι δ' ἁπλοῦν οὐδὲ τὸ πάσχειν, ἀλλὰ τὸ μὲν
φθορά τις ὑπὸ τοῦ ἐναντίου, τὸ δὲ σωτηρία μᾶλλον τοῦ
δυνάμει ὄντος ὑπὸ τοῦ ἐντελεχείᾳ ὄντος καὶ ὁμοίου
οὕτως ὡς δύναμις ἔχει πρὸς ἐντελέχειαν· (417b1–5)

To suffer or to be acted upon, too, is a term of more
than one meaning. Sometimes it means a sort of destruc-
tion by the contrary, sometimes it is rather a preser-
vation of what is potentially existent by what is actually
existent and like it, so far as likeness holds of poten-
tiality when compared with actuality.

Aristotle, *De Anima (trans. R. D. Hicks)*

"The Ritual Icon" completes the argument of *American Apocalypses*—and yet, in the very inadequacy of the argument's striving toward completion it also insists upon incompletion, and upon continuation of the argument elsewhere. The expected location for such a continuation would be here, of course, in the Conclusion, which by the conventions of book writing is a resumption and extension of a book's argument beyond its apparent end, a summation of the argument in which its temporal movement halts in a timeless moment that encompasses all that preceded it. But I am afraid I have no such "eternal" perspective to offer; indeed, the nature of my subject would appear to preclude one. If my method throughout the study has seemed to mire the discussion in inconclusiveness, always skirting the temptations of thematic summations, I suggest that it is a characteristically American brand of inconclusiveness, one that remains all too aware of the impossibility of conclusions. And so my Conclusion is anything but a syllogistic one; this study has no teleology, no entelechy whose inexorable progress toward self-actualization would give a coherent meaning to all the details of "potentiality" that constitute it. To end a book in the strong American apocalyptic tradition is a skeptically grounded act of faith: a statement of hope that one has at least cleared the way for understanding even if one has not attained it and that ultimate knowledge therefore lies just beyond the last page. At the same time it is an admission that one has failed, that one has only stalled off the recognition that no ultimate knowledge exists to be found.

Even so, the radical skepticism of American apocalypses never wholly undermines the hope. What I want to offer in this Conclusion is thus no image of failure at all, but an image of transition whose success will, I hope, lie precisely in its failure to conclude. What does this reading of American apocalypses imply, not about American literature but about the *interpretation* of American literature? More specifically, if the literary work becomes the "communal tie" by which the American writer engages a collective communication across time (Faulkner) and across moral discriminations (Barth), how can the critic use it to define and explore not only a critical community but a significant relation between criticism and the larger community?

The two tales through which I want to consider this question are again by Poe—"Ligeia" and "The Man of the Crowd," which provide two different perspectives on the fundamental problems of interpretation and community. Ligeia's very name is our first and perhaps richest clue to the complexity of the problem. Ligeia is one of the sirens in Milton's *Comus* (l. 880) and a dryad in Vergil's *Georgics* (4:336), and so in either case inhabits a medial ontological ground between human beings and the gods.[1] As siren, Ligeia sings *of* the gods, promising absolute knowledge of them but without the power or the will to disclose that knowledge, thereby enmeshing her song in deception. And though the Greek *ligeia* means clear-voiced or sweet-sounding, "siren" comes from *seira* (cord), which renders the sirenic promise of clarity itself an entanglement or bondage. Indeed, while the etymological root for *ligeia* is *ligus* (clear-voiced), it is surely conceivable that Poe was thinking also of the Latin verb *ligare* (to bind), from which we derive "religion," a rebinding; for a religion is expressly the binding of individual men and women into a community, through a collective bond to the divinity—a "bond" that, in Christianity, is a divine-human person, Jesus Christ, whose bond to humanity is conceived symbolically as marital. The "ligament" or religious bond in poetic tradition since the time of the Greeks has of course been the Muse, or the nine Muses, the daughters of Zeus who inspire artistic creation by singing to men, like the sirens, of the gods. It is also worthy of note that one of Homer's typical adjectives for the sweet voices of the Muses is *ligeia* (compare *Odyssey* 24:62, *Mousa ligeia*).

What Poe's choice of name involves his readers in, then, is the problem of interpreting voices that would bind a community by speaking of the beyond. Both the sirens and the Muses sing sweetly, promising absolute knowledge; but the sirens deceive, and by deceiving lure men to their deaths. On what grounds is one to make the essential discrimination between false sirenic promises and the true promises of the Muses? If the sweet voices of artistic creation can convey promises that are true *and* false, by what authority can one assert the truth of any voice? What truth is to "authorize" or organize a community?

In "Ligeia" Poe explores the interpretive dilemmas implicit in the idea of a medium or ligament between human beings and God mainly by the optical/vocal images with which I have been concerned throughout. Having wondered, "What was it—that something more profound than the well of Democritus—which lay far within the pupils of my beloved?",[2] Poe's narrator goes on to transform both Ligeia's eyes and her voice into mediatory icons that go between the limitations of his knowledge and the mysteries of the cosmos: "And of such passion I could form no estimate, save by the miraculous expansion of those eyes which at once so delighted and appalled me—by the almost magical melody, modulation, distinctness and placidity of her very low voice—and by the fierce energy (rendered doubly effective by contrast with her manner of utterance) of the wild words which she habitually uttered" (2:253). And yet the entire tale is conceived as the evocation of an interpretive mediation that is never achieved and may not be achievable on earth:

There is no point, among the many incomprehensible anomalies of the science of mind, more thrillingly exciting than the fact— never, I believe, noticed in the schools—that, in our endeavors to recall to memory something long forgotten, we often find our- selves *upon the very verge* of remembrance, without being able, in the end, to remember. And thus how frequently, in my in- tense study of Ligeia's eyes, have I felt approaching the full knowledge of their expression—felt it approaching—yet not quite be mine—and so at length entirely depart! (2:252)

Upon the very verge: this, of course, is the critical transition, the barrier that interpretation both must and cannot cross. Whether one conceives the interpretive act Platonically, as *anamnesis,* as Poe does here, or biblically, as proleptic intuition, as he does in *Eureka,* the act is profoundly eschatological in the root sense of the word: for it faces the necessity of crossing an apparently uncrossable threshold, a boundary between present lack of understanding and true knowledge. The apocalypse in its strict theological sense involves the crossing of that threshold collectively, by the instantaneous transformation of the earth and all its inhabitants; and while American apocalypses are rarely willing to destroy so much in their quest for understanding, there is clearly an ultimacy or an intensity about the apocalyptic act of inter- pretation that implicates even the least destructive of these works in the will to destroy.

Poe ties interpretation to will powerfully but problematically in the bogus quotation from Joseph Glanvill that stands as the epi- graph to "Ligeia" and is reiterated obsessively (four times) in the tale itself: "AND the will therein lieth, which dieth not. Who knoweth the mysteries of the will, with its vigor? For God is but a great will per- vading all things by nature of its intentness. Man doth not yield himself to the angels, nor unto death utterly, save only through the weakness of his feeble will" (2:248). In this formulation, will is the agent by which desire is fulfilled; and since God is sheer will, that fulfillment is potentially boundless. *Eureka*'s argument indicates that "Glanvill" here speaks for Poe; but the rhetoric of the quotation also reveals Poe's profound awareness of the restrictions on his belief. Of the four sen- tences in the epigraph, the first and last are negative definitions, which suggests that the boundless fulfillment of desire relies upon the linguistic inversion of lack: human beings die and so can be saved only by some- thing that does *not* die. The middle two sentences set up a question- answer movement in which the logical transition between question and answer is conspicuously missing. The answer to the question, "Who knoweth the mysteries of the will, with its vigor?" is obviously "No one," and the logical premises that would ground the conclusion, "For God is . . . ," are omitted. The juxtaposition of the question mark and the conclusive conjunction "for" thus places at the center of the quotation a *disjunction* that conditions the negative definitions and so prefigures the story itself.

Indeed, Poe begins and ends his tale with much the same class of negations. "I cannot, for my soul," the narrator begins, "remember how, when, or even precisely where, I first became acquainted with the Lady Ligeia" (2:248). The narrator's acquaintance with Ligeia is the ground of interpretation, the "ligament" or marital bond by which he seeks to understand the cosmos as will; to forget how it began, then, is to ambiguate interpretive origins and thereby also interpretive ends. This problematic transition from origins to the deathly absence that is mortal existence, and from that absence to ends, is further undermined by the narrator's apparently casual oath, "for my soul," since one of the questions the story seeks to ask concerns the implications of interpretive will "for my soul." If I can so construe the mediatory icon as to permit absolute interpretation, can my will perpetuate my soul's existence beyond death? If the narrator cannot *remember* for his soul, his chances of *willing an interpretation* for his soul are slight.

The tale also closes on a note of interpretive ambiguity, heightened by the narrator's immoderate use of opium and the absence of witnesses: "And now slowly opened *the eyes* of the figure which stood before me. 'Here then, at least,' I shrieked aloud, 'can I never—can I never be mistaken—these are the full, and the black, and the wild eyes—of my lost love—of the lady—of the LADY LIGEIA'" (2:268). "Can I never be mistaken": the negative question embedded in the narrator's wild shriek seems to imply that he *wants* to be mistaken but knows he is not. But the will to be mistaken implies a will *not* to be mistaken; whether the narrator willfully mistakes a dead Rowena for a living Ligeia or a living Rowena for a dead Ligeia, his will to interpret implicates his perception of the metempsychosis in desire. The narrator both does and does not want the revived wife to be Ligeia, in the same internal conflict of wills by which he was earlier both delighted and appalled by her otherworldly eyes. "Glanvill" to the contrary, that is, who spoke only of "the will," the tale seems to posit in each of its protagonists *two* wills, one to life and one to death, Eros and Thanatos—though in a rather enhanced Freudian sense. The will to death is specifically a will not to surrender to death "utterly," which is to say, a will to continue to live even in and beyond death—to die, but not utterly—while the will to life involves a kind of absolute repression, by which the fear of death reduces life to a marble funereality, a placid *image* of death. "An *intensity* in thought, action, or speech, was possibly, in her, a result, or at least an index, of that gigantic volition which, during our long inter-course, failed to give other and more immediate evidence of its exis-tence. Of all the women whom I have ever known, she, the outwardly calm, the ever-placid Ligeia, was the most violently a prey to the tumul-tuous vultures of stern passion" (2:253). The narrator says that her in-tensity signals "her wild desire for life,—for life—*but* for life" (2:255), but it is not immediately clear what sort of life it is: a life that forestalls death or a life that transcends it. If passion and intensity are signs of "that gigantic volition," who or what is the "she" that is a prey to those passions?

The duality in both husband and wife suggests that their mar-riage enacts the conflict of wills in a single composite individual, Ligeia willing a visionary, transcendental death, her husband a repressive and regressive clinging to a childhood state of dependence: "Without Ligeia I was but as a child groping benighted" (2:254), he says, implying that *with* her he was as a child guided ("I was sufficiently aware of her in-finite supremacy to resign myself, with a childlike confidence, to her guidance through the chaotic world of metaphysical investigations" [2:254]). One is in fact tempted to follow Marie Bonaparte here, and to read the narrator's metaphysical investigations as aimed toward an absolute and permanent union with Ligeia in the flesh, which is to say, a literal return to the womb,[3] as reflected in the narrator's words: "With how vast a triumph—with how vivid a delight—with how much of all that is ethereal in hope—did I *feel,* as she bent over me in studies but little sought—but less known—that delicious vista by slow degrees expanding before me, down whose long, gorgeous, and all untrodden path, I might at length pass onward to the goal of a wisdom too di-vinely precious not to be forbidden!" (2:254). The narrator does not see but *feels,* as the wife-mother bends over him in little sought and less known "studies," a delicious vista expanding before him: a uterine vista, it seems, in which the apocalyptic paradise is sought not in a paternal exteriority (the New Jerusalem) but in a maternal interiority (the womb). The narrator wills life as a deathly stasis; Ligeia wills death as a vital transformation.

The interpretive dilemma that plagues the marriage is that as "ligament," as the mediatory bond by which "delicious vistas" into the cosmos can be gained, the marriage must be preserved against death, in a deathly freezing of time. But since it is the possibility of death trans-cended that opens those vistas, any such freezing or fixing in time would necessarily close off the attainment of the very visionary victory over death mediated by the marriage. Self-actualization requires, in Aristotle's terms from my epigraph, the preservation of the potentially existent by the actually existent (by the *entelecheia ontos,* that is, the perfection of the self toward which the potential of the self is constantly striving); but, Aristotle to the contrary, that *entelecheia ontos* is not "like" (*homoion*) the potentially existent but rather is its "contrary" (*enantion*). The fulfillment of desire, the attainment of true being, can be *imagined* only by the preservation of the potentially existent, which for Poe in this tale is a marriage of two living humans, man and wife; but it can be attained only by the destruction of the potentially existent, the destruction of the marriage in the death of one of its members, by a contrary that is revealed now as the very image of fulfilled desire, self-actualization. Preservation at once anticipates and is negated by destruction; destruction is at once the culmination and the ironic parody of preservation.

Poe's implicit revision of Aristotle's terms might tempt us to assimilate them to their NT use; *soteria,* or preservation, there is Christ's salvation, *phthora,* or destruction, the decay or corruption of the flesh when not quickened by the spirit, which would suggest that life as "mere" preservation, as sheer material existence, is a deathly cycle of decay that must be transcended in a spiritual salvation. But the simple opposition of spirit to matter will not suffice here. What is needed is a physical and material "salvation" in which destruction by the contrary is reified as the preservation of desire by its fulfillment; or, put differently, what is needed is a fulfillment of desire in which the fulfillment is not a *negation* of the state in which desire was conceived (the marital state of lack or fear of death), but an enhanced *return* to that state. And the spouses' solution to the dilemma (whether actually achieved by Ligeia, with or without her husband's imaginative aid, or only hallucinated by the narrator) is metempsychosis, in which the marriage is reconstituted through the visionary reincarnation of Ligeia's will in an expendable body. It is a daring solution to the old problem—but it is also, of course, a ghastly one, in which *bodies* are wasted (first Ligeia's, then Rowena's) in an obsessive attempt to render bodies proof against time and death. The ideal, of course, would be the sudden transformation of the body in *life,* without the destructive passage through death— that, certainly, is the attraction behind the Christian idea of the Rapture. Second best, perhaps, would be the revivification of a dead body by its *own* soul, as in the resurrection of Christ. The waste that begins to proliferate in Poe's tale bespeaks both an exacerbated awareness of the impossibility of an economical ideal and the escalating sense that any and all means must be employed to achieve the fulfillment of desire anyway, against all odds. The next step beyond "Ligeia," one surmises, is something like Mary Shelley's *Frankenstein,* in which an entire laboratory is filled with bodies from the charnel house in an effort to infuse *one* of them with life. And the culmination of the sequence is the destruction of *all* human flesh in order to ensure the fulfillment of a single human desire—a gruesome thought whose apocalyptic realization is at least logically implicit in Poe's "Ligeia."

■

"The Man of the Crowd" offers us a rather different image of desire fulfilled. In place of the fierce intensification of desire and its reification as its own fulfillment, here the image is diffused until it is emptied into absolute otherness. The tale's narrator, a somewhat calmer narrator than in "Ligeia," begins his tale with an explicit rejection of the possibility of total revelation:

> It was well said of a certain German book that *"es lässt sich nicht lesen"*—it does not permit itself to be read. There are some secrets which do not permit themselves to be told. Men die nightly in their beds, wringing the hands of ghostly confessors, and looking them piteously in the eyes—die with despair of heart and convulsion of throat, on account of the hideousness of mysteries which will not *suffer themselves* to be revealed. Now and then, alas, the conscience of man takes up a burthen so heavy in horror that it can be thrown down only into the grave. And thus the essence of all crime is undivulged. (4:134)

It is a rather drastic leap from "Now and then" to "the essence of *all* crime"; but the direction of Poe's leap, this time away from the absolute fulfillment of apocalyptic desire, signals this tale's difference from "Ligeia." Indeed, crime figures only in the tale's first and last paragraphs; it becomes, one might say, essentially a trope for the *social* human condition, which is thus revealed as impenetrable. Whereas in "Ligeia" Poe transforms a minicommunity of two, a marriage, into a complex medium for visionary seeing, in "The Man of the Crowd" he transforms a locus of visionary seeing into a vista onto the human community:

> Not long ago, about the closing in of an evening in autumn, I sat at the large bow window of the D---- Coffee-House in London. For some months I had been ill in health, but was now convalescent, and with returning strength, found myself in one of those happy moods which are so precisely the converse of *ennui*— moods of the keenest appetency, when the film from the mental vision departs—the ἀχλὺς ἣ πρὶν ἐπῆεν—and the intellect, electrified, surpasses as greatly its everyday condition, as does the vivid yet candid reason of Leibnitz, the mad and flimsy rhetoric of Gorgias. (4:134)

What follows is crucial: this strikingly Poeian description, with its apocalyptic invocation of the removal of mental veils, the *achlus he prin epeen* or "mist that before was on them" from the *Iliad* (5:127, where Athene gives Diomede an unobstructed vision of the gods while he fights), sets the stage for a very Hawthornean view of the evening crowd, rushing past the window.

Interestingly, however, even as Poe submits his narrator to realistic social description, he conceives that description in diacritical terms that bring to mind the day of doom. Lodged securely behind his window (that exterior "film of mental vision" which has not yet been removed), the narrator moves progressively down "the scale of what is termed gentility" (4:138), from "noblemen, merchants, attorneys, tradesmen, stock-jobbers" (4:136), all those "pointedly termed the decent" (4:136), through clerks, pickpockets, gamblers, dandies, military men, beggars, prostitutes, until at last he lights upon a singular figure whose expression "Retzsch, had he viewed it, would have greatly preferred . . . to his own pictural incarnations of the fiend" (4:140). The narrrator's diacritical observation of the community has led him down the rings of Dante's hell to the frozen figure of Satan at the center, realistically displaced into a potential model for a pictorial incarnation of the fiend.

But "I felt singularly aroused, startled, fascinated" (4:140): the sight of the strange old man brings the narrator out of his diacritical reverie, out of his serene seclusion behind the window, and into the street, where he sets himself to shadowing the old man for the next twenty-four hours, from dusk to dusk. It is a remarkable physical performance for a convalescent; but one might say that the disease from which the narrator is convalescing is the disease of Ligeia's husband, and he moves decisively out of it in the direction of what the society calls health: a concern for his fellow man, physical exercise in the open air, a plunging into the hustle and bustle of the city. The old man he follows—"close at his elbow through fear of losing sight of him" (4:141)—becomes his bond or "ligament" to the urban community; the excuse of observing the old man permits him to imitate him, and by this "ligation" he too becomes the "man of the crowd."

Significantly, however, that state is anything but healthy. The old man is not the crowd personified, but the crowd particularized; he does not simply "represent" the crowd, he cannot be apart from it. So long as he is surrounded by people, his gait is determined, his path apparently directed; but the direction is circular, or random, since the *crowd* never goes anywhere, however much individual people may move from one place to another. The old man's intensity of purpose is a wholly mechanical expression of the "press" of people; when the press slackens, he becomes aimless, wanders without object. The press of the crowd, perhaps, serves the old man as the "ligament" or bond that construes the urban "religion"—but it is an emptied-out religion, for the old man notices no one's face, but simply needs the presence of bodies, the sheer sensation of physical contact, living but depersonalized, for the semblance of stability.

David Riesman's popular term from the 1950s, "other-direction," is exactly right here: the old man is "the man of the crowd" because his essence is expressed only by and in the crowd, his direction determined not only by but *as* other.[4] The man of the crowd is emptied out in the sense that his self *is* wholly other; his interiority is displaced into sheer exteriority, his personality possessed by the impersonality of the crowd. He is man *as* the crowd. And this is the "health" to which the old man binds the narrator: the removal of the films of mental vision that separate self from other, the individual from the mass, entails a loss without gain, a dissipation of personal identity into objectified alienation. To venture out of diacritical seclusion is to escape the prisonhouse of solipsism and so to allow for the transformation of the self; but mediated by the crowd, that transformation is simply the loss of self, a conversion of self into an unrecognizably alien other. The narrator's act of identificatory observation mobilizes him out of passivity, but into a meaningless activity, a random tracing of the collective paths of an undifferentiated mass. The urban "religion" in this tale is a religion of crowdness, in which the self is bound to other selves by being locked firmly outside of itself.

■

Taken together, then, "Ligeia" and "The Man of the Crowd" chart the two extremes of a dual vision of community as an interpretive stay against death: one either confronts death by the ligation of an intensely personal beloved to a shadowy but somehow brilliant beyond, and is burned out; or one defers death (the old man is ageless; Ligeia dies young) by the ligation of a depersonalized stranger to a physically present but impenetrably alien and colorless crowd, and is emptied out. Poe offers us two "religions," two communal bindings, as bases for interpretation: a religion of the self, in which the duality of marriage becomes a mystical unity, husband and wife becoming a superpersonality whose intensity as fullness bursts all vessels; and a religion of the city, in which the multiplicity of the crowd becomes a unity that is not mystical but alien, an impersonality whose diffusion as emptiness binds through alienation.

What the two images of communal interpretation offer, I suggest, is a radical exploration of the values and dangers implicit in alternative models of criticism. What is the relation, these stories ask, between desire (or will) and interpretation? To what extent should interpretive will be intensified, regardless of the distortions such intensification requires, in the interest of confronting directly and paradigmatically one's personal stakes in the ethical and ontological concerns of the community? To what extent, and in what context, is it preferable to neutralize or displace interpretive will in quest of objectivity—to see things not as one wants them to be but, so far as possible, as they really are—in the interest of checking will with circumstantial exigency? To what extent should the critic offer his or her voice as the visionary incorporation of the multiplicity of communal voices, containing and lending coherence to all—how far as simply one more, anonymous like the rest, but at least adding something factual, a verifiable core—however small—of truth?

Most importantly, it seems to me, the conjunction of radical hopes and self-doubts in the American apocalyptic drive to places of mediation points us to the role of the literary work as a kind of dialogical medium, as at once a bone of contention and a forum that implicitly *contains* the contention. Something like this notion is Evan Watkins's insistence in *The Critical Act* that there is a reciprocal relation between poem and critic—"that a poem is more than an object of thought to be defined, explained, and interpreted. It must be understood as an object with a unique capacity to 'talk back,' to study in turn the critic who would analyze it."[5] Watkins's term for this reciprocity is *dialectic:* "For the basic movement of dialectical thinking remains the process whereby subject and object exchange roles, where a static antimony dissolves into the sheer relationality of a development with no fixed point of reference—neither the object itself, as in older theory, nor the critical act alone, as in more recent criticism—and no coordinates that can be mapped out in advance" (4-5). But a more accurate term for this reciprocal engagement I think is *dialogue,* which at least sidesteps the Hegelian implication of a progress toward a telos.[6] American apocalypses engage their critics in a dialogue about the ways and possibilities of knowing, just as critics engage those works in a dialogue about the ways and possibilities of meaning. But in so doing, writers and critics are also driven face to face with the self-reflexive problem of dialogue itself: to what extent is the very idea of a dialogue the solipsistic projection of individual imaginations, which construe opponents in order to internalize and so master the exchange; or, on the other hand, to what extent is the idea of dialogue the ritual enactment of a faceless community, which subsumes and so anonymitizes, neutralizes opponents and their oppositions?

If American apocalypses fail to provide answers to these questions, that failure is itself a spur to critics both to join in the dialogue on the ground established and explored by those works, and dialogically to *shift* that ground in directions that seem, to the individual critic at historically limited points in time, fruitful and exciting. In this creative and responsive conception of the literary act, there is at once no room for hubristic assertion and all the room in the world. The effort will, after all, soon enough be damped out, but may in the process reconstrue the ground of the debate.

CHAPTER 1: APOCALYPTIC HERMENEUTICS

1. Leslie Fiedler, *Love and Death in the American Novel* (1960; repr., New York: Stein & Day, 1975), p. 23.

2. Saul Bellow, *Herzog* (New York: Viking Press, 1964), pp. 316–17.

3. Henry James, *The Art of the Novel: Critical Prefaces* (New York: Charles Scribner, 1934), pp. 256–57. See also Burton R. Pollin, "Poe and Henry James: A Changing Relationship," *Yearbook of English Studies* (1973), pp. 232–43; and Adeline R. Tintner, "James Corrects Poe: The Appropriation of *Pym* in *The Golden Bowl*," *American Transcendental Quarterly* 37 (Winter 1978), pp. 87–91.

4. R. W. B. Lewis's "Days of Wrath and Laughter" appeared in his essay collection, *Trials of the Word* (New Haven: Yale University Press, 1965), pp. 184–235; Robert Alter's "The Apocalyptic Temper" in *Commentary* 41 (June 1966), pp. 61–66; Bernard Bergonzi's discussion of contemporary "comic-apocalyptic" fiction on pp. 98–120 of *The Situation of the Novel* (Harmondsworth, England: Penguin Books, 1972); and Nathan A. Scott, Jr.'s, " 'New Heav'ns, New Earth'—The Landscape of Contemporary Apocalypse" in *Journal of Religion* 53 (January 1973), pp. 1–35, esp. 24–27. See also Walter Cummins, "Inventing Memories: Apocalyptics and Domestics," *The Literary Review* 23, no. 1 (Fall 1979), pp. 127–33.

5. Alter, "The Apocalyptic Temper," pp. 62–63. For Alter's later applications of this position to other contemporary novels, see "The New American Novel," *Commentary* 60, no. 5 (November 1975), pp. 44–51, and "The American Political Novel," *New York Times Book Review*, August 10, 1980, pp. 3, 26–27.

6. Richard Chase, *The American Novel and Its Tradition* (1957; repr., Baltimore: Johns Hopkins University Press, 1980), p. 13.

7. Northrop Frye, *Anatomy of Criticism: Four Essays* (1957; repr., Princeton: Princeton University Press, 1973), pp. 186–205.

8. For later applications of Chase's unproblematic account of American romance to the question of apocalypse, see Elaine B. Safer, "The Allusive

Mode and Black Humor in Barth's *Giles Goat-Boy* and Pynchon's *Gravity's Rainbow*," *Renascence* 32, no. 2 (1980), pp. 89–104; and Lois Parkinson Zamora, "The Apocalyptic Myth and the American Literary Imagination," in *The Apocalyptic Vision in America: Interdisciplinary Essays on Myth and Culture*, ed. Lois Parkinson Zamora (Bowling Green, Ohio: Bowling Green University Popular Press, 1982), pp. 97–138. Both Safer and Zamora adopt the conservative readings of American apocalypses offered by Lewis, Alter, and others, without either derogating these apocalypses or perceiving in them the problematic nature that the conservative reaction attempted to elicit.

The most recent example of this sort of reading, which appeared after this book was written, is Zbigniew Lewicki's *The Bang and the Whimper: Apocalypse and Entropy in American Literature* (Westport, Conn.: Greenwood Press, 1984). Lewicki is a purist who would define American apocalypses by means of an ideal formalistic (structural and imagistic) correspondence with the Book of Revelation. Citing R. W. B. Lewis's formulation of the ten phases of the apocalyptic process, he writes:

> If these are indeed the main apocalyptic "moments," and there seems to be little quarrel with Lewis' assumptions, then apocalyptic fiction perhaps can best be identified by the presence and intensity of related images. Ideally, a novel would include situations that can be traced back to all these elements of the apocalyptic vision. However, this is very rarely the case. It is therefore important to establish which of these images must be present in a work of fiction if it is to be classified as apocalyptic literature. It seems that the indispensable elements are the Antichrist figure, the battle between the forces of light and the powers of darkness, and the destruction of the book's world by violent means. The last element is particularly crucial, and no other image can be substituted for it. (xiii–xiv)

The result is a mode of interpretation in which American apocalypses are reduced to pale imitations of the biblical apocalypse. According to Lewicki, *Moby-Dick*, for example, gives us the entire pattern, since Ishmael's survival of the catastrophe signals his redemptive translation into paradise:

> Although at first Ishmael does not seem to be among the elect, his behavior gradually convinces us that he is. He befriends Queequeg but refuses to participate in the savage's pagan ceremonies; goes to church before sailing; keeps his distance from Ahab; and favors Stubb and Starbuck, who at least try to challenge their iconoclastic captain. Ultimately, Ishmael is rewarded with salvation, which also completes the apocalyptic structure. (27)

Lewicki does not, I should add, offer this reading parodically; he is perfectly serious.

9. See Kenneth Burke, *The Rhetoric of Religion: Studies in Logology* (1961; repr., Berkeley and Los Angeles: University of California Press, 1970), pp. 1–42, esp. 13–14.

10. See Northrop Frye, *Fearful Symmetry: A Study of William Blake*

(Princeton: Princeton University Press, 1947); Harold Bloom, *Blake's Apocalypse: A Study in Poetic Argument* (Ithaca: Cornell University Press, 1963); Geoffrey Hartman, *Wordsworth's Poetry, 1787-1814* (New Haven: Yale University Press, 1964) (all subsequent quotations are from this edition); Ross Grieg Woodman, *The Apocalyptic Vision in the Poetry of Shelley* (Toronto: University of Toronto Press, 1964); Thomas J. J. Altizer, *The New Apocalypse: The Radical Christian Vision of William Blake* (East Lansing, Mich.: Michigan State University Press, 1967); M. H. Abrams, *Natural Supernaturalism: Tradition and Revolution in Romantic Literature* (New York: W. W. Norton & Co., 1971) (all subsequent quotations are from this edition); and Harvey Stahl, *William Blake: The Apocalyptic Vision* (New York: Wittenborn, 1974).

11. Harold Bloom, *Agon: Toward a Theory of Revisionism* (New York: Oxford University Press, 1982), p. 335. This notion of "negative" or "antithetical" criticism has been one of Bloom's major critical tenets since *The Anxiety of Influence* (1973; repr., New York: Oxford University Press, 1981). Kenneth Burke's pronouncement on God and language that Bloom paraphrases is from *Language as Symbolic Action: Essays on Life, Literature, and Method* (Berkeley and Los Angeles: University of California Press, 1966), p. 469: "Everything that can be said about 'God' has its analogue in something that can be said about *language.*"

12. See Sidney P. Moss, "Poe's Apocalyptic Vision," in *Papers on Poe*, ed. Richard P. Veler (Springfield: Chantry Music Press, 1972), pp. 42-53; Todd M. Lieber's chapter "The Apocalyptic Imagination of A. Gordon Pym" in *Endless Experiments* (Columbus: Ohio State University Press, 1973), pp. 165-89; and two books by David Ketterer, *New Worlds for Old: The Apocalyptic Imagination, Science Fiction, and American Literature* (Bloomington: Indiana University Press, 1974), pp. 50-75, esp. 70 (all subsequent quotations are from this edition), and *The Rationale of Deception in Poe* (Baton Rouge: Louisiana State University Press, 1979), pp. 125-41.

13. See esp. R. H. Charles's *Eschatology: The Doctrine of a Future Life in Israel, Judaism and Christianity* (1899; repr., New York: Schocken Books, 1963), and *A Critical and Exegetical Commentary on the Book of Revelation of St. John* (Edinburgh: T. & T. Clark, 1920). For later exegetical studies of the apocalyptic writings, see H. H. Rowley's *The Relevance of Apocalyptic: A Study of Jewish and Christian Apocalypse from Daniel to the Revelation* (1944; rev. ed., London: Lutterworth Press, 1963); D. S. Russell's *The Method and Message of Jewish Apocalyptic* (Philadelphia: Westminster Press, 1964); and Paul D. Hanson's *The Dawn of Apocalyptic: The Historical and Sociological Roots of Jewish Apocalyptic Eschatology* (Philadelphia: Fortune Press, 1975). An extremely helpful overview of twentieth-century theological studies of the apocalypse may be found in Klaus Koch, *The Rediscovery of Apocalypse*, trans. Margaret Kohl (London: SCM Press, 1972). Other useful works on individual apocalypses include Austin Farrer, *A Rebirth of Images: The Making of St. John's Apocalypse* (London: Dacre, 1949); and John J. Collins, *The Apocalyptic Vision of the Book of Daniel* (Missoula, Mont.: Scholars Press, 1977). The classic sociological study of Lewis's "Lutheran" strain of apocalypse in modern times is *When Prophecy Fails,* by Leon

Festinger, Henry W. Riecker, and Stanley Schachter (New York: Harper & Row, 1964). And the central study of the entire historical ground for this discussion (the main source, in fact, for Lewis's distinction between "Augustinian" and "Lutheran" phases of apocalyptic belief) is Ernest Lee Tuveson, *Millennium and Utopia: A Study in the Background of the Idea of Progress* (Berkeley: University of California Press, 1949).

14. See Harold Bloom, *A Map of Misreading* (New York: Oxford University Press, 1975). For a concise literary-critical account of midrash, see Frank Kermode, *The Genesis of Secrecy: On the Interpretation of Narrative* (1979; repr., Cambridge: Harvard University Press, 1982), pp. 81-83.

15. Hal Lindsey's most famous book (a 10-million-copy bestseller) is, with C. C. Carlson, *The Late Great Planet Earth* (Grand Rapids: Zondervan Publishing House, 1970). Lindsey has published numerous other books propounding the same theories of imminent apocalypse as well, and apparently is available on cassette tape. Lindsey's stature in the field of imminent end-prediction is no doubt due in large part to his calm, "scholarly" approach; he is by far the most rhetorically restrained and scholastically cautious of recent prophets of doom.

16. I refer to Jeremiah's famous unfulfilled prophecy (Jer. 25:12) that Israel's restoration would come 70 years after the rebuilding of the temple. By the time of the writing of the Book of Daniel (ca. 165 B.C.), several hundred years had passed without restoration, and so the writer addresses himself to the hermeneutical problem: "I, Daniel, perceived in the books the number of years which, according to the Word of the Lord to Jeremiah the prophet, must pass before the end of the desolations of Jerusalem, namely, seventy years" (Dan 9:2). In accordance with the prophetic tradition at the supposed time of writing (Nebuchadnezzar's reign during the Exile), the pseudonymous writer attributes the delay to Israel's sin, and launches into an over-dramatic prayer to spare his holy nation. But then an angel appears, "to give you wisdom and understanding" (9:22), and explains that "seventy weeks of years are decreed concerning your people and your holy city" (9:24) before the restoration. Seventy years are thus revised by midrash into 70 heptads, 70 times 7 years, or 490 years, bringing the end roughly into the time of the book's writing. The period of the end is significantly not contingent upon Israel's repentance, as it had been for the prophets, but is *decreed,* predestined, a central feature of apocalyptic. At the end of his book, "Daniel" revises the "decreed" time still further, predicting a restoration in 1,260, 1,290, and 1,335 days (12:5-13). But each prediction is disconfirmed in its turn, and by the time John of Patmos comes to write his Apocalypse, the entire notion of 70 heptads is obsolete. "Daniel's" series of four beasts (chapter 7) culminates in Greece; but by A.D. 95 Greece has been superseded by Rome, and John of Patmos adopts "Daniel's" imagery of beasts in midrashic revision, calling the last beast a Roman emperor.

17. Bernard McGinn, *Visions of the End: Apocalyptic Traditions in the Middle Ages* (New York: Columbia University Press, 1979), p. 25. Due to this resistance in Augustine to imminent prediction, McGinn describes him as "the fountainhead of all anti-apocalyptic eschatology in the Middle Ages"

(p. 26); historically, to deny the imminence of the end is to deny the apocalypse.

18. The stark contrast I set up here between the conservatism of
Augustine and the medieval church on the one hand and the revolutionary
thrust of apocalypticism on the other is Norman Cohn's vision of millenarian-
ism in *The Pursuit of the Millennium: Revolutionary Millenarians and Mystical
Anarchists of the Middle Ages* (1957; rev. ed., New York: Oxford University
Press, 1970), which as Bernard McGinn points out in *Visions of the End*
(pp. 29-31) has been partially discredited by later scholarship. Medieval
apocalypticism was not *merely* revolutionary; it was also, McGinn shows, frequently employed to support existing temporal institutions. This is an important historical qualification; certainly end-predictive apocalyptic sects
today too can be revolutionary, but more often (as in the case of Hal Lindsey)
they represent a kind of conservative orthodoxy. Ideologically, however,
Cohn is right in an important sense: the apocalyptic transformation is by
definition a radical revolution, whether the power locus it overthrows is one
of authority or of a challenge to authority. End-predictive apocalypticism
invariably projects the destruction of political opposition and the survival and
transformation of self, and in that broad sense *is* always revolutionary.

19. R. W. B. Lewis's *The American Adam: Innocence, Tragedy, and
Tradition in the Nineteenth Century* (Chicago: University of Chicago Press,
1955) was the classic "myth-symbol" study of the central American myth in
nineteenth-century thought; I discuss its importance to an understanding of
American apocalypses in chapter 3 of this book. Charles Reich's *The Greening of America* (New York: Random House, 1970), a rhapsodic account of
new Adams and Eves in jeans and long hair and a transformed consciousness
("Consciousness III"), stood squarely in the grand Emersonian tradition of
"hope" that Lewis traced in the earlier book.

20. John R. May, *Toward a New Earth: Apocalypse in the American Novel* (Notre Dame: University of Notre Dame Press, 1972), p. 35. All
subsequent quotations are from this edition.

21. Letter to Thomas Butts, July 6, 1803, in *The Complete Poetry
and Prose of William Blake*, ed. David V. Erdman (1965; rev. ed., Garden
City, N.Y.: Doubleday & Co., 1982), p. 730. All subsequent quotations are
from this edition.

22. Northrop Frye, *Anatomy of Criticism*, p. 119. Frye's herme-
neutical opposition to the "wrong" or reductive literal interpretation of the
Apocalypse is clearest in his recent book on the Bible, *The Great Code*
(New York: Harcourt Brace Jovanovich, 1982):

> We are greatly simplifying the vision [of the Book of Revelation],
> however, if we think of it simply as what the author thought was
> soon going to happen, as a firework show that would be put on for
> the benefit of the faithful, starting perhaps next Tuesday. For
> him all these incredible wonders are the inner meaning or, more
> accurately, the inner form of everything that is happening now.
> Man creates what he calls history as a screen to conceal the working

of the apocalypse from himself. . . . What is symbolized as the destruction of the order of nature is the destruction of the way of
seeing that order that keeps man confined to the world of time and
history as we know them. This destruction is what the Scripture
is intended to achieve. (136)

"Intended": i.e., my interpretation of the Bible is no mere interpretation, but
the true meaning of the Scripture.

23. For a fuller account of centers and circumferences in Blake, see
Hazard Adams, *Blake and Yeats: The Contrary Vision* (Ithaca: Cornell University Press, 1955), pp. 290-96.

24. I quote from Robert Scholes's book on science fiction, *Structural
Fabulation: An Essay on Fiction of the Future* (Notre Dame: University of
Notre Dame Press, 1975), p. 29; Scholes first defined fabulation for literary
criticism in his highly influential book, *The Fabulators* (New York: Oxford
University Press, 1967).

25. *The Education of Henry Adams*, ed. Ernest Samuels (1906; Boston: Houghton Mifflin Co., 1973), p. 63. All subsequent quotations are from
this edition.

26. Ketterer, *New ·Worlds for Old*, pp. 94-95. Ketterer's claim that
nuclear weaponry has rendered the theological sense of apocalyptic obsolete
is essentially an extreme version of Perry Miller's discussion of the atomic
blast at Hiroshima and its consequences for the apocalyptic imagination in
Miller's essay, "The End of the World," in *Errand into the Wilderness* (Cambridge, Mass.: Belknap Press, 1956), pp. 217-39, esp. 238. Indeed, the notion
is rapidly becoming a critical commonplace; Ketterer develops it out of
references to Miller in Lewis's "Days of Wrath and Laughter," pp. 205-6,
and May's *Toward a New Earth*, pp. 3-4.

27. See, for example, Lindsey and Carlson's discussion of the coming
nuclear holocaust in *The Late Great Planet Earth*, pp. 149-50. In the funda-
mentalist imagination, it doesn't really matter who *builds* the instruments of
destruction; whether they are bowls made in heaven or bombs made on earth,
God wields them and therefore controls his apocalypse.

28. See citation for Abrams in note 10. In *Natural Supernaturalism*,
Abrams lists four Romantic apocalypses—crisis-autobiography, apocalypse by
revolution, apocalypse by imagination, and apocalypse by cognition—as well
as the biblical apocalypse and the secular vision of total annihilation, the
latter of which actually lies outside the scope of Abrams's subject but is mentioned in passing late in the book (pp. 426-27). Martha Banta offers a range
of categories for organizing the various visions of apocalypse; most important
are the vision of perfection, which projects an image of paradise; the vision of
cessation, which predicts a secular annihilation; and the vision of continuation,
which confronts the possibility of an end only to reject its likelihood. More
than any other student of the American apocalypse, Banta stresses the importance of the third, or continuative, vision for American writers: the
antiapocalyptic *restriction* of apocalyptic vision, which I explore in detail
throughout Part II. See Banta's *Failure and Success in America: A Literary*

Debate (Princeton: Princeton University Press, 1978), parts V and VI, and "American Apocalypses: Excrement and Ennui," *Studies in the Literary Imagination* 7, no. 1 (Spring 1974), pp. 1-30.

29. See Frank Kermode's *The Sense of an Ending* (New York: Oxford University Press, 1967), *passim*.

30. For a concise discussion of the importance of "antiapocalpyses" in American literature, especially among the contemporary novels that Lewis brands "comic apocalypses," see my "Visions of *No* End: The Anti-Apocalyptic Novels of Ellison, Barth, and Coover," *American Studies in Scandinavia* 13 (1981), pp. 1-16. Another framework for understanding the interrelationships of apocalyptic hermeneutics is presented in my "Poe's Mini-Apocalypse: 'The Conversation of Eiros and Charmion,' " *Studies in Short Fiction* 19, no. 4 (Fall 1982), pp. 329-37, esp. 335-37.

CHAPTER 2: SIGNS OF THE TIMES

1. Jacques Derrida, "Differance," in *Speech and Phenomena*, trans. David Allison (Evanston: Northwestern University Press, 1973), p. 138. All subsequent quotations are from this edition. See also Derrida's recent discourse on the apocalypse itself, "Of an Apocalyptic Tone Recently Adopted in Philosophy," trans. John P. Leavey, Jr., *Semeia* 23 (1982) (an entire issue devoted to Derrida and biblical studies), pp. 63-97. Unfortunately, I came to this rich essay of Derrida's only after my manuscript was completed. Toward the end of his essay, Derrida ponders:

> I have also asked myself why, to what ends, with a view to what, did the Apocalypse itself, I mean the historic writings thus named and first the one signed by John of Patmos, install itself little by little, above all for six or seven years, as a theme, a concern, a fascination, an explicit reference, and the horizon for me of a work or a task, although I know very badly these rich and secret texts. (90)

Although he offers no answer to his own question, it seems clear that the apocalyptic imagination fascinates Derrida precisely as the "purest" form, the most mythical expression or the most extreme statement of the metaphysics of presence:

> Whoever takes on the apocalyptic tone comes to signify to, if not to tell, you something. What? The truth, of course, and to signify to you that it reveals the truth to you; the tone is the revelator of some unveiling process. Unveiling or truth, apophantics of the imminence of the end, of whatever returns at the limit, at the end of the world. Not only truth as the revealed truth of a secret on the end or of the secret of the end. Truth itself is the end, the destination, and that truth unveils itself is the advent of the end. Truth is the end and the instance of the Last Judgment. The structure of truth here would be apocalyptic. And that is why there would not be any truth of the apocalypse that is not the truth of truth. (84)

Derrida ends his essay eloquently, rising to a high apocalyptic tone in order to place into question the apocalyptic tone—a strategy that, I will suggest in this book, American writers emulate up to a point and then swerve away from:

> Now here, precisely, is announced—as promise or threat—an apocalypse without apocalypse, an apocalypse without vision, without truth, without revelation, of *dispatches* [des envois] (for the 'come' is plural in itself, in oneself), of addresses without message and without destination, without sender or decidable addressee, without last judgment, without any other eschatology than the tone of the 'Come' itself, its very difference, an apocalypse beyond good and evil. . . . But then what is someone doing who tells you: I tell you this, I have come to tell you this, there is not, there never has been, there never will be an apocalypse, the apocalypse deceives, disappoints? There is the apocalypse *without* apocalypse. The word *sans, without,* I mention here in Blanchot's so necessary syntax, who often says *X without X.* The *without,* the *sans* marks an internal and external catastrophe of the apocalypse, an overturning of sense [*sens*] that does not merge with the catastrophe announced or described in the apocalyptic writings without however being foreign to them. Here the catastrophe would perhaps be *of* the apocalypse itself, its *pli* and its end, a closure without end, an end without end. . . .
>
> The end approaches. Now there is no more time to tell the truth on the apocalypse. But what are we doing, you will still insist, to what ends do we want to come when we come to tell you, here now, let's go, 'come,' the apocalypse, it's finished, that's all, I tell you this, that's what happens, that's what comes. (94–95)

Apocalypse without apocalypse: this might stand as the implicit motto of American apocalypses as well, with the crucial proviso that in American literature an apocalypse without apocalypse is still an apocalypse, by which I mean that American apocalyptists seek not to tear away the veil presented by the apocalyptic unveiling, as Derrida would, but to preserve the unveiled veil. Derrida retains the apocalyptic tone in order to destroy it; but in his urgency to expose the unveiling of presence he necessarily implicates himself in that same unveiling, as the unveiling of the *sans* comes finally to look, as Derrida's ironic conclusion indicates he knows, like the unveiling of the truth. American apocalyptists, one might say, destroy the apocalyptic tone in order to retain it, but in retaining it transform it; the American apocalypse is an apocalypse *with* vision, *with* truth, *with* revelation, *with* eschatology, but it is a vision, a truth, a revelation, an eschatology with a difference—a difference that will inform my discussion of American apocalypses throughout.

2. Eric LaGuardia,"Derrida's 'Differance,'" *Cahiers roumains d'études littéraires* 3 (1981), p. 37.

3. Martin Heidegger, *Holzwege,* cited in Derrida, "Differance," pp. 155–56.

4. Northrop Frye, *Anatomy of Criticism: Four Essays* (1957; repr., Princeton: Princeton University Press, 1973), p. 104.

5. Carol Balizet, *The Seven Last Years* (1979; repr., New York: Bantam Books, 1980). All subsequent quotations are from this edition.

6. Lindsey needs the two phases for a familiar reason: the unfulfillment of prophecy. The 70 heptads (70 times 7 years) are of course "Daniel's" midrash of the famous unfulfilled prophecy of Jeremiah, that the messianic restoration would come 70 *years* after the rebuilding of the temple. Because "Daniel's" prediction too remained unfulfilled, Lindsey is forced to invent a historical bifurcation of the 70 heptads into two phases, one before Christ lasting 69 heptads (483 years), the other (a single heptad, 7 years long) in the 1980s and 1990s. Note that, weak as this link may be, it is absolutely characteristic of apocalyptic predictions in this mode. Somehow the dates must be manipulated in order to place the end in the writer's own imminent future.

The doctrine of a pretribulation Rapture, in which the saints are taken up before the sufferings begin and so are spared the pains reserved for sinners, is quite another matter. Here we confront a dogmatic tradition whose fundamental premise is that God will not let his people suffer, a premise that is historically and ideologically tied to the Calvinist belief that worldly prosperity was God's reward for virtue and that poverty or other suffering was his punishment for sin. There is, of course, no scriptural warrant for the pretribulation Rapture; the passages usually quoted in support of the idea (1 Cor 15, 1 Thess 4, etc.) say that the Christians will be taken up, but not *when.* Indeed, in the key text, 1 Thess 4:13–18, to which Lindsey, with C. C. Carlson (in *The Late Great Planet Earth* [Grand Rapids, Mich.: Zondervan Publishing House, 1970], pp. 130–31) refer without quoting, the narrative sequence is (1) the Lord's Coming, (2) the resurrection of the dead, (3) the Rapture, all of which follow the tribulation in the Book of Revelation.

7. See Herman Melville's *The Confidence-Man: His Masquerade,* ed. Elizabeth S. Foster (1857; New York: Hendricks House, 1954), p. 271.

8. My discussion of Balizet's "phantasy of the reversal of generations" is indebted to John T. Irwin's discussion of that phantasy as posited by Ernest Jones. See Irwin's *Doubling and Incest/Repetition and Revenge: A Speculative Reading of Faulkner* (1975; repr., Baltimore: Johns Hopkins University Press, 1980), pp. 64–67. I will discuss the phantasy in greater detail in connection with Faulkner's *Absalom, Absalom!* in chapter 6.

9. William Carlos Williams, "The American Background," in *Selected Essays* (New York: New Directions, 1954), p. 134. All subsequent quotations are from this edition.

10. Cited in Sacvan Bercovitch, *The Puritan Origins of the American Self* (New Haven: Yale University Press, 1975), pp. 142–43. All subsequent Bercovitch quotations are from this edition.

11. Jonathan Edwards, *The Nature of True Virtue* (1765; Ann Arbor: University of Michigan Press, 1960), pp. 8–9.

12. Cited in Kenneth Murdock's "Introduction" in Michael Wiggles-

worth, *The Day of Doom* (1662; New York: Russell & Russell, 1966), p. ix. All quotations from the poem are from this edition.

13. Kenneth Burke, *The Rhetoric of Religion: Studies in Logology* (1961; repr., Berkeley and Los Angeles: University of California Press, 1970), p. 218. All subsequent quotations are from this edition.

CHAPTER 3: REVISING THE AMERICAN DREAM

1. David Ketterer, *New Worlds for Old: The Apocalyptic Imagination, Science Fiction, and American Literature* (Bloomington: Indiana University Press, 1974), p. 332.

2. See H. Richard Niebuhr, *The Kingdom of God in America* (Chicago: Willett, Clark & Co., 1937); Perry Miller, "The End of the World," in *Errand into the Wilderness* (Cambridge, Mass: Belknap Press), pp. 217–39; Frederic I. Carpenter, *American Literature and the Dream* (New York: Philosophical Library, 1955); R. W. B. Lewis, *The American Adam: Innocence, Tragedy, and Tradition in the Nineteenth Century* (Chicago: University of Chicago Press, 1955); David W. Noble, *The Eternal Adam and the New World Garden: The Central Myth in the American Novel Since 1830* (New York: George Braziller, 1968); Ernest Lee Tuveson, *Redeemer Nation: The Idea of America's Millennial Role* (Chicago: University of Chicago Press, 1968); Cushing Strout, *The New Heavens and the New Earth: Political Religion in America* (New York: Harper & Row, Publishers, 1974); Sacvan Bercovitch, *The Puritan Origins of the American Self* (New Haven: Yale University Press, 1975), and *The American Jeremiad* (Madison: University of Wisconsin Press, 1978); James H. Moorhead, *The American Apocalypse: Yankee Protestants and the Civil War, 1860–1869* (New Haven: Yale University Press, 1978). Both Moorhead and Bercovitch provide highly useful bibliographies. See also two essays in Lois Parkinson Zamora, ed., *The Apocalyptic Vision in America: Interdisciplinary Essays in Myth and Culture* (Bowling Green, Ohio: Bowling Green University Popular Press, 1982): Ernest Cassara, "The Development of America's Sense of Mission" (pp. 64–96) and Charles H. Lippy, "Waiting for the End: The Social Context of American Apocalyptic Religion" (pp. 37–63). All subsequent quotations to the references in this note are from the editions cited.

3. Frederick I. Carpenter, " 'The American Myth': Paradise (To Be) Regained," *PMLA* 74 (December 1959), pp. 599–606.

4. Cited from Mark Twain's Notebook #18 in Henry Nash Smith, *Mark Twain's Fable of Progress: Political and Economic Ideas in "A Connecticut Yankee"* (New Brunswick, N.J.: Rutgers University Press, 1964), p. 41.

5. See Harold Bloom, *A Map of Misreading* (1975; repr., New York: Oxford University Press, 1980), pp. 101–3. All subsequent quotations are from this edition. My terminological borrowings from Bloom's map throughout this chapter are "assimilative" (or piratical), but by that token are made in much the same spirit as Bloom's own borrowings from Freud. "I grant that my method is precariously assimilative," Bloom writes in *A Map of Misreading*,

"and that my transfers from Freudian theory to poetry may seem curiously literal. But I seek to take back from Freud precisely what he himself took from the poets (or from Schopenhauer and Nietzsche, who themselves had taken it from the poets). This is what Freud called *Bedeutungswandel,* which Hartman translates as either 'tropism of meaning' or 'wandering signification' " (89). Since I trope Bloom's meanings by assimilating them to Twain's *A Connecticut Yankee,* it may be useful here to review Bloom's terms in their original context. Bloom reads the Romantic crisis-lyric as a series of three revisionary dialectics, each substituting for a mode of limitation a mode of representation. The first dialectic moves from the trope of *irony* or the revisionary ratio of *clinamen* (characterized by the psychic defense of reaction-formation and the poetic imagery of presence and absence) to the trope of *synecdoche* or the revisionary ratio of *tessera* (characterized by the psychic defense of reversal or turning against the self and the poetic imagery of part and whole). The ephebe's sense of his own absence in relation to the precursor's presence is thus relativized by the synecdochic perception that the precursor's presence is part of a larger and disfigured whole. The second dialectic moves from the trope of *metonymy* or the revisionary ratio of *kenosis* (characterized by the psychic defenses of undoing, isolation, and regression and the poetic imagery of fullness and emptiness) to the trope of *hyperbole* or the revisionary ratio of *daemonization* (characterized by the psychic defense of repression and the poetic imagery of high and low). Here the ephebe's self-limitation, self-reduction to a stance of humility or emptiness before the fullness of the precursor, is hyperbolically transformed, like Satan in the emptiness of the abyss, into an image of the Sublime (high) or the Grotesque (low). The third dialectic, finally, moves from the trope of *metaphor* or the revisionary ratio of *askesis* (characterized by the psychic defense of sublimation and the poetic imagery of inside and outside) to the trope of *metalepsis* or the revisionary ratio of *apophrades* (characterized by the psychic defenses of introjection and projection and the poetic imagery of early and late). The perspectivizing movement of metaphorical resemblance, in this last dialectic, is triumphantly overcome in an early/late reversal in which the son becomes his father's father and so achieves a victory over time and the precursor both. See Bloom's tabulation of the map on p. 84 of *A Map of Misreading* and his discussion throughout chapter 5, pp. 83–105.

6. Smith, *Mark Twain's Fable of Progress,* p. 92.

7. Justin Kaplan, "Introduction," in Mark Twain, *A Connecticut Yankee in King Arthur's Court* (Harmondsworth, England: Penguin Books, 1980), p. 17.

8. Kenneth Burke, *The Rhetoric of Religion: Studies in Logology* (1961; repr., Berkeley and Los Angeles: University of California Press, 1970), p. 180.

9. For a related approach to the discussion of "terms" that follows, see Harold Bloom's reading of Emily Dickinson's lyric, "Our Journey Had Advanced" (#615), in *Wallace Stevens: The Poems of our Climate* (Ithaca: Cornell University Press, 1977), p. 16–19.

10. Erich Auerbach, *"Figura,"* in *Scenes from the Drama of European*

Literature, trans. Ralph Manheim (New York: Meridian Books, 1959), pp. 28–49. For useful discussions of typological concerns in American literature, see Ursula Brumm, *American Thought and Religious Typology* (New Brunswick: Rutgers University Press, 1970), and the essays in Sacvan Bercovitch, ed., *Typology in Early American Literature* (Amherst: University of Massachusetts Press, 1972), esp. Thomas M. Davis, "The Traditions of Puritan Typology" (pp. 11–45).

11. Bloom, *A Map of Misreading,* p. 100.

12. Mark Twain, *A Connecticut Yankee in King Arthur's Court* (1889; repr., New York: Harper & Bros., 1917), p. 61. All subsequent quotations are from this edition.

13. Smith, *Mark Twain's Fable of Progress,* p. 39.

14. Kenneth Burke, *A Grammar of Motives* (1945; repr., Berkeley and Los Angeles: University of California Press, 1969).

15. Martha Banta, *Failure and Success in America: A Literary Debate* (Princeton: Princeton University Press, 1978), p. 435. All subsequent quotations are from this edition.

16. Smith, *Mark Twain's Fable of Progress,* pp. 87–88.

17. See J. H. Kahn, *Job's Illness: Loss, Grief, Integration: A Psychological Interpretation* (New York: Pergamon Press, 1975). For a related reading of Job, see Victor White's theological answer to C. G. Jung's *Answer to Job* in "Jung on Job," Appendix V to *Soul and Psyche* (London: Collins & Harvill Press, 1960), pp. 233–40.

18. The text that until very recently was read and criticized as "The Mysterious Stranger" was the joint creation of Twain's first literary executor, Alfred Bigelow Paine, and Paine's editor at Harper & Bros., Frederick A. Duneka (1916). With the publication of John S. Tuckey's close study of the manuscript material in *Mark Twain and Little Satan: The Writing of The Mysterious Stranger* (West Lafayette, Ind.: Purdue University Press, 1963), of W. M. Gibson's edition of *Mark Twain's Mysterious Stranger Manuscripts* (Berkeley and Los Angeles: University of California Press, 1969), and of Sholom J. Kahn's *Mark Twain's Mysterious Stranger: A Study of the Manuscript Texts* (Columbia: University of Missouri Press, 1978), critical opinion seems increasingly to be turning against the Paine-Duneka text, which Gibson denounces as a "fraud" (1) and Kahn dismisses more calmly as "a literary curiosity illustrative of the special taste and editorial practices prevalent in the second decade of the twentieth-century United States" (11). Paine and Duneka did, it appears, take rather excessive liberties with Twain's text; a good example is their invention of an evil astrologer to take the heat off the bad priest (Father Adolf) whom Twain attacks in the manuscript, because Twain's attack offended Duneka's Catholic sensibilities. (See Tuckey, *Mark Twain and Little Satan,* pp. 19–20.)

More importantly, close analysis of the manuscript texts has shown that there are three distinct "Mysterious Stranger" drafts, of which only the third is reasonably complete and coherent. In fact, only the third draft is even *titled* "The Mysterious Stranger"; the first is "The Chronicle of Young Satan," the second "Schoolhouse Hill," and the third "No. 44, The Mysterious

Stranger." The "all is a dream" chapter is the conclusion to "No. 44," where the mysterious stranger is not Satan but a mysterious "44," and the narrator is not Theodor Fischer but August Feldner. Paine and Duneka based their edition of *The Mysterious Stranger* on "The Chronicle of Young Satan," Twain's first and rejected draft of the book, making such editorial emendations as their literary and ideological judgments suggested were necessary, and grafting onto the unfinished ending the concluding chapter from "No. 44."

As should be obvious, I agree with Tuckey, Gibson, and Kahn that the Paine-Duneka text is corrupt and should be superseded by "No. 44," or even by the manuscript texts in their present state. Certainly considerable support for my reading of the concluding chapter could be adduced from "No. 44" taken as a coherent whole; but my reading is also convincing in isolation from "No. 44," and even in conjunction with "Young Satan," in the Paine-Duneka text. I have therefore thought it politic to treat the chapter as if it were a separate narrative entity. All quotations to *The Mysterious Stranger* are from Gibson's edition of the manuscript texts, pp. 403-5.

19. R. W. B. Lewis, "Days of Wrath and Laughter," in *Trials of the Word* (New Haven: Yale University Press, 1965), p. 212.

20. John R. May, *Toward a New Earth: Apocalypse in the American Novel* (Notre Dame: University of Notre Dame Press, 1972), p. 90.

21. Ralph Waldo Emerson, *Nature, Addresses, and Lectures,* ed. Robert E. Spiller and Alfred R. Ferguson (1971; repr., Cambridge, Mass. Belknap Press of Harvard University Press, 1979), p. 45.

22. "The Power of Words," in *The Complete Works of Edgar Allen Poe,* ed. James A. Harrison (1902; repr., New York: AMS Press, 1965), 6:143-44.

CHAPTER 4: DREAM'S BODY

1. F. O. Matthiessen, *American Renaissance: Art and Expression in the Age of Emerson and Whitman* (1941; repr., London: Oxford University Press, 1979), p. xii, note 3.

2. See T. S. Eliot's "From Poe to Valéry," *The Hudson Review* 11 (Autumn 1949), pp. 327-42; and Allen Tate's "The Angelic Imagination: Poe as God," in *The Forlorn Demon* (Chicago: Henry Regnery Co., 1953), originally in *Kenyon Review* 14 (1952), pp. 455-75. Both essays are reprinted in Eric W. Carlson, ed., *The Recognition of Edgar Allan Poe: Selected Criticism since 1829* (Ann Arbor: University of Michigan Press, 1966), pp. 205-21 (Eliot) and 235-54 (Tate).

3. See esp. Jacques Lacan's "Seminar on 'The Purloined Letter,'" originally the opening text of the *Écrits* (Paris: Seuil, 1966) and published in partial English translation in *Yale French Studies* 48 (1973), pp. 39-72; Jacques Derrida's deconstruction of Lacan's reading in "The Purveyor of Truth," originally "Le Facteur de la Vérité," *Poétique* 21 (1975), and published in partial English translation in *Yale French Studies* 52 (1975), pp. 31-113. Barbara Johnson critiques both readings in "The Frame of Reference: Poe, Lacan, Derrida," *Yale French Studies* 55-56 (1977), pp. 457-505. The

standard study of Poe in France is Patrick F. Quinn, *The French Face of Edgar Poe* (Carbondale: Southern Illinois University Press, 1957).

4. See John Lynen's chapter on Poe in *The Design of the Present: Essays on Time and Form in American Literature* (New Haven: Yale University Press, 1969), pp. 205-71; and Paul John Eakin's "Poe's Sense of an Ending," *American Literature* 45 (1973), pp. 1-22. All subsequent Eakin quotations are from this article.) Burton R. Pollin's source studies are far too numerous to list here; a good introduction to his work is his recent edition of *The Imaginary Voyages,* vol. 1 of *The Collected Writings of Edgar Allan Poe* (Boston: Twayne Publishers, 1981), with extensive annotations and commentary. Barton Levi St. Armand has studied Poe's Gnostic, deistic, and alchemical backgrounds in a number of articles; see for example " 'Seemingly Intuitive Leaps': Belief and Unbelief in *Eureka,*" *American Transcendental Quarterly* 26 (Spring 1975), pp. 4-15 (all subsequent St. Armand quotations are from this article); "Usher Unveiled: Poe and the Metaphysic of Gnosticism," *Poe Studies* 5, no. 1 (June 1972), pp. 1-8; and "The Dragon and the Uroborus: Themes of Metamorphosis in *Arthur Gordon Pym,*" *American Transcendental Quarterly* 37 (Winter 1978), pp. 57-71.

5. Letter to James Russell Lowell, July 2, 1844, in *The Letters of Edgar Allan Poe,* ed. John Ward Ostrom (New York: Gordian Press, 1966), p. 257. All subsequent quotations from Poe's letters are from this edition, abbr. "L."

6. "The Poet," in *Centenary Edition of the Complete Works of Ralph Waldo Emerson,* ed. Edward Waldo Emerson (Cambridge: Riverside Press, 1903) 3:11. The Belknap Press edition (two volumes completed), *Nature, Addresses, and Lectures,* 1971 (repr., 1979), and *Essays: First Series,* 1979 (Cambridge, Mass.: Belknap Press of Harvard University Press), will be used whenever possible, abbr. "B." For other volumes, the Riverside Press edition, cited first in this note (abbr. "R") will be used. I will also be using the Belknap Press edition of *The Journals and Miscellaneous Notebooks of Ralph Waldo Emerson,* chief ed. Ralph H. Orth, 16 vols. (Cambridge, Mass.: Belknap Press of Harvard University Press, 1960-1982), abbr. "JMN." References are to volume and page.

7. Mark Twain, *A Connecticut Yankee in King Arthur's Court* (1889; repr., New York: Harper & Bros., 1917), p. 417.

8. Norman O. Brown, *Love's Body* (New York: Random House, 1966). For an interesting application of *Love's Body* to literature, see Cary Nelson, *The Incarnate Word: Literature as Verbal Space* (Urbana: University of Illinois Press, 1973).

9. For the definitive study of Coleridge's "plagiarisms" from German philosophers, see Gian N. G. Orsini, *Coleridge and German Idealism* (Carbondale: Southern Illinois University Press, 1969). For the contemporary American response to that "plagiarism," see, for example, George Allen's letter to James Marsh, Jan. 18, 1841, in *Coleridge's American Disciples: The Selected Correspondence of James Marsh,* ed. John J. Duffy (Amherst: University of Massachusetts Press, 1973), pp. 250-51, and the editor's note (no. 9) on p. 253.

10. See Joseph Esposito, *Schelling's Idealism and Philosophy of Nature* (Lewisburg, Pa.: Bucknell University Press, 1977), p. 195. See *The Dial* 3, no. 3 (1843), pp. 398–404, and no. 4 (1843), pp. 541–44.

11. Peter Carafiol, *Transcendent Reason: James Marsh and the Forms of Romantic Thought* (Tallahassee: University Presses of Florida, 1982), p. 108.

12. F. W. J. Schelling, *System of Transcendental Idealism (1800)*, trans. Peter Heath (Charlottesville: University Press of Virginia, 1978), p. 236.

13. Kenneth Burke, "I, Eye, Ay—Concerning Emerson's Early Essay on 'Nature' and the Machinery of Transcendence," in *Language as Symbolic Action: Essays on Life, Literature, and Method* (Berkeley and Los Angeles: University of California Press, 1966), p. 189.

14. Barbara L. Packer, *Emerson's Fall: A New Interpretation of the Major Essays* (New York: Continuum, 1982), p. 62.

15. *The Four Zoas*, in *The Complete Poetry and Prose of William Blake*, ed. David V. Erdman (1965; rev. ed., Garden City, NY: Doubleday & Co., 1982), 129:14–130:1, p. 398.

16. I have here conflated two translations with a slight modification: The RSV, from which I take the basic translation, does not have "as in a mirror," which appears as "as in a glass" in the AV. The original Greek for "beholding" is *katoptrizomenoi*, from *katoptron* (mirror); and Bible scholars agree that the meaning is simultaneously to see and to reflect or mirror, hence to behold as in a mirror.

17. Eric Cheyfitz, *The Trans-Parent: Sexual Politics in the Language of Emerson* (Baltimore: Johns Hopkins University Press, 1981), p. 29.

18. Frederic I. Carpenter, *American Literature and the Dream* (New York: Philosophical Library, 1955), p. 95.

19. Letter to Henry James, Jan. 28, 1894, cited in Esposito, *Schelling's Idealism*, p. 203. Also in this volume Esposito notes that Peirce elsewhere described himself as "a Schellingian, of some stripe," the developer of a "Schelling-fashioned idealism which holds matter to be mere specialized and partially deadened mind" (202). In discussing his early influences, Peirce denied the influence of Emerson on his thought, but with telling irony:

> I may mention, for the benefit of those who are curious in studying mental biographies, that I was born and reared in the neighborhood of Concord—I mean in Cambridge—at the time when Emerson, Hedge, and their friends were disseminating the ideas that were caught from Schelling, and Schelling from Plotinus, from Boehm, and from God knows what minds stricken with the monstrous mysticism of the East. But the atmosphere of Cambridge held many an antiseptic against Concord transcendentalism; and I am not conscious of having contracted any of that virus. Nevertheless, it is probable that some cultured bacilli, some benignant form of the disease was implanted in my soul, unawares, and that now, after long incubation, it comes to the surface, modified by mathematical conceptions and by training in physical investigations. (Esposito, *Schelling's Idealism*, 202; and Carpenter, *American Literature*, 94)

20. Charles Sanders Peirce, cited in Carpenter, *American Literature*, p. 96, who comments:

> James would not agree, and would not "correct" his doctrine. And Peirce publicly disowned the new pragmatism of James, coining the term "pragmaticism" to describe his original variety of idealism. "If pragmaticism really made Doing the Be-all and End-all of life, that would be its death. For to say that we live for the mere sake of action, regardless of the thought it carries out, would be to say that there is no such thing as rational purport." (96)

21. *Eureka*, in *The Complete Works of Edgar Allan Poe*, ed. James A. Harrison (1902; repr., New York: AMS Press, 1965), 16:205. All subsequent quotations are from this edition. References are to volume and page.

22. St. Armand, " 'Seemingly Intuitive Leaps,' " p. 11.

23. David Ketterer, *New Worlds for Old: The Apocalyptic Imagination, Science Fiction, and American Literature* (Bloomington: Indiana University Press, 1974), p. 50.

24. See my discussion in "Reading Poe's Novel: A Speculative Review of *Pym* Criticism, 1950–1980," *Poe Studies* 15, no. 2 (December 1982), pp. 47–54.

25. This is Charles O'Donnell's reading in "From Earth to Ether: Poe's Flight into Space," *PMLA* 77 (1962), pp. 85–91, which he supports on the grounds that Pym and his companions have always been rescued by ships before and therefore must be so rescued again. For a rather surprising importation of this naturalistic reading into a visionary interpretation of Poe, see David Ketterer's chapter on *Pym* in *The Rationale of Deception in Poe* (Baton Rouge: Louisiana State University Press, 1979), pp. 125–41.

26. John T. Irwin, *American Hieroglyphics: The Symbol of the Egyptian Hieroglyphics in the American Renaissance* (New Haven: Yale University Press, 1980), p. 213. All subsequent quotations are from this edition.

27. J. V. Ridgely and Iola S. Haverstick, "Chartless Voyage: The Many Voyages of Arthur Gordon Pym," *Texas Studies in Language and Literature* 7 (1966), pp. 63–80.

CHAPTER 5: CALL ME JONAH

1. Ralph Waldo Emerson, *Nature, Addresses, and Lectures*, vol. 1 (1971; repr., Cambridge: Belknap Press of Harvard University Press, 1979), p. 10. All subsequent quotations are from this edition, abbrev. "B." References are to volume and page.

2. For a discussion of the apocalypse as linguistic cessation or annihilation, see Ihab Hassan, *The Literature of Silence: Henry Miller and Samuel Beckett* (New York: Alfred A. Knopf, 1967), pp. 4–8. The American literature of linguistic annihilation, in which the image of the end of the world as *figure* disfigures itself and leaves behind only a record of its own impossibility, is, I realize, a significant gap in my study; there are others. There are a

number of interesting things to be said, in this context, about Henry Miller in relation to Emerson, say, or about William Burroughs in relation to Poe.

3. Herman Melville, *Moby-Dick*, ed. Harrison Hayford and Hershel Parker (New York: W. W. Norton, 1967), p. 379. All subsequent quotations are from this edition.

4. Sharon Cameron, *The Corporeal Self: Allegories of the Body in Melville and Hawthorne* (Baltimore: Johns Hopkins University Press, 1981). All subsequent quotations are from this edition. Cf. p. 26:

> We are told Pip sees "wondrous" sights, and we are told he sees "eternities," but in the very same sentence these eternities are declaimed as "heartless." Melville's insistence on Pip's isolation from, rather than on his transcendence of, the human condition he survives is revealed in the following chapter, "A Squeeze of the Hand," which works itself into a passion in a hopeless effort to salve the terror previously scripted. And lest we have any doubt that terror comes from transcendence, that isolation overwhelms wonder, we are diligently reminded by the pathetic recurrence of Pip's own emphasis on a solitude so terrible it is actually self-annihilating.

This is excellent, except for Cameron's rather misleading suggestion that Pip's isolation from and transcendence of the human condition are two different things. The false dichotomy seems to stem from a desire to establish Pip's fall as negative ("isolation") rather than positive ("transcendence"), as it has often been read. But read in the context of Melville's revision of Emerson, the dichotomy collapses: Emerson's transcendence *is* an isolation from the human condition, as indeed Cameron's last sentence in the passage just cited indicates she knows.

5. I cite from *The Complete Poems of Emily Dickinson*, ed. Thomas H. Johnson (Boston: Little, Brown & Co., 1955).

6. René Girard, *Violence and the Sacred*, trans. Patrick Gregory (1977; repr., Baltimore: Johns Hopkins University Press, 1981), p. 167.

7. Grace Farrell Lee, *"Pym* and *Moby-Dick:* Essential Connections," *American Transcendental Quarterly* 37 (Winter 1978), pp. 73-86. See also Patrick Quinn, *The French Face of Edgar Poe* (Carbondale: Southern Illinois University Press, 1957), pp. 205-14, the first discussion of the striking parallels between the two sea novels, and the analysis Lee is thinking of in subtitling her piece *"Essential* Connections."

8. Martha Banta, *Failure and Success in America: A Literary Debate* (Princeton: Princeton University Press, 1978), p. 503.

9. "A Descent into the Maelström," in *The Complete Works of Edgar Allan Poe*, ed. James A. Harrison (1902; repr., New York: AMS Press, 1965), 1:239. All subsequent quotations are from this edition. References are to volume and page.

10. Richard D. Finholt, "The Vision at the Brink of the Abyss: 'A Descent into the Maelstrom' in the Light of Poe's Cosmology," *Georgia Review* 27, no. 2 (Summer 1973), p. 362. All subsequent quotations are from

this article. Cf. also Paul John Eakin, "Poe's Sense of an Ending," *American Literature* 45 (1973), pp. 9-14.

11. Daniel Hoffman's essay, "Moby Dick: Jonah's Whale or Job's?," appeared originally in *Sewanee Review* 69, no. 2 (April-June 1961), pp. 205-24, and was incorporated into chapter 13 of his *Form and Fable in American Fiction* (1961; repr., New York: W. W. Norton 1973), sections 5-7, pp. 256-78. This and all subsequent quotations are from *Form and Fable*.

12. Nathalia Wright, "Moby-Dick: Jonah's or Job's Whale?," *American Literature* 37, no. 2 (May 1965), pp. 190-95.

13. R. W. B. Lewis, "Days of Wrath and Laughter," in *Trials of the Word* (New Haven: Yale University Press, 1965), p. 219.

14. Ralph Ellison, *Invisible Man* (1952; repr., New York: Signet Books, 1965), p. 490. All subsequent quotations are from this edition.

15. Kurt Vonnegut, *Cat's Cradle* (1963; repr., New York: Dell Publishing, 1973), p. 13. All subsequent quotations are from this edition.

16. Bainard Cowan, *Exiled Waters: Moby-Dick and the Crisis of Allegory* (Baton Rouge: Louisiana State University Press, 1982), p. 85.

17. I should note that Daniel Hoffman in *Form and Fable* is certainly aware of the conclusion to the Book of Jonah; he simply seems at a loss to know what to do with it. "When we compare Father Mapple's sermon to the Book of Jonah," he writes, "we are struck by Melville's suppression of the sequel to Jonah's deliverance from the whale; his Jonah does not propose to God vengeance against the sinners of Nineveh, nor is he chastened by the parable of the gourd, illustrating God's infinite mercy" (260). By "his Jonah" does Hoffman mean Father Mapple's Jonah, or Melville's Jonah—i.e., Ahab, Ishmael, and the other Jonah-figures in the novel? It is true that the scene outside the walls of Nineveh does not appear in Father Mapple's sermon. Does it figure elsewhere in the novel? Because Hoffman takes the point of this scene to be merely "God's infinite mercy," he finds himself constrained to shift from Jonah to Job to explain Ishmael's ultimate vision of the supernatural: Ishmael's God is no loving father but a mysterious and unpredictable force. This is true, of course, although it might be argued that Jonah's God and Job's God are also congruent in their rejection of both moral rebellion and pious platitudes. The lesson of both books, at one level, is that God is not subject to human control and cannot be forced to conform to the image of him offered by the prophets. He will not punish the Ninevites for their sins, and Job's comforters are wrong to think Job's sufferings are punishment for his sins; but neither is he bound to reward Job or Israel for their self-righteous piety.

These reflections are relevant to the question of Israel's survival, of course; but my concern in the remainder of this chapter is less with Melville's (or Ishmael's, or Ahab's) image of God than with the visionary's dilemma of how to live in the world. Does one cling to one's vision exclusively, seeking to impose it on God, mankind, and beast, as Job, Jonah, and Ahab do? Or does one learn to compromise with vision, to reduce it to the mere image or representation of a vision, as Ishmael learns to do? Jonah, praying to God in the whale's belly, remains just as much a solipsist as Narcissus, though he doesn't die of his self-love; the path out of solipsism must begin in the community, in Nineveh, where privative vision—the vision of apocalypse— must compromise with collective demands.

18. Talus is the cyborg from Melville's short story, "The Bell Tower"; see Herman Melville, *Selected Tales and Poems*, ed. Richard Chase (New York: Holt, Rinehart & Winston, 1950), pp. 190-205, esp. 202.

19. My discussion of the coffin life-buoy, of Queequeg, and of the whale as metonymies of Ishmael's book is indebted to John T. Irwin, *American Hieroglyphics: The Symbol of the Egyptian Hieroglyphics in the American Renaissance* (New Haven: Yale University Press, 1980), esp. pp. 185-89; and Edgar A. Dryden, *Melville's Thematics of Form: The Great Art of Telling the Truth* (1968; repr., Baltimore: Johns Hopkins University Press, 1981), pp. 81- 113. Cf. esp. p. 84: "Surrounding and structuring Ishmael's encyclopedic treatment of whaling is the metaphor of the whale as book, a device which always serves to remind the reader that he is encountering an imaginative reality which is the invention of an isolated consciousness."

CHAPTER 6: THE HOUSE OF FICTION

1. Bainard Cowan, *Exiled Waters: Moby-Dick and the Crisis of Allegory* (Baton Rouge: Louisiana State University Press, 1982), p. 178.

2. Edgar A. Dryden, *Melville's Thematics of Form: The Great Art of Telling the Truth* (1968; repr., Baltimore: Johns Hopkins University Press, 1981), p. 117.

3. Frank Lentricchia, *After the New Criticism* (Chicago: University of Chicago Press, 1980), pp. 56-57. All subsequent quotations are from this edition.

4. William Faulkner, *Absalom, Absalom!* (1936; repr., New York: Modern Library, 1964), p. 145. All subsequent quotations are from this edition.

5. Evan Watkins, *The Critical Act: Criticism and Community* (New Haven: Yale University Press, 1978), pp. 202-3. All subsequent quotations are from this edition.

6. Evan Watkins's emphasis on the centrality of Miss Rosa is salutary, given the standard critical denigration of her to the caricature with which chapter 1 begins, as a Gothic "demonizer" who systematically reduces everything to the simplistic terms of her moral indignation. For a useful discussion of Miss Rosa and the critics, see Watkins, *The Critical Act*, pp. 191-203.

7. John T. Irwin, *Doubling and Incest/Repetition and Revenge: A Speculative Reading of Faulkner* (1975; repr., Baltimore: Johns Hopkins University Press, 1980), p. 119. All subsequent quotations are from this edition.

8. My brief summary of Irwin's complex argument simplifies it unduly, perhaps; one should add that Quentin's fainting like a girl in Dalton's arms displaces hatred into a shameful image of love, while his attempted *Liebestod* displaces frustrated love into an image of hatred. For Irwin's discussion of the brother-seducer/sister/brother-avenger triad of spatial doubling, see pp. 37-50.

9. See Norman O. Brown, *Life Against Death: The Psychoanalytical Meaning of History* (1959; repr., Middletown, Conn.: Wesleyan University Press, 1972), pp. 78ff.

10. Leroy Searle, "Opening the Door: Truth in Faulkner's *Absalom, Absalom!*," an unpublished essay to which my reading of the novel is heavily indebted.

11. Ralph Waldo Emerson, *Nature, Addresses, and Lectures*, ed. Robert E. Spiller and Alfred R. Ferguson (1971; repr., Cambridge, Mass.: Belknap Press of Harvard University Press, 1979), pp. 44–45.

12. "The Fall of the House of Usher," in *The Complete Works of Edgar Allan Poe*, ed. James A. Harrison (1920; repr., New York: AMS Press, 1965), 3:283. All subsequent quotations are from this edition. References are to volume and page.

13. See Earl J. Wilcox's "Poe's Usher and Ussher's Chronology," *Poe Newsletter* 1, no. 2 (1968), p. 31.

14. For the definitive discussion of *figura* as plastic form, see Erich Auerbach, *"Figura,"* in *Scenes from the Drama of European Literature*, trans. Ralph Manheim (New York: Meridian Books, 1959), pp. 11–12.

15. There is a significant parallel to this movement of figure through disfiguration to transfiguration in another of Paul's uses of the word *schema*, which is in fact the source of Harold Bloom's term *kenosis:*

> Have this mind among yourselves, which is yours in Christ Jesus, who, though he was in the form of God [*morphe theou*], did not count equality with God a thing to be grasped, but emptied himself [*heauton ekenosen*, whence *kenosis*], taking the form of a servant, being born in the likeness of men. And being found in human form [*schemati heurestheis hos anthropos*] he humbled himself and became obedient unto death, even death on a cross. Therefore has God highly exalted him and bestowed on him the name which is above every other name, that at the name of Jesus every knee should bow, in heaven and on earth and under the earth, and every tongue confess that Jesus Christ is Lord, to the glory of God the Father. (Phil 2:5–11)

Here the form or figure of God is emptied out (from *kenon* [void]), leaving the figural husk or shell that is the human being: the fullness of internal presence becomes the emptiness of absence, a terrible loss whose transcendental reversal is prefigured for Paul by God's exaltation of Jesus in death. As Jesus' disfiguration by emptying-out becomes a transfiguration-by-refilling in his resurrection, so too can we expect Christ to "transfigure the body" (*metaschematisei to soma*, Phil 3:2) in death. Poe realizes, however, that all we perceive evidentially is "disfigure," which is to say not even disfiguration, for that would imply a perceived shift from meaningful figure to its emptying out into absence. The "evidence" for transfiguration in biblical terms is the constitution of "disfigure" or *state* of loss as "disfiguration" or *movement* of loss, which is then completed by the reattainment of the primordial figural state. For Bloom's discussion of this passage in Paul, see *The Anxiety of Influence:*

A Theory of Poetry (1973; repr., New York: Oxford University Press, 1981), pp. 91–92; Bloom says (p. 91) that "in the archetypal *kenosis,* St. Paul found a pattern that no poet whatever could bear to emulate, as poet," for where Jesus had God to refill him, the poet has only himself-as-god, and so must remain full even as he empties himself. Note that in *A Map of Misreading* (New York: Oxford University Press, 1975), p. 84, Bloom links *kenosis* with metonymy, which works in an inverted sense, since Jesus' transfiguration or exaltation in Paul's description is imaged as a renaming; the disfiguration that empties him out, however, is involved specifically in the presence/absence imagery of irony and the inside/outside imagery of metaphor.

16. See Joseph Riddel's "The 'Crypt' of Edgar Poe," *boundary 2* 7, no. 3 (Spring 1979), pp. 117–44, esp. 125–30; and John Lynen's discussion of "Usher" in *The Design of the Present* (New Haven: Yale University Press, 1969), pp. 229–36.

17. Cleanth Brooks, *William Faulkner: The Yoknapatawpha Country* (New Haven: Yale University Press, 1964), p. 298.

18. See Maurice Beebe's "The Fall of the House of Pyncheon," *Nineteenth Century Fiction* 11 (1956), pp. 1–17.

19. *The House of the Seven Gables,* vol. 2 of *The Centenary Edition of the Works of Nathaniel Hawthorne,* ed. William Charvat et al. (Columbus: Ohio State University Press, 1974), p. 3. All subsequent quotations to this novel and to other works by Hawthorne are from this edition. References are to volume and page.

20. My discussion of this passage is indebted to Edgar A. Dryden, *Nathaniel Hawthorne: The Poetics of Enchantment* (Ithaca: Cornell University Press, 1977), pp. 138–40.

21. For a discussion of Hawthorne and his dealings with the Pynchon family after the publication of *The House of the Seven Gables,* see Mathew Winston, "The Quest for Pynchon," in *Mindful Pleasures: Essays on Thomas Pynchon,* ed. George Levine and David Leverenz (Boston: Little, Brown & Co., 1976), p. 255–56.

22. I discuss Hawthorne's metafiction at some length in the context of an early tale in my "Metafiction and Heartfelt Memory: Narrative Balance in 'Alice Doane's Appeal,'" *ESQ* 28, no. 4 (1982), pp. 213–19. For a counterargument to my reading of Hawthorne as always insistently metafictional, always seeking to balance vision against its ironic undermining, see Nina Baym, *The Shape of Hawthorne's Career* (Ithaca: Cornell University Press, 1976), in which metafiction (not Baym's term) is seen as an early device reflecting less conscious strategy than authorial uncertainty, out of which Hawthorne has matured by his major period in the 1850s. See pp. 15–52, esp. 19:

> After the first few unself-conscious forays into publication, his early writing developed a characteristic atmosphere of ambivalence and caution. In a typical early work Hawthorne appears to try to discover the nature and value of his enterprise even while presenting it, despite his doubts, in the most favorable manner he can. The narrator

explores, expresses and conceals his doubts all at once. Significantly, this apologetic stance disappears in "The Custom House" and *The Scarlet Letter* and does not return until the final years of his career.

Whether this metafictional stance is a sign of artistic failure (as Baym maintains) or a deliberate effort to embody the nature of his artistic endeavor and thus is a successful reflection of the complexity of his perceived task (as I argue) is perhaps a matter of preference; but to claim, as Baym does, that this stance disappears in the major novels of the 1850s is quite simply to misread Hawthorne, as indeed Edgar A. Dryden's book on Hawthorne amply documents.

23. "The Jolly Corner," *The Short Stories of Henry James*, ed. Clifton Fadiman (New York: The Modern Library, 1945), p. 633.

24. For a useful discussion of *Absalom, Absalom!* as epistemological irony, see Judith Bryant Wittenberg, *Faulkner: The Transfiguration of Biography* (Lincoln: University of Nebraska Press, 1979), pp. 142-60. A similar reading is offered by Donald M. Kartiganer in *The Fragile Thread: The Meaning of Form in Faulkner's Novels* (Amherst: University of Massachusetts Press, 1979).

25. Frederick L. Gwynn and Joseph L. Blotner, eds., *Faulkner in the University* (Charlottesville: University of Virginia Press, 1959), pp. 273-74.

CHAPTER 7: THE RITUAL ICON

1. Nathaniel Hawthorne, *The Blithedale Romance*, vol. 3 of *The Centenary Edition of the Works of Nathaniel Hawthorne*, ed. William Charvat et al. (Columbus: Ohio State University Press, 1974), pp. 140-41.

2. *The Tempest*, in *The Riverside Shakespeare*, textual ed. G. Blakemore Evans (Boston: Houghton Mifflin Co., 1974), 4.1.147-58, p. 1630. All subsequent quotations are from this edition. References are to act, scene, and line.

3. The seminal discussion of Poe's allusions to *The Tempest* in this tale is Kermit Vanderbilt, "Art and Nature in 'The Masque of the Red Death,'" *Nineteenth-Century Fiction* 22, no. 4 (March 1968), pp. 379-89.

4. "The Masque of the Red Death," in *The Complete Works of Edgar Allan Poe*, ed. James A. Harrison (1902; repr., New York: AMS Press, 1965), 4:255-56. All subsequent quotations are from this edition. References are to volume and page.

5. See Jacques Ellul, *Apocalypse: The Book of Revelation*, trans. George W. Schreiner (New York: Seabury Press, 1977); and René Girard, *Violence and the Sacred*, trans. Patrick Gregory (Baltimore: Johns Hopkins University Press, 1981). Both books, in fact, implicitly align themselves ideologically with Augustine.

6. Frank Kermode, *The Sense of an Ending: Studies in the Theory of Fiction* (1967; repr., New York: Oxford University Press, 1979), *passim*.

7. Daniel Hoffman, *Poe Poe Poe Poe Poe Poe Poe* (1972; repr., New York: Avon Books, 1978), p. 209.

8. John Barth, *Lost in the Funhouse: Fiction for Print, Tape, Live Voice* (1968; repr., New York: Bantam Books, 1969), p. 76. All subsequent quotations are from this edition.

9. John Barth, "Muse, Spare Me," *Book Week*, Sept. 26, 1965, p. 28.

10. See John Gardner's *On Moral Fiction* (New York: Basic Books, 1978).

11. *The Complete Poetical Works of John Milton*, ed. Douglas Bush (Boston: Houghton Mifflin Co., 1965), 1.7, p. 464. All subsequent quotations are from this edition. References are to book and line. I find, after writing my discussion of *Miss Lonelyhearts*, that Harold Bloom has recently linked West's novel to *Paradise Regained* as well, as a ground for a revisionary reading of the work that, substantially different though it is, finally reaches a position that is not far from my own: that West is seeking to revise the Miltonic rage for order. See Bloom's *The Breaking of the Vessels* (Chicago: University of Chicago Press, 1982), pp. 21-25.

12. *The Complete Works of Nathanael West* (New York: Farrar, Strauss & Cudahy, 1957), p. 132. All subsequent quotations from West's works are from this edition.

13. John R. May, *Toward a New Earth: Apocalypse in the American Novel* (Notre Dame: University of Notre Dame Press, 1972), p. 126. All subsequent quotations are from this edition.

14. T. S. Eliot, *Four Quartets* (New York: Harcourt, Brace & Co., 1943), p. 5. The seminal discussion of the Romantic image of the dance in Yeats and the moderns is Frank Kermode, *Romantic Image* (New York: Chilmark Press, 1961).

15. Norman O. Brown, *Life Against Death: The Psychoanalytic Meaning of History* (1959; repr., Middletown, Conn.: Wesleyan University Press, 1972), pp. 90-91.

16. Donald R. Torchiana, "The Painter's Eye," in *Nathanael West: The Cheaters and the Cheated; A Collection of Critical Essays*, ed. David Madden (DeLand, Fla.: Everett/Edwards, 1973), p. 252.

17. I borrow the term *decreation* from Charles Altieri, "Motives in Metaphor: John Ashbery and the Modernist Long Poem," *Genre* 11 (Winter 1978), p. 661:

Decreation I take to be a deliberate poetic act intending to disclose possible forms of relatedness, and consequently other possible grounds for identity and value, sharply different from the host forms, the dramatic lyrics, which the decreation parasitically restructures. Decreation, in essence, is a means for working within the seams and expectations of dominant modes of discourse by disclosing fresh ways of making sense. It blends the parodic and the transcendental because it continues to seek qualities of perception and forms of poetic knowledge by at once cleansing and transforming outmoded expressive or descriptive vehicles. Decreation alters the economy of consciousness by exploring new modes of exchange among its used and various coins. Deconstruction, on the other hand, invokes the spirit of sceptual lucidity without a lyric counterpressure. Deconstruction is primarily a critical act devoted to displaying the irreducible interchange of sense and nonsense in the overlapping codes on which any discourse is ultimately dependent. Deconstruction shows contradictions in intentions while decreation intentionally posits contradictions to suggest new integrations.

Altieri opposes his notion of decreation to deconstruction in terms that are remarkably congruent with Harold Bloom's poetic revisionism, in which the poet creates new (though short-lived) meaning by troping on his or her predecessors: ephebes "parasitically restructure" their precursors by at once parodying and transcending them, at once cleansing and transforming their expressive vehicles or images. I find the notion congruent also with my sense that American writers characteristically seek to restrict the force of their predecessors' apocalyptic visions by writing new self-restrictive apocalypses. This would suggest that the decreative impulse is operative not just in the postmodern poetry Altieri is concerned with, and not just in the postmodern novels of Barth and his contemporaries, but in the entire self-conscious tradition of American apocalypses. It also suggests that decreation, or poetic revisionism, or metafiction is no postmodern invention, no contemporary aberration, but an impulse that lies at the heart of literary creation. The aberration, perhaps, was the brief (century-long) attempt to reduce the novel to a pure form by pruning off its "artifice," an attempt that culminated in the French new novel and heavily influenced the deconstruction of Jacques Derrida. See also my "Oscar Wilde and the Postmodernist Novel," in *Literature and Science*, ed. Matti Palm (Jyväskylä, Finland: University of Jyväskylä, 1982), pp. 255-66.

18. See John Barth's *LETTERS*, where the "Author" refers in a letter to A. B. Cook VI to "the Tragic View of history, to which in fact I subscribe" (New York: G. P. Putnam's Sons, 1979), p. 431.

19. Barth revealed his mythographic sources for *Giles*, with specific emphasis on Campbell's *The Hero with a Thousand Faces* (1949; repr., Princeton: Princeton University Press, 1973), in an interview with John Enck some eighteen months before the novel was released ("John Barth: An Interview," *Wisconsin Studies in Contemporary Fiction* 6 [Winter-Spring 1965], p. 12). The novel's use of the hero myth is self-conscious in the sense that not only Barth and the reader but the characters as well know that they are following the mythographic pattern of the hero-quest. For more detailed discussions of the mythological framework for the novel's sacrifice motif, see Robert Scholes, *The Fabulators* (New York: Oxford University Press, 1967), pp. 150-73, reprinted in Scholes's *Fabulation and Metafiction* (Urbana: University of Illinois Press, 1979), pp. 75-102; John Tilton, "*Giles Goat-Boy*: An Interpretation," *Bucknell Review* 18 (Spring 1970), pp. 93-119; and my *John Barth's Giles Goat-Boy: A Study* (Jyväskylä, Finland: University of Jyväskylä, 1980), pp. 179-257. The germ for this present book lay in my work on Barth; see pp. 168-78 for a discussion of the novel's antiapocalyptic thrust.

20. John Barth, *Giles Goat-Boy: or, The Revised New Syllabus* (Garden City, N.Y.: Doubleday & Co., 1966), pp. 695–96. All subsequent quotations are from this edition.

21. Compare Raymond Olderman's account of the novel's "double ending," as he calls it: "Giles wants to redeem everybody; he is not satisfied with symbolic affirmation. For that reason there is a 'posttape' to his first-person narrative, and it contradicts what seems to be the achieved peace, affirmation, and success of the story proper." *Beyond the Wasteland: A Study of the American Novel in the Nineteen-Sixties* (New Haven: Yale University Press, 1972), p. 72. Throughout his chapter on Barth's novel, Olderman clings to a notion of "maturity" as mystical affirmation of unity, which George gains briefly with Anastasia in WESCAC's Belly and then loses in the Posttape: a reading that is congruent with J.B.'s.

22. The hoax reading, whether offered in praise or censure, has become something like an established interpretation, though many readings (including those of Tilton and Scholes cited here in note 19) steer past it. For early statements of this position, see Beverly Gross, "The Anti-Novels of John Barth," *Chicago Review* 20 (November 1968), pp. 95–109; Richard Poirier, "The Politics of Self-Parody," *Partisan Review* 35 (Summer 1968), pp. 339–53; and Tony Tanner, "The Hoax That Joke Bilked," *Partisan Review* 34 (Winter 1967), pp. 102–9; for a later version, see John Stark, *The Literature of Exhaustion: Borges, Nabokov, Barth* (Durham, N.C.: Duke University Press, 1974), pp. 118–75, esp. 120–21: "[In *Giles Goat-Boy*] Barth accomplishes his purpose of writing a novel, gradually shucking away all his material and leaving only the process of writing."

23. See my *John Barth's Giles Goat-Goy*, e.g., pp. 21–33, 253–54.

CONCLUSION: COMMUNAL TIES

1. I am indebted for these sources, as well as for Poe's allusions to the *Iliad* in "The Man of the Crowd" mentioned later in the chapter, to Thomas Ollive Mabbott's annotations to vol. 2 of *The Collected Works of Edgar Allan Poe, Tales and Sketches, 1831–1842* (Cambridge, Mass.: Belknap Press of Harvard University Press, 1978), pp. 330–31 ("Ligeia") and 516 ("The Man of the Crowd").

2. "Ligeia," in *The Complete Works of Edgar Allan Poe*, ed. James A. Harrison (1902; repr., New York: AMS Press, 1965), 2:251. All subsequent quotations from "Ligeia" and other Poe tales are from this edition. References are to volume and page.

3. See Marie Bonaparte, *The Life and Works of Edgar Allan Poe: A Psycho-Analytic Interpretation*, trans. John Rodker (London: Imago Books, 1949), pp. 224–36, esp. 229–30.

4. See David Riesman, with Reuel Denney and Nathan Glazer, *The Lonely Crowd: A Study of the Changing American Character* (New Haven: Yale University Press, 1950).

5. Evan Watkins, *The Critical Act: Criticism and Community* (New

Haven: Yale University Press, 1978), p. 4. All subsequent quotations are from this edition.

      6. I use the term *dialogue* here in the sense developed by Thomas R. Whitaker in *William Carlos Williams* (New York: Twayne Publishers, 1968), esp. pp. 77-91.

ABOUT THE AUTHOR

Douglas Robinson is associate professor of English philology
at the University of Tampere in Finland
and is author of John Barth's
Giles Goat-Boy: A Study

THE JOHNS HOPKINS UNIVERSITY PRESS

American Apocalypses

Designed by Cynthia W. Hotvedt.
Linocut illustrations by Erik Sandgren.
Composed in Baskerville text and Helvetica display
by A. W. Bennett, Inc., Windsor, Vermont.

Printed on 50 lb. Sebago Eggshell Cream paper
and bound in Kivar by BookCrafters,
Chelsea, Michigan.